When Victims Become Killers

MAHMOOD MAMDANI

WHEN VICTIMS BECOME KILLERS

Colonialism, Nativism, and the Genocide in Rwanda

PRINCETON UNIVERSITY PRESS

PRINCETON AND OXFORD

Third printing, and first paperback printing, 2002
Paperback ISBN 0-691-10280-5

The Library of Congress has cataloged the cloth edition of this book as follows

Mamdani, Mahmood, 1946–
When victims become killers : colonialism, nativism,
and the genocide in Rwanda / Mahmood Mamdani.
p. cm.
Includes bibliographical references and index.
ISBN 0-691-05821-0 (alk. paper)
1. Genocide–Rwanda–History–20th century. 2. Rwanda–
Politics and government. 3. Rwanda–Ethnic relations–
History–20th century. 4. Tutsi (African people)–
Crimes against–Rwanda–History–20th century.
5. Hutu (African people)–Rwanda–Politics and
government. I. Title.
DT450.435 .M35 2001
967.57104–dc21   00-065213

This book has been composed in Galliard

Printed on acid-free paper. ∞

www.pupress.princeton.edu

Printed in the United States of America

10 9 8 7 6 5 4

FOR

ZOHRAN

Contents

List of Abbreviations

ADP	Alliance Démocratique des Peuples
APROSOMA	L'Association pour la Promotion Sociale de la Masse
CDR	Coalition pour la Défense de la République
CMS	Church Missionary Society
CNS	Conférence Nationale Souveraine
CODESRIA	Council for the Development of Social Research in Africa
FRONASA	Front for National Salvation
HCR	Haut Conseil de la République
IMF	International Monetary Fund
KM	Kikosi Maalum
MAGHRIVI	Mutualité des Agriculteurs du Vironga
MDR	Mouvement Démocratique Républicain
MRND	Mouvement Révolutionnaire National pour le Développement(et la Démocratie)
NGO	Nongovernmental organization
NRA	National Resistance Army
NRM	National Resistance Movement
PARMEHUTU	Parti du Mouvement et d'Emancipation Hutu
PDC	Parti Démocrate-Chrétien
PL	Parti Libéral
PSD	Parti Social-Démocrate
RADER	Rassemblement Démocratique Rwandais
RANU	Rwandese Alliance of National Unity
RPA	Rwanda Patriotic Army
RPF	Rwanda Patriotic Front
RTLM	Radio Télévision Libre des Mille Collines
SAP	Structural Adjustment Program
SIDER	Syndicat d'Initiative pour le Développement de la Zone de Rutshuru
TRAFIPRO	Travail, Fidélité, Progrès
UDPS	Union pour la Démocratie et le Progrès Social
UNAMIR	United Nations Assistance Mission to Rwanda
UNAR	Union Nationale Rwandaise

UNHCR	United Nations High Commissioner for Refugees
UNLA	Uganda National Liberation Army
UPC	Uganda Peoples Congress
USAID	United States Agency for International Development

Preface and Acknowledgments:
Decolonizing Area Studies

Fᴏʀ ᴍᴜᴄʜ of my life, I lived just over a hundred miles from the Uganda-Rwanda border. Only once can I recall going to colonial Rwanda. When I was a child of four, my maternal grandfather came to Masaka, which is where we then lived, and announced that he had come to take my mother and her two sons to Bujumbura (Burundi) for his daughter's wedding. The drive over and back took us through Kigali and Astrida (contemporary Butare).

As we grew up, mostly in Kampala, less than another hundred miles from Masaka, Rwanda was seldom a part of our lived reality. That was until the genocide of 1994. Following reports of mass killings, we heard of bodies floating into Lake Victoria. Evidence of gruesome torture could be seen from the shores of the lake. Often, peasants would bring the bodies on shore, followed by periodic mass burials. I remember one occasion when busloads of people went from Kampala to a lakeside village, to attend a large burial and honor the dead. When they returned, word spread that several peasants involved in bringing and burying the bodies on shore had gone mad.

In the next few months, the Council for the Development of Social Research in Africa (CODESRIA) called a major Africa-wide conference in Arusha (Tanzania) to reflect on the tragedy. I was asked to write a paper, and decided that I must go to Kigali before doing so. I had little idea whom I would meet in Kigali. Imagine my surprise when I found a number of my former Makerere University (Kampala) students—whom I had always assumed were Ugandan like the rest—holding important positions in the Rwanda Patriotic Army (RPA), the Front (RPF), and even in the reorganized gendarmerie and police. I met them individually, and as a group. The times were difficult, and the road ahead not easy to see. I was someone they knew from a comfortable past, and yet I was a safe outsider. The more we talked, the more they shared doubts and anxieties with me.

That was in 1995. I visited Kigali, Butare, and the church at Ntarama. It was a short visit, roughly ten days, but one that I could not and would not easily forget. Rwanda turned into a preoccupation. Most obviously, it was a metaphor for postcolonial political violence. Less obviously, it was a political challenge, a vantage point from which to think through the postcolonial political crisis. Even though the conference was over, and I had no immediate academic agenda in which Rwanda would feature, I kept on returning to Rwanda, usually a couple of times a year. When the RPF crossed the border into Zaire in 1997, I too went to Gisenyi, and then crossed the border with an RPA commander into Goma, to go and meet Laurent Kabila, the head of the anti-Mobutu rebellion.

Later that year, CODESRIA asked Jacques Depelchen, a Congolese intellectual then in Kinshasa, and me to undertake a research trip to eastern Congo. The object was to speak to non-governmental organizations about the citizenship crisis that had become publicly identified with the plight of the Banyamulenge. By then, the name Banyamulenge had ceased to identify simply those Tutsi living on the hills of Mulenge; instead, it had become a generic term for the Kinyarwanda-speaking minority in Congo. Depelchen was an old friend from the 1970s when we had both taught at the University of Dar-es-Salaam, and we traveled well together. We went from Kinshasa to Goma, Bukavu, Kisangani, and then back to Kinshasa. I was pleased to find out that Kiswahili was a popular lingua franca in the whole of eastern Congo, and that I could talk directly to those I met. Yet, the language of academic discourse was French, and I did not speak it. Jacques was fluent in French and was patient enough to translate for me so I could take notes every time we had an extended discussion with some-one in French, which turned out to be often. When I returned to the University of Cape Town, which is where I had started teaching in 1996, I sought out a French teacher, to pick up from the one year of French that I had learned during my undergraduate years. Thus began the slow and laborious task of learning a new language in middle age.

The move to South Africa for the first time put me in an academic milieu in which Africa (which is how South Africans tend to refer to the continental land mass to their north) was defined as an "area" to be studied by "area" specialists. The move to Columbia University in 1999 both thickened the experience of area studies and brought me into conversations with postcolonial scholars increasingly critical of it. Finally, as the encounter with Rwanda gradually turned into one with Rwanda experts, it fed my own growing discontent with the methodological underpinnings of area studies.

The area studies enterprise is underpinned by two core methodological claims. The *first* sees state boundaries as boundaries of knowledge, thereby turning political into epistemological boundaries. Even when radical area studies linked developments in the colony to those in imperial centers, it did not cross boundaries *between* colonies. It soon became clear to me that just because the genocide took place within the boundaries of Rwanda, it did not mean that either the dynamics that led to it or the dynamics it unleashed in turn were confined to Rwanda. The *second* methodological claim is that knowledge is about the production of facts. This view translates into a stubborn resistance to theory in the name of valorizing the fact. From this point of view, the claim is that theory is deadening: instead of illuminating, it manipulates the fact. The assumption is that facts speak for themselves. But facts need to be put in context, and interpreted; neither is possible without a theoretical illumination.

This dual methodological underpinning highlights two ways in which this book breaks out of the constraint of area studies. *One*, the book breaks through the rules of area studies where every "expert" must cultivate his or her own "local" patch, where geography is forever fixed by contemporary political boundaries. Thus, we have experts on Rwanda, and others on Uganda, but not on both. Instead of breaking free of this intellectual claustrophobia, the radical impetus in area studies has linked local outcomes to colonialism historically, but not to broader regional developments. The book breaks through this constraint by historicizing geography. In doing so, it combines a critical appropriation of existing literature—particularly historical literature on Rwanda—with original work (on post-colonial Uganda, Kivu, and lived experiences in the genocide). I assert the *critical* nature of the appropriation in two instances in particular. In the first instance, I show the ways in which history writing has been complicit with imperialism, particularly in *naturalizing* political identities, Hutu and Tutsi, and in considering facts about place of origin (migration) as key to history making. Second, I show the ways in which key texts on the 1959 Revolution failed to *problematize* the object of their analysis; instead of addressing critically the ways in which the postcolonial state reproduced and reinforced colonially produced political identities in the name of justice, they ended up once again treating these identities as if they were natural constructs.

The book also breaks out of a *second* limitation of area studies. This is the profoundly antitheoretical thrust that links expertise to the search for new facts. The area is mined over and again in the ongoing hunt for the new fact. Every new book is read for evidence as to what new fact, if any, it contributes. In the process, the empirical is detached and set up in opposition to the theoretical. And yet, it is self-evident that the more you go beyond the local—without necessarily letting go of the local—the more you will need to appropriate secondary material. But this appropriation need not turn into a mindless reliance on others. To the extent you rely on others, better to stand on their shoulders than to lean against them, the more to see beyond the horizon where their sights came to rest. Thus, my claim that the theoretical framework of this book—particularly as regards colonially generated political identities and the crisis of postcolonial citizenship—goes beyond a simple critique to a reinterpretation of, if you will, borrowed facts. This book is more than just an attempt to dig up new facts by expanding the scale of investigation; rather, it is an attempt to rethink existing facts in light of rethought contexts, thereby to illuminate old facts and core realities in new light.

My knowledge of the enterprise called "area studies" did not really begin until I moved from Makerere University in Kampala to the University of Cape Town, and then to Columbia University in New York. To the extent the enterprise of area studies was driven by a search for the latest empirical facts, it needed native informants—not native intellectuals—in the area of expertise. The result, at best, was a polite coexistence whereby local intellectuals and area study experts acknowledged one another through what has been called benign neglect in a different context. This was not simply because local intellectuals would appear as competitors to an outside expert claiming empirical expertise of an area. It was even more the outcome of a fundamental difference in the methods through which locals sought to produce knowledge and the method of the area experts, a fact that did not really dawn on me until I moved out of the area. Whether at Dar-es-Salaam or Makerere, we were never really practitioners of area studies. In the pursuit of knowledge, we knew no boundaries. It never occurred to us to translate political boundaries into boundaries of knowledge production. Our reach extended to the whole world, from China to Nicaragua, and from the Soviet Union to South Africa. The only difference was that we never lost sight of location: we looked at the world *from within Africa.*

The single-most important failing of area studies is that it has failed to frame the study of the "third-world" in broad intellectual terms. If the "area" in area studies was perceived through narrow colonial and Cold War lenses, then the end of apartheid regionally and the Cold War globally offers us an opportunity to liberate the study of Africa from the shackles of area studies. To do so, however, we need to recognize that decolonization in one sphere of life does not necessarily and automatically lead to decolonization in other spheres. If dependency theory taught us that political decolonization did not automatically lead to decolonization of the

economy, postcolonial studies brings home the fact that intellectual decolonization will require no less than an intellectual movement to achieve
this objective. I hope this can explain to the reader why this book, immediately the result of an endeavor to make the Rwandan genocide thinkable,
·is also guided by a broader quest: What can the study of Africa teach us
about late modern life?

IN WRITING this book, I have incurred several intellectual debts. The
funding that made it possible for me to put together the research base of
this book came from the South-South Exchange Program for Research
on the History of Development (SEPHIS), a government-funded body
in Holland which is dedicated to promoting research-related activities in
resource-constrained "third world" contexts. For the generous three-year
grant from SEPHIS, I am indeed grateful. The preliminary effort that
preceded this book-length project was funded by a grant from the MacAr-
thur Foundation. My early research in Rwandan politics and history was
carried out at the Centre for Basic Research in Kampala. I continued the
endeavor at the University of Cape Town, where I was A. C. Jordan Professor of African Studies from 1996 to 1999, and completed writing at the
Department of Anthropology in Columbia University, which I joined later
in 1999.

People are often reluctant to reveal the identity of their financial debtors, but not usually of their intellectual debtors. Not withstanding the
tendency of area studies, which translates the endless search for the new
fact into a prejudice against borrowing, could it be that the effect of intellectual debts is more likely to be enriching than impoverishing? It is thus
with pleasure that I acknowledge those who read through earlier drafts of
this book and helped me identify and address some of its shortcomings,
even if I did not always accept every advice that came my way: Robert
Meister at the University of California in Santa Cruz; David Newbury at
the University of North Carolina in Chapel Hill; Carlos Forment at
Princeton University; Abdullah Ibrahim at University of the Western
Cape; Mamadou Diouf at CODESRIA and then the University of Michigan at Ann Arbor; Michael Ignatiff at Harvard; Rûth Iyob at the University of Missouri—St. Louis; Nick Dirks and Andreas Huyssen at Columbia
University; Tom Keenan at Bard College; Ian Shapiro at Yale; Justus Mu-
gaju at Fountain Publishers in Kampala; and Mary Murrell at Princeton
University Press.

From the wise and patient editorial guidance of Mary Murrell, to the copyediting of Alice Calaprice, I have benefited greatly from support at Princeton University Press. Augustine Ruzindana and Wafula Oguttu in Kampala, friends for decades, acted as reliable and fearless critics. Jacques Depelchen was a friend and guide in Kivu, Kisangani, and Kinshasa. Faustin guided me on my first visit to postgenocide Rwanda and explained ' every detail patiently as I groped for meaning. Christopher Brest produced the maps I needed; and Sofian Merabet, Ravi Sriramachandran, Poomima Paidipathy and Ngozi Amu, students and assistants at Columbia University, provided invaluable help: from bibliographical support to translations to compiling the index and reading the proofs late into the night. To all of them, my thanks.

The writing of this book marks a different transition in the confines of our family, a time when our son Zohran crossed the boundary from a fascination with the image, whether on the video or the computer screen, to familiarity with the written word. The more Harry Potter he read, the more curious he became of what I was writing, and whether I would read some of it to him as he retired in the evening. When my efforts to explain that my kind of writing would not make ideal bedtime reading were unsuccessful, I looked for portions that could be read to an eight-year-old without harm. It was not always easy. I dedicate this book to Zohran—and of course to Mira—in the hope that he may one day choose to read it for benefit.

WHEN VICTIMS BECOME KILLERS

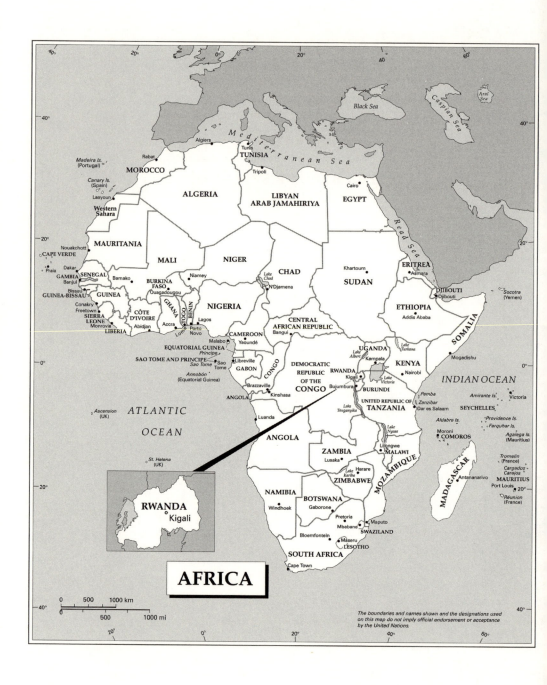

40°   20°   0°   20°   40°   60°

Black Sea

Caspian Sea

Aral Sea

40°   40°

Mediterranean Sea

Madeira Is. (Portugal)   Rabat   Algiers   Tunis
                          MOROCCO   TUNISIA
Canary Is. (Spain)   Tripoli
  Praia   Laayoun
Western   ALGERIA   LIBYAN   Cairo
Sahara   ARAB JAMAHIRIYA   EGYPT

20°   Nouakchott   MAURITANIA   Red Sea   20°
CAPE VERDE
  Dakar   MALI   NIGER   Khartoum   Asmara   ERITREA
GAMBIA SENEGAL Bamako   Lake   Asmara
Banjul   BURKINA   Niamey   Chad   DJIBOUTI
Bissau GUINEA   FASO   N'Djamena   SUDAN   Djibouti   Socotra
GUINEA-BISSAU   Ouagadougou   CHAD   (Yemen)
Conakry   ETHIOPIA
Freetown CÔTE   NIGERIA   Addis Ababa
SIERRA   D'IVOIRE   SOMALIA
LEONE   Lagos   CENTRAL
Monrovia Abidjan Accra Porto   AFRICAN REPUBLIC
LIBERIA   Lomé   Novo   Bangui
                  CAMEROON   Lake
          Malabo Yaoundé   Turkana
EQUATORIAL GUINEA   UGANDA   Lake   Mogadishu
        Principe   Kampala   Albert
SAO TOME AND PRINCIPE Sao   DEMOCRATIC   KENYA
        Sao Tomé Tomé   REPUBLIC RWANDA Nairobi   INDIAN OCEAN
Annobón   GABON Libreville OF THE   Kigali Lake
(Equatorial Guinea)   CONGO Bujumbura Victoria
0°   Brazzaville   BURUNDI   0°
Ascension   Kinshasa ANGOLA   UNITED REPUBLIC OF Pemba
(UK)   Zanzibar Amirante Is. Victoria
                                          TANZANIA Dar es Salaam SEYCHELLES
ATLANTIC   Luanda   Aldabra Is. Providence Is.
                                          Lake   Farquhar Is.
OCEAN   Nyasa   Agalega Is.
        St. Helena   Moroni   (Mauritius)
        (UK)   ANGOLA   ZAMBIA   Lilongwe COMOROS
                                   Lusaka   MALAWI   Tromelin
                                          Lake   (France)
                                   Harare Kariba   Cargados
20°   ZIMBABWE   Carajos   MAURITIUS
                          NAMIBIA   Port Louis   20°
RWANDA   BOTSWANA   MOZAMBIQUE Réunion
Kigali   Windhoek Gaborone   (France)
                                   Pretoria Maputo
                                   Mbabane SWAZILAND
                          Bloemfontein Maseru
                                        LESOTHO
                          SOUTH AFRICA
                          Cape Town

AFRICA

40°   0   500   1000 km   40°
       0   500   1000 mi

       The boundaries and names shown and the designations used
       on this map do not imply official endorsement or acceptance
       by the United Nations.

       20°   0°   20°   40°   60°

Thinking about Genocide

I visited Rwanda roughly a year after the genocide. On July 22, 1995, I went to Ntarama, about an hour and a half by car from Kigali, on a dirt road going south toward the Burundi border. We arrived at a village church, made of brick and covered with iron sheets. Outside there was a wood and bamboo rack, bearing skulls. On the ground were assorted bones, collected and pressed together inside sacks, but sticking out of their torn cloth. The guard explained that the bones had been gathered from the neighborhood. A veteran of similar sites in the Luwero Triangle in Uganda roughly a decade ago, I felt a sense of déjà vu. Even if the numbers of skulls and sacks were greater in quantity than I had ever seen at any one site, I was not new to witnessing the artifacts of political violence.

The church was about twenty by sixty feet. Inside, wooden planks were placed on stones. I supposed they were meant as benches. I peered inside and saw a pile of belongings—shoulder sacks, tattered clothing, a towel, a wooden box, a *suferia* (cooking pot), plastic mugs and plates, straw mats and hats—the worldly goods of the poor. Then, amidst it all, I saw bones, and then entire skeletons, each caught in the posture in which it had died. Even a year after the genocide, I thought the air smelled of blood, mixed with that of bones, clothing, earth—a human mildew.

I scanned the walls with their gaping holes. The guide explained these were made by the Interahamwe (youth militia of the ruling party) so they could throw grenades into the building. He said that those in the church were lucky. They died, almost instantly. Those outside had a protracted, brutal death, in some cases drawn out over as long as a week, with one part of the body cut daily.

I raised my eyes, away from the skeletons, to look at the church wall. Much of it was still covered with some old posters. They read like exhortations common to radical regimes with a developmental agenda, regimes that I was familiar with and had lived under for decades. One read: "Journée Internationale de la Femme." And below it, was another, this time in bold: "ÉGALITÉ—PAIX—DÉVELOPPEMENT."

I was introduced to a man called Callixte, a survivor of the massacre in Ntarama. "On the 7th of April [1994], in the morning," he explained, "they started burning houses over there and moving towards here. Only a few were killed. The burning pushed us to this place. Our group decided to run to this place. We thought this was God's house, no one would attack us here. On the 7th, 8th, up to the 10th, we were fighting them. We were using stones. They had *pangas* (machetes), spears, hammers, grenades. On the 10th, their numbers were increased. On the 14th, we were being pushed inside the church. The church was attacked on the 14th and the 15th. The actual killing was on the 15th.

"On the 15th, they brought Presidential Guards. They were supporting Interahamwe, brought in from neighboring communes. I was not in the group here. Here, there were women, children, and old men. The men had formed defense units outside. I was outside. Most men died fighting. When our defense was broken through, they came and killed everyone here. After that, they started hunting for those hiding in the hills. I and others ran to the swamp."

I asked about his *secteur*, about how many lived in it, how many Tutsi, how many Hutu, who participated in the killing. "In my *secteur*, Hutu were two-thirds, Tutsi one-third. There were about 5,000 in our *secteur*. Of the 3,500 Hutu, all the men participated. It was like an order, except there were prominent leaders who would command. The rest followed."

I asked whether there were no intermarriages in the *secteur*. "Too many. About one-third of Tutsi daughters would be married to Hutu. But Hutu daughters married to Tutsi men were only 1 per cent: Hutu didn't want to marry their daughters to Tutsi who were poor and it was risky. Because the Tutsi were discriminated against, they didn't want to give their daughters where there was no education, no jobs . . . risky. Prospects were better for Tutsi daughters marrying Hutu men. They would get better opportunities.

"Tutsi women married to Hutu were killed. I know only one who survived. The administration forced Hutu men to kill their Tutsi wives before they go to kill anyone else—to prove they were true Interahamwe. One man tried to refuse. He was told he must choose between the wife and himself. He then chose to save his own life. Another Hutu man rebuked him for having killed his Tutsi wife. That man was also killed. Kallisa— the man who was forced to kill his wife—is in jail. After killing his wife, he became a convert. He began to distribute grenades all around.

"The killing was planned, because some were given guns. During the war with the RPF, many young men were taken in the reserves and trained and given guns. Those coming from training would disassociate them-

selves from Tutsi. Some of my friends received training. When they returned, they were busy mobilizing others. They never came to see me. I
am fifty-seven. Even people in their sixties joined in the killing, though
they were not trained. The trained were Senior 6 or Technical School
leavers." I asked how such killers could have been his friends. "I was a
friend to their fathers. It was a father-son relationship. I think the fathers
must have known."

Who were the killers in Ntarama? Units of the Presidential Guard came
from Kigali. The Interahamwe were brought in from neighboring communes. Youth who had been trained in self-defense units after the civil war
began provided the local trained force. But the truth is that everybody
participated, at least all men. And not only men, women, too: cheering
their men, participating in auxiliary roles, like the second line in a street-
to-street battle.

NO ONE can say with certainty how many Tutsi were killed between
March and July of 1994 in Rwanda. In the fateful one hundred days that
followed the downing of the presidential plane—and the coup d'état
thereafter—a section of the army and civilian leadership organized the
Hutu majority to kill all Tutsi, even babies. In the process, they also killed
not only the Hutu political opposition, but also many nonpolitical Hutu
who showed reluctance to perform what was touted as a "national" duty.
The estimates of those killed vary: between ten and fifty thousand Hutu,
and between 500,000 and a million Tutsi.[1] Whereas the Hutu were killed
as individuals, the Tutsi were killed as a group, recalling German designs
to extinguish the country's Jewish population. This explicit goal is why
the killings of Tutsi between March and July of 1994 must be termed
"genocide." This single fact underlines a crucial similarity between the
Rwandan genocide and the Nazi Holocaust.[2]

In the history of genocide, however, the Rwandan genocide raises a difficult political question. Unlike the Nazi Holocaust, the Rwandan genocide was not carried out from a distance, in remote concentration camps
beyond national borders, in industrial killing camps operated by agents
who often did no more than drop Zyklon B crystals into gas chambers
from above. The Rwandan genocide was executed with the slash of machetes rather than the drop of crystals, with all the gruesome detail of a
street murder rather than the bureaucratic efficiency of a mass extermination. The difference in technology is indicative of a more significant social
difference. The technology of the holocaust allowed a few to kill many,

but the machete had to be wielded by a single pair of hands. It required not one but many hacks of a machete to kill even one person. With a machete, killing was hard work, that is why there were often several killers for every single victim. Whereas Nazis made every attempt to separate victims from perpetrators, the Rwandan genocide was very much an intimate affair. It was carried out by hundreds of thousands, perhaps even more, and witnessed by millions. In a private conversation in 1997, a minister in the Rwanda Patriotic Front–led government contrasted the two horrors: "In Germany, the Jews were taken out of their residences, moved to distant far away locations, and killed there, almost anonymously. In Rwanda, the government did not kill. It prepared the population, enraged it and enticed it. Your neighbors killed you." And then he added, "In Germany, if the population participated in the killing, it was not directly but indirectly. If the neighbor's son killed, it is because he joined the army."[3]

The Rwandan genocide unfolded in just a hundred days. "It was not just a small group that killed and moved," a political commissar in the police explained to me in Kigali in July 1995. "Because genocide was so extensive, there were killers in every locality—from ministers to peasants—for it to happen in so short a time and on such a large scale." Opening the international conference on Genocide, Impunity and Accountability in Kigali in late 1995, the country's president, Pasteur Bizimungu, spoke of "hundreds of thousands of criminals" evenly spread across the land:

> Each village of this country has been affected by the tragedy, either because the whole population was mobilized to go and kill elsewhere, or because one section undertook or was pushed to hunt and kill their fellow villagers. The survey conducted in Kigali, Kibungo, Byumba, Gitarama and Butare Préfectures showed that genocide had been characterized by torture and utmost cruelty. About forty-eight methods of torture were used countrywide. They ranged from burying people alive in graves they had dug up themselves, to cutting and opening wombs of pregnant mothers. People were quartered, impaled or roasted to death.
>
> On many occasions, death was the consequence of ablation of organs, such as the heart, from alive people. In some cases, victims had to pay fabulous amounts of money to the killers for a quick death. The brutality that characterised the genocide has been unprecedented.[4]

A political commissar in the army with whom I talked in July 1995 was one of the few willing to reflect over the moral dilemma involved in this situation. Puzzling over the difference between crimes committed by a minority of state functionaries and political violence by civilians, he recalled: "When we captured Kigali, we thought we would face criminals in the state; instead, we faced a criminal population." And then, as if reflecting on the other side of the dilemma, he added, "Kigali was half empty when we arrived. It was as if the RPF was an army of occupation." His sense of ambiguity was born of the true moral and political dilemma of the genocide. Just pointing at the leadership of the genocide left the truly troubling question unanswered: How could this tiny group convince the majority to kill, or to acquiesce in the killing of, the minority?

The violence of the genocide was the result of both planning and participation. The agenda imposed from above became a gruesome reality to the extent it resonated with perspectives from below. Rather than accent one or the other side of this relationship and thereby arrive at either a state-centered or a society-centered explanation, a complete picture of the genocide needs to take both sides into account. For this was neither just a conspiracy from above that only needed enough time and suitable circumstance to mature, nor was it a popular *jacquerie* gone berserk. If the violence from below could not have spread without cultivation and direction from above, it is equally true that the conspiracy of the tiny fragment of *génocidaires* could not have succeeded had it not found resonance from below. The design from above involved a tiny minority and is easier to understand. The response and initiative from below involved multitudes and presents the true moral dilemma of the Rwandan genocide.

In sum, the Rwandan genocide poses a set of deeply troubling questions. Why did hundreds of thousands, those who had never before killed, take part in mass slaughter? Why did such a disproportionate number of the educated—not just members of the political elite but, as we shall see, civic leaders such as doctors, nurses, judges, human rights activists, and so on—play a leading role in the genocide? Similarly, why did places of shelter where victims expected sanctuary—churches, hospitals, and schools—turn into slaughterhouses where innocents were murdered in the tens and hundreds, and sometimes even thousands?

THREE SILENCES: A STARTING POINT

Accounts of the genocide, whether academic or popular, suffer from three silences. The first concerns the *history* of genocide: many write as if genocide has no history and as if the Rwandan genocide had no precedent, even in this century replete with political violence. The Rwandan genocide thus appears as an anthropological oddity. For Africans, it turns into a Rwandan oddity; and for non-Africans, the aberration is Africa. For both, the temptation is to dismiss Rwanda as exceptional. The second silence concerns the *agency* of the genocide: academic writings, in particular, have highlighted the design from above in a one-sided manner. They hesitate to acknowledge, much less explain, the participation—even initiative— from below.[5] When political analysis presents the genocide as exclusively a state project and ignores its subaltern and "popular" character, it tends to reduce the violence to a set of meaningless outbursts, ritualistic and bizarre, like some ancient primordial twitch come to life. The third silence concerns the *geography* of the genocide. Since the genocide happened within the boundaries of Rwanda, there is a widespread tendency to assume that it must also be an outcome of processes that unfolded within the same boundaries. A focus confined to Rwandan state boundaries inevitably translates into a silence about regional processes that fed the dynamic leading to the genocide.

We may agree that genocidal violence cannot be understood as rational; yet, we need to understand it as thinkable. Rather than run away from it, we need to realize that it is the "popularity" of the genocide that is its uniquely troubling aspect. In its social aspect, Hutu/Tutsi violence in the Rwandan genocide invites comparison with Hindu/Muslim violence at the time of the partition of colonial India. Neither can be explained as simply a state project. One shudders to put the words "popular" and "genocide" together, therefore I put "popularity" in quotation marks. And yet, one needs to explain the large-scale civilian involvement in the genocide. To do so is to contextualize it, to understand the logic of its development. My *main* objective in writing this book is to make the popular agency in the Rwandan genocide thinkable. To do so, I try to create a synthesis between history, geography, and politics. Instead of taking geography as a constant, as when one writes the history of a given geography, I let the thematic inquiry define its geographical scope at every step, even if this means shifting the geographical context from one historical period to another. By taking seriously the historical backdrop to political events, I hope to historicize both political choices and those who made these choices. If it is true that the choices were made from a historically limited menu, it is also the case that the identity of agents who made these choices was also forged within historically specific institutions. To benefit from a historically informed insight is not the same as to lapse into a politically irresponsible historicism. To explore the relationship between history and politics is to problematize the relationship between the historical legacy of colonialism and postcolonial politics. To those who think that I am thereby trying to have my cake while eating it too, I can only point out that it is not possible to define the scope—and not just the limits—of action without taking into account historical legacies.

COLONIALISM AND GENOCIDE

The genocidal impulse to eliminate an enemy may indeed be as old as organized power. Thus, God instructed his Old Testament disciples through Moses, saying:

> Avenge the children of Israel of the Medianites: afterward shalt thou be gathered unto thy people. And Moses spake unto the people saying, Arm ye men from among you for the war, that they may go against Median, to execute the LORD's vengeance on Median. . . . And they warred against Median, as the LORD commanded Moses, and they slew every male. . . . And the children of Israel took captive the women of Median and their little ones; and all their cattle, and all their flocks, and all their goods, they took for a prey. And all their cities in the places wherein they dwelt, and all their encampments, they burnt with fire. And they took all the spoil, and all the prey, both of man and of beast. . . . And Moses said unto them, Have you saved all the women alive? Behold, these caused the children of Israel, through the counsel of Balaam, to commit trespass against the LORD in the matter of Peor, and so the plague was among the congregation of the LORD. Now therefore kill every male among the little ones, and kill every woman that hath known man by lying with him. But all the women children that have not known man by lying with him, keep alive for yourselves.[6]

If the genocidal impulse is as old as the organization of power, one may be tempted to think that all that has changed through history is the technology of genocide. Yet, it is not simply the technology of genocide that has changed through history, but surely also how that impulse is organized and its target defined. Before you can try and eliminate an enemy, you must first define that enemy. The definition of the political self and the political other has varied through history. The history of that variation is the history of political identities, be these religious, national, racial, or otherwise.

I argue that the Rwandan genocide needs to be thought through within the logic of colonialism. The horror of colonialism led to two types of genocidal impulses. The first was the genocide of the native by the settler.

It became a reality where the violence of colonial pacification took on extreme proportions. The second was the native impulse to eliminate the settler. Whereas the former was obviously despicable, the latter was not. The very political character of native violence made it difficult to think of it as an impulse to genocide. Because it was derivative of settler violence, the natives' violence appeared less of an outright aggression and more a self-defense in the face of continuing aggression. Faced with the violent denial of his humanity by the settler, the native's violence began as a counter to violence. It even seemed more like the affirmation of the native's humanity than the brutal extinction of life that it came to be. When the native killed the settler, it was violence by yesterday's victims. More of a culmination of anticolonial resistance than a direct assault on life and freedom, this violence of victims-turned-perpetrators always provoked a greater moral ambiguity than did the settlers' violence.

More than any other, two political theorists, Hannah Arendt and Frantz Fanon, have tried to think through these twin horrors of colonialism. We shall later see that when Hannah Arendt set out to understand the Nazi Holocaust, she put it in the context of a history of one kind of genocide: the settlers' genocide of the native. When Frantz Fanon came face-to-face with native violence, he understood its logic as that of an eye for an eye, a response to a prior violence, and not an invitation to fresh violence. It was for Fanon the violence to end violence, more like a utopian wish to close the chapter on colonial violence in the hope of heralding a new humanism.

Settlers' Genocide

It is more or less a rule of thumb that the more Western settlement a colony experienced, the greater was the violence unleashed against the native population. The reason was simple: settler colonization led to land deprivation. Whereas the prototype of settler violence in the history of modern colonialism is the near-extermination of Amerindians in the New World, the prototype of settler violence in the African colonies was the German annihilation of over 80 percent of the Herero population in the colony of German South West Africa in a single year, 1904.[7] Its context was Herero resistance to land and cattle appropriation by German settlers and their *Schutztruppe* allies. Faced with continuing armed resistance by the Herero, German opinion divided between two points of views, one championed by General Theodor Leutwein, who commanded the army in the colony, and the other by General Lothar von Trotha, who took over the military command when General Leutwein failed to put down native resistance. The difference between them illuminates the range of political choice in a colonial context.

General Trotha explained the difference in a letter:

> Now I have to ask myself how to end the war with the Hereros. The views of the Governor and also a few old Africa hands [*alte Afrikaner*] on the one hand, and my views on the other, differ completely. The first wanted to negotiate for some time already and regard the Herero nation as necessary labour material for the future development of the country. I believe that the nation as such should be annihilated, or, if this was not possible by tactical measures, have to be expelled from the country by operative means and further detailed treatment. This will be possible if the water-holes from Grootfontein to Gobabis are occupied. The constant movement of our troops will enable us to find the small groups of the nation who have moved back westwards and destroy them gradually.

Equally illuminating is General Trotha's rationale for the annihilation policy: "My intimate knowledge of many central African tribes (Bantu and others) has everywhere convinced me of the necessity that the Negro does not respect treaties but only brute force."[8]

The plan Trotha laid out in the letter is more or less the fate he meted to the Herero on the ground. To begin with, the army exterminated as many Herero as possible.[9] For those who fled, all escape routes except the one southeast to the Omeheke, a waterless sandveld in the Kalahari Desert, were blocked. The fleeing Herero were forcibly separated from their cattle and denied access to water holes, leaving them with but one option: to cross the desert into Botswana, in reality a march to death. This, indeed, is how the majority of the Herero perished. It was a fate of which the German general staff was well aware, as is clear from the following gleeful entry in its official publication, *Der Kampf*: "No efforts, no hardships were spared in order to deprive the enemy of his last reserves of resistance; like a half-dead animal he was hunted from water-hole to water-hole until he became a lethargic victim of the nature of his own country. The waterless Omaheke was to complete the work of the German arms: the annihilation of the Herero people."[10]

Lest the reader be tempted to dismiss General Lothar von Trotha as an improbable character come to life from the lunatic fringe of the German officer corps, one given a free hand in a distant and unimportant colony, I hasten to point out that the general had a distinguished record in the annals of colonial conquest, indeed the most likely reason he was chosen to squash a protracted rebellion. Renowned for his brutal involvement in the suppression of the Chinese Boxer Rebellion in 1900, and a veteran of bloody suppression of African resistance to German occupation in Rwanda, Burundi, and Tanzania, General Trotha often enthused about his own methods of colonial warfare: "The exercise of violence with crass terrorism and even with gruesomeness was and is my policy. I destroy the African tribes with streams of blood and streams of money. Only following this cleansing can something new emerge, which will remain."[11]

Opposition to Trotha's annihilation policy had come from two sources: colonial officials who looked at the Herero as potential labor, and church officials who saw them as potential converts.[12] Eventually, the Herero who survived were gathered by the German army with the help of missionary societies and were put in concentration camps, also run by missionaries along with the German army. By 1908, inmates of these concentration camps were estimated at 15,000. Put to slave labor, overworked, hungry, and exposed to diseases such as typhoid and smallpox, more Herero men perished in these camps. Herero women, meanwhile, were turned into sex slaves. At the same time, those who survived were converted en masse to Christianity. When the camps were closed in 1908, the Herero were distributed as laborers among the settlers. Henceforth, all Herero over the age of seven were expected to carry around their necks a metal disk bearing their labor registration number.

The genocide of the Herero was the first genocide of the twentieth century. The links between it and the Holocaust go beyond the building of concentration camps and the execution of an annihilation policy and are worth exploring. It is surely of significance that when General Trotha wrote, as above, of destroying "African tribes with streams of blood," he saw this as some kind of a Social Darwinist "cleansing" after which "something new" would "emerge." It is also relevant that, when the general sought to distribute responsibility for the genocide, he accused the missions of inciting the Herero with images "of the bloodcurdling Jewish history of the Old Testament."[13] It was also among the Herero in the concentration camps that the German geneticist, Eugen Fischer, first came to do his medical experiments on race, for which he used both Herero and mulatto offspring of Herero women and German men. Fischer later became chancellor of the University of Berlin, where he taught medicine to Nazi physicians. One of his prominent students was Josef Mengele, the notorious doctor who did unsavory genetic experiments on Jewish children at Auschwitz.[14] It seems to me that Hannah Arendt erred when she presumed a relatively uncomplicated relationship between settlers' genocide in the colonies and the Nazi Holocaust at home: When Nazis set out to annihilate Jews, it is far more likely that they thought of themselves as natives, and Jews as settlers. Yet, there is a link that connects the genocide of the Herero and the Nazi Holocaust to the Rwandan genocide. That link is *race branding*, whereby it became possible not only to set a group apart as an enemy, but also to exterminate it with an easy conscience.

Natives' Genocide

In the annals of colonial history, the natives' genocide never became a historical reality. Yet, it always hovered on the horizon as a historical possibility. None sensed it better than Frantz Fanon, whose writings now read like a foreboding. For Fanon, the native's violence was not life denying, but life affirming: "For he knows that he is not an animal; and it is precisely when he realizes his humanity that he begins to sharpen the weapons with which he will secure its victory."[15] What distinguished native violence from the violence of the settler, its saving grace, was that it was the violence of yesterday's victims who have turned around and decided to cast aside their victimhood and become masters of their own lives. "He of whom they have never stopped saying that the only language he understands is that of force, decides to give utterance by force." Indeed, "the argument the native chooses has been furnished by the settler, and by an ironic turning of the tables it is the native who now affirms that the colonialist understands nothing but force."[16] What affirmed the natives' humanity for Fanon was not that they were willing to take the settler's life, but that they were willing to risk their own: "The colonized man finds his freedom in and through violence."[17] If its outcome would be death, of settlers by natives, it would need to be understood as a derivative outcome, a result of a prior logic, the genocidal logic of colonial pacification and occupation infecting anticolonial resistance. "The settler's work is to make even dreams of liberty impossible for the native. The native's work is to imagine all possible methods for destroying the settler. . . . For the native, life can only spring up again out of the rotting corpse of the settler . . . for the colonized people, this violence, because it constitutes their only work, invests their character with positive and creative qualities. The practice of violence binds them together as a whole, since each individual forms a violent link in the great chain, a part of the great organism of violence which has surged upwards in reaction to the settler's violence in the beginning."[18]

The great crime of colonialism went beyond expropriating the native, the name it gave to the indigenous population. *The greater crime was to politicize indigeneity in the first place*: first negatively, as a settler libel of the native; but then positively, as a native response, as a self-assertion. The dialectic of the settler and the native did not end with colonialism and political independence. To understand the logic of genocide, I argue, it is necessary to think through the political world that colonialism set into motion. This was the world of the settler and the native, a world organized around a binary preoccupation that was as compelling as it was confining. It is in this context that Tutsi, a group with a privileged relationship to power before colonialism, got constructed as a privileged *alien settler* presence, first by the great nativist revolution of 1959, and then by Hutu Power propaganda after 1990.

In its motivation and construction, I argue that the Rwandan genocide needs to be understood as a natives' genocide. It was a genocide by those who saw themselves as sons—and daughters—of the soil, and their mission as one of clearing the soil of a threatening *alien* presence. This was not an "ethnic" but a "racial" cleansing, not a violence against one who is seen as a neighbor but against one who is seen as a foreigner; not a violence that targets a transgression across a boundary into home but one that seeks to eliminate a foreign presence from home soil, literally and physically. From this point of view, we need to distinguish between racial and ethnic violence: ethnic violence can result in massacres, but not genocide. Massacres are about transgressions, excess; genocide questions the very legitimacy of a presence as alien. For the Hutu who killed, the Tutsi was a settler, not a neighbor. Rather than take these identities as a given, as a starting point of analysis, I seek to ask: When and how was Hutu made into a native identity and Tutsi into a settler identity? The analytical challenge is to understand the historical dynamic through which Hutu and Tutsi came to be synonyms for native and settler. Before undertaking this analysis, however, I propose to discuss both how native and settler originated as political identities in the context of modern colonialism, and how the failure to transcend these identities is at the heart of the crisis of citizenship in postcolonial Africa.

ORGANIZATION AND SCOPE

Chapter One elaborates the theoretical perspective that guided my research, at the same time as it got modified as I learned of new fact. and relationships. I begin with the need to differentiate political identities from cultural and market-based identities, so as to understand them as a direct consequence of the process of state formation. I focus on two forms of the colonial state in Africa. Characterized by direct and indirect rule, these state forms legally enforced race and ethnicity as two salient political identities. I also contrast the experience of Uganda and Congo, both the sites of indirect rule colonialism, with that of Rwanda, which Belgian rule turned into more of a halfway house between direct and indirect rule. Unlike in Uganda and Congo, colonial law in Rwanda recognized only race, and not ethnicity, as a political identity.

Studies on African politics have been relatively silent on the question of race, whereas a vigorous discussion has developed on that of ethnicity.[19] This discussion has swung from one extreme to another; the colonial presupposition that ethnicity was a primordial identity has given way to an instrumentalist notion that it is manipulated by special interests. The claim that political ethnicity is an outcome of elite manipulation resembles the nationalist conviction that ethnicity ("tribalism") was no more than a colonial prejudice. I disagree with both the primordial and the instrumentalist notions. By understanding political identities as embedded in particular institutions, I conceptualize them as historical and not primordial, and institutionally durable as opposed to being available for instant manipulation by those in power or seeking power. By treating race and ethnicity as identities that are legally enforced and institutionally reproduced, I analyze both as political identities.

Chapter Two begins by tracing the long debate in Rwandan studies on the origins of Hutu and Tutsi. Why is it that contending positions in this debate—whether between colonial officials and nationalist intellectuals, or among church officials, or between different categories of "disinterested" scholars—have come to be identified with a Hutu versus a Tutsi position? Besides acknowledging important differences that mark the stakes in this contest, I argue that both share a common concern with facts of conquest and migration as central to understanding Rwandan history. More than anything else, this preoccupation with *origins* reflects how colonial power sketched the boundaries of colonial and postcolonial scholarship.

In contrast to this mainstream preoccupation in Rwandan studies, I discuss Hutu and Tutsi as political identities that have changed from one historical period to another, each period indicating a different phase in the institutional development of the Rwanda state. There can, thus, be no single answer to the question posed so often: Who is a Hutu and who is a Tutsi? True, the association of Tutsi with power, and with privilege underwritten by power, can be traced to the period before colonialism;

yet, this fact should not detract us from the critical change that takes place with the colonial period. It is Belgian reform of the colonial state in the decade from the mid-1920s to the mid-1930s that constructed Hutu as *indigenous* Bantu and Tutsi as *alien* Hamites. It is also Belgian colonialism that made for a political history in Rwanda different from that in standard indirect rule colonies, like Uganda and Congo, in tropical Africa.

Chapter Three traces the history that racialized the Hutu/Tutsi difference in Rwanda. It does this in two ways, first, as an ideological discourse, by tracing the notion of race to the grand colonial discourse—called the Hamitic hypothesis—which explained away every sign of civilization in tropical Africa as a foreign import, no doubt an appealing claim at a time when humanity in the black skin was being devalued through capture and exchange for commercial gain. And it does this, secondly, by showing how notions of racial difference got embedded in and reproduced through durable institutions, why it would take more than just an intellectual challenge to cast this legacy aside. What did it mean for the difference between Hutu and Tutsi to be *racialized* rather than to be *ethnicized*? What did it mean for Tutsi to be constructed as nonnatives, even if colonized, and thus occupy a contradictory middle ground between settler citizens and nativized subjects?

Chapter Four focuses on the revolution of 1959 and on the intellectuals who tended to eulogize it. Unlike some who write after the genocide of 1994 and caricature the Revolution, I take its social claims seriously. But unlike those who turn the social and economic record of the revolution as reason enough to embrace it, I turn to its political record to *problematize* the revolution. The single most important failure of the revolution was its inability to transform Hutu and Tutsi as political identities generated by the colonial power. If anything, the revolution built on and reinforced these identities in the name of justice. The underside of the Rwandan revolution, its political tragedy, was that this relentless pursuit of justice turned into a quest for revenge. That quest was the hallmark of the First Republic.

Chapter Five is concerned with the political record of the Second Republic, ushered into power in 1973 with the Habyarimana coup. I take a fresh look at the Second Republic through a single fact whose significance has gone unnoticed by most: the Second Republic redefined the Tutsi from a race to an ethnicity. The Habyarimana regime tried to join the First Republic's discussion of justice in the aftermath of the "Hutu Revolution" to the need for reconciliation to give the revolution a truly national character. In this context, it began a discussion of the Tutsi as an indigenous ethnic group as opposed to a nonindigenous race, and of Tutsi rights as minority rights. But the more it tried to carve a niche for the "internal" Tutsi in the civil and political life of Rwanda, the more precarious became the situation of the "external" Tutsi—exiles from 1959, 1963, and 1973. The failure to address the citizenship demands of the "external" Tutsi marked the single most important failure of the Habyarimana regime. While the reconciliation pursued by the Second Republic softened the critique from the "internal" Tutsi, it tended, if anything, to exacerbate the critique from the "external" Tutsi.

Chapter Six focuses on postcolonial Uganda, the location from which the "external" Tutsi launched their critique in 1990. It is in Uganda, more than anywhere else, that the 1959 Tutsi exiles cast their lot with indigenous citizens who sought to reform the state inherited from colonialism, in the hope that the reformed state will give them political room to make a new home. As they reformed local power in "liberated" areas, the guerrillas of the National Resistance Army redefined the basis of citizenship from indigeneity to residence. In line with this revolutionary heritage, the victorious leadership of the post-1986 government redefined the requirement of citizenship from ancestry to a ten-year residence, thus extending citizenship to 1959 Tutsi exiles. The chapter explains how this remarkable innovation was jettisoned when the National Resistance Movement (NRM) faced its first political crisis in power. The decision to return to ancestry as the basis of citizenship was taken in August 1990 in the face of the Mawogola uprising; a month later, the Rwanda Patriotic Front (RPF) crossed the border into Rwanda. I argue that the crossing needs to be understood as both an invasion of Rwanda and an armed repatriation from Uganda. With the repatriation, the NRM government exported its first political crisis to Rwanda, why the invasion needs to be understood as a confluence of a dual crisis of postcolonial citizenship, in both Rwanda and Uganda.

Chapter Seven is concerned with a single aspect of the political violence that developed in the aftermath of the civil war and grew into massacres that took on the proportions of genocide. My central concern is with *mass participation* in the Rwanda genocide. Defeat in the civil war provided the context for at least three different types of killings in Rwanda in the hundred days between January and April 1994: *first*, the killing of combatants (and civilians) on both sides, killings that were directly an outcome of the civil war; *second* the killing of Hutu by Hutu, whether for political reasons (as when Hutu nationalists killed "moderate" Hutu as RPF collaborators) or for social reasons (as when poor Hutu killed rich ones and appropriated or redistributed their property); and *third*, the killing of Tutsi civilians by civilian Hutu mobs, whether or not organized by state authorities. The Rwanda genocide refers to the third type of killing, that of Tutsi by Hutu. It is this killing *alone* that is the focus of my concern. I begin with the understanding that the genocide was not a local but a Rwanda-wide affair. To be sure, there was a difference between localities, as there was between killers—those enthusiastic, those reluctant, and those coerced—but the killing was not a local affair. Too many experts on Rwanda have shied away from this troubling fact, the "popular" agency in the genocide, by casting the genocide as a state project and not also as a social project. To show how the unthinkable becomes thinkable is my central objective. It is this fact that needs confronting, not because of what it can tell us of Rwanda and Rwandans, but because of what it can tell us about ourselves as political beings—as agents with a capacity to tap both the destructive and the creative potential in politics.

Chapter Eight turns from Rwanda to Congo. The genocide gave birth to Tutsi Power in Rwanda, a power shaped by a diasporic sense of obligation for the welfare of all Tutsi globally. As with the crisis that engulfed Rwanda from 1990, it is the confluence of this external factor with the internal crisis of citizenship in postcolonial Congo that explains the growing crisis in eastern Congo after 1994. In tracing the historical thread to this crisis, and documenting its dimensions through interviews, I seek to press home a conclusion both intellectual and political. Just as when it first crossed the border from Uganda into Rwanda in 1990, the RPF's second crossing, that from Rwanda into Congo in 1997, calls for a regional analysis to be understood.

The *Conclusion* returns to Rwanda as the epicenter of a regional crisis and argues that the political nature of the crisis demands a political solution, just as its regional manifestation calls for a regional approach. If the postcolonial pursuit of justice turned into revenge and built on the colonial legacy, one needs to be aware lest postgenocidal reconciliation also turns into an embrace of the colonial legacy. To steer clear of both horns of the dilemma, I argue for the need to rethink different forms of justice— victors' justice and survivors' justice—this time in the context of democracy, so as to recognize that each would build on and reinforce different political identities, and a different political future.

Defining the Crisis of Postcolonial Citizenship: Settler and Native as Political Identities

Iɴ ᴛʜᴇ decade that followed African political independence, militant nationalist intellectuals focused on the expropriation of the native as the great crime of colonialism. Walter Rodney wrote *How Europe Underdeveloped Africa*. But no one wrote of how Europe *ruled* Africa. The great contribution of underdevelopment theorists was to historicize the construction of colonial markets and, thereby, of market-based identities.[1] The popularity of political economy spread like a forest fire in the postindependence African academy precisely because it historicized colonial realities, even if in a narrowly economic way. Political economy provided a way of countering two kinds of anthropological presumptions embedded in various theories of modernization. The first was that identities in colonized societies were not grounded in historical processes. The second was that the beginning of a history for these societies was precisely colonialism, the point at which they were said to be historically animated by "cultural contact" with the West.[2]

The limits of political economy as a framework for political analysis became clear in the face of postcolonial political violence. For political economy could only explain violence when it resulted from a clash between market-based identities: either class or division of labor. From this point of view, political violence had to be either revolutionary or counterrevolutionary. In the face of political violence that cut *across* social classes rather than between them, and that was animated by distinctions crafted in colonial law rather than those sprouting from the soil of a commodity economy, explanations rooted in political economy turned arid. Animated by noneconomic distinctions, this violence was neither revolutionary nor counterrevolutionary; it was simply nonrevolutionary. It is this limit that seems to have provided an opening for a second coming of cultural explanations of political conflict.

Simply put, cultural theories claim that conflict arises from the difference between cultures. We are thus said to be in the grip of ethnic conflict locally and—more ominously—a clash of civilizations globally.[3] As cultures and civilizations appear armor-plated, the colonial promise of cultural contact is said to have soured into postcolonial cultural conflict. If we are to come to analytical grips with the spread of nonrevolutionary political violence, I suggest we recognize that the process of state formation generates political identities that are distinct not only from market-based identities but also from cultural identities. Faced with a growing tendency to root causes of violence in cultural difference, however, the more pressing need is to differentiate between cultural and political identities, so as to distance oneself analytically from a growing culture-coded racism.

To focus on the construction of political identity is not to deny significant overlaps—or interrelations or even determinations—among cultural, economic, and political processes. No Chinese Wall exists between the political and other domains. Political identities may originate from the cultural or the economic domain.[4] This much is clear from a reading of theorists of both social class and the nation-state. It was, after all, Marx's prediction, and Lenin's endeavor, that economic class would become political class through self-consciousness and self-organization. Similarly, all those who paid homage to the nation-state assumed that the cultural would become the political through the self-determination of the nation. As they heralded the "nation" in the Western world, anthropologists described "tribe" in Africa—like "caste" in India—as the cell form of social life. In both cases, they presumed a lack of historical dynamism. To understand how "tribe" and "race"—like "caste"—got animated as political identities, we need to look at how the law breathed political life into them.

Yet, no one historicized the political legacy of colonialism, of the colonial state as a legal-institutional complex that framed and set in motion particular political identities. The tendency was to discuss agency in an institutional void, by focusing on how it was harnessed to the colonial project; Marxists called the agents "compradors" and nationalists called them "collaborators." Both bemoaned "tribe" and "tribalism" as a colonial concoction while assuming "race" and "racism" to exist as something real, in a positivist sense. Neither tried to historicize race and ethnicity as political identities undergirded and reproduced by institutions of colonial vintage—perhaps because neither had yet managed sufficient analytical distance from that legacy.

Identities: Political, Cultural, and Market Based

In an era when political crisis and civil war have come to be seen as ubiquitous, it is surprising how little academic writing there has been on the question of political identity.[5] The tendency, rather, has been the opposite: to see political identity as derivative of either market-based or cultural identities. An earlier intellectual left tended to see political identity as derivative of market-based class identities such as worker and capitalist or landlord and tenant or merchant and peasant.[6] The intellectual right had a habit of arguing that "real" identity was cultural, and that political identity was in reality an expression of cultural identity.[7] The left had its verifying literature on class struggle and revolution, and the right had its counterpart literature on nationalism and tribalism.

The middle ground, where the two overlapped, was defined by the notion of the "nation-state." Everyone—that is, everyone from Max Weber to V. I. Lenin—agreed that "self-determination" meant the right to one's own state, and that the "self" in "the right of self-determination" was a cultural self. Even when Stalin orchestrated a Marxist consensus around the notion that the nation was not any cultural community, but one that had come to self-consciousness by virtue of a common economy, his point was to highlight the single market as a web of material relations knitting together a single cultural community.[8] The bottom line was still that the nation was a common cultural community, and that self-determination made of it a political community. Cultural identity remained the bedrock of political identity.

The mainstream Marxist left assumed that market-based identities would come to self-consciousness as political identities within the context of the nation-state. That this did not happen was taken as evidence of either a false consciousness or a refracted consciousness. In the post–Cold War period, however, the focus of left analysis shifted from class movements (movements of workers, peasants) to social movements (movements of women, youth, ethnic and racial minorities). As the literature on class struggle gives way to that on social movements, it is no longer the right intelligentsia alone, but also many on the left, who now calls for self-determination for ethnicities. To that extent, too, there has been a growing tendency to presume that political identities either are or should be derivative of cultural identities.

If we are to understand the specificity of political crisis and the possibility of political action, we will need to distinguish political identity from both cultural and market-based identities. Political identities exist in their own right. They are a direct consequence of the history of state formation, and not of market or culture formation. If economic identities are a consequence of the history of development of markets, and cultural identities of the development of communities that share a common language and meaning, political identities need to be understood as a specific consequence of the history of state formation. When it comes to the modern state, political identities are inscribed in law. In the first instance, they are legally enforced.

If the law recognizes you as member of an ethnicity, and state institutions treat you as a member of that ethnicity, then you become an ethnic being legally and institutionally. In contrast, if the law recognizes you as a member of a racial group, then your relationship to the state, and to other legally defined groups, is mediated through the law and the state. It is a consequence of your legally inscribed identity. If your inclusion or exclusion from a regime of rights or entitlements is based on your race or ethnicity, as defined by law, then this becomes a central defining fact for you the individual and your group. From this point of view, both race and ethnicity need to be understood as political—and not cultural, or even biological—identities.

The tendency on the left has been to think of the law as individuating or disaggregating classes, and thus creating false identities. But the law does not just individuate; it also collates. It does not just treat each person as an abstract being—the owner of a commodity in the market, a potential party to a contract—it also creates group identities. Legally inscribed and legally enforced, these identities shape our relationship to the state and to one another through the state. In so doing, they also form the starting point of our struggles.

Political identities are the consequence of how power is organized. The organization of power not only defines the parameters of the political community, telling us who is included and who is left out, it also differentiates the bounded political community internally. This it does by acknowledging different kinds of identities in law. It is identities so acknowledged in law—and thus legally enforced—that form the basis of different political identities. Legal enforcement makes these identities the basis of participation in state-organized institutional and political life. By so doing, it encapsulates them, but without freezing them. Though legally enforced identities constitute the starting point of political action, they do not necessarily limit or even map the course of that political action.

It is not only political identities enforced by power, and thus defined "from above," that are framed in legal definitions. These definitions also form a starting point for the forging of identities "from below"—for the simple reason that this forging "from below" is not in isolation but in contention with power. Even the most radical political action, such as action that accompanies the rise of insurgent identities, has to take as its starting point identities enforced by law, even if to break out of a legal straightjacket. This is why, whether officially enforced or insurgent, political identities need to be understood in relation to the process of state formation.

To sharpen the distinction between cultural and political identities, it will be useful to underline a point of contrast between cultural and political communities. More than anything else, a common cultural community signifies a common past, a common historical inheritance. In contrast, a political community testifies to the existence of a common project for the future. The distinction is often blurred because the past flows into the future, as it always does, creating a significant overlap between cultural and political communities. Yet, there are instances when there is a radical rupture between the two, as in the case of diasporic and immigrant communities. As we shall see, these instances most clearly illuminate the difference between cultural and political identities.

Even when defined as binaries in law, political identities are not always polarized. To understand the dynamic that polarizes political identities, we need to look at polarized identities as the end point of a historical dynamic, rather than positing them as its starting point. At the same time, it is when political identities do become polarized that they become most unlike cultural identities. Whereas cultural identities tend to shade into one another, with plenty of middle ground to nurture hybridity and ambiguity, there is no middle ground, no continuum, between polarized identities. Polarized identities give rise to a kind of political difference where you must be either one or the other. You cannot partake of both. The difference becomes binary, not simply in law but in political life. It sustains no ambiguity.

Every state form generates specific political identities. I shall illustrate this, first, with regard to two forms of the colonial state, characterized by direct and indirect rule. Direct rule tended to generate race-based political identities: settler and native. Indirect rule, in contrast, tended to mitigate the settler-native dialectic by fracturing the race consciousness of natives into multiple and separate ethnic consciousnesses. Once we have understood the dynamic whereby distinctive forms of the colonial state tend to generate distinctive types of political identities, we shall be in a position to understand the process of formation of Hutu and Tutsi as political identities through different periods in the history of the Rwandan state.

COLONIALISM AND POLITICAL IDENTITY

From the outset, modern Western colonialism presented itself as a civilizing project. In Kipling's well-known phrase, colonialism was "the white man's burden." Said to signify the pinnacle of Western civilization, the modern state was considered testimony to the organizing genius of Western man.[9] The architecture of the modern state was inscribed in modern law, Western law. And rule of law was in turn central to the construction of civilized society, in short, civil society.

Wherever in the non-Western world the white man carved out colonies, the civilizational project was marked by a turn-key import: Western law. At its outset, the Western colonial project was no less than to wipe clean the civilizational slate so as to introduce Western norms through Western law; modernization would have to be Westernization. Whatever the differences in practice between colonial powers, one single claim defined a shared civilizational project: whether rulers or ruled, Westerners or non-Westerners, all those subject to the power of the state would be governed through imported Western law. To be sure, there were discriminations that set the colonizers apart from the colonized, and even different groups of colonized apart from one another, within this single universe of modern law. The legal basis of group discrimination was *race*.

The shift from direct to indirect rule marked the first major retreat from this shared civilizational project. In contrast to the single legal universe of direct rule, indirect rule constituted separate legal universes. In addition to a *racial* separation in civil law between natives and nonnatives, as under direct rule, indirect rule divided natives into separate groups and governed each through a different set of "customary" laws. Every ethnic group was now said to have its own separate set of "customary" laws, to be enforced by its own separate "native authority," administering its own "home area." Thereby, the very category "native" was legally dismantled as different groups of natives were set apart on the basis of *ethnicity*. From being only a cultural community, the ethnic group was turned into a political community, too. The political project of the regime of "customary" laws was to fracture a racialized native population into different *ethnicized* groups. The basis of group distinction under indirect rule was both *race* and *ethnicity*.

The shift from direct to indirect rule was eventually made by every colonial power.[10] To understand the sort of compulsion that made for the shift, one needs to reflect on the astonishingly arrogant claim with which modern colonialism announced itself to the world at large. Under direct rule, the colonial state justified the hierarchy of colonial society as a civilizational imperative. Within a single legal order—one based on modern law—it distinguished a political minority from a political majority. The language of the law tried to *naturalize* political differences in the colony by mapping these along a civilizational ladder. As the litmus of a civilizational test, the law separated the minority of civilized from the majority of those yet-to-be-civilized, incorporating the minority into a regime of rights while excluding the majority from that same regime.[11] The law thus enfranchised and empowered as citizens the minority it identified as civilized, and at the same time disempowered and disenfranchised the majority it identified as yet-to-be-civilized. The *unintended* consequence of direct rule was to produce a bipolar identity between the colonizer and the colonized and to mark this difference by race. Its tendency was to divide colonial society into two racialized groups and thereby to turn *race* into the primary difference between these groups.

It is this unintended consequence that made for a fundamental crisis of direct-rule colonialism. As those excluded from the regime of rights made sense of the basis of their exclusion, they tended to organize along racial lines, more or less submerging all other differences as secondary. The more this marker of colonial civilization was turned into a standard for the anticolonial struggle, the more race turned into an anathema. This development posed a new question for colonial rule: how to dismantle and fragment race, and thus the colonized majority, into several political minorities. Indirect rule was the response to this dilemma. Alongside race, indirect rule introduced another political marker: ethnicity. Instead of treating the colonized as a single racialized mass, indirect rule sliced them over, not once but twice. The first division separated the nonindigenous—governed through civil law as nonnatives—from the indigenous, the natives. The second division sliced the natives into so many separate ethnicities. With each ethnicity governed through its own "customary law," the plural legal order among the colonized not only produced plural political identities—as ethnicities—it also claimed that they in turn reflected just as many preexisting cultural identities.

The cultural policy of the colonial power augmented the distinctions written into colonial law. As in law, so in culture, policy in the civic sphere was based on the principle of *identity* and discrimination. The civic sphere was culturally assimilationist, with the culture of the colonized considered the hallmark of civilization, the destiny of all those considered capable of being civilized, and thus becoming citizens. In contrast, cultural policy in the customary sphere was based on the principle of *difference*: it claimed to reproduce "ethnic" difference through an ethnicized "customary" law, not to soften "racial" difference through the application of a uniform civil law. In its legal and cultural policy, the civic sphere was characteristic of direct-rule colonialism, and the customary sphere of indirect-rule colonialism. The amalgam of the two in the actual colonial experience in twentieth-century tropical Africa supplemented racial exclusion in the civic sphere with ethnic fragmentation in the customary sphere, thereby combining direct rule in the civic sphere with indirect rule in the customary sphere.

Said to spring from biology and culture, the difference between races and ethnicities involved two kinds of claims: one about hierarchy, the other concerning diversity. Claims about cultural difference and hierarchy were at the same time turned into foundation stones for building and reproducing legal and political differences. *Culturally,* races were said to be a civilizing influence and ethnicities in dire need of being civilized. Whereas race claimed mainly to reflect a *civilizational hierarchy,* ethnicity was said to be primarily about a *cultural diversity.* Neither claim excluded the other. Thus, the discourse on hierarchy did not preclude a statement about the diversity of unequal races. Similarly, the discussion on ethnic diversity did not mean that some ethnic groups (such as those with an internal hierarchy and a state) were not considered more civilized than others (usually those considered stateless). Yet, as representation, race was vertical but ethnicity horizontal. *Legally,* races were ruled through a single law: riddled with racially discriminatory provisions, civil law was an amalgamation of imported law and local initiative under colonial conditions. In contrast, each ethnicity was ruled through a separate set of customary laws. While civil law discriminated against the lower races in the civil sphere, customary law discriminated against ethnic strangers in the ethnic sphere. *Politically,* ethnicities lived under separate Native Authorities, each reinforcing its version of customary law in its own ethnic homeland, whereas races lived under a single civic authority. Governed under a single law, living under institutions designed for cultural assimilation, and subjugated to a single administrative authority, races were meant to have a common future—but not so ethnicities. In reality, the distinction between race and ethnicity illuminated the political difference between the nonindigenous and the indigenous.

What did it mean to be constructed as a race as opposed to an ethnicity? In the African colonies, only "natives" were said to belong to ethnic groups. "Nonnatives" were identified as races. While ethnicities were said to be indigenous, races were presumed to be nonindigenous. Ethnicity was said to mark an *internal* difference among those constructed by colonial law as indigenous to the land. Race marked an *external* difference, a difference with others, those legally constructed as nonindigenous. Through its discourse on race and ethnicity, the colonial state tried to *naturalize* political differences, not only between the colonizer and the colonized, but also—and this is the important point here—between two kinds of colonized: those indigenous and those not.

Subject Races as Virtual Citizens

Race was about nonnatives and ethnicity about natives; yet, the legal distinction between nonnatives and natives was not quite the same as the political difference between the colonizer and the colonized. By making a distinction between two kinds of colonized groups, those indigenous and those not, the legal system blurred the colonial difference rather than illuminating it. This it did by highlighting the commonality between the colonizer and a minority among the colonized: that both were nonindigenous. It thus created a contradictory middle ground between the colonizer and the colonized. This middle ground was occupied by *subject races*, those from the colonized who were identified as nonindigenous.

Though all races were presumed to be a civilizing influence, some were said to be more so than others. We have seen that the hierarchical distinctions between races were expressed in civil law as so many internal discriminations. Instead of a universal citizenship, civil law gave rise to different categories of citizens. Alongside the master and colonizing race, the law constituted subject races. While members of the master race were the only full citizens in the colony, members of subject races were *virtual citizens*, deprived of rights of citizenship, yet considered to have the potential of becoming full citizens. Though colonized, they came to function as junior clerks in the juggernaut that was the civilizing mission. Without being part of colonial rulers, they came to be integrated into the machinery of colonial rule, as agents, whether in the state apparatus or in the marketplace. As such, they came to be seen as both instruments and beneficiaries of colonialism, however coerced the instrumentality and petty the benefits. Though part of the colonized population, the subject races received preferential treatment under the law. In contrast, subject ethnicities were set apart, and literally sat upon, legally. They were the core victims of colonial rule.

The subject race experience was marked by both petty privilege and petty discrimination. Elevated to the point that they were governed through civil law, subject races were at the same time the target of specific forms of racial discrimination under the same law. Theirs was a contradictory experience: on the one hand, they were elevated above natives and treated as virtual citizens, part of the hierarchy of civilized races; on the other hand, they were subjected to racial discrimination, which emphasized their position in the lower rungs of that hierarchy. They thus became the source of both collaborators with the colonial enterprise and nationalists who agitated against it. The legal and political distinction that cut through the colonized—native subjects and subject races, the majority ethnicized and the minority racialized—evokes the distinction that Malcolm X drew between the House Negro and the Field Negro in a different historical circumstance. As one with access to petty privilege and preferential treatment, the House Negro was prone to identifying with the master: as a clone who would mime "we sick" if the master was sick. And so did many among the subject races.

The subject races of colonial Africa were many. The best known of these were the Asians of East Africa, the Indians and "Coloureds" of South Africa, the Arabs of Zanzibar, and the Tutsi of Rwanda and Burundi. Historically and culturally, they represented a mishmash. The Asians of East Africa, like the Indians of South Africa, were obviously nonindigenous in origin. But South African "Coloureds," Zanzibari "Arabs," and Tutsi of Rwanda and Burundi were not at all obviously alien. The category "Arab" included both those ancestrally Arab and those culturally Arab, both immigrants and children of the soil. To the extent that one could become an Arab, Arab was more of a hybrid identity, as was obviously the identity "Coloured." But the law brooked no hybridity, or ambiguity. At the other end of this list of subject races were the Tutsi. Though wholly indigenous to Africa, we shall see that the Tutsi were constructed by colonial ideology as well as law as nonindigenous Hamites. The claim that the Tutsi—or, for that matter, the Arabs or the "Coloureds"—were nonindigenous, part of the hierarchy of *nonindigenous* races, apart from the Bantu who were said to be indigenous, needs to be understood more as a legal and political construct than as representation of a historical and cultural reality.

POSTCOLONIAL CITIZENSHIP

The political legacy of indirect-rule colonialism in Africa was a bifurcated state: civic and ethnic, the former governed through civil law and the latter through customary law. But the colonial legacy went beyond legal pluralism to a set of institutionally entrenched discriminations: civil law was racialized and customary law ethnicized. At the basis of two different political identities, race and ethnicity, were two sets of discriminations. Racial discrimination in the civic sphere reproduced race as a political identity, just as ethnic discrimination in the customary sphere translated ethnicity from a cultural to a political identity. This twofold discrimination, civic and ethnic, became the basis of a distinction between two types of citizenship in the postcolonial period: civic and ethnic.

Civic and Ethnic Citizens

Civic citizenship is a consequence of membership of the central state. Both the qualifications for citizenship and the rights that are its entitlement are specified in the constitution. These rights are mainly individual and are located in the political and civil domain. In contrast, *ethnic citizenship* is a result of membership in the Native Authority. It is the source of a different category of rights, mainly social and economic. Further, these rights are not accessed individually but by virtue of group membership, the group being the ethnic community. The key socioeconomic right is the right to use land as a source of livelihood.

Ethnic citizenship does not just evoke a cultural difference. It has material consequences also. A civic citizen may acquire land—like any other material good—only through a market transaction, by purchasing it. For a civic citizen, a kin-based property transaction is more or less limited to inheritance. But an ethnic citizen can claim land as a "customary" right, a kin-based claim that is a consequence of membership in an ethnic group. It is also how most peasants access land in a Native Authority. The immediate practical consequence of being defined a citizen of nonindigenous origin is this: since they do not have their own Native Authority, nonindigenous citizens are denied "customary" access to land. No wonder a land-poor peasant sees the struggle for land as part of a struggle for ethnic belonging.

The postcolonial stranger was racial in the civic sphere, and ethnic in the customary sphere. When you said you were citizen of, say, Uganda or Congo, the claim was that you were a citizen of the central state, a civic citizen. Your rights as a civic citizen were specified in the constitution of the republic. But it did not necessarily mean that you were an ethnic citizen. To be an ethnic citizen was to belong to one of the ethnicized Native Authorities so as to claim "customary" rights. Only those considered ethnically indigenous to the republic could claim ethnic citizenship and thus a Native Authority as an ethnic home. In the indirect-rule state, citizens were divided into those indigenous and those not. The former enjoyed both civic and ethnic citizenship; the latter were only civic citizens. At the same time, whereas civic citizenship could be accessed individually, ethnic citizenship could only be exercised as a group.

Who qualified as indigenous? The colonial state considered as indigenous all those who were resident on the territory it seized at the time of colonization, and only those. Anyone who came after was treated as a stranger: if they were indigenous to Africa, they were racially branded as "native" but ethnically as strangers; if they were from outside Africa, they were considered nonnative in race but—and this is the important point— were not ascribed an ethnic identity in law. Most states in Africa continue to adhere to this claim, considering as "native" only those who were present on native soil at the time of colonization, with all others considered nonindigenous. The irony is that for a postcolonial state to make this claim is to uphold the colonial state as its true parent.

Ethnic Citizenship as a Native Prerogative

Given this legacy, any power with a democratic state project in postcolonial Africa confronted a dual task: first, simultaneously to deracialize civil power and deethnicize customary power; and then, to join the two spheres in a single authority. Without creating an undivided civic authority, it would not be possible to create a single and unified citizenship.

Given this monumental task, it is not surprising that the postindependence story is mixed. On the positive side, no independent state was content to reproduce the colonial legacy wholly unreformed. Everywhere, the world of the racialized citizen and the ethnicized native changed after independence. All postindependence regimes were determined, to one degree or another, to do away with the stigma of race they associated with colonial rule. The tendency of the postcolonial state was to deracialize civic identity. Civic citizenship ceased to recognize any difference based on race or place of origin. To deracialize civic citizenship was to end the legal prerogative of the settler. That struggle continued right up to the southern tip of the continent, to apartheid South Africa. The end of apartheid marked an African achievement because it set the future of Africa apart from that of the Americas. Whereas the Americas remain a land of settler independence, nowhere in Africa has settler power survived the end of colonialism.

That is where similarities ended, and differences sprouted among different kinds of postcolonial reform agendas. On the negative side, the conservative variant of the postcolonial state—also its mainstream—continued to reproduce the native identity as ethnic, while enforcing an ethnic version of law as "customary." The irony was that deracialization without deethnicization continued to reproduce a bifurcated citizenship. So long as Native Authorities continued to function with an ethnically defined membership, the state continued to make a distinction between two kinds of citizens: the ethnically indigenous and ethnic strangers. Even if the civic sphere ceased to make a distinction between citizens who were indigenous and those who were not, the ethnic sphere continued to make this distinction. Indigenous citizens continued to have an ethnic home (a "Native Area") governed by an ethnic administration (a "Native Administration"). Thus, the conservative variant of the postcolonial state accepted as "authentic" the colonial construction of the native: as an ethnic being ruled by a patriarchal authority with an authoritarian and unchanging custom that needed to be enforced officially as "customary" law. Conservative postcolonial power thus replaced the settler's prerogative with the native's prerogative. The outcome, however, was proof enough that you could not do away with settler identity without also doing away with native identity, for settler and native were as Siamese twins born of the same colonial parent. Even if conservative nationalism turned the world designed by the settler upside down, it did not change it.

POSTCOLONIAL SETTLERS AND POSTCOLONIAL JUSTICE

If the anticolonial struggle was about deracializing the state, the postcolonial debate was about deracializing civil society. If the anticolonial struggle was preoccupied with the question of rights across racial boundaries, the postcolonial preoccupation was with justice and entitlement. If deracialization meant political equality between erstwhile settlers and natives, justice meant nothing less than a turning of the tables at the expense of the settler and in favor of the native. If to deracialize society was to achieve a measure of social equality between settler and native, the state would have to assert the prerogative of the native at the expense of the settler.

Defining Settlers

The struggle for justice, for redress of colonial wrongs, raised afresh the question of colonial power and the distinctions it made in society. What kinds of differences in civil society were legitimate and what kinds were not? Which differences were directly and predominantly an effect of colonial power asserting the settlers' prerogative, and which ones an effect of market differentiation? In each case, the answer turned around a more basic question: Who is a settler? For unlike "native," "settler" was not a legal identity. Everywhere, the law spoke of "natives" and "nonnatives," not of settlers. Settler was an insurgent assertion, a libel hurled back by natives at the core beneficiaries of colonial rule. Settler was a political identity, of those identified with the conquest state. This is why there was never one single definition of "settler," but as many as there were perspectives among natives. As nationalism differentiated—between the narrow and the inclusive, the cultural and the political, the reactionary and the progressive, and so on—each tendency arrived at a different understanding of "settler" as a political identity. As this process unfolded, the contradictory middle ground occupied by subject races turned into a political battlefield shaping the political future of anticolonial nationalism. What was at the heart of the settler experience: immigration or conquest? Were the settlers only those directly linked to colonial power and thus its core beneficiaries, or did they include all those legally constructed as nonnatives and thus legally entitled to preferential treatment, no matter how petty the preference? Was the key political difference between colonizer and colonized, or between indigenous and nonindigenous? If settlers were created by conquest and reproduced through a form of the state that enforced a settler's prerogative, then the very abolition of that prerogative—and of the state that enforced it—would deflate settlers and natives as political identities.[12] But if settlers were created by migration, then nothing less than repatriation would erase the settler identity.

My point is that every nationalist movement was called upon to determine its attitude to the subject races; similarly, those occupying the middle ground found themselves having to declare their preference for future membership of a political community. The variety of answers on both sides testified to a dynamic that rapidly differentiated nationalism. In the range of answers that emerged during the anticolonial movement of the late fifties, two leaders—Nyerere in Tanzania and Kayibanda in Rwanda—marked the extremes. Nyerere stood for a single unified citizenship, both deracialized and deethnicized.[13] Kayibanda championed a racialized nationalism—of the Hutu—built on the very political identities institutionalized by colonialism: Hutu and Tutsi.[14] Tanzania came to be a paragon of political stability in the region, the one postcolonial state that did not turn entire groups into refugees. Rwanda signified a postcolonial pursuit of justice so relentless that it turned into revenge as it targeted entire groups from the previously colonized population, groups it first victimized and turned into refugees, and later annihilated.

Political Identity and Political Violence

By politicizing indigeneity, the colonial state set in motion a process with the potential of endlessly spawning identities animated by the distinctions indigenous and nonindigenous, and polarizing them. This indeed set the context in which political violence unfolded in Africa, colonial as well as postcolonial. The starting point of that violence was colonial pacification, which took on genocidal proportions where settlers set out to appropriate native land, as in southern Africa and Congo. Settler colonies continued to be the main focus of political violence during the anticolonial struggle, though the initiative shifted from the settler to the native. While it has been widely noted that Africa's most violent anticolonial struggles unfolded against the master race in the settler colonies, few have noted that Africa's worst postindependence violence targeted its subject races: the Tutsi in Rwanda in 1959, the Arabs in Zanzibar in 1963, the Asians in Uganda in 1972, and finally, the Tutsi in Rwanda in 1994. And even fewer have noted the line along which the settler/native dialectic has unfolded in postcolonial Africa, as it has moved from targeting racial strangers in the civic sphere to targeting ethnic strangers in the Native Authorities.

If the master races of colonial Africa were the first group to be defined as settlers, the subject races were the second, and the ethnic strangers in Native Authorities the third, to be targeted as settlers. The more the native/settler dynamic proliferated, the more groups of settlers it created: first the master race, then the subject races—both racial strangers—and finally ethnic strangers from the erstwhile native population. The more this happened, the more the nationalist movement built up through the anticolonial struggle unraveled in the postcolonial period. It is conservative nationalism, with its nativist notions of political identity, that was intent on branding every immigrant, whether racial or ethnic, as a "settler." Victimized in 1959–63, 1973 and 1991–94, the Tutsi of Rwanda belonged to the second category of postcolonial settlers, whereas the Banyarwanda expelled from Uganda in 1982–83 and 1990 and the Banyamulenge of Congo, targeted in 1994, belonged to the third and last category of postcolonial settlers. As we shall see, the case of the Tutsi—considered racial strangers in Rwanda and ethnic strangers in Uganda and Congo—brought together both outcomes in an explosive combination.

HUTU AND TUTSI

My analysis of Hutu and Tutsi as identities differs from the mainstream literature on Rwanda in two important ways. First, whatever other disagreements they may have, historians and political analysts of Rwanda have been preoccupied with finding a *single* answer to the question: Who is a Hutu and who is a Tutsi? In contrast, I argue that Hutu and Tutsi have changed as political identities along with the state that has enforced these identities. There cannot therefore be a single answer that pins Hutu and Tutsi as transhistorical identities. Second, unlike those preoccupied with the *search for origins*—whether biological or cultural—of Hutu and Tutsi, I argue that the clue to Hutu/Tutsi violence lies in two rather contemporary facts. The origin of the violence is connected to how Hutu and Tutsi were constructed as political identities by the colonial state, Hutu as indigenous and Tutsi as alien. The reason for continued violence between Hutu and Tutsi, I argue, is connected with the failure of Rwandan nationalism to transcend the colonial construction of Hutu and Tutsi as native and alien. Indeed, if anything, the revolutionaries of 1959 confirmed the Tutsi minority as aliens and the Hutu majority as natives—in the well-known phrase, *Rwanda nyamwinshi*[15]—finally and rightfully come to power.

A Halfway House

Colonial Rwanda was a halfway house between direct and indirect rule, combining features of both. Like elsewhere in colonial Africa, in Rwanda too, Belgian power constructed "customary law" and "Native Authorities," alongside civic law and civic authorities. But, unlike elsewhere in Africa, neither this law nor this authority were ethnicized. After the Belgian colonial reform of 1926–36, Hutu were not ruled by their own chiefs, but by Tutsi chiefs. The same reforms constructed the Tutsi into a different race: the Hamitic race. This made for two important differences with indirect-rule colonialism. *One*, the bulk of the colonized population was not fragmented along ethnic lines into so many ethnically diverse identities, each with its own "customary" law and enforcing authority; instead, they were made into a single mass—the Hutu, said to be indigenous Bantu—who cut across all Native Authorities. *Two*, this Bantu majority was not ruled through their own chiefs but through those constructed as racially different and superior, the Hamites. Unlike indirect rule elsewhere, but like British rule in Zanzibar, the colonial state in Rwanda produced bipolar racial identities, and not plural ethnic identities, among the colonized. A single binary opposition split the colonized population into two: a *nativized* majority opposed to several *nonnative* minorities. In Zanzibar, this opposition pitted African against Arab and Asian, not just British power; in Rwanda, it pitted Hutu against Tutsi, not just Belgian power.

This difference cannot be explained as either a simple carryover from the precolonial era or its inevitable consequence. It has to be seen as a specific outcome of the articulation between precolonial and colonial institutions and ideologies. We shall see that while Tutsi privilege had its genesis in the period immediately preceding colonialism—it was not unlike Hima privilege in the neighboring kingdom of Ankole that became part of colonial Uganda—the difference between Uganda and Rwanda in forms of colonial rule made for a world of difference between the postcolonial future of the Ugandan Bahima and that of the Rwandan Tutsi. Nor can it be seen as an inevitable effect of colonial racism, the ideological perversion called the "Hamitic hypothesis." To account for the difference that Belgian colonialism made to Rwanda, as opposed to Congo, we shall need to consider not simply its ideological, but also its institutional impact.

The Hamitic hypothesis was not articulated with reference to Rwanda only. In fact, it claimed to explain all signs of civilization in Bantu Africa—from monotheism to the use of iron and other material artifacts to the development of statecraft. Not only the Tutsi, but also the Bahima and the ruling stratum in Baganda, too, for example, were considered Hamites. The important point is that only the Tutsi—and not the Bahima elite, nor the Baganda, nor any other group considered Hamitic—were constructed as a race as opposed to an ethnic group. Only in Rwanda and Burundi did the Hamitic hypothesis become the basis of a series of institutional changes that *fixed* the Tutsi as a race in their relationship to the colonial state.

THE GENOCIDE IN A REGIONAL CONTEXT

More than any other, the Rwandan genocide brings two events into sharp focus: the 1959 "social" revolution and the 1990 RPF invasion. More than ever before, a postgenocidal analysis demands that we take a second, and a third, look at each so that we may draw from it lessons appropriate to a postgenocide politics.

I will argue that both events are indicative of a deep-seated crisis: 1959 signals a crisis of subaltern nationalism, and 1990 a crisis of postcolonial citizenship. The promise of 1959 turned sour not because 1959 was a false revolution, as proponents of "Tutsi Power" often allege. It turned sour in spite of real social gains, because 1959 repudiated only the consequences of colonial rule, but not the native/settler dynamic that was its institutional premise. Instead of pioneering a way beyond colonially shaped identities and destinies, 1959 locked Rwanda's fate within the world of political identities constructed by colonialism. Instead of the promised first act in a revolutionary drama that would close the curtain on the colonial era, 1959 turned into a final act desperately trying to breathe life into racialized identities born of the colonial state. Indeed, 1959 ushered in a pursuit of justice so focused that it turned into revenge.

While the crisis of nationalism can be made sense of in a single-country context, the crisis of citizenship cannot be grasped fully outside of a regional context. The RPF invasion of Rwanda from Uganda was the first signal that the crisis of citizenship had indeed taken on a regional dimension. The 1990 invasion, I argue, needs also to be understood as an armed repatriation of Banyarwanda refugees from Uganda. It signified a citizenship crisis on both the Ugandan and the Rwandan sides of the border. The RPF's crossing of the Uganda-Rwanda border in 1990 had a double significance: on the one hand, the National Resistance Movement (NRM) in Uganda exported its first political crisis since coming to power to Rwanda; on the other, the postrevolutionary Second Republic in Rwanda got its first taste of revolutionary chickens returning home. Neither the 1990 invasion nor the dynamic that led to the 1994 genocide can be understood outside of a regional context.

Specifically, a regional approach has three advantages. *First*, it allows us to contrast the process of identity formation in colonial Rwanda with some aspects of identity formation in Congo and Uganda. The salient political identities in Rwanda were Hutu and Tutsi; but in Congo and Uganda, Hutu and Tutsi tended to belong to a single political identity, the Banyarwanda. While Hutu and Tutsi were exclusively political identities, Banyarwanda was a cultural identity that also became political in the context of indirect-rule colonialism in Uganda and Congo. While Hutu and Tutsi in Rwanda were racialized identities—Tutsi as nonindigenous Hamites and Hutu as indigenous Bantu—Banyarwanda was an ethnicized identity in

Congo and Uganda. The consequence was that while the Tutsi were considered racial strangers in colonial and postcolonial Rwanda, the Banyarwanda were considered ethnic—but not racial—strangers in colonial and postcolonial Uganda and Congo.

This does not mean that the identity Banyarwanda did not exist on the Rwandan side of the border, or that, as they crossed to the Ugandan or Congolese sides of the border, migrants and refugees somehow ceased to think of themselves as Hutu or Tutsi and miraculously began to think of themselves as Banyarwanda only. To be sure, there were always multiple identities on all sides of the border. The same persons came to see themselves as both Hutu (or Tutsi) *and* Banyarwanda. And yet, the important fact—the politically salient fact—is that the law considered this same person as Hutu (or Tutsi) on the Rwandan side of the border but as Munyarwanda on the Congolese or Ugandan side of the border.

Second, the regional approach not only makes for a comparative understanding of the crisis of postcolonial citizenship, it also allows for a comparative insight into initiatives that tried to address this crisis. These initiatives came from both above and below. The initiatives from below came from Congo and Uganda, contexts where the Banyarwanda were branded ethnic strangers even if they were granted civic citizenship. Defined as ethnic strangers, the Banyarwanda of Congo and Uganda sought to make a political home where they were resident. But the initiatives they took differed. Those in South Kivu pressed for an ethnic home (Native Authority) by redefining their identity from Banyarwanda to Banyamulenge, from ethnic strangers to an ethnically indigenous community. In contrast, the political refugees in Uganda who were the spearhead of the National Resistence Army (NRA) guerrilla struggle went so far as to challenge the very system of Native Authorities by redefining the very basis of rights from ethnicity to residence. Theirs was indeed a radical attempt whose objective was to deethnicize citizenship.

The initiative from above came from the Habyarimana government in Rwanda and the Museveni government in Uganda, two regimes that were often publicly at loggerheads with each other. Unlike the postrevolutionary government of Kayibanda (also known as the First Republic), which continued the racial branding of Tutsi as Hamites, the Second Republic identified with Habyarimana sought to soften Hutu/Tutsi relations by redefining Tutsi from a race to an ethnicity. But while Habyarimana was willing to remove the stigma of being alien from those Tutsi living in Rwanda, thereby even letting them participate in the political sphere, he was not willing to grant the same opening to the political diaspora of exiles and refugees spread throughout the region, and indeed the globe. The limits of the Habyarimana initiative were that the Tutsi resident outside Rwanda must find a way to regularize their stay outside. That way was indeed found with the NRA reforms that redefined the basis of rights from ancestry to residence. It is indeed this reform that the Museveni government translated into law, both when it changed the legal requirement for civic citizenship from two generations to ten years of residence, and when it replaced the very notion of ethnic citizenship by residence-based rights within local councils throughout the country. But the first major political crisis of the Museveni government also brought this very reform into question. The price of surviving that crisis was to repudiate the very reform that had promised a future beyond colonially crafted political horizons: the exiles of 1959 found their new citizenship no more than a paper promise. Thrown back to an exile status, the Tutsi guerrilla fighters in the Uganda state army, the National Resistance Army, found themselves between the Rwandan devil and the Ugandan deep sea. The invasion of 1990 was their attempt to escape the closing scissors of a postcolonial citizenship crisis in Rwanda and Uganda.

Finally, a regional approach allows us to understand the regional consequences of the Rwandan genocide. It will allow us to see how the cross-border passage from racialized to ethnicized identities, and vice versa, has made the Banyarwanda diaspora—first the Tutsi and then the Hutu—the most volatile of all diasporic networks in the region. If it were the tensions of the Ugandan civil war and its aftermath that spilled over into Rwanda in October 1990, we shall see that it was the tensions of the Rwandan civil war and genocide that spilled into Kivu that same decade. Somewhat like the Zionist state born of the Holocaust, the diasporic state born of the genocide saw itself as morally accountable for the welfare of all surviving Tutsi globally. One consequence of the genocide was to dissolve the Banyarwanda ethnicity in North and South Kivu into the by-now volcanic crucible of Rwandan politics. Out of that process of dissolution emerged ultimately hostile Hutu and Tutsi partisans.

More than any other development, the Rwandan genocide is testimony to both the poisoned colonial legacy and the nativist nationalist project that failed to transcend it. Written with an eye on both developments, this book is concerned both with the nature of political identities reproduced by the colonial state and with identity formation in the postcolonial period. To understand how the colonial and the postcolonial articulated politically, I ask questions such as the following: To what extent did the identities implanted by colonial institutions get reproduced in the nationalist move-ment, and to what extent did the nationalist movement and the postcolo-nial state manage to transcend the colonial institutional/ideological legacy?

The Banyarwanda diaspora is today the largest and the most active of all diasporic networks in the region of the African Great Lakes. Infected by civil war and genocide in Rwanda, it has over the past decade split into two distinct and antagonistic networks: one Hutu, the other Tutsi. In this form, Hutu and Tutsi identities have functioned like so many carriers that have taken the virus of political conflict from one side of the border to the next. If the Hutu demand democracy, a recognition that they are the political majority, the Tutsi demand justice, a claim that the right to life must precede any recognition of a political majority. Is it possible to recon-cile these seemingly conflicting demands: democracy and justice? To do so, I argue, requires going beyond the notion of victors' justice to that of survivors' justice. Without a notion of justice appropriate to a postgeno-cide situation, it will not be possible to construct a political identity other than Hutu and Tutsi in postgenocide Rwanda.

If the Nazi Holocaust was testimony to the crisis of the nation-state in Europe, the Rwandan genocide is testimony to the crisis of citizenship in postcolonial Africa. But if the Nazi Holocaust breathed life into the Zion-ist demand that Jews too must have a political home, a nation-state of their own, few have argued that the Rwandan genocide calls for the building of a Tutsi-land in the region. While Europe "solved" its political crisis by exporting it to the Middle East, Africa has no place to export its political crisis. That need not necessarily turn into a dilemma. If taken hold of, it can be an opportunity to marshal Africa's resources to address the crisis of citizenship in postcolonial Africa. I aim to probe that possibility in the hope that life must be possible after death—why this book is more about politics than about history, why it is ultimately a book that wrestles with the question of political reform after political catastrophe.

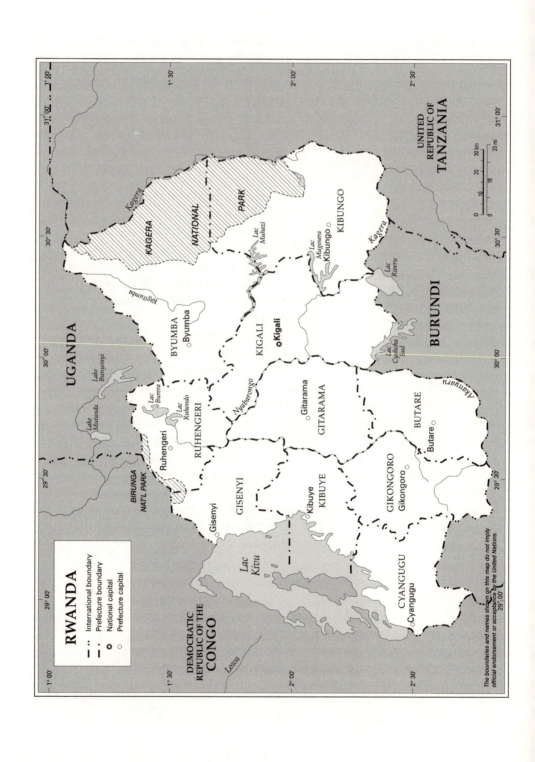

Chapter Two

The Origins of Hutu and Tutsi

W<small>HO ARE</small> the Hutu and who the Tutsi? Are they the same people, as many a militant in the Rwanda Patriotic Front (RPF) is prone to insist? Or are they distinct ethnic—even racial—groups, as proponents of Hutu Power claim? In my visits to postgenocide Rwanda, the question came up in literally every discussion. The answers were many. At one end were those who claimed the difference did not exist or that it was simply a "normal" socioeconomic difference: either a class difference between poor and rich, or a division of labor between agriculturalists and pastoralists. In either case, they said it was a type of difference that would exist "normally" within a single people, anywhere. At the other end were those who maintained the difference to be sociobiological: Hutu and Tutsi, they said, were two distinct peoples with separate histories, until Tutsi migrants conquered the settled Hutu communities and reduced them to the status of a servile population.

The genocide consolidated two opposed points of view: one Tutsi, the other Hutu. A Nigerian colleague made the point boldly at a conference organized by the Dakar-based Council for the Development of Social Research in Africa (CODESRIA) in Arusha early in 1995. If he went to a discussion on Rwanda and Burundi, he said, he could close his eyes and tell the identity of a speaker by the twist of his or her argument: if a person claimed there was no difference between Hutu and Tutsi, or that the difference was one of class, the speaker was most likely a Tutsi. A Hutu intellectual was more likely to argue otherwise, that the difference was one between distinct groups, ethnic or even racial. The "no difference" (or class difference) point of view has come to be identified with a pro-Tutsi orientation, the "distinct difference" point of view with partiality to the Hutu. In the inflamed atmosphere of postgenocide Rwanda studies, even the tiny coterie of Rwanda specialists among Western academics—mostly Belgian, French, and North American—has not escaped this litmus test. Depending on one's point of view, each gets tagged as pro-Hutu or as pro-Tutsi.

Within the region of the African Great Lakes, the diversity of views on this question can be mapped around a dialectic defined by two opposed viewpoints: colonialism and nationalism. European explorers and missionaries who entered the region at the turn of the century began with what seemed a commonsense observation: Tutsi aristocrats *looked* different from Hutu commoners. As we shall see, colonial scholarship built on this observation and *constructed* Hutu and Tutsi as different. Faced with an accent on difference, the intellectuals of the anti-colonial movement took as their starting point a second common sense observation: no matter how different they looked, Hutu and Tutsi were part of a single economic and cultural community. Ergo, they were the same.

When I returned from my first visit to postgenocide Rwanda in 1995, I was perplexed by the same question: Who were the Hutu and who the Tutsi? My forays into Rwandan history brought me to two observations that form the point of departure of this book. *First*, I noticed that the colonial and the anticolonial standpoints, one highlighting difference and the other sameness, had given rise to distinct scholarly traditions, each with its own overall consensus and internal controversies. While the "distinct difference" point of view highlights *separate origins* of ancestors of Hutu and Tutsi, the "no difference" point of view emphasizes subsequent processes leading to *cultural integration* on the one hand, and *occupational and wealth differentiation* on the other—both within the framework of a single cultural and economic community. The relationship between scholarship and politics has been dialectical: grounded in scholarship, political perspective has in turn influenced the development of scholarship. This, it seemed to me, was reason to take the scholarship more, and not less, seriously.

I became one of a growing number of African academics who, though new to Rwandan scholarship, was beginning to think of the relationship between political power and political violence in the 1994 genocide. The more I delved into it, the more convinced I was of how effectively power had mapped the parameters within which scholars had pursued knowledge of Rwanda. This gruesome event not only stripped from scholarship the veil of objectivity with which it habitually claims a distance from the world of power and practice, it also threw specific light on how complicit history-writing on Rwanda had become in the imperialist project in twentieth-century Africa. If power *classified* the population of Rwanda into three "races"—Hutu, Tutsi, and Twa—then scholars accepted race as a transhistorical reality and wrote the history of Rwanda as a history of the coming together of three races. If power assumed that migration was central to the

spread of civilization, particularly of statecraft, in Africa, then scholarship
became preoccupied with the *search for origins*. If power read racial differences as cultural artefacts, and translated cultural into political differences,
few indeed were the scholars who pointed out that what was at work was
really a political project trying to *naturalize* political difference as a simple
and unproblematic reflection of cultural and biological difference.

Precisely because the discussion on origins was from the outset framed
in political terms by the colonial state, it took on a partisan character that
goes beyond the intentions of any one author. The most esoteric debates
unfolded in political terms framed by the colonial power, even the most
"disinterested" scholars observed those parameters and got implicated,
their intentions not withstanding. If postgenocide sobriety can teach us
one thing, it is how colonial power has become etched on the pages of
scholarly books no less than on the surface of public life in the region. As
we shall see, competing interpretations got linked to changes in sociopolitical context in the region. When it came to major shifts in interpretation,
they followed events that signaled a crisis of political power no less than
that of intellectual perspective, such as the 1959 Revolution, and now, the
1994 genocide.

My *second* observation followed from this reflection. To the extent that
it saw political difference as a simple consequence of cultural or biological
difference, neither scholarly tradition had much to say about the question
that interested me: the *political* difference between Hutu and Tutsi. To
make that point, and to begin my own exploration into the meaning of
Hutu and Tutsi, I first need to sum up the main tendencies in both scholarly traditions.

SEARCH FOR ORIGINS: THE MIGRATION HYPOTHESIS

At least four different kinds of studies have tended to buttress the
"distinct difference" school of thought. All four highlight particular facts
of history. Chronologically, the first is a literature from physical anthropologists that takes as its starting point differences in *phenotype*, mainly in
physical height. Akin to this, but more recent, is a second type of literature
originating from a combination of physical anthropologists and natural
scientists. Its focus is *genotype:* blood factors, the presence of the sickle cell
trait, and the prevalent ability among adults to digest lactose, a milk sugar.
The third type of literature comes from cultural anthropology, and takes
as its source material the *memory* of the peoples of the region as its cultural
archive. The final branch of this scholarship is constituted by the work of

the more conventional historians. In the absence of written archival sources that go back more than a century, and a recognition that it is difficult to stretch the reliability of oral sources for more than a few generations, historians have looked for other source materials, mainly *archaeological* and *linguistic*, to piece together a narrative. Let us briefly look at each of these scholarly endeavors.

Colonial anthropologists began with a commonsense observation concerning a difference in physique between those who lived in Rwanda: the Twa, the Hutu, and the Tutsi. The Twa were short, like pygmies. The Hutu were squat and of medium height, and the Tutsi were slender and tall. Since the Twa were insignificant numerically, hardly a few percentage of the total population, attention focused on the Hutu and the Tutsi. The data physical anthropologists gathered confirmed the visual evidence: on average, Tutsi tended to be taller than Hutu. Working in the early part of this century, a German anthropologist found a 12-centimeter difference in average height between Hutu and Tutsi.[1] Over a decade after independence, Jean Hiernaux, the director of research at the Paris-based National Center for Scientific Research (CNRS), confirmed: "The Tutsi are taller than the Hutu by nearly ten centimetres."[2] From the observation that Hutu and Tutsi were indeed different in some respects, colonial scholars concluded that they were indeed different peoples who must indeed have come from different places. Thus was born the *migration hypothesis*, that the ancestors of the Hutu and the Tutsi migrated as different peoples into the region of the African Great Lakes.

The critique of colonial anthropology came in two rounds. The first was also the more polemical: it denied the very possibility of migration and argued that physical differences originated in social selection, that is, the tendency of privileged elites to breed and feed selectively. The second round came as more evidence was gathered, this time from natural scientists showing the plausibility of migration as a historical fact. Rather than deny the possibility of migration, critics questioned the contemporary significance of this historical fact. Walter Rodney best represents the first round of response, a militant nationalist critique of colonial racial ideology. His writing was standard reading for RPF cadres in the late 1980s and early 1990s. In his influential work, *How Europe Underdeveloped Africa*, Rodney explained physical differences in Rwanda as evidence of different levels of social development. The Twa, he claimed, remained "pygmies" because "they wandered around in small bands, hunting and digging roots, thereby failing to assure themselves of plentiful or rich food." The Hutu "were more socially advanced than the Batwa" because "they did not live entirely on the whims of nature." But compared to the Tutsi, the Hutu remained "short and stocky" because "the quality of their food fell short of the protein-rich Tutsi diet." And so the pastoralist Tutsi, "subsisting on a constantly accessible and rich diet on milk and meat" turned out to be "one of the tallest human groups in the world."[3] Writing after the genocide, a captain in the RPF repeated that same argument: "Science can account for the differences in physical traits which are explained in terms of diet and natural selection."[4]

While Walter Rodney emphasized social selection in the form of selective feeding, others have coupled it with selective breeding. More recently, Dominique Franche, a French social geographer, had pointed out that a 12-centimeter difference in average height said to differentiate Hutu from Tutsi was "exactly the same difference that existed in France between a conscript and a senator in 1815." On this basis, he concludes: "The difference in height can be explained by their different lifestyles and eating habits, and by the fact that Tutsi noblemen, unlike Hutus, did not till the land." To this, he adds the reinforcing influence of sexual selection: "Ideals of beauty vary amongst different social groups."[5]

More recent studies pay less attention to phenotype such as body height and width of nose, and more to genotype: blood factors, the presence of the sickle cell trait, and the prevalent ability among adults to digest lactose, a milk sugar. A 1987 survey, "Genetics and History of Sub-Saharan Africa," concluded that "though surrounded by Bantu populations," the Tutsi and Hima are "closer genetically to Cushites and Ethiosemites."[6] Another study concluded that while the sickle cell trait was "about as common" among Rwandan Hutu "as [it was] in neighbouring populations," it was virtually absent among Rwandan Tutsi. Previously taken as a marker of "race"—a point of view now discredited—the presence of the sickle cell trait is now considered evidence of survival in malarial environments through natural selection over centuries, even millennia. This finding thus reinforced the first: that the ancestors of Tutsi had indeed moved from a relatively malaria-free environment.[7] A third genetically determined characteristic said to differentiate Rwandan Tutsi from Hutu—and both from all surrounding peoples in the Great Lakes region—is the prevalent ability among adults to digest lactose, a milk sugar.[8]

Lactose is "a biologically unique sugar" which occurs "as a free molecule only in milk." The ability to digest lactose is limited in most human populations, except in "milk-dependent nomadic desert populations" which, through natural selection over millennia, have a gene (allele) that accounts for their high lactose absorption capacity.[9] Studies in the Great

Lakes region bring out three contrasting sets of empirical findings. They
highlight, at one end of the spectrum, the Tutsi of Rwanda and Burundi
among whom three out of four adults display a high ability to digest lactose; and at the other end, the neighboring Shi people of eastern Congo,
among whom only 5 percent of adults display this ability. In the middle
are the Hutu, among whom one out of three adults shows that same ability. Could the explanation for the high prevalence of lactose digestion
among as many as a third of the Rwandan Hutu be centuries of intermarriage between Hutu and Tutsi?

The migration hypothesis was further reinforced by regional myths that
predated the colonial period and were recorded by early colonial anthropologists and explorers. They have recently been strung together and
framed into a single grand hypothesis by Archie Mafeje in a recent work,
The Theory and Ethnography of African Social Formations.[10] The central
myth concerns the Bachwezi dynasty in the kingdom of Bunyoro in western Uganda. The Bachwezi are said to have "migrated from south eastern
Ethiopia and southern Somalia with their long-horned cattle," but moved
on after "a few generations" when "chased out by Babito invaders" from
the north. Following the myth, Mafeje suggests a migration in "a south-
westerly direction where ecological conditions are ideal for cattle-keep-
ing." Mafeje thus links the Bachwezi of Bunyoro with the Bahima of Ankole and the Tutsi of the Great Lakes. While many may be reluctant to
accept the restatement of myth as historical fact, few would dare dismiss
it as outright fiction.[11] At the same time, one needs to beware that public
memory—in this case, myth—also changes and that this change is not
entirely unrelated to official discourse. A context in which official discourse
privileged some because they were said to have migrated from elsewhere
was certainly an incentive to those concerned to embellish stories about
their having come from elsewhere.

Writing in the UNESCO *General History* in 1988, Bethwell Ogot, the
leading East African historical authority on the subject, both accepted that
pastoralists and agriculturalists had long inhabited the region and noted
that the number of pastoralists increased "sharply" from "about the fifteenth century." Whence did these pastoralists—among the ancestors of
contemporary Tutsi—come? This is where views differed among those
who supported the thesis of separate origins. The first group comprised
a combination of colonial anthropologists, explorers, and missionaries.
Anthropologists were led by John Seligman, explorers by Hohn Hanning
Speke, and missionaries followed Father Léon Classe; all subscribed to
the "Hamitic hypothesis." Discredited with the first onslaught of militant

nationalism, this point of view nonetheless animated the political institutions of both colonial and revolutionary Rwanda. The second group comprised several trends in nationalist and postnationalist historiography. The "older view" (Roland Oliver) was that the Tutsi—and the Bahima—came "from the north-east, probably from southern Ethiopia." A later theory (Chris Ehret) put forward the possibility that the Bahima/Tutsi could have come from "the east rather than the north," testifying to the "late continuation of Southern Cushites as important pastoralists in the southern half of the lacustrine region."[12] The most interesting amongst these was Jean Hiernaux, who argued on the basis of genetic and archaeological evidence that the Tutsi may be ancient East Africans—"elongated East Africans"—whose physical distinctiveness attested to successful adaptation to and survival in a dry arid climate over millennia.

Among the physical anthropologists who wrote on the Hutu/Tutsi difference, Jean Hiernaux occupies a notable position because he combined explicitly antiracist convictions with the view that Hutu and Tutsi had separate origins. Based on studies of blood factors and on archaeological evidence, Hiernaux argued that the Tutsi were one extreme of humanity as it developed under African conditions, just as pygmies were the other extreme. He thus disagreed sharply with the Hamitic hypothesis—identified in anthropology with Seligman, a formulation we shall encounter in detail in the next chapter—that Tutsi were a civilizing Caucasian influence in Negro Africa. He began with the observation that, though Tutsi were on the average taller than Hutu, they were in most respects more different from Europeans than were Hutu: after all, they were darker than the Hutu in skin color, had thicker lips, while their hair was almost as "spiraled" as that of the Hutu.[13] Hiernaux maintained that what had struck European explorers was a feature specific to Tutsi and related populations. This was "a tendency towards general elongation of the physical features: long and narrow heads, faces and noses, narrow thorax and shoulders relative to the stature; even the limb diameters are small when related to limb length." He described this population as "elongated East African," and located "the area of differentiation of these people in the interior of East Africa," not outside it: "Fossil record tells of tall people with long and narrow heads, faces and noses who lived a few thousand years B.C. in East Africa at such places as Gambles Cave in the Kenya Rift Valley and at Olduvai in northern Tanzania. There is every reason to believe that they are ancestral to the living elongated East Africans." He then concluded: "Neither of these populations, fossil and modern, should be considered to be closely related to Caucasoids of Europe and West Asia, as they usually are in the literature." Similar to the contrast between Hutu and Tutsi, Hiernaux pointed out, were the differences found in Kenya between "the elongated Masaii herders of the dry plains and the Kikuyu farmers of the well-watered mountainous areas nearby." Along with the Masai of Kenya and the Tutsi of Rwanda and Burundi, Hiernaux classified the Fulani of West Africa in a single group—"elongated Africans"—and postulated "that they owe much of their constitution to a peculiar evolution in the semi-arid or arid crescent which caps sub-Saharan Africa to the north and the northeast," and added that their most conspicuous features represent "genetic adaptations to dry heat." It is not "an extra-African 'Caucasoid' element in their gene pool," nor selective feeding or breeding, but genetic adaptation that explained for Hiernaux how such strikingly different physiques as those of the "elongated Africans" and the pygmies could be produced in tropical Africa: "These two opposite poles of morphological differentiation correspond to the two climatic opposites of tropical Africa," one "hot and dry, with well-marked seasons," the other "uniformly hot and wet."[14] The adaptation had to have occurred not only over centuries, but over millennia. The ancestors of Hutu and Tutsi, Hiernaux remained convinced, had to have had separate origins: "The Tutsi are evidently not Hutu transformed by selection."[15]

I have argued that the critique of colonial anthropology came in two rounds. Written in direct response to colonial racial ideology, the earlier critique was the more polemical. It simply generalized backwards from the commonsense observation that—whatever the physical differences between them—Hutu and Tutsi lived in a single cultural and economic community and thus argued that they had always been a single people. A later response—the second round, so to speak—shifted ground. Without denying the possibility that ancestors of Hutu and Tutsi may have had separate origins, it questioned the significance of this historical fact in explaining contemporary realities. Historians suggested that contemporary cultural facts such as pastoralism, statecraft, or a common language could be the outcome of entirely different processes, with contradictory outcomes. Four kinds of studies made this point. The *first* proceeded by making a distinction between migration and conquest: that, whereas both can lead to cultural integration, they involve dramatically different political consequences. Migrations can be peaceful and protracted, but invasions are often a bloody and dramatic affair leading to political polarization. A *second* type of study questioned the presumed link between the Tutsi migration and the origin of pastoralism and statecraft in the region, thereby devaluing the significance of pastoralist migrations. A *third* type questioned the presumption that cultural exchange, in this case the spread of a common language, necessarily has to involve a movement of peoples, either via conquest or migration. An exchange of ideas or practices is possible without physical displacement of humans involved in the exchange. A *fourth* and final type questioned the presumption that contemporary Hutu and Tutsi are necessarily "pure" offspring of Hutu or Tutsi ancestors, whether these migrated or not, given widespread practices of cohabitation and intermarriage over generations, a historical fact otherwise erased by the patriarchal transmission of cultural identity.

Jan Vansina was the first historian to draw the distinction behind migration and conquest. Gathering his evidence from oral testimony, Vansina countered hitherto court-centered explanations of cultural assimilation based on conquest with popular accounts stressing a process of two-way cultural integration rather than a one-way assimilation. While we shall later see how this altered the prevailing account of the founding of Rwanda, it suffices to point out here that Vansina's contribution almost immediately revived the migration controversy in the writing of African history. The context of the debate was the essay on Bantu expansion in volume 3 of the UNESCO *General History*, coauthored by Jan Vansina with the Ugandan historian S. Lwanga-Lunyiigo. While the authors had no trouble agreeing on devaluing the conquest-and-assimilation thesis, they could not agree on an alternative explanation. The body of the article cited the majority view among linguists and historians—advocated in the essay by Vansina—that "the Bantu languages originated in the West" and spread to most of subequatorial Africa through migrations. This, in other words, was the "migration-and-acculturation" view—that cultural transmission was the consequence of migration. Articulated by linguists and buttressed by genetic evidence, it gave primacy to the movement of peoples over linguistic borrowing. Instead of earlier notions implying one or several dramatic waves of migration, Vansina argued that migration must have occurred in dribs and drabs over two or three thousand years.[16]

In an appendix he penned under his name, Lwanga-Lunyiigo disagreed. Questioning whether the spread of language had necessarily to be the result of migration, he wondered whether it could not just as easily be the result of the borrowing of language. His conclusion called into question the entire migration hypothesis: "Basing myself on archaeological evidence, I suggested recently that the speakers of Bantu languages occupied from very early times a broad swath of territory running from the Great Lakes region of East Africa to the shores of the Atlantic in Zaire and that the supposed movement of Bantu-speakers from West Africa to central,

eastern and southern Africa did not take place."[17] Whatever the merits
of his specific argument, the important point about Lwanga-Lunyiigo's
contribution was that he questioned the prevalent tendency among historians to assume that every "development" within Africa had to be the
result of an external impulse. In the process, even if unwittingly, he exposed the original and persistent sin of Western history writing when it
came to Africa: *the search for origins.* The important question he raised
was: Why presume that cultural development was the result of migration,
of peoples, rather than the exchange of ideas?

In any specific instance, such as Rwanda, the question could not be
answered without adequate historical information. The more historical
information was gathered, the more the significance of earlier migrations
was brought into question: both in explaining the origin of pastoralism
and statecraft, and in the presumption that those who emigrated separately
must have remained biologically separate and pure over centuries, so that
those identified as Tutsi today must naturally be the offspring of those
who may have come in as Tutsi centuries earlier. Even if historical research
buttressed the notion that ancestors of Tutsi and Hutu had separate origins, it was forced to contend with a far more contemporary fact: that
Tutsi and Hutu did not live as separate cultural communities in Rwanda,
but spoke the same language, practiced the same religion, and lived on
the same territory. This, too, was an outcome of historical processes, one
that no historian could ignore.

A COMMON CULTURAL COMMUNITY:
RECONSIDERING THE MIGRATION HYPOTHESIS

Recent historical research tends to deemphasize dramatic ruptures
and to bring to light more integrative processes over the past five centuries. In this context, the tendency is to diminish the exaggerated significance attributed to migration by earlier historians, but without denying
its possibility. J. K. Rennie's summation of the state of research in the
1960s is still a consensus: while we do not know "whether the Bantu-
speaking agriculturalists settled in Rwanda before the pastoralists," we do
know that "pastoralist groups began immigrating in considerable numbers
from at least the 15th century."[18] It is research bearing on the five centuries since, and not the migration hypothesis, that has yielded results that
can provide a truly fruitful starting point for further work. The focal point
of this research is the formation of two communities: one economic, the
other cultural.

An Economic Community

When the ancestors of today's Hutu and Tutsi came together, they created different types of communities: economic, cultural, and political. The economic community was that of pastoralists and agriculturalists. The simple notion that Hutu were agriculturalists and Tutsi pastoralists is no longer sustainable in light of recent research which challenges the equation of Tutsi with pastoralism: more and more evidence has come to light that the predecessors of the Hutu had cattle long before the Tutsi appeared on the scene.[19] Such a finding questions the long-held assumption that the Hutu were always agriculturalists and the Tutsi always pastoralists. Agricultural and pastoral activities were hardly exclusive; they tended to be carried out jointly in most regions. Many Hutu had cattle, and many Tutsi farmed the land.[20] Certainly, if Hutu had in fact had a natural and timeless aversion to cattle rearing and had always been cultivators, it would have made little sense for those in power to put restrictions on Hutu owning cattle.[21] One needs to question the tendency to equate the origin of cattle keeping and pastoralism with the arrival of the Tutsi. These identifications—of Tutsi with cattle and Hutu with land—need to be understood less as mere facts unrelated to power than as historical artefacts created alongside the institutionalized power of the Rwandan state. The division of labor observed between the two at the onset of the colonial period is better thought of as a division *enforced* through the medium of political power rather than as a timeless preoccupation of two separate groups. The economic community was less a natural than a historical artifact, less a biological predisposition than a political creation.

A Community of Language

If we are to grasp fully the significance of historical research on processes of cultural integration, we need to think of the cultural community, too, as distinct both from this economic community of agriculturalists and pastoralists and from the political community of those living within the boundaries of a single state. From this point of view, the cultural community of those who speak a single language, Kinyarwanda, can be thought of as separate from the political community of those who have lived within the boundaries of the state of Rwanda since sometime in the sixteenth century. The parameters of the cultural community that speaks Kinyarwanda are much larger than the domain of the state called Rwanda.[22] The disparity in their respective sizes was even greater in the

precolonial period than it is today. The cultural community of Kinyarwanda speakers is substantial by any reckoning. Outside of Kiswahili, Kinyarwanda is said to have the largest group of speakers among the Bantu
languages in the region. Speakers of Kinyarwanda number over ten million. Put alongside mutually intelligible languages, the pool expands to
nearly 20 million.[23] People speaking variants of Kinyarwanda had settled
widely in the region long before the consolidation of the Nyiginya dynasty
as the state of Rwanda in what is known as the central court complex.
Today, the Banyarwanda—the speakers of the language, Kinyarwanda—
are spread over Rwanda, Burundi, Uganda, Congo, and Tanzania. If we
understand an ethnic group to mean a cultural group, comprising those
who speak a common language, then the Banyarwanda must be considered
East Africa's largest ethnic group.[24]

As members of the cultural community of Kinyarwanda speakers, the
Banyarwanda are distinct from members of the political community
framed by the state of Rwanda, variously called Rwandans or Rwandese.
The cultural community of Kinyarwanda speakers long predated the political community framed by the state called Rwanda. Thus, we come to the
point that the people called Tutsi, and those who came to be called Hutu,
spoke the same language, lived on the same hills, and had more or less the
same culture,[25] depending on the cultural zone in which they lived. But
they had yet to become one people.

Central Rwanda was the historical location of the precolonial Rwandan
state. Outside it, there were at least two major zones that were culturally—
but not politically—Banyarwanda. The first of these is today divided between northern Rwanda and western Uganda, settled by a people known
as the Bakiga—"the people of the mountains"—who shared the same language but not the same social and political institutions with those who
lived within the ambit of the Rwandan state. Not only did they have different settlement patterns, clan categories, and marriage forms, their political
life was also highly decentralized and community based, in sharp contrast
to the centralized hierarchy of the state of Rwanda. Here there were no
Hutu and no Tutsi, at least not until German colonialism integrated part
of this area into the Rwandan polity.

The second major cultural zone that lay outside the precolonial state
of Rwanda is today divided between western Rwanda and eastern Congo.
These speakers of Kinyarwanda live south and west of Lake Rweru (Edward), and north and south of Lake Kivu, in Congo. Unlike the Bakiga
of the north, the Banyabwisha and Banyarutshuru of the west had long

accepted delegates from the central court and thus their social institutions closely resembled those in the central region. Here, there *were* Hutu and Tutsi.

Two persons may possess the same broad cultural identity—Banyarwanda—and yet be marked by different political identities: Hutu or Tutsi. The cultural identity—Munyarwanda in the singular, Banyarwanda in the plural—exists alongside aเd in tension with the political identity, Hutu/Tutsi, whether in the singular or the plural. There is no Chinese Wall separating them. The middle ground is structured by several institutions that both contain and express the tension between cultural and political identities. The most important of these institutions are the family, the lineage, and the clan. All three have come to be shaped by the political power of the Rwandan state over centuries. We can see this in the social identity produced in Rwanda, through both intermarriage and clan affiliation. In some instances, there is evidence to contrast the outcome with practices among the Banyarwanda in the cultural Diaspora. The difference will illuminate some of the ways in which politics has come to shape culture since the sixteenth century.

Cohabitation and Marriage

Hutu and Tutsi lived together, not just as neighbors but also intimately, often through cohabitation, sometimes through intermarriage.[26] The history of cohabitation and of intermarriage spans centuries. And yet, that history cannot be glimpsed from contemporary social identities. If you go to Rwanda or Burundi, the purity of social definition is striking: everyone you meet identifies as either Hutu or Tutsi; there are no hybrids, none is "Hutsi." When cohabitation takes the form of marriage, the wife takes on the identity of the husband.[27] The social identity is passed on through patrilineal descent.[28] If the father is a Tutsi, then the child will be socially identified as Tutsi; and if the father is a Hutu, the child will be identified as Hutu. As the child takes on a unidimensional identity, that of the father, the identity of the mother—whether Hutu or Tutsi—is systematically erased. So it happens that the child of generations of intermarriage and cohabitation between Hutu and Tutsi comes into this world unequivocally Hutu or Tutsi.

One begins to understand the puzzled reaction of those new to the region, such as a visiting Sudanese intellectual:

I had come to know, more or less, the stereotypical description of the short Negroid Hutu and the tall, fine-featured Hamitic Tutsis. As I looked at my audiences, I saw a few who were clearly Tutsis and a few who were clearly Hutus. But most were somewhere in between, and I could not identify them. I later asked the Burundese, including senior government officials and ministers, whether they could tell a Tutsi from a Hutu. The response of the Foreign Minister, which represented the general tone, was a confident "Yes," but "with a margin of error of 35 percent"—a remarkable margin given the confidence of the affirmative answer.[29]

"There's been so much inter-marriage over the years that you often cannot tell who's who," said a presidential aide from Burundi to a Western reporter, and then added as an afterthought, "but everybody knows, anyway."[30]

I have been unable to find comprehensive data on the extent of inter-marriage. Yet, all accounts I have heard of or read speak of considerable intermarriage: anywhere from a significant minority to a majority of con-temporary Rwandans are likely to be children of Hutu and Tutsi intermar-riages over the centuries. This means that we cannot equate the identities Hutu and Tutsi with those identified as Hutu and Tutsi when this process set in motion. Rather than being biological offspring of Tutsi of centuries ago, today's Tutsi need to be understood as children of mixed marriages who have been constructed as Tutsi through the lens of a patriarchal ideol-ogy and the institutional medium of a patriarchal family.

Kin Groups

Both Hutu and Tutsi recognized patrilineal kin groups, such as the *inzu*, the *umulyango*, and the *ubwoko*. The smallest of these was the *inzu* (lineage), and the largest was the *ubwoko* (the clan). The difference was this: the lineage had a shallow depth and comprised no more than four or five generations with a link to a recognized original ancestor; in contrast, the clan was supposed to have a common ancestor many more generations ago. In Rwanda, however, clan members "were definitely unable to trace their relationship" to a common ancestor. Although the lineage was either Hutu or Tutsi, never mixed, the clan—which comprised different Hutu and Tutsi lineages—came to be the only mixed kin group in Rwandan society: all eighteen major clans in Rwanda include Hutu and Tutsi (and Twa). While the lineage head had definite powers—such as presiding over its collective activities, judging internal disputes, supervising tax contribution, and meeting obligation for military service—the clan had neither a head nor any collective activities. Unsurprisingly, while members of a lineage behaved as kin with mutual obligations, Hutu and Tutsi clansmen "did not exhibit any solidarity at all and behaved towards each other as complete strangers."[31]

The existence of mixed Hutu/Tutsi clan corporations, each composed of exclusively Hutu or Tutsi (or Twa) lineages, has led to an ongoing discussion seeking to explain their genesis. To explain the paradox of mixed Hutu/Tutsi clans in an otherwise divided society, Maquet asked his respondents (all Tutsi) whether the absence of a purely Hutu or Tutsi clan meant that "Tutsi and Hutu of the same clan descended from the same ancestor." He noted that "the Tutsi answered that it did not. They explain it by the relationships which have linked Hutu to Tutsi as clients or servants. After some time the Hutu were identified with the group of their master. Such identification was particularly easy since Tutsi frequently emigrated from one region of Rwanda to another with their Hutu clients and servants."[32] In other words, Hutu clients simply adopted the clan identity of their Tutsi patron. Since the original clientship (*umuheto*)—whereby Hutu lineages gave a cow to a Tutsi patron in return for protection—was lineage based, it made sense that the incorporation of the client into the clan of the patron would also be lineage based, thereby explaining the existence of exclusively Hutu or Tutsi lineages inside otherwise mixed Hutu/Tutsi clans.

David Newbury has reformulated this hypothesis on the basis of comparative research that shows differences in clan identity among populations who lived on two sides of Lake Kivu, one on the island of Ijwi and the other on the Rwandan mainland.[33] The importance of the Ijwi community is that while it is part of the *cultural* community of Kinyarwanda speakers, it is not part of the *political* community living within the borders of the state of Rwanda. It is significant that "no group on Ijwi—nor anywhere else west of Lake Kivu—retains a clan identity presently found among the eighteen largest clans of Rwanda." Differences between Ijwi and Rwanda, he suggests, are likely to have arisen as a result of different developments in the two places since the clans of Ijwi migrated "from areas now part of Rwanda but formerly autonomous of direct Rwandan political penetration." Newbury links the expansion in the size of clans in Rwanda to the process of state formation: "Centralized state penetration in the Rwandan case appears to have encouraged, maintained and perhaps extended broader identities." The hypothesis makes sense of data gathered by d'Hertefelt in his 1971 study of clans in Rwanda: it explains why very small clans constitute "a much higher proportion of the population" precisely in those parts of the country where Rwandan state penetration has been "most recent and least intensive."

The Newbury hypothesis gives greater weight to a number of claims put forth by Alexis Kagame, the historian of the central court in the colonial period. Kagame considered Rwandan clans "purely political" ("clans purement politiques"), and claimed that all Rwandan clans were Tutsi in origin; as Newbury points out, it makes better sense to think of them as artifacts of state construction, and thus as "dynastic" rather than Tutsi in origin. The point is brought home brilliantly with the case of the Renge,[34] a group variously mentioned in Rwandan tradition both as a part of the Singa clan and as an autonomous group that was neither Hutu nor Tutsi. Whereas the two claims have hitherto been seen as contradictory, Newbury's historical hypothesis dissolves the contradiction by showing the two identities as having existed at different points in history. Once we recognize that Renge was "a general term applied to formerly autonomous populations which were later incorporated within a system of state (in this case Rwandan central court) identities," the contradiction ceases to exist. This underlines the point that we need to understand Hutu and Tutsi as *changing* political identities by linking both to the history of the Rwandan state.

We shall see that the Rwandan state was a powerful political engine that restructured social relations wherever its tentacles took hold. The tendency was for social relations to follow rather than to precede or accompany the spread of political authority. The outcome was testimony to the primacy of politics. A whole array of institutions—from the army to clientship—enforced and undergirded the reproduction of Hutu and Tutsi as binary political identities. If we are to understand Hutu and Tutsi as changing political identities, we need to move away from notions of an unchanging Rwandan state in the "precolonial" period, and instead draw a historical outline of its institutional development.

Let me sum up this review of the existing literature as it bears on the question: Who is a Hutu and who a Tutsi? We have gathered the many answers to this question under two broad heads: one point of view claiming "no difference" (or "normal difference") and the other a "distinct difference" between Hutu and Tutsi. Each is identified with a distinct political tendency, "no difference" with Tutsi power and "distinct difference" with Hutu power. Each is also anchored in one of the two broad perspectives that has guided scholarship on Rwanda: the "no difference" point of view explaining that the Hutu/Tutsi difference is an outcome of social selection characteristic of privileged classes throughout history, and the "distinct difference" perspective holding that the difference actually began with separate migrations into the African Great Lakes region.

The "no difference" point of view holds the Hutu/Tutsi difference to be socioeconomic, either a class difference or a division of labor.[35] Yet, the Tutsi comprise different classes. The identification of Tutsi noble families—the "well-born Tutsi," as colonial and Church officials used to say—with all Tutsi was erroneous, for it ignored the poor Tutsi to whom these officials usually referred as "*petits* Tutsi," and who clearly belonged to a different class. Similarly, the notion that the Hutu/Tutsi difference is really a division of labor also does not hold in light of evidence that pastoralism was really a local development in the region and that the *equation* of pastoralism with a Tutsi migration needs to be rejected.[36]

At the other extreme is the "distinct difference" point of view, which holds the Hutu/Tutsi difference to be one between sociobiological groups.[37] We have seen that this point of view tends to freeze Rwandan history in its misty beginnings. In so doing, it discounts the entire history of physical mixing (through cohabitation and intermarriage) and of cultural integration that spanned subsequent centuries. It thus innocently equates Tutsi of a few centuries ago with the patriarchal construct of Tutsi in spite of—or maybe because of—the widespread practice of social cohabitation. There is undoubtedly much truth in the refrain that RPF cadres were fond of repeating to every foreign visitor to postgenocide Kigali: "We speak the same language, have the same culture, and live on the same hills; we are the same people."

The two points of views—one stressing separate origins as the source of the Hutu/Tutsi difference and the other highlighting the cultural integration that created a single Banyarwanda cultural identity from the diverse groups that migrated into the region at different times—need not be seen as incompatible. They can be seen as complementary rather than alternative accounts, each highlighting a different aspect of history. While neither is able to account for the history underlined by the other, each is incomplete without the other. In considering the plausibility of the two hypotheses before us—migration and social selection—I suggest we move away from an unequivocal embrace of either by distinguishing between a "strong" and a "weak" version of each. My point is that a weak version of the migration hypothesis is entirely compatible with a weak version of the social selection hypothesis. In a context where the historical evidence in both cases is slim, such a resolution has the merit both of taking the available evidence into account and of leaving the door open for future and even incompatible evidence.[38]

Let me begin with the migration hypothesis. While the strong version suggests an invasion or a mass migration in one or a few dramatic waves, the weak version disassociates the notion of migration from that of invasion. It then conceives of migration as a gradual infiltration, a cumulative result of a movement that unfolded in so many dribs and drabs over centuries and that had multiple outcomes. Jan Vansina, for example, has pointed out that there was evidence of peaceful coexistence between pastoralists and agriculturalists in the northeast, northwest, and west of Rwanda: "There was little raiding, no system of vassalage and no state formation to incorporate both groups." On this basis, he conjectured that this represented "an early, continuing and quite stable relationship between the two cultures." Noting that this hypothesis "corresponds with what we know of other areas such as Nkore," J. K. Rennie argued that it made greater sense to think of the migration hypothesis as a series of separate propositions. The first of these, he suggested, would be that of a relatively peaceful coexistence between cultivators and pastoralists,[39] giving way to a tension-ridden relationship only "with competition for land, or raiding and feuding if pastoralists moved in and dispossessed the cultivator of some land." Similarly, he suggested that an "economic integration of the two groups by the exchange of cattle in a vassalage arrangement" be thought of as a distinct third set of relationships. All three possibilities, he suggested, can be thought of as distinct from a fourth—"the incorporation of the peoples into a centralized state"—that they "might follow or precede."[40] Such a hypothesis suggesting numerous migrations stretched out over centuries in no way rules out a weak version of social selection whereby rulers inbreed and reproduce on the basis of notions of social selectivity and physical beauty.

While this kind of account highlights the grain of truth in each hypothesis, it still fails to address the issue at hand. That issue arises from a *third* commonsense observation about contemporary Rwanda. It is, after all, the very political conflict and political violence that pit Hutu against Tutsi that has in the first place focused attention on the question: Who is a Tutsi and who a Hutu? Faced with the genocide, the social demographer Dominique Franche, previously cited, suggests that we think of Hutu and Tutsi as different communities: "The best term is 'community.' What we have here are two recently constituted communities, one Hutu, the other Tutsi, united by their hatred and fear of each other and thirst for revenge. What is now going on is a civil war between elites, who are fighting for power."[41] While Dominique Franche gets closer to understanding the Hutu/Tutsi divide, he still begs the question: What type of communities?

To answer this question, one needs to go beyond a simple aggregation of insights found in the existing literature. That simple aggregation brought us to the realization that even if we accept that Hutu and Tutsi have different and distinct historical origins, we still have to take into account a subsequent history that made of them a cohesive cultural group: one that not only lived on a common territory, but also spoke a common language and practiced a common religion. This, in turn, posed a question: Even if we start with the recognition that Hutu and Tutsi belong to a common *cultural* group, we still need to explain that they have yet to create a common *political* community, one based on consent. Is it possible to arrive at a third point of view, an overarching one, that can take the first two into account by incorporating their respective insights, but without reproducing the limitation contained in each? To do so, I suggest two propositions.

First, we need to make an analytical distinction between three different kinds of identities: market-based, cultural, and political. For Hutu and Tutsi are best understood, not as market-based or cultural identities, but as *political identities* reproduced first and foremost through a form of the state.

Second, political identities—and the state institutions that undergird them—need to be historicized so they may also be understood as *changing identities*. There has not been one single and constant definition of Hutu and Tutsi through Rwandan history. Rather, the definitions have shifted as a consequence of every major change in the institutional framework of the Rwandan state.

In what follows, I will show the usefulness of differentiating political from cultural identities by contrasting two tendencies in Rwandan history. Having traced the tendency to cultural integration from separate origins, I will now highlight the countertendency: to a political differentiation, even polarization, notwithstanding the cultural integration. Later, when I deal with the colonial and the postcolonial periods, I shall show how the meaning of Hutu and Tutsi has shifted every time a new power has seen it fit to reorganize the institutions of rule. The real challenge, I will argue, is to go beyond understanding Hutu and Tutsi as *political identities*, to grasping the process whereby they have turned into *polarized identities* with no middle ground between them.

POLITICAL POLARIZATION

The most striking thing about the African Great Lakes region is the contradictory nature of cultural and political developments. The very people who came to be integrated into a common cultural community—the speakers of Kinyarwanda—became polarized into two distinct and even antagonistic political identities, Hutu and Tutsi. While the historical origin of the Hutu and the Tutsi may be shrouded in mystery, the nature of the state they built is not. The history of the encounter between Tutsi and Hutu is important, not because of where their ancestors came from, but because in their coming together they created certain political institutions which outlived that history and shaped a tragic future.

The Early Rwandan State

Rwandan historiography has been so caked with orthodoxy that it has usually taken a profound political crisis—such as the 1959 Revolution or the 1994 genocide—to crack the crust. Following the 1959 Revolution, the key challenge to orthodoxy was to understand the process of state formation. Whereas pre-1959 historians gave a "court interpretation" from the point of view of the centralized power that emerged at the end of this process, post-1959 writers tended to view the expansion of Rwanda from the standpoint of the societies that were incorporated into it. Whereas pre-1959 studies tended to emphasize a more or less complete assimilation of conquered peoples by a system of vassalage in which they received the use of cattle in return for services and loyalty, post-1959 writing paid more attention to pre-Rwandan kingdoms and gave a much less functionalist or harmonious interpretation of the vassalage system in the state of Rwanda.

The crowning text in the pre-1959 corpus came from the historical sociologist Jacques Maquet. The first major post-1959 reinterpretation to challenge the accepted version came from the pen of Jan Vansina, the second from that of Catharine Newbury. Jan Vansina reinterpreted the process leading to the founding of the Rwandan state; Catharine Newbury historicized the institution of clientship rather than presume it to be a transhistorical Rwandan or African affliction. Both checked the tendency to read history backwards from the present. I shall first deal with the significance and consequence of Vansina's work, and then turn to Newbury. Following in the footsteps of the Ibadan historians, Vansina subjected oral histories to a criticism of form and transmission, thereby subjecting them to rules of evidence while establishing their credibility.[42] His conclusions challenged the notion that the Rwandan state was an artifact singularly constructed by the Tutsi aristocracy. Instead, he suggested an understanding of state evolution in which ritual institutions were borrowed from the earlier pre-Rwandan states and military organization from the Nyoro. He argued for a more protracted process of expansion and a less complete assimilation of subject peoples into Rwanda. In my view, this aspect of Vansina's research has an important methodological significance. As I have already pointed out, it both discredits the view which sees the making of Rwandan state and society as the outcome of a process of one-sided *assimilation* and invites us to see this as the outcome of a process of two-sided *integration*.

The immediate consequence of Vansina's research was to devalue the significance of the conquest-and-assimilation hypothesis: that state formation in the region began with conquest by a group external to the region, the pastoralists who began migrating into the region in large numbers since at least the fifteenth century.[43] As others followed Vansina's pioneering leadership, the regional history of states and statelets constructed by surrounding agriculturalists before the rise of Rwanda came to light. The post-Vansina consensus was modified by J. K. Rennie in a major interpretive essay,[44] and it was adopted by Bethwell Ogot in his essay on the Rwanda kingdom in volume 4 of the UNESCO *History of Africa*. According to this account, "the first inhabitants were almost certainly forest hunters and gatherers, represented by the Batwa." The agriculturalists arrived later and began to clear forests for permanent settlements. By the fifteenth century, "many of the Bantu-speakers were already organised into small states." They included at least three: "the oldest state in Rwanda" for which posterity has preserved no name but, which "was probably established by the Renge lineages of the Singa clan" and covered "most of modern Rwanda except the eastern section;" the Mubari state of the Zigaba clan, "which apparently covered an extensive area"; and the powerful state of Gisaka in southeast Rwanda, which managed to maintain its independence until the middle of the nineteenth century. Only the strongest of these found a place in Tutsi tradition as recorded by Kagame. Although Ogot spoke of the foundation of the Rwanda kingdom sometime in the fifteenth century, we should note that the founding date, established mainly on the basis of an oral tradition referring to a solar eclipse at the time of a royal coronation, has been subject to much debate, from 1312 (Kagame) to 1468 (Nkurikiyimfura) to 1482 (Vansina) to 1532 (Rennie).[45]

No matter the precise date of its expansion, it is clear that Abanyiginya clan expanded "not only into areas populated by fiercely independent lineages of Kiga hill-dwellers, but also into a myriad of states, some tiny and some quite powerful." These states had institutions of kingship and regalia (drums, royal hammers, etc.), and they had "developed ritual power over the land and over rain," features that scholarly orthodoxy had come to identify with only or mainly the state of Rwanda.[46] The more the local history of state formation came to light, the more it deflated the significance of the conquest hypothesis associated with the rise of Rwanda. The more the presumed link between pastoralism and power was challenged, the more it became possible to put the history of the state of Rwanda within a broader regional context. Instead of a singular rupture, the Tutsi conquest, it now became possible to investigate elements of continuity in state development before and after the expansion of the Abanyiginya dynasty. In the words of one born-again historian, "It looks as if the newcomers found nothing better to do than to lie in the bed which had already been made by their predecessors."[47]

The balance of scholarly opinion today is that the state of Rwanda emerged as did many a state in the region, through the amalgamation of several autonomous chiefships into a single nuclear kingdom, under the leadership of a royal clan. This royal clan was the Abanyiginya clan. The location of early Rwanda was near Lake Muhazi, in open savanna country between Lake Victoria and Lake Kivu. This was pastoral country, and the various states which gradually formed in that region "were originally built on the alliance of pastoralist groups." The period was probably the fifteenth century. From this location, and through "several centuries of turbulent political history," the center of gravity of the state gradually shifted westward to the forested highland area near the Nile-Congo divide, quite different from its original open savanna homeland in the east.[48]

The Rwandan state had a distinctive ideological and institutional characteristic. A mark of the very circumstances of its birth was that it associated "Hutu supernatural powers with Tutsi military powers." This ritual basis was institutionalized "at the very heart of the state."[49] A narrative associated with Cyilima Rugwe, considered the founder of the state, testifies to its historical significance. According to this narrative, Cyilima Rugwe was advised by his counselors that the way to rid his territory of "rebels" was to go to a famous "Hutu" diviner and take him gifts of butter, goats, and honey. The diviner, however, demanded, before anything else, a blood brotherhood pact, which Cyilima refused on grounds that he could not enter into one with a "Hutu." In the face of continuing difficulties, however, he relented. In return, he got advice from the diviner, advice he followed and from which he benefited. Thus began the chain of events that led to the creation of the independent state of Rwanda—at least according to this account.

The ritual prescriptions that the king was periodically required to carry out for the welfare of the country were known as the *ubiiru*. The guardians of the *ubiiru*, those who laid down the principles of rule but did not themselves rule, were known as the *abiiru*. They advised the king on whether or not to conduct wars and designated the heir apparent and the family from which he was to come. The most important *abiiru* positions are said to have been created at the time of Rugwe (1559–86) and his successor, Mukobanya (1586–88). The three topmost *abiiru* were from the lineages of Tsobe, Tege, and Kono. The story of the origin of the Tsobe relates how its founder, Rutsobe, was a "Hutu." J. K. Rennie suggests that the story of the origin of different *abiiru* is the most important clue we have of how predominantly agriculturalist (later "Hutu") political units were incorporated into the state of Rwanda.

The formative period of this state, the period of its distinctive development, is associated with a series of wars that, beginning with the rule of Rujugira (1756–65), spanned several reigns.[50] To understand the growing social polarization between Hutu and Tutsi, we need to focus on three ideological and social institutions—the court rituals (*ubiiru*) through which important Hutu lineages were incorporated into the court as ritualists (*abiiru*), the patron-client relationships through which the pastoralist hierarchy was organized, and the military and administrative systems that were the true backbone of the state—as they changed over the next century. Together, these changes suggest both a centralization of state power and a reorganization of society along hierarchically exploitative lines. We shall see that these changes not only happened simultaneously, they also reinforced one another. The political tendency to free the king's power from restraint exercised by countervailing institutions had important social effects. The *abiiru* who set the rules of governance, but without themselves governing, were also the institution through which important Hutu lineages were incorporated into the Rwandan state. Then there was the parallel tendency whereby a new form of corvée clientship was imposed on newly subjugated Hutu populations. Both came to a head under the rule of Rwabugiri in the late nineteenth century. Together, they made for a double and related development: just as power was increasingly defined as Tutsi, the political and social position of Hutu was getting progressively degraded. Yet, the relation between Hutu and Tutsi was far from polarized even under Rwabugiri. It was mitigated by the military and administrative systems, both of which provided avenues—albeit limited—for Hutu participation in the state, while at the same time allowing for a form of organization that made for countervailing tendencies placing a check on administrative power at all levels.

ABIIRU RITUALISTS

Let us recall that a distinctive ideological feature of the Rwandan state was that it associated Hutu supernatural powers with Tutsi military powers. The supernatural powers were said to be the preserve of the *abiiru*. The heyday of the *abiiru* as a courtly power seems to have been the seventeenth and the early eighteenth centuries. A corollary of their predominance was that the king's powers were limited. The progressive emancipation of the king from ritual prescriptions of the *abiiru* began with the reign of the fighting king, Rujugira (1756–65). He first undermined the spiritual monopoly of the *abiiru* by bringing to court a possession cult (the *mandwa*) said to have emerged among politically and militarily defeated lineages. Thereby, Rujugira was able to coopt into the service of the central court a ritual authority that might otherwise have operated against it. By the end of the nineteenth century, the *abiiru* had been so weakened that King Rwabugiri could afford to demonstrate publicly how little he cared for their ritual prescriptions.

PATRON-CLIENT RELATIONS

Clientship was the *second* distinctive institution characteristic of the Rwandan state. I have already pointed out that our understanding of clientship has been profoundly affected by post-1959 research, particularly the work of Catharine Newbury.[51] The pre-1959 assumption was that everyone, except the king at the top and those at the bottom, was simultaneously a patron and a client in an unending and unvarying chain of patron-client relationships. This claim about clientship as a transhistorical institution subsequently came to dominate African Studies in the West. As a corrective, Newbury carried out a bottom-up examination of changes in clientship in a peripheral region as it was incorporated into the kingdom of Rwanda in the last quarter of the nineteenth century. Her work underlined the importance of historicizing institutions in the face of a widespread tendency to read history backward from the present. That tendency had been epitomized by the work of Jacques Maquet. Those who followed Maquet's ahistorical and functionalist lead assumed that

clientship was the key social institution holding Rwandan society together. After all, it made for a structure in which everyone but the king
was the client of someone else.

To counter this claim, Newbury studied the changing forms of clientship in Kinyaga, a region that had been outside firm control of the
central court until the last quarter of the nineteenth century. Going back
a hundred years from 1960, she studied changes in three types of clientship—*umuheto, ubuhake,* and *ubureetwa*—particularly as these affected
reciprocity and inequality in the relationship between patron and client.
In the *umuheto* form in which it first existed, cattle clientship involved the
periodic gift of cattle from client lineages to patrons in return for regular
protection. This meant, first, that this relationship was necessarily confined to those who owned cattle, leaving out the growing number of the
cattle-less poor. It meant, second, that in spite of the inequality inherent
in it, the relationship was more like a historical version of a modern protection racket, which explained more the social cohesion of elites than any
bond between the rich and the poor, the powerful and the disempowered.
The larger significance of Newbury's work is that it diminished the importance of cattle clientship as an explanation of social cohesion even in the
kingdom of Rwanda.

It does this by allowing us to identify two key changes in the institution
of clientship from the time of Rujugira. The first was a shift in the form
of cattle clientship from *umuheto* to *ubuhake*. It was a shift whose effect
was to erode reciprocity while intensifying the inequality in the relationship. Between *umuheto* and *ubuhake*, there were at least two important
differences. Whereas *umuheto* had linked an entire lineage as a group to
an *umuheto* chief or his delegate, *ubuhake* most commonly linked an individual to his patron. Also, while the *umuheto* clientship involved the gift
of a cow at regular intervals from a client lineage to its patron, *ubuhake*
involved exactly the opposite: a patron ceding the use of a cow to a client.
This means that while the *umuheto* clientship was limited to cattle-owning
lineages, for only they had the cows from which to give one as a regular
gift to a patron, *ubuhake* clientship was more likely to involve families
with no cattle. Ultimately, *ubuhake* exposed the clients to "more arbitrary
forms of exploitation," including possible confiscation of any personal cattle at the pleasure of the patron.

Changes in the nature of clientship were closely affected by changes in
the nature of land tenure, particularly from lineage control over land (*ubukonde*) to control by the king who then decided to assign it as pasturage

(*igikingi*) to his closest subjects through the administrative appointment of chiefs. Whereas the claim *ubukonde* emphasized the right of a lineage over the land it had cleared, the basis of *igikingi* was a political grant from the King. The latter system is supposed to have started in the first half of the nineteenth century, in the reign of Yuhi Gahindiro, and most certainly led to a decline in the social position of the Hutu. For so long as lineages controlled land, the lineage head—the person having effective right to land—was appointed as the land chief (or subchief), since the role of the land chief was to gather agricultural tribute. This is how one got to the point where many land chiefs in early Rwanda were Hutu.[52] As control over land passed from lineages to the king, and thus its effective control from the lineage head to the administrative chief, there was no guarantee that the lineage head would continue to function as the land chief.

It is the loss of land rights by the mass of cultivators that explains the introduction of *ubureetwa*, a form of clientship, that was almost entirely without an element of reciprocity, in fact one that starkly underlined the serflike status of the Hutu population. In contrast to *ubuhake*, a form of clientship that attracted all those with an interest in access to a cow, usually Tutsi more than Hutu, *ubureetwa* was a form of clientship that was imposed only on the Hutu.[53] *Ubureetwa* originated under the reign of Rwabugiri: it was imposed on Hutu lineages by hill chiefs, who replaced lineage heads and took their land by right of occupation. *Ubureetwa* entailed manual labor for the local hill chief, performed as "payment" for occupation of the land. While his regime imposed a harsh rule on the formerly semiautonomous Hutu and Tutsi lineages, Rwabugiri imposed corvée-type labor obligations only on the Hutu, thereby polarizing the social difference between Hutu and Tutsi.[54] As a result, more than at any other time in its history, the state of Rwanda appeared as a Tutsi power under Rwabugiri.

THE MILITARY SYSTEM

While the effect of changes in court rituals and forms of clientship was to polarize relations between Hutu and Tutsi, we also need to note countertendencies that mitigated the polarization for a time. These countertendencies stemmed from both the military and the administrative systems in the state.

More than any other, it was the *military system* that began to develop during the reign of Rujugira (1756–65) that explains the distinctiveness of the state of Rwanda in the region of the Great Lakes. It was a time when Rwanda was faced with the combined military threat of three neighbors. The external wars led to a reorganization of the state internally. The internal reorganization was the real source of Rwanda's growing strength in the region. Triggered by the spectacular military expansion that began under Rujugira, the military reorganization had administrative consequences of long-term significance.[55] Armies were permanently posted to outlying areas, making it possible both to occupy a conquered area and to use it as a staging ground for cattle raids. Army members were drawn from geographically diverse areas and assigned for a number of years of common service outside their home region. This gave endurance to the *umuheto* groups that constituted the army and turned them into a key institution for socialization. In the standard literature, these groups are referred to as *umuheto* ("social armies"). At the outset, *umuheto* (meaning "bow") incorporated mainly Tutsi and required of them some form of military service.[56] Gradually, there was a blurring of the distinction between supplying the central court with spoils from military raids outside the territorial domain of Rwanda and supplying it with tribute from the population within the territory. As internal tribute gained in significance over external booty, the administrative functions of these *umuheto* groups came to predominate over their military functions. This was particularly the case by the middle of the nineteenth century.

Increase in state capacity was thus the result of both horizontal and vertical growth, the former through the incorporation of newly conquered territories, and the latter through a restructuring of state relationships in hitherto central areas. Army membership came to include all social groups. The first Hutu sections of the army were noted from the time of Rujugira in the second half of the eighteenth century. At that time, most Hutu were not yet warriors, but were associated with administrative structures of the army and were required to provide prestations on a permanent basis. Subjugation was characterized less by exclusion from the army, more by the differentiated manner of their incorporation into the army. By the end of the nineteenth century, every Rwandan male—Twa, Hutu, or Tutsi—was affiliated to the army. Every unit in the army had a distinctive name, evocative of a dynastic or historical event: "the tough ones" (*abashakamba*), "the first to be praised" (*imbanzamihigo*), or "the fearless ones" (*inzirabwoba*). As the army expanded, the forms of subordination of Twa and Hutu also changed. The more they were used in a fighting capacity, the less their participation was confined to nonmilitary activities such as herding. Contradictory claims by different writers about the social nature of the army make sense if we realize that their informants may be referring to different historical periods. Thus, Maquet's claim that only the Tutsi had a fighting role in the army seems to refer to an earlier period.[57] But it is in no way contradicted by De Lacger pointing out that the great conqueror Kigeri IV Rwabugiri preferred to recruit mainly Hutu armies when he went into battle.[58] In the herding section, the army recruited entire lineage groups rather than individuals. In this arrangement, the head of the lineage performed an intermediary function between the army chief and individual members of the army coming from his lineage. The result was to tie every Munyarwanda to the state structure through the kinship structure, at the same time limiting the authority of the kin head by his incorporation into the military structure. The military system combined in a single organization economic, political, and military functions through a combination of state cattle keeping, provincial government, and fighting. It socialized Tutsi youth into dominant positions in the army at the same time as it gave the army a vested interest in state expansion.

Rwanda was an expansionist state. Starting from roughly the geographical center of present-day Rwanda, the Abanyiginya dynasty expanded its dominion aggressively and progressively. Its court history thus reads like an account of successive annexation wars. This was not only a fighting but also a looting army: besides going to battle to defend or to annex, the army also regularly raided neighbors for cattle. To the limited extent that the state managed to create one people of the Twa, Hutu, and Tutsi of Rwanda, it did so more on the battlefield than anywhere else.

THE ADMINISTRATIVE SYSTEM

While Rwabugiri's reform centralized power, we need to bear in mind that power was nowhere near as absolute as it would come to be in the colonial period. In theory, the *mwami* (king) of Rwanda was said to be an absolute monarch, who was said to be both the supreme judge and the legislator with the right to change any custom.[59] In practice, however, the country was administered through a threefold hierarchy: running from province to district to hill. Each province was entrusted to an army chief. Known as the *chief of men*, he was in charge of recruiting soldiers. The province was in turn demarcated into districts, each with two chiefs independent of one another. The *chief of landholding* was in charge of agricultural land and production; accordingly, he collected dues from agriculture. His counterpart was the *chief of pastures;* he ruled over grazing land and collected dues from stock. Finally, each district was divided into hills, each with a single hill chief.

The chiefs did not claim their position by virtue of right or inheritance; they were bureaucrats who were appointed to their position by a superior, either the *mwami* or a superior chief. The kings were considered sacred, and all were Tutsi. So were all army commanders, chiefs of pasture, and provincial chiefs. The occasional presence of Hutu chiefs could be noticed among chiefs of landholding, more so the lower one went down the hierarchy. The lowest ranks of administrators, the hill chiefs, could be Tutsi, Hutu, or Twa. The administrative system of the Kingdom of Rwanda toward the end of the nineteenth century was notable for two features. *One,* the rule of the monarchy was less absolute in practice than were its claims in theory. In practice, the monarch ruled through two sets of parallel hierarchies: at the level of the smallest administrative unit, the hill, every subject was linked to the monarch through the hill chief and the army chief; at the district level, the cattle chief and the land chief functioned as two parallel hierarchies. The existence of parallel administrative hierarchies made it possible for peasants to find breathing space by playing off one set of officials against another when the need arose. *Two,* while power was visibly Tutsi the higher one reached in the military and administrative hierarchy, it was still true that the lower ranks of administration, where officials were most involved in face-to-face contact with subjects, continued to include a significant presence of Hutu and Twa officials.

The Reign of Rwabugiri

The final and the most spectacular expansion of the boundaries of the Rwandan state took place under the reign of Mwami Kigeri Rwabugiri (1860–95), one of the most prestigious historical figures of the Rwandan court. Rwabugiri led a series of military campaigns that led to the incorporation of "Hutu" statelets in both eastern and western Rwanda; the northern and southwestern parts, however, remained largely autonomous.[60] He further centralized the state structure, but through a series of reforms that had a contradictory outcome: at the same time as it expanded Hutu participation in the army from nonmilitary to fighting roles—and appointed Hutu to administrative positions while taking on the power of uppity Tutsi aristocratic lineages—these reforms debased the social position of the Hutu outside the army and administration and further polarized the social opposition between Hutu and Tutsi.

Research on the expansion of the Rwandan state during the reign of Rwabugiri and the early colonial period gives us critical insight into the transethnic nature of the Hutu identity. For Hutu, it appears, were simply those from a variety of ethnic backgrounds who came to be subjugated to the power of the Rwandan state. Take, for example, Catharine Newbury's study of Kinyaga in southwestern Rwanda from 1860 to 1960. Its population became Hutu only in the last quarter of the nineteenth century, through gradual Tutsi military occupation and as a consequence of absorption into the institutions of the expanding state of Rwanda. This story of previously autonomous communities being absorbed within the boundaries of an aggressively expanding state focuses on the process of state expansion and its contradictory outcome. On the one hand, as local chiefs were dismissed and replaced by incoming collaborators, identified as Tutsi, land and cattle gradually accumulated into Tutsi hands. On the other hand, as those subjugated lost land and were forced to enter into relations of servitude to gain access to land, the "Hutu identity came to be associated with and entirely defined by inferior status."[61]

The same can be said of the fiercely autonomous communities of Kinyarwanda speakers in northwestern Rwanda who were only brought under the fold of the state of Rwanda by a collaboration between German troops and the mwami's soldiers. They, too, never really saw themselves as Hutu before their forcible incorporation into Rwanda. Before that, as we have seen, they were the Bakiga, the people of the mountains. And they used the term *Banyanduga*, not Hutu, to refer to the southern Hutu who joined the Tutsi in the war of conquest.[62]

One institution in precolonial Rwanda prevented the Hutu/Tutsi distinction from hardening into feudal-type orders, just as it prevented the formation of a Hutu counterelite that would in time challenge Tutsi domination. This was *kwihutura*: the rare Hutu who was able to accumulate cattle and rise through the socioeconomic hierarchy could *kwihutura*—shed Hutuness—and achieve the political status of a Tutsi.[63] Conversely, the loss of property could also lead to the loss of status, summed up in the Kinyarwanda word *gucupira*. Both social processes occurred over generations. Of little significance statistically, their social and political significance cannot be overstated. Noting that the process of "accession to the nobility" accelerated as did the expansion of the state, Jean-Népomucène Nkurikiyimfura astutely observed that "this 'ennoblement' prevented the birth of a distinct Hutu chiefly stratum which could have become a privileged intermediary between the court and the larger population."[64]

The strongest proof of this is that when organized protest did emerge against Tutsi Power at the outset of colonial rule, it did not take the form of a struggle for Hutu Power. Instead, the protest, which drew its strength from the participation of those newly subjugated as Hutu, was led by none other than the Tutsi excluded from power. The protest arose on the basis of a joining of two forces: the Tutsi excluded from Tutsi Power, and the Hutu newly subjugated to it. The *first* was the consequence of a struggle for accession to the throne on the death of Mwami Rwabugiri in 1895. The struggle turned into a prolonged civil war between two clans, the Abeega and the Abanyiginya, and culminated in 1896 with the coup of Rucunshu in favor of the Abeega. According to Kagame, "countless members of the defeated party were massacred" and "new chiefs were appointed to fill the posts vacated by the death of the incumbents." The pro-Abanyiginya legitimists sought refuge in the north and the east. The *second* ingredient that made for the protest, initially against Tutsi Power and then against colonial rule, was the dissatisfaction among the Bakiga people of the north, who had been formally incorporated into the kingdom scarcely a decade before the coup of Rucunshu.

The Cult of Nyabingi

Protest against Rwandan aggression and expansion at the time of Rwabugiri was widespread on the periphery of the kingdom. Two important sites of protest were the island of Ijwi and the kingdom of Ndorwa. Ndorwa is said to be the home of Nyabingi. Though the origins of the cult are obscure, its stamina is renowned.[65] Beginning at the time of Rwabugiri, Nyabingi continued well into the colonial period. Though he "killed several leading mediums," Rwabugiri "could not destroy the spirit," for it "simply moved on to another host, infusing him or her with all the authority held by those fallen."[66] The cult survived into colonialism and "succeeded in immobilizing the administrative efforts of three colonial powers for nearly two decades, until its final suppression in 1928."[67]

Nyabingi made an easy transition into the colonial period, for one reason: colonial rule simply added on to precolonial impositions. To the demands of occupying nobles were added the demands of European overlords. When first appointed in 1907, the German Resident for northern Rwanda wanted to build a European-style capital at Kigali. So he called for "hundreds of labourers" to work daily to construct a road into the north, and "thousands of days of labour" to cut northern forests and transport the wood. The missionaries, too, needed "800 labourers a day" to build the church at Rwaza, and more to build homes that would "reflect the scale and solidity of their civilization." While missionaries and administrators paid a regular salary to regular workers, they "usually paid nothing" to "unskilled labourers whom they requisitioned through the notables."[68]

When defeated claimants to the throne rose up against those they considered usurpers of royal power, there was no shortage of popular discontent from which to harness support. After the death of Rwabugiri in 1895, the resistance went through three phases, each associated with a different leadership. The best known of these was the opening phase under the leadership of Muhumusa, one of Rwabugiri's wives, who took shelter in the rugged mountains of the north. In J. M. Bessel's words: "Herself an outstanding personality, possessing great powers of leadership and organisation, and far more brains than probably any Tutsi woman before or since, she was in intelligence quite up to the standards of her late husband." And then he adds: "Not only in intelligence but in ambition: in 1911 she proclaimed herself Queen of Ndorwa and promised her followers that she would soon liberate the country from the yoke of the Europeans." Muhumusa was captured in 1911 by British authorities in Bufumbira, Uganda. This inaugurated the second phase of the resistance under Ndungutse, accepted by most authorities as a son of Muhumusa and Rwabugiri. Now the chief spokesman of the legitimist faction laying claim to the Rwandan throne, Ndungutse was nonetheless "viewed by the local populations as their saviour, as the prophet who would restore peace to the country and free the labouring masses from the servitude of the corvée (*ubureetwa*)." Lemarchand's comment is worth noting: "Though himself a Tutsi, Ndungutse's name became a symbol of anti-Tutsi sentiment, and by implication of anti-European sentiment as well."[69]

Though German troops killed Ndungutse and his comrades in April 1912, the northern region remained the site of recurrent outbreaks against chiefs and the central administration for many years, right into the period of Belgian rule. The thread that knit together the protest movement, from its origins under Muhumusa and Ndungutse to its recurrence in subsequent years, what I call the *third* phase, was a possession cult of messianic proportions that went by the name *Nyabingi*. Nyabingi literally means "one who possesses great riches." It is believed to have been the title of an eighteenth-century queen of Karagwe who ruled until she was murdered by a Hima chief of Mpororo named Ruhinda. One tradition had it that the Nyabingi sect was a vehicle through which the queen's spirit enacted vengeance upon her murderers and disloyal subjects.

The Nyabingi cult presents a paradox. On the one hand, it was regarded as a powerful anti-Tutsi protest. J.E.T. Philipps, a British district commissioner of Kigezi who claimed firsthand knowledge of it, described it as "revolutionary in method and anarchic in effect," and added: "The whole appeal is to fear and the lowest instincts, to the masses, Hutu, against the classes, Tutsi and Batwa."[70] Historians who have written of the fiercely independent spirit of the Bakiga of northern Rwanda and western Uganda have seen Nyabingi as a crucial ingredient in the making of this culture. Thus wrote P.T.W. Baxter: "The proud boast of the Kiga is that they never were, as a people, subjugated by either Tutsi or Hima."[71] And yet this resistance against the combination of Tutsi power and colonial rule—one that spanned decades and whose regional claim to being the most powerful rebellion in recent history is unrivalled—was for the most part led by disaffected elements from the Tutsi monarchy and aristocracy of Rwanda. The answer to this paradox lies in an understanding of the difference between the kingdom of Rwanda, even at its most repressive moment under Rwabugiri, and the colonial state of Rwanda under the Belgians. The answer lies in the changing nature of Hutu and Tutsi as political identities from the kingdom to the colonial state, even if both went by the name Rwanda.

CONCLUSION

There cannot be a single answer to the question we began with: Who are the Hutu and who the Tutsi? Not only do the identities Hutu and Tutsi have a history, they have also changed in the course of this history. Although seeds of an alternative hypothesis can be found in the writings of several authors, writings from which I will quote extensively, they have yet to be worked out fully.[72] As part of that endeavor, I would like to suggest that Hutu and Tutsi be seen as *political* identities that changed with the changing history of the Rwandan state. This has two implications. *First*, if Hutu and Tutsi are *historical* identities, then we need to be open to the possibility that the definition of Hutu and Tutsi may have changed over time, and that there may therefore not be any single answer to the question asked so often: Who is a Hutu and who a Tutsi? *Second*, if Hutu and Tutsi are *political* identities, then their history is likely to be coterminous with that of the institutions of power, particularly the state of Rwanda. While we may be able to speak of Tutsi as an ethnic identity preceding the formation of the state of Rwanda, we certainly cannot speak of Hutu with the same historical depth. For as a political identity, Hutu was constructed as a consequence of the formation and expansion of the state of Rwanda. If subject populations only came to be defined as Hutu after being incorporated into Rwandan state structures, we cannot speak of these as Hutu before that incorporation.

My historical overview leads to three conclusions. The *first* is that the search in migrations in dim history for the origins of Hutu and Tutsi is likely to be fruitless since Hutu and Tutsi are political, not cultural, identities. Ancestors of Hutu and Tutsi most likely had separate historical origins. Hutu did not exist as an identity outside of the state of Rwanda; it emerged as a transethnic identity of subjects in the state of Rwanda. The predecessors of the Hutu were simply those from different ethnicities who were subjugated to the power of the state of Rwanda. Tutsi, in contrast, *may* have existed as an ethnic identity before the establishment of the state of Rwanda. With formal mechanisms in the Rwandan state that allowed rulers to absorb the most prosperous of their subjects into their own ranks through intermarriage, Tutsi too became more and more a transethnic identity.

My *second* conclusion is that the predecessors of today's Hutu and Tutsi indeed created a single cultural community, the community of Kinyarwanda speakers, through centuries of cohabitation, intermarriage, and cultural exchange. That cultural community is to be found today both within the borders of the state of Rwanda and outside of it. It is a regional community. From this point of view, the speakers of Kinyarwanda who today live outside of the borders of Rwanda can be considered a cultural diaspora.

My *third* conclusion is that Hutu and Tutsi emerged as state-enforced political identities. The context of that development is the emergence of the state of Rwanda. It is the history of that state that ultimately made of Hutu and Tutsi *bipolar* political identities. This definition happened over time. Its context was twofold. One was the process of state centralization, whereby the powers of the king grew at the expense of the ritual powers of the *abiiru* and the army emerged as the central administrative institution. The other was social processes, particularly changes in clientship, that led to the social degradation of Hutu.

With the Tutsi identity sufficiently porous to absorb successful Hutu through ennoblement and Hutu clearly a transethnic identity of subjects, the Hutu/Tutsi distinction could not be considered an ethnic distinction. Neither could it be considered a socioeconomic distinction, one between exploiters and exploited or rich and poor. This is because of the "*petits* Tutsi" who could not be told apart from many Hutu in their socioeconomic circumstances, and who were substantial in number and continued to reproduce through intermarriage. At the same time, the *petits* Tutsi could always be told apart from the Hutu socially, on account of both the petty privileges and the more substantial exemption from forced labor (*ubureetwa*) they were entitled to as Tutsi under Rwabugiri. It was also not a division of labor between pastoralists and agriculturalists, once again because the *petits* Tutsi were usually as cattle-less as the majority of Hutu, and the "*moyens* Tutsi" tended to combine herding a few cattle with cultivating a modest garden.

To be a Tutsi was thus to be in power, near power, or simply to be identified with power—just as to be a Hutu was more and more to be a subject. By subjecting only the Hutu to a serflike tribute, *ubureetwa*, and by eroding the spiritual powers of the *abiiru*, Rwabugiri's reforms highlighted the growing bipolarity of the identity just as they did the social difference between a *petit* Tutsi and a Hutu. It was toward the end of the nineteenth century, as Rwabugiri's rule was drawing to a close, that the Hutu/Tutsi distinction clearly began to appear as a political distinction that divided the subject population from those identified with power. Yet, when contrasted with Belgian rule, which was soon to follow, one is struck by two mitigating features. *First*, the Hutu continued to be present at lower levels of officialdom. *Second*, the boundary between Hutu and Tutsi was softened by a degree of social mobility; no matter how low its quantitative significance, this would prove to be a fact of great social and ideological importance.[73] If Hutu/Tutsi evoked the subject-power distinction in the precolonial Rwandan state, the colonial state gave it an added dimension: by racializing Hutu and Tutsi as identities, it signified the distinction as one between indigenous and alien. By making of Tutsi and Hutu identities evocative of colonial power and colonial subjugation—and not just local power relations—colonialism made them more volatile than ever in history.

Chapter Three

The Racialization of the Hutu/Tutsi
Difference under Colonialism

IN THE aftermath of the Second World War, a leading European Jewish intellectual set out to understand what in the trajectory of European history had made possible an event as full of horror as the Holocaust. Unlike many who had tried to closet this event to the internal history of Europe, Hannah Arendt's great merit was to locate it within the context of a wider history, that of Europe's global conquest and expansion. She recognized the confluence of two institutions, scientific racism and scientific bureaucracy, as key to shaping the nature of German power as it expanded into Europe. But she also recognized that neither of these institutions was uniquely German. Both were forged in the course of an earlier European expansion into the non-European world.[1]

> Of the two main political devices of imperialist rule, race was discovered in South Africa, and bureaucracy in Algeria, Egypt and India; the former was originally the barely conscious reaction to tribes of whose humanity European man was ashamed and frightened, whereas the latter was a consequence of that administration by which Europeans had tried to rule foreign peoples whom they felt to be hopelessly their inferiors and at the same time in need of their special protection. Race, in other words, was an escape into an irresponsibility where nothing human could any longer exist, and bureaucracy was the result of a responsibility that no man can bear for his fellow-man and no people for another people.

Hannah Arendt recognized, generally, that genocide had a history and, more specifically, that modern genocide was nurtured in the colonies: the "elimination of Hottentot tribes, the wild murdering by Carl Peters in German Southwest Africa, the decimation of the peaceful Congo population—from 20 to 40 million reduced to 8 million people and . . . worst of all . . . the triumphant introduction of such means of pacification into ordinary, respectable foreign policies."[2]

Although the race idea found free reign in the colonies, Europe was the land of its conception, its prehistory, as it was of its culmination. The prehistory of the race idea in Europe had more of a French than a German imprint. At its core lay a notion nurtured by the French nobility in times of crises: that class differences were natural in origin, and that its taproot was none other than race difference. In its origin, race was an attempt to biologize and naturalize class difference at a time of crisis. Race doctrine in France came to a fruition in the writings of Comte Arthur de Gobineau, whose major work appeared in 1853 and who identified, step by step, the fall of the aristocracy with the fall of France, then of Western civilization, and then of the whole of humanity.[3] He looked forward to a "race of princes," the Aryans, which he hoped would replace the aristocracy and build on its privileges. Ever since French noblemen found themselves pitted against the French bourgeoisie in a struggle for political supremacy, they discovered that they belonged to a separate "race." The view that the nobility were the descendants of Germanic Franks and the Third Estate of the native Gallo-Romans played a significant role in the development of the revolutions of 1789 and 1830. Nonetheless, the self-proclaimed "Germanism" of the nobility was not quite the same as the "Latinism" of the Third Estate: while the former was a race doctrine, the latter claimed a spiritual and not a biological inheritance from Rome.

Was Hannah Arendt right to posit biology and culture as opposites? Even if she was, in the context of France of the revolutions of 1789 and 1830, what is striking about postrevolutionary developments, as Republican France turned to an imperialist project, was the confluence of culture and biology and the emergence of a discourse on civilization that was nothing less than a culture-coded racism. To identify the link between biology and culture, between the language of race and that of civilization, is to fill in the shaded transition from Republicanism at home to a full-bodied imperialism abroad. Born of an internal class crisis, the race idea took full form in the context of an external imperial crisis. Race spread from a marginal to a mainstream doctrine in the context of modern imperialism, that single most important transformative experience in recent human history. In that same context, race moved from being a preoccupation of a rapidly declining aristocracy to being the fascination of an increasingly bourgeois Europe. Race became the marker dividing humanity into a few superhuman and the rest less than human, the former civilized, the latter putty for a civilizational project. This bipolar division of humanity provided the rationale for the elimination of entire peoples. More than the design to eliminate an entire people, it was the fact that this ghastly endeavor for the first time targeted a people in the heart of Europe that made the Holocaust unique in the imagination of the West. Nazi ideology having cast the Jewish people as a race apart from Europeans, Nazi power set out to eliminate them as a people. The imperial chickens, as it were, had come home to roost.

Hannah Arendt was right that genocide had to be linked to race ideology and bureaucratic efficiency if it was to be brought within the realm of comprehension. But she was mistaken in thinking that race was a singular South African, Boer, discovery. Had she added to the list of imperial horrors the genocide of the Amerindians and the centuries-long trans-Atlantic slave trade, she would have come to a different conclusion. For the nurturing ground of scientific racism was not as much the Boer experience in South Africa as the imperial encounter with continental Africa. The trans-Atlantic slave trade racialized notions of Africa. It fueled the conceptual tendency to divide Africa in two: that above the Sahara and that below it. From a bridge that had for centuries facilitated a regular flow of trading camel caravans between civilizations to its north and south, the Sahara was now seen as the opposite: a great civilizational barrier below which lay a land perpetually quarantined, "Negro Africa." "True" Africa, "real" Africa, was now seen as identical with tropical ("sub-Saharan") Africa geographically and Negro ("Bantu") Africa socially.

The racialized understanding of Africa in the era of the trans-Atlantic slave trade is summed up, most systematically, even if not most originally, in the writings of the great philosopher Georg Wilhelm Friedrich Hegel.[4] Hegel separated the land from where the slaves were captured, which he called "Africa Proper" from north Africa ("European Africa") and northeast Africa ("the land of the Nile"), which was for him "closely connected with Asia."[5] In this vision, "European Africa" was seen as a land that though "not itself a theatre of world-historical events" had "always been dependent on revolutions of a wider scope."[6] Similarly, the "land of the Nile" was seen as attached to Eurasia, "a focus" that was "destined to become the centre of a great and independent culture." In contrast was "Africa Proper" to the south. In Hegel's words: "Africa proper, as far as history goes back, has remained—for all purposes of connection with the rest of the world—shut up; it is the gold-land compressed within itself— the land of childhood, which lying beyond the day of conscious history is enveloped in the dark mantle of Night."[7]

Although the origin of European race doctrines about Africa lay in the period of the trans-Atlantic slave trade, these doctrines grew in complexity in the period that followed, that of "discovery" and colonial conquest.

The more Europeans got to know Africa, the less credible became the notion of the Sahara as a great civilizational barrier, and the more they were confronted with—and had to explain—growing evidence of organized life on the continent before the encounter with Europe. Every sign of "progress" on the Dark Continent was now taken as evidence of a civilizing influence of an outsider race. This race of civilizers, it was said, were Caucasians who were black in color without being Negroid in race. Thus were born the Hamites of Africa, separated from the Bantu, so-called real Africans.

THE HAMITIC HYPOTHESIS

The Tutsi may have emigrated from elsewhere, but they did not see this as a politically significant fact. It is worth noting that while royal myths claimed a sacred origin for the *mwami* (king), they never claimed a foreign origin. Mythology had it that the two royal clans (the *Abanyiginya* and the *Abeega*) from which the mwami was chosen had a sacred origin. We shall see that the sacral sanction evoked in mythology was not limited to the monarchy; it extended to Tutsi supremacy.

Three oft-cited royal myths are relevant here. The most commonly cited myth about the sacral nature of kingship and the origin of human settlement in Rwanda has it that the monarchy originated from a heavenly king, *nkuba*, meaning thunder.[8] Nkuba lived in heaven with his wife, Nyagasani; their two sons, Kigwa and Tutsi; and their daughter, Nyampundu. One day the three siblings fell from heaven and settled on a Rwandan hill. There, Kigwa married his sister. Their descendants are said to constitute the Abanyiginya clan. Tutsi, Nyampundu's and Kigwa's brother, married one of his nieces. Their descendants were the Abeega clan. This, in a nutshell, is why the two royal clans are said to prefer to intermarry, with Abanyiginya boys usually taking Abeega girls.

The subject of the second myth is the social difference between the three differentiated groups. Kigwa's three sons—Gatwa, Gahutu, and Gatutsi—were said to be deprived of a social faculty. One day, Gatutsi, the firstborn, suggested that they go to *Imana* (God) and ask for a social faculty. Gatutsi went first, and Imana offered him the faculty of anger. When Gahutu arrived, Imana let him know that only the faculty of disobedience and labor was left, and Gahutu agreed to accept it. Gatwa was the last to arrive and was offered the only remaining faculty, gluttony, which he gladly embraced.

The third legend refers to Kigwa, the son of Nkuba and the first Rwandan king on earth.[9] To test the ability of his three sons—Gatwa, Gahutu, and Gatutsi—Kigwa carried out an experiment. Entrusting each of his sons with a calabash filled with milk, he told them to watch over it for a night. The morning after, Gatwa was found to have drunk all the milk, and Gahutu to have spilled his; only Gatutsi had kept his milk intact. So, the king entrusted Gatutsi to command the glutton serf Gatwa and the clumsy peasant Gahutu. Thus did the Tutsi aristocracy, like the Tutsi monarchy, claim a sanction based on a sacred, and not an alien, origin.

The idea that the Tutsi were superior because they came from elsewhere, and that the difference between them and the local population was a *racial* difference, was an idea of colonial origin. It was an idea shared by rival colonists, Belgians, Germans, English, all of whom were convinced that wherever in Africa there was evidence of organized state life, there the ruling groups must have come from elsewhere. These mobile groups were known as the Hamites, and the notion that they were the hidden hand behind every bit of civilization on the continent was known as the "Hamitic hypothesis." We shall see that its genealogy goes deeper than the colonial period, to the era of trans-Atlantic slavery, and even deeper. The paradox of the slave trade was this: the more the slave trade grew in volume, the more it increased the value of the slave while debasing his or her humanity. The more this trend accelerated, the more the ideologues of the period were determined to keep the ancestors of slaves from contaminating the origin of civilization. The Hamitic hypothesis easily appealed to such a sensibility.

The raw material from which the Hamitic hypothesis was manufactured can be dated back to Judaic and Christian myths of biblical and medieval vintage. Scholars of the period say the word Ham appears for the first time in Genesis, chapter 5, of the Bible.[10] The account in Genesis tells of Ham's contempt for his father, whom he saw drunk and lying naked in a stupor. While Noah's other sons covered their father's nakedness, averting their eyes so as not to witness his shame, Ham did not look away. Noah blessed the descendants of Shem and Japhet, but cursed those of Ham. While Genesis says nothing about the descendants of Ham being black, the claim that they were cursed by being black first appeared in the oral traditions of the Jews when these were recorded in the sixth-century Babylonian Talmud; that same myth depicts Ham as a sinful man and his progeny as degenerates.[11] This notion persisted in the Middle Ages, when a rabbinical elaboration on the Genesis story had it that Ham had emasculated Noah, who cursed him thus:

Now I cannot beget the fourth son whose children I would have ordered to serve you and your brothers! Therefore it must be Canaan, your firstborn, whom they enslave. And since you have disabled me . . . doing ugly things in blackness of night, Canaan's children shall be borne ugly and black! Moreover, because you twisted your head around to see my nakedness, your grandchildren's hair shall be twisted into kinks, and their eyes red; again because your lips jested at my misfortune, theirs shall swell; and because you neglected my nakedness, they shall go naked, and their male members shall be shamefully elongated!

The commentary continues: "Men of this race are called Negroes, their forefather Canaan commanded them to love theft and fornication, to be banded together in hatred of their masters and never to tell the truth."[12]

The biblical myth was that descendants of Ham were Negro Africans. Though a part of humanity—as descended from Noah—they were considered an *accursed* part, having descended from a cursed son of Noah. It was in this vein that Leo Africanus, the great North African traveler and one-time protégé of Pope Leo X, identified Negro Africans as having descended from Ham. Scholars of Hebrew myths note that these oral traditions "grew out of a need of the Israelites to rationalize their subjugation of Canaan." In a different age, that of the sixteenth-century Atlantic slave trade, it was turned into raw material and put to a different use. The biblical curse—"a servant of servants shall he be"—was taken to mean that the Negro was clearly preordained for slavery. So, the Negro could be degraded while remaining a part of humanity—without disturbing Christian sensibilities formally.

The biblical and the Rwandan myths share an important similarity. Both identify social differences as differences between those whose ancestors were brothers, thus the differences continue to be within a single humanity. It is this assumption, this myth, of a single humanity, that came under question over the first two centuries of the trans-Atlantic slave trade. The more the Western world grew rich on the institution of slavery, the less it was willing to accept Negros as brothers and sisters under the skin. This tension was reflected in a growing intellectual debate about the origin of humanity, spurred by the *philosophes* who were at the epicenter of the Enlightenment. Two schools of thought mushroomed.[13] On one side were the monogenists who emphasized that humanity had a single origin: they explained the degradation of the Negro as the result of a "degeneration" due to adverse environmental conditions, not any biblical curse. On the other side were the polygenists who argued in favor of multiple origins:

they claimed that the Negro was subhuman. Though for opposite reasons, neither had room for the notion that the Negro was descended from the accursed Ham. A parallel debate also emerged in theological circles with a dissident school claiming the existence of pre-Adamite beings from whom nonwhite races were said to have descended.[14]

By the end of the eighteenth century, the myth that the Negro was the accursed descendant of Ham had been turned upside down. The catalyst behind the second incarnation of the Hamitic hypothesis was Napoleon's invasion of Egypt in 1798. Napoleon shared a passion for science and antiquities with intellectuals of the Enlightenment, so he invited archaeologists and other scientists to join him on the expedition. The immediate impact of the discoveries they made was to disturb Europe's view of Africans profoundly. V. Denon, a member of Napoleon's expedition, described the predominant physical features of Egyptians: "a broad and flat nose, very short, a large flattened mouth . . . thick lips, etc."[15] How could the producers of a civilization that had nurtured Greece and Rome be black? Another French traveler who had a decade earlier spent four years in Egypt and Syria had remarked on this paradox in a well-known book:[16] "How are we astonished . . . when we reflect that to the race of negroes, at present our slaves, and the object of our contempt, we owe our arts, sciences, and . . . when we recollect that, in the midst of these nations who call themselves the friends of liberty and humanity, the most barbarous of slaveries is justified; and that it is even a problem whether the understanding of negroes be of the same species as that of white men!"

The answer to this paradox was disarmingly simple: it was to turn the curse of Noah upside down and to claim that the Hamites (including the Egyptians) were actually Caucasians under a black skin. Rather than Negroes, Hamites were seen as other than Negroes, those who civilized the Negroes and were in turn corrupted by the Negroes. In this scheme of things, the ancient Egyptians were considered Hamitic, not Negroid, as were the Nubians and the Ethiopians (who were preferably called Abyssinians, a name less evocative of blackness than was Ethiopian). This is how Comte de Gobineau, that respectable nineteenth-century reactionary who later came to be considered the father of European racism, explained it all.[17] According to him, the three races represented by the sons of Noah—Ham, Shem, and Japhet—had all originated in some region of Central Asia and set out to seek their fortunes—all rather like the Three Little Piglets, to repeat Martin Bernal's amusing quip. The first to head south were the Hamites. The Hamites were said to be the genius behind ancient

Egypt and behind the Phoenicians. But after founding some civilizations and attempting to keep their blood pure, they had become hopelessly mongrelized by the native and inferior blacks. Next to leave were the Semites, who also got polluted in the course of time, partly from direct contact with the blacks, but mostly from contact with the "mulatto" Hamites. Only the Aryans, the Japhites, had stayed in the north and retained their purity. In this version, the one that is generally accepted, the sons of Noah were the predecessors of the three main races in humanity: the Europeans were begotten from Japhet, the Semites from Shem, and the Hamites from Ham. No longer Hamites, but a pre-Hamitic species that were said to have corrupted the Hamites, the Negroid Africans were finally beyond the pale of humanity.

This second version of the Hamitic hypothesis was reconciled to the biblical story in the early nineteenth century. It was remembered that Noah had, after all, cursed Canaan, son of Ham, but not Ham or his other sons, Cush the Ethiopian, Mizrahim the Egyptian, and Put. The Egyptians, it was also remembered, were born of Mizrahim, a different son of Ham. So, the Egyptians were salvaged, unscathed, black but not Negroid, and thus not cursed. The high regard in which Egypt was held in the European imagination at the beginning of nineteenth century is clear from the enormous popularity of *Aida*, the national opera that Mohamed Ali's grandson Ismail commissioned from Giuseppe Verdi, the composer of the Italian *Risorgimento*. The opera's plot was devised by the French Egyptologist Auguste Mariette, and it glorified Ancient Egypt in a Western manner, advancing a favorable view of Egypt "as essentially white and as a fount of civilisation."[18]

But "the Egyptian problem"—how could Africans have produced such a high civilization?—did not disappear with the whitening of Egypt. When equatorial Africa was colonized and European explorers were running its length and breadth, the question appeared in bold, this time in the public mind. One way to answer that question, a way that found great favor in those times, was to devalue Egyptian civilization doubly. The first was to deny its links to what was claimed as the cradle of modern Europe: Ancient Greece. And the second was to confirm it nominally as a part of Africa, as part of it geographically but not organically; considered African but not Negroid, both Egyptians and Ethiopians could be presented as external civilizers of "Negro Africa." As the nineteenth century drew to a close, Egyptians were brought lower down the ladder, and the civilization known as Ancient Egypt was similarly devalued. French writers such as

Maspero made the point bluntly: "Thothmes III and Rameses II resemble Mtesa [Mutesa] of Central Africa more than they do Alexander or Ceasar." The English Egyptologist Wallis Budge concluded in the same vein:

> The Egyptians, being fundamentally an African people, possessed all the virtues and vices which characterised the North African races generally, and it is not to be held for a moment that any African people could become metaphysicians in the modern sense of the word. In the first place, no African language is suitable for giving expression to theological and philosophical speculations, and even an Egyptian priest of the highest intellectual attainments would have been unable to render a treatise of Aristotle into language which his brother priests, without teaching, could understand.

Martin Bernal has shown how the European view of Egyptians changed through history.[19] In classical times, Egyptians were considered "both black and white and yellow." Herodotus referred to them as having "black skins and woolly hair." In the fifteenth century, in the era before Atlantic slavery, Egyptians could both be admired and be seen as black. The Talmudic interpretation that "the curse of Ham" was blackness became widespread in the seventeenth century. With increased racism amid growing respect for Ancient Egyptians in the late seventeenth century, their image tended to be whitened. In the second half of the eighteenth century, the tendency was to pull Egyptians back to Africa, just as there was growing enthusiasm for Ethiopia. By the end of the eighteenth century, however, the predominant view—as in Mozart's *The Magic Flute*—was that Egyptians were neither Negro nor essentially African, but Asian. Following Napoleon's expedition, however, pictorial representations of Ancient Egyptians became available to Europeans, and they showed "a thoroughly mixed" population.

To make room for a revised notion of Hamites as Caucasian, the hierarchy of race was stretched further. The top of the Caucasian ladder continued to be occupied by the Teutonic Anglo-Saxons. But its bottom rungs, previously occupied by the Slavs, were now stretched to include the African Hamites. Just as Egyptians were devalued in the hierarchy of Caucasians—put at its lower rung as Hamites, whites in black skin—they were rejoined to Africa and acclaimed as the historical summit of the African pyramid. They constituted, as it were, the front line of the Hamites marching through the length and breadth of the African continent, spreading civilization.[20] Corruptors of civilization in the original thesis, the Hamites had now become its dispensers.

Writing in 1955, the Senegalese savant Cheikh Anta Diop crisply summarized the shifts in how scholars understood the Hamitic hypothesis:

What we cannot understand, however, is how it has been possible to make a white race of *Kemit*: Hamite, black, ebony, etc. (even in Egyptian). Obviously, according to the needs of the cause, Ham is cursed, blackened, and made into the ancestor of the Negroes. This is what happens whenever one refers to contemporary social relations.

On the other hand, he is whitened whenever one seeks the origins of civilization, because there he is inhabiting the first civilized country in the world.

It is important to link the notion of Hamites, as we labour to understand it in official textbooks, with the slightest historical, geographical, linguistic or ethnic reality. No specialist is able to pinpoint the birthplace of the Hamites (scientifically speaking), the language they spoke, the migratory route they followed, the countries they settled, or the form of civilization they may have left. On the contrary, all the experts agree that this term has no serious content, and yet not one of them fails to use it as a kind of master-key to explain the slightest evidence of civilization in Black Africa.[21]

Cheikh Anta's observation was astute and his rebuttal poignant. And yet, one reflects to the extent to which the Hamitic hypothesis influenced the contours of his own scholarly claim: that the decline of ancient Egypt led to the dispersal of its population, an Egyptian diaspora, as it were, in turn leading to the "peopling of Africa."

The colonial official whose writings were central to the second incarnation of the Hamitic hypothesis was John Hanning Speke. "I profess to describe naked Africa—Africa in those places where it has not received the slightest impulse, whether for good or for evil, from European civilization," so Speke began his *Journal of the Discovery of the Source of the Nile*, as if picking up where Hegel had left off, but then continued in a vein more evocative of post-Genesis mythology: "If the picture be a dark one, we should when contemplating these sons of Noah try and carry our mind back to that time when our poor elder brother Ham was cursed by his father, and condemned to be the slave of both Shem and Japhet; for as they were then, so they appear to be now—a strikingly existing proof of the Holy Scriptures."[22] When he discovered the kingdom of Buganda with its complex political organization, Speke attributed this "barbaric civilization" to the Hamitic Galla from Ethiopia.[23] The Hamite had now become African Caucasians. By 1870, fathers of the Catholic Church gathered in the Vatican I Council were calling on fellow Caucasians to mount a rescue operation for "hapless Hamites caught amidst Negroes."[24]

The Hamites were not just ascribed physical attributes. Soon, they were given other attributes: first language, and then a wider cultural identity. In line with the claim that race and language were inextricably bound together, the Hamites were seen as speakers of the Hamitic language. This was said to be the case regardless of whether they retained the language, as the Ethiopians and the Berbers were said to, or lost it, wholly or partially, as was said to be the case with the Egyptians, the Tutsi, the Bahuma, or the Masai. Just as they were said to share a single family of languages, the Hamitic languages, the Hamites were also said to share a single culture, a way of life: unlike the Negroes who were said to be agriculturalists, the Hamites were said to be pastoralists. Few were bothered by the contradiction that racial groups were first based on language, if for no other reason than to give the claim a scientific grounding; but when some were found to have lost the original language, they were said to be left with nothing but their original race! The real irony was that the racial classification "Hamite" no longer corresponded to a color line. It came to include a wide range of peoples, from fair-skinned, blond, and blue-eyed Berbers to black Ethiopians. Even more glaring was the contradiction that Hamites could continue to be seen as practitioners of a pastoralist culture even if more and more of their numbers were without cattle.

But these contradictions did not seem to matter, not so long as the hypothesis could explain away the growing evidence of civilization within the Dark Continent as European adventurers took to "exploring" it. The Hamites were now confirmed as the great "civilizers" of Africa. With every move, these pastoralists were said to have brought a wider range of innovations to local agriculturalists: not only technical ones such as iron working and irrigation, but more so the political arts ranging from the age-grade system to the very capacity for state organization and, in some cases, even monotheism. With its status raised from a biblical myth to a scientific claim, the Hamitic hypothesis found support from much of anthropology. The key text was Charles Gabriel Seligman's famous *Races of Africa*, first published in 1930, and then reprinted, basically without revision, in several editions until 1966. From his chair of ethnology in the University of London, Seligman pronounced the Hamites "Europeans" for they "belong to the same great branch of mankind as the whites." And then he opined: "Apart from the relatively late Semitic influence—whether Phoenician (Carthaginian) and strictly limited, or Arab (Muhammedan) and widely diffused, the civilizations of Africa are the civilizations of the Hamites, its history the record of these peoples and their interaction with the other two African stocks, the Negro and the Bushmen, whether this influence was exerted by highly civilized Egyptians or by such wider pastoralists as are represented at the present day by the Beja and the Somalis."[25]

Now we come to the final paradox, one that directly concerns our study. The Hamites had now become an entire branch of the race of Caucasians; the Tutsi were said to be but one of many Hamitic groups. Recall that Speke had first employed the Hamitic hypothesis to explain the Buganda kingdom, not the kingdom of Rwanda. Why was it that it was only in Rwanda (and Burundi) and not anywhere else—not with the Baganda in Uganda, the Bahima in Ankole, the Bahuma in Bunyoro, or the Masai in Kenya and Tanganyika—that the Hamitic hypothesis retained a political potency decades later? My answer is simple: only in Rwanda was the notion that the Tutsi were a *race* apart from the majority turned into a rationale for a set of institutions that reproduced the Tutsi as a *racialized* minority. The Tutsi were racialized, not just through an ideology but through a set of institutional reforms that the ideology inspired, in which it was embedded, and which in turn reproduced it. This set the Tutsi apart from other so-called Hamites in Africa, just as it ruptured the link between race and color in Rwanda.

THE RACIALIZATION OF THE TUTSI/HUTU DIFFERENCE

The racialization of the Tutsi/Hutu was not simply an intellectual construct, one which later and more enlightened generations of intellectuals could deconstruct and discard at will. More to the point, racialization was also an institutional construct. Racial ideology was embedded in institutions, which in turn undergirded racial privilege and reproduced racial ideology. It is this political-institutional fact that intellectuals alone would not be able to alter. Rather, it would take a political-social movement to be dismantled.

As a process both ideological and institutional, the racialization of the Tutsi was the creation of a joint enterprise between the colonial state and the Catholic Church. Missionaries were "the first ethnologists" of colonial Rwanda.[26] As such, they were the primary ideologues of colonization. For Father Léon Classe, the future bishop of Rwanda and the key architect of missionary policy, the Tutsi were already in 1902 "superb humans" combining traits both Aryan and Semitic, just as for Father

François Menard, writing in 1917, a Tutsi was "a European under a black skin."[27] If the Church heralded the Tutsi as "supreme humans" in 1902, the same Church would turn into a prime site for the slaughter of Tutsi in 1994.

The colonial state called upon missionary knowledge from early on. Soon after colonization, the Belgian state ordered a reflection on Rwanda from the White Fathers.[28] The purpose was to elaborate and implement "race policies." In response, Fathers Arnoux, Hurel, Pagès, and Schumacher—Church fathers with expertise—prepared anthropological treatises. A consolidated document was then drawn up by Léon Classe, the head of the Catholic Church in Rwanda, and then presented to government authorities. This 1916 document had a wide readership. Not surprisingly, it gave vent to the kind of race thinking that the Church hierarchy had come to hold as a deeply felt conviction. "Race policy" became such a preoccupation with the colonial power that from 1925 on, annual colonial administration reports included an extensive description of the "races" in a chapter called "race policy."[29] By then, the Church had become integral to the workings of the state: since 1925, annual colonial reports included sections devoted exclusively to reports written by the heads of the Catholic Société Belge de Missions Protestantes au Congo (SBMPC, former Bethel mission), Church Missionary Society (CMS), and Adventists missions.[30]

It took Belgian rule a little over a decade to translate its vision of a civilizational mission in Rwanda into an institutional imprint. Central to that translation was the Hamitic hypothesis. Summed up in Kinyarwanda as other than *Rubanda Nyamwinshi*[31]—meaning the majority, the ordinary folk—Belgian power turned Hamitic racial supremacy from an ideology into an institutional fact by making it the basis of changes in political, social, and cultural relations. The institutions underpinning racial ideology were created in the decade from 1927 to 1936. These administrative reforms were comprehensive. Key institutions—starting with education, then state administration, taxation, and finally the Church—were organized (or reorganized, as the case may be) around an active acknowledgment of these identities. The reform was capped with a census that classified the entire population as Tutsi, Hutu, or Twa, and issued each person with a card proclaiming his or her official identity. We shall look at each of these to get a sense of the institutional matrix through which the Tutsi found themselves in a contradictory position, privileged in relation to the Hutu but oppressed in relation to Europeans.

Race Education

If the theory was that the Tutsi were "a civilizing race," then there would have to be institutions that would discriminate in favor of the Tutsi so as to make the theory a reality. Two institutions were key to ensuring this outcome: the school system and local administration. Of the two, the creation of a school system that could act as a womb of racial ideology was a priority. While the starting point of this enterprise was the notion of Tutsi supremacy that had both justified and sustained Tutsi privilege under Rwabugiri in the Rwanda of the late nineteenth century, its end product was to construct a far more comprehensive ideology of the Tutsi as a *race*, the "Hamites," both *civilizing* and *alien*. Without a cadre incubated with a Hamitic ethos, it would not be possible to create a local administrative hierarchy steeped in a self-conscious racialized elitism.

The first Western-style school in Rwanda was opened by the White Fathers in 1905 in Nyanza.[32] By 1908, it had twenty-six pupils, all sons of chiefs. In July 1907, Fathers Dufays and Classe had started the construction of another school in Kabgayi. To "surely reach the sons of the chiefs Batoutsi, there has been opened a special school for them," so they explained as their objective. In 1910, the policy of "favouring the Mututsi of Rwanda" was formulated and addressed by Father Schumacher as a report to the Superior General. The point was underlined by Father Classe in his extended study of 1911. The objective was to turn the Tutsi, the "born rulers" of Rwanda, into an elite "capable of understanding and implementing progress," and thus functioning as auxiliaries to both the missionaries and the colonial administration. There followed schools, no longer just for sons of chiefs but specifically for sons of Tutsi chiefs: in Nyanza in 1912, Kabgayi and Rwaza in 1913, Kigali in 1914 and 1916, Save in 1917, and Rwamagana in 1919. The obsession with a Tutsi-focused education was so strong that the White Fathers decided to move the school in Nyanza to Kabgayi on the grounds that "in Nyanza there were many sons of the Hutu being recruited." The trend culminated with the creation of the Groupe Scolaire d'Astrida in 1929 by the colonial authorities.

By the early 1930s, government schools were phased out and the missions assumed control of the education system. The system they created had two tiers. The tendency was to restrict admission mainly to Tutsi, especially to the upper schools.[33] But where both Tutsi and Hutu children were admitted, there was a clear differentiation in the education meted out to each. The Tutsi were given a "superior" education, taught in French in a separate stream. The *assimilationist* education prepared them for administrative positions in government and testified to their preparation for citizenship, even if at the lowest orders. In contrast, the Hutu were given an education considered "inferior," since they were taught in a different stream, one where the medium of instruction was Kiswahili. The point of the *separatist* education was not simply to prepare them for manual labor but also to underline the political fact that educated Hutu were not destined for common citizenship. The products of the French stream identified themselves as "Hamites" and those of the Kiswahili stream as "Bantu."

State Administration

The reform of the 1920s had a triple objective: *first*, to shift power from the monarch to chiefs as local authorities; *second*, to reorganize the powers of local authorities both to remove any form of accountability to communities below or any check and balance internal to the administrative bureaucracy, leaving in place only an accountability to the colonial administration above; and *third*, to racialize the local authority. The three objectives were not always in harmony. They gave rise to contradictory consequences at the start of reform, creating widespread discontent among both the chiefs and the monarch, and undermining the racialization policy. Ultimately, they led to a wholesale displacement of many of the leading chiefs and the mwami.

The reform of the 1920s began by centralizing the powers of chiefs and deflating those of the mwami. Both moves reinforced the same end: to augment colonial power in a despotic fashion. Even before Mwami Musinga was deposed in 1930, the powers of the office of the mwami were reduced in two important ways.[34] In 1922, the mwami lost his juridical supremacy and was obliged to take the advice of the colonial resident—through a delegate—in juridical affairs. The next year the mwami's administrative powers were curtailed as he lost the right to appoint chiefs, first at the regional and then the district level, without the consent of the Belgian Resident Representative. In 1926, the structure of local government was "streamlined" and powers of chiefs were redefined. The traditional trinity of chiefs had consisted of the *chief of the pastures* who was always a Tutsi, the *chief of the land* who was often a Hutu, and the *chief of the men* who was usually a Tutsi. The trinity of powers was abolished. Powers hitherto separate and differentiated were fused in a single agent. René Lemarchand noted in his study of colonial Rwanda that the streamlining abolished "the old balance of forces between cattle chiefs, land chiefs and army chiefs, which in previous times had served to protect the [Ba]hutu peasantry against undue exactions." The resulting "concentration of powers in the hands of a single chief, exercising unfettered control over his people, was bound to lead to abuses: not only did it deprive the Hutu of opportunities to play one chief off against another, but it also eliminated the channels of appeal offered by the previous arrangement."[35] Such institutional change not only augmented state power, it also made it more despotic in character.

The deflation in the power of the mwami and the redefinition of the powers of chiefs bred discontent among many chiefs. As we shall see, the tension between the colonial administration and the old chiefs was exacerbated in a context where both church missionaries and state officials were exerting great pressures on the elite to convert to Christianity. In the face of resistance, the response of the Belgian administration was to depose those they saw as unredeemable, even if they numbered in the hundreds. But when Tutsi chiefs and subchiefs were substituted by Hutu appointees, Catholic missionaries were aghast, and alarmed. Concerned about the "vacillation of the colonial authorities with regard to the traditional hegemony of the well-born Tutsi," Monseigneur Classe categorically warned the administration against any attempt to "eliminate the Tutsi caste."[36] In Lemarchand's opinion, "the Church posed as the strongest advocate of Tutsi supremacy."

And Tutsi supremacy in the local administration is precisely what the Church assured. The 1920s saw a Tutsification of the chiefship as an institution. This was the result of a double development. The trend had begun with local chiefs being dismissed from all the newly incorporated principalities—such as the Ndorwa, Mutara, and Mulera regions in the north, and Busozo, Bushinzi, and Bukiru regions in the northwest—and replaced by Tutsi freshly parachuted into each region. Later, all Hutu chiefs in the central kingdom were systematically deposed and replaced by Tutsi chiefs. The new Tutsi chiefs were the products of schools for the sons of Tutsi chiefs. Nourished on a steady diet of Hamitic supremacy, they were appointed chiefs as if by birthright.

Tutsi power in local administration was consolidated by a further institutional reform. This was a judicial reform that introduced the Native Tribunals in 1936. These reforms further augmented the powers of the single, centralized chiefship, in every case headed by Tutsi chiefs. To the executive power to implement every government directive, and legislative

power to proclaim a by-law so long as it did not violate an existing government policy or directive, the reform added a judicial power that allowed
the chief literally to sit in judgment of himself. So were the parameters of
local administrative power rounded off into a local despotism.[37]

The Church and Conversion

It was one thing to incorporate the Tutsi hierarchy in the colonial
power structure, quite another to Christianize it.[38] To do this successfully
took over three decades of colonial rule. German officials tended to defer
to missionaries, especially the Catholic White Fathers, *first*, because they
were too few in numbers, and *second*, because they were mindful that missionaries had an advantage over state administration not only in numbers
but also in the longevity of their stay in Rwanda. The missionaries, on
their part, had been delighted to find a country where there were neither
Muslims nor Protestants—in other words, no competition.[39] Now, in return for service to the state, they wanted their proverbial pound of flesh:
the freedom to evangelize for themselves augmented by the freedom to
convert for their subjects. Belgian power obliged in 1917 when it compelled the *mwami* to sign a bill on the "liberty of conscience."[40] Formal
liberties aside, the *mwami* and his chiefs had their own ideas. Besides restricting evangelical access to the Tutsi elite—while directing it to the
Hutu peasantry—the *mwami* also opened the door to Protestant missions.
For the White Fathers, this constituted a double injury: it went against
the grain of their policy that they convert the rulers first, and it violated
their expectation that as an officially Catholic colony Rwanda would naturally be a Catholic evangelical monopoly.

That the mwami had an important role in the traditional religion proved
an obstacle to converting the Tutsi hierarchy to Christianity. The court
and the majority of chiefs resisted conversion well up to 1930. When per-
suasion did not work, missionaries called upon the power of the state to
clear the ground for successful evangelization. Those among the chiefs
"who would not convert" were branded "sorcerers, diviners and superstitious and were deposed."[41] The trend came to a head in 1926, when "hundreds of Rwandese chiefs were dismissed from office and in some cases
temporarily replaced by chiefs of Hutu extraction."[42] The bill on liberty
of conscience notwithstanding, the king, who did not convert, was constantly considered a threat, not only to evangelization but also to colonization; so he was deposed in 1930 and exiled to Congo, where he died in

1943. Among other things, Mwami Musinga was accused of closeness with Protestants and the Adventists, whom he had allowed to open stations in Kirinda and Rubengera, two symbolic ritual areas, and in Gitwe, only a half-hour drive from the capital of the monarchy in Nyanza.

It is notable that Musinga was deposed without significant popular protest. This testified to his growing estrangement, not only from Belgian power and missionaries, but also from an expanding rank of Tutsi chiefs, particularly those with a keen appreciation of the changes entailed by the new colonial order. Among this latter group, there was a growing awareness that the defense of their own position required a recognition of the Church as part of the new forces shaping the destiny of Rwanda.[43] The event that seemed to have given them a particular fright was the ordination of five Hutu to priesthood in 1919. It signaled a possibility they dared not entertain: that the Hutu could be emancipated and ennobled as Hutu, rather than in the traditional way, which required them to take on a Tutsi identity.

Passing over tradition which required that the new king be enthroned by the *abiiru* ritualists, Monseigneur Classe and Governor Voisin enthroned Rudahigwa as the new king, symbolizing, in Gatwa's words, "the alliance of the altar and the throne." The "pagan monarch" done away with, the new young king and the Tutsi hierarchy converted to Catholicism. The effect on the mass of the population was electric. Believing that the new king had given an order to convert, many did just that.[44] The mass conversion came to be known as the "Tornado" in missionary literature. It was said to transform Rwanda into the second "Christian Kingdom" after that of "Priest Jan." Decades later, the change would be summed up in a popular Kinyarwanda saying: "Church preaching replaced culture."[45]

A Regime of Compulsions

Rwanda was an agrarian colony with little urban settlement before this century. From the very outset, Belgians signaled that the agrarian political economy would be developed mainly along agricultural, and not pastoral, lines. This meant that in any tension between cultivators and herders over use of common resources, the state would come down on the side of cultivators. The message was conveyed in unmistakable terms by decree no. 791/A/53, which levied a fine—twice the amount of damage caused—on every Tutsi taking the harvest of a Hutu or sending his herd to graze in a cultivated field. A later decree compelled the mwami to double the size of the arable land at the disposal of Hutu families, thereby emphasizing the tilt in resource use in favor of agriculture and away from cattle-rearing.[46]

In spite of reforms favouring agrarian production, the Hutu peasantry experienced Belgian rule as harsher than any previous regime in living memory. For this, there were two reasons. *First*, there was the reorganization of state administration, particularly local administration. We have seen that the reorganization went beyond a simple incorporation of the precolonial state machinery into the lower rungs of the new order. By creating a single hierarchy of chiefs, it accentuated the despotic aspect of state administration. *Second*, this despotic machinery was enabled by a highly administrative version of "customary" law, one which sanctified as "customary" any exercise of force by authorities simply because they too were considered "customary." As "customary" authorities and "customary" law became central to the Belgian project of colonial development, a combination of market mechanisms and extra/economic compulsions became central to propelling the project forward. The key point for our purposes is that the authority decreeing these compulsions was inevitably the hierarchy of Tutsi chiefs.

The Belgian administration began by confirming and, where possible, individualizing taxes previously introduced by the Germans, and then followed by adding on to these. This included a Minimum Personal Contribution, levied as an individual tax on every adult male. The Church, too, in the person of Monseigneur Classe, introduced its own tax, being 1 franc per person per year. But there was a limit to monetary exactions, especially in the early decades when it was assumed that market relationships were the privilege of officialdom, whether Belgian or Tutsi. This was so prevalent that "until about 1930 it was common practice throughout Rwanda for chiefs who recruited workers to take wages for themselves."[47]

When it came to the regime of exactions, monetary taxes were but the tip of the iceberg. This is why it is not the range of monetary taxes but that of nonmonetary exactions that convey the real harshness of Belgian rule. These exactions constituted nothing less than a regime of force, ranging from forced labor to forced crops. These could be demanded of individuals for "educational" reasons, or of entire groups for "developmental" reasons. The standard punishment for anyone who reneged on an administrative requirement—whether it was forced labor, forced crops, or forced sales—was the *kiboko*, eight strokes with hippopotamus cane.[48]

Force was integral to the process of exploitation—particularly *forced labor*. At first, the colonial power found it convenient simply to pass on every demand—say, the upkeep of roads—to "customary" chiefs so they would use their "customary" prerogative to get the job done without payment and with a minimum of disruption of order. The chiefs, too, found it convenient to add their own demands to this list of "customary" exactions. So the list grew: the land tax—*butake*—traditionally said to be one day of labor for the chiefs in every five, was increased by chiefs to two or even three days in every six. Soon, this was supplemented by other forms of corvée that had never before existed, such as an obligation to construct chiefs' houses from durable materials. Under these conditions, "work" came to be synonymous with "force." Commenting on the interwar period, the historian Kagame wrote: "Thus for several decades the country became a vast camp of forced work of a new type. The very notion of work came to be practically synonymous with corvée, to the point that the representatives of Authority themselves, natives as well as Europeans, understood it as such and interpreted it with this transformed nuance."[49]

Forced labor soon led to *forced crops*. The cultivation of "famine" crops was first made an administrative compulsion in the 1920s. Ironically, the compulsory cultivation of famine-resistant but protein-deficient tubors came as an antidote to a string of famines that began as early as 1904, never mind that recurring famines bore a relationship to the onset of a regime of force worse than any in Rwandan memory. In 1932, one missionary complained that "the authorities had requisitioned his parishioners so often they scarcely had time to grow food, and famine threatened." He complained of "the coffee drive, the buckwheat drive, the cassava drive, tree planting, construction work, road cleaning, and more." He calculated that "of 2,024 available male villagers in his area, 1,375 were requisitioned each day."[50] The response to the famine of the 1920s was not a program of public relief through public works, giving a monetary income to the worker, but a program where public work became a compulsion to work for the public power without any reward. The series of programs introduced to counteract the famine "required vastly increased demands on rural manpower and set forth an explicit policy of reinforcing the power of the chiefs, who were responsible for seeing that each directive was carried out in all its details." The measures included the "compulsory cultivation of famine-resistant food crops (cassava, sweet potatoes and, in some areas, European potatoes), reclamation of marshes to provide additional land for cultivation, the introduction of required cash crop production (primarily coffee) and reforestation programs."[51] While the compulsion to grow food crops as an "antifamine" measure became administrative practice in the 1920s, it was formulated into law in 1931, mandating "that each farm family cultivate a certain area in root crops as a means of preventing seasonal food crises and famines."[52] In most of Rwanda, the root crop of choice was the sweet potato, with cassava grown only at the lowest elevations and white potatoes at high elevations. Similarly, coffee was introduced as a compulsory cash crop for reasons of "development."

Force so permeated the arena of law defined as "customary" that *forced sales* also came to be considered as part of civilized behavior. At the beginning of colonial rule, a refusal to sell assets was considered uncivil, and even rebellious, behavior. Here, for example, is an entry from the diary of a colonial official, dated 14 January 1905: "The movement of resistance (see 1904) to 'the opening of the region to commerce' grows; 'Mwami Musinga forbids all breeders to sell cattle.' Learning of this interdiction, two European traders (the Austrian Fritz Schindelar and the Boer Praetorius) accompanied by armed escorts 'seize the cattle in Gisaka and Nduga'; they take 'women hostages in order to force the people to sell or else they steal the cattle and burn the houses.' "[53]

Two decades later, in 1928, when the administrator Hendrix was asked to provide thousands of porters to carry beans procured in Gisaka, Rugari made the following observation in his diary about how the beans had been "bought": "The chiefs are ordered to bring their sub-chiefs and subjects ladden with food" and that "it is more or less forced sale."[54] Similarly, tax levies, even if in cash, were turned by chiefs into opportunities "to gather cows, goats, hoes, etc."[55] The more a chief became indispensable as an instrument of local government, the more he had opportunities for extralegal exactions. An administrative report from 1926 explained how these abuses proliferated:

In the territories where food supplies are requested from chiefdoms, the notables sometimes proceed in the following manner: In the case of beef, cattle are requisitioned from various hills or from a variety of abagaragu. The notable who requisitions these animals delivers one to the [administrative] post where he collects the payment, and places the others in his herds or sells them to the traders. A similar method is used in the case of food supplies. . . .

When porters are requested from chiefdoms, it happens that a certain number of these are not used. These are sometimes used by the notables for cultivating the latter's fields.[56]

To be sure, many a chief was deposed, and just as many received corporal punishment from Belgian authorities, for failure to deliver. Tutsi overseers were often required to force Hutu commoners to work. "If you didn't meet your targets, the Belgians would whip you," recalled John Kanyambo, age seventy-eight. Recalling massive terracing schemes and road projects, elderly Tutsi refugees in Uganda told Catherine Watson of how little choice the regime of forced labor gave them. The Belgian attitude was simple: "You whip the Hutu or we will whip you."[57] And yet the chiefs were no simple cogs in the colonial wheel. For the chief willing to collaborate, colonialism turned into a profitable partnership: the chief could and did add his own exactions on top of whatever the colonial power demanded, and then proceeded to apply the degree of force necessary to ensure compliance with demands he inevitably presented as "traditional." The smaller the chief, the more arbitrary the imposition: as one Church observer noted, a *petit* Tutsi chief and his wife "could take almost anything they please—bananas, yams, etc.—and the Hutu must comply lest he be expelled from his fields."[58]

Every so often, the Belgian authorities would try to rationalize the system, mainly to reduce the chiefly scope for levying extralegal exactions. At first, this took the form of codifying and thus setting specific limits on forced measures. The prime example was the codification in 1924 of *ubureetwa* (forced labor) that had earlier been introduced by Mwami Rwabugiri. It was now fixed at 42 days a year, as opposed to the earlier practice, irregular but said to be extending in some instances to as many as 142 days a year. Though its weight was formally reduced in law, the practical effect of legal codification was otherwise: previously a practice only where Tutsi power had been a reality for some time, this form of unpaid labor for chiefs became generalized throughout Rwanda, becoming rigidly enforced as a legal compulsion, only during the colonial period.[59]

Later, Belgian authorities sought to concentrate on different forms of corvée, so as to replace each with an annual tax to be paid in cash. But, as often as old forms of corvée were converted to a cash levy, new exactions in kind would be levied, justified as "antifamine" or "development" measures. Throughout this see-saw between the monetization of old exactions and the introduction of new impositions in kind, there was one form of corvée the colonial power refused to convert into a monetary payment. This was *ubureetwa*, one "imposed specifically on Hutu" and left unreformed because officials argued that to do away with it would be to "undermine the chiefs' authority over the population."[60] The chief who came out of the interwar period was expected to enforce and supervise obligatory cultivation of food and export crops; to mobilize labor for road building, reforestation, and any rural project like a dispensary; and even to become major coffee producers by using corvée labor. Not surprisingly, this chief resembled more a local despot than a government official.[61]

Ubureetwa was a forced imposition on the Hutu only. More than any other, it testified to the existence of Tutsi privilege in colonial Rwanda and highlighted the social separation between the *petit* Tutsi and the average Hutu. Just as white privilege in colonial Africa separated poor whites from all "natives," no matter what class they belonged to, so Tutsi privilege in colonial Rwanda set *all* Tutsi apart from *all* Hutu in their relation to power.

Census and Classification

To issue a decree was one thing, to effect it was quite another. Belgian power could issue decrees making an official distinction between Tutsi and Hutu,[62] but Belgian administration could not treat the subject population as Tutsi and Hutu so long as it had not classified every individual as Tutsi or Hutu, apart from the tiny number of Twa. This happened only with the official census of 1933–34.

There is an ongoing debate on the criteria that were used to distinguish Tutsi from Hutu in that census. The prevalent view has been that the 1933–34 census identified Tutsi as separate from Hutu on the basis of the ten-cow rule: whoever owned ten or more cows was classified as a Tutsi.[63] This is also the basis of the claim that Tutsi is in reality the identity of a social class. This conclusion has been subjected to a criticism on empirical grounds, based on an overall calculation of the numbers classified as Tutsi against the number of cows at the time. The total number of cattle around 1930 was said to fluctuate between 500,000 and 600,000. Many were held in royal or chiefly herds and could not be claimed by individuals. The census estimated the 1933 population of Rwanda at 1.8 million, and the number of Tutsi as between 250,000 and 300,000. No matter how one calculates, the figures simply do not tally if one assumes that the 10-cow rule held in every case. This conclusion is reinforced by the fact that many Tutsi owned few or no cows. These were the *petits* Tutsi. It is difficult to see how these *petits* Tutsi, whose average income was calculated at no more than 5 percent above the average Hutu income, could have been classified as Tutsi if the ten-cow rule held in every instance, or even in most.[64]

The ten-cow rule both holds a kernel of truth and has been turned into fodder for a polemic that holds that the Belgian authority arbitrarily cooked up the Hutu/Tutsi distinction at the outset of colonial rule. The kernel of truth is that the ten-cow rule *was* applied, but it was neither the only nor even always the main basis for identification of Tutsi. The state relied heavily on data provided by the Church, whose local servants knew very well their neighbors and their genealogy. Tharcisse Gatwa would seem to be closer to the point when he claims that the administration relied on three major sources of information: oral information mainly provided by the church, physical measurements, and ownership of large herds of cows.[65] In the final analysis, when it came to breathing institutional life into the Hamitic hypothesis, the colonial Church acted as both the brains and the hands of the colonial state. In this instance, at least, the Church did both the strategic thinking and the dirty work for the state. The fact is that Belgian power did not arbitrarily cook up the Hutu/Tutsi distinction. What it did do was to take an existing sociopolitical distinction and racialize it.

Racializing the Hutu/Tutsi Difference

The census marked the end point of a process through which the colonial power constructed the Tutsi as nonindigenous and the Hutu as indigenous. Through this distinction between alien and indigenous, the Tutsi came to be defined as a race—the Hamitic race—different from the Hutu, who were constructed as indigenous Bantu. I have argued earlier that Rwanda shared the broad legal framework of indirect rule with other tropical African colonies, at the same time as its colonial experience represented a distinct trajectory. On the one hand, the legal divide between civic and customary spheres prevailed in Rwanda. On the other hand, there was no corresponding political divide, fragmenting the subject population into a multitude of ethnic groups, each with its separate "customary law" enforced by an ethnically defined Native Authority. *In colonial Rwanda, there were no ethnic groups, only races.* The Belgian authority considered Tutsi and Hutu as two distinct *races*, in the manner of direct rule, without deconstructing the Hutu into so many ethnicities in the manner of indirect rule. The Information Bulletin on Ruanda-Urundi, issued by the Public Relations Office in Belgium in 1960, thus spoke of "the inhabitants" of Rwanda as belonging "to two main *racial groups*: the Tutsi feudal stock-breeders, comprising 14% of the population, and the Hutu farmers, amounting to 85%" (emphasis mine).[66]

In Rwanda, district authorities did not correspond to so many ethnic powers. Instead, the bulk of the subject population was battered into a single identity said to be indigenous: the Hutu. There were no Hutu chiefs; the chiefs were all Tutsi. The Tutsi were not defined as an ethnic group with its own Native Authority and "customary law," but were spread over the entire society: the "well-born Tutsi" like a creamy layer, and the "*petits* Tutsi" an adjunct to it. Even if the *petits* Tutsi were not clearly set apart from the Hutu poor by a higher standard of living, their racialized status entitled them to petty privilege, specifically, Tutsi privilege.

That Rwanda was a halfway house—halfway between direct and indirect rule—had an important political consequence. Unlike direct rule, which was organized around the pivotal difference between colonizer and native, indirect rule legally fractured natives into so many ethnicities, and this mitigated the tension between the colonizer and the colonized. Indirect-rule colonialism thus had no racially branded majority in law; the colonized were legally constructed as so many ethnic minorities. It is here that Rwanda was different from all indirect-rule colonies in equatorial Africa. Because the boundaries of Native Authorities did not correspond to ethnic boundaries, the halfway house that was the Belgian colony of Rwanda ended up with the same fatal flaw of *all* direct-rule colonies: it constructed the colonized along a majority/minority axis, an indigenous majority and a so-called nonindigenous minority. This political outcome was far more characteristic of direct-rule colonies from the nineteenth century, be these in Africa (South Africa) or in Asia (India, Sri Lanka), where the presumed difference between an indigenous majority and a nonindigenous minority—Hindu and Muslim in India, Sinhalese and Tamil in Sri Lanka—was in reality a construction more political than historical.

The resulting position of the Tutsi was analogous, not to that of ethnicities in colonial Africa, but to that of *subject races*. Like the Indians of East Africa, the Arabs of Zanzibar, and the Indians and the Coloureds of South Africa, the Tutsi occupied the contradictory ground of a subject race. But, unlike them, the well-born Tutsi were also the chiefs who defined "custom" in the ethnic sphere, even though they were not subject to its worst manifestations. Along with the *petits* Tutsi, they were exempt from *ubu-reetwa*, the corvée that was the lot of the core colonial subject. The Tutsi had a leg in both the civic and the ethnic spheres. The contradictory position of the Tutsi was signified by their privileged status in the customary sphere and their nearly rightless status in the hierarchy of race in the civic sphere. This contradictory position meant that the Tutsi were simultaneously the target of popular resistance in the customary sphere and the source of popular resistance in the civic sphere. As we shall see in the next chapter, they were at the same time the target of Hutu "tribalism" in the customary sphere and the spearhead of Rwandan "nationalism" in the civic sphere.

To sum up, what then were the institutions that undergirded the identity "Tutsi"? *To begin with*, there was the *political regime* that issued official identities confirming every individual as Hutu or Tutsi, thereby seeking to naturalize a constructed political difference between Hutu and Tutsi as a legislated racial difference. After the 1933 census, Hutu and Tutsi were enforced as legal identities. This had a crucial social effect: neither *kwihutura* (the social rise of an individual Hutu to the status of a Tutsi) nor *gucupira* (the social fall from a Tutsi to a Hutu status) was any longer possible. For the first time in the history of the state of Rwanda, the identities "Tutsi" and "Hutu" held permanently. They were frozen. Then, *second*, there was the *administrative regime*, which, at its lowest rungs, was inevitably a Tutsi power. *Finally*, there was the *legal regime* whereby a Tutsi had a special relationship to the sphere of "customary" law. While the *petits* Tutsi were exempt from the extraeconomic exactions that went with the "customary" regime, the "well-born Tutsi" not only organized the regime of extraeconomic coercion but were also among its beneficiaries. The legal exemption of the *petits* Tutsi from corvée testified to the existence of a form of Tutsi privilege. It underlined that to be a Tutsi was to have a privileged relationship to power, to be treated preferentially, whether as part of power, in proximity to power, or simply to be identified with power—but in all cases, to be exempt from its worst exactions. In addition, colonialism branded Tutsi privilege, which had existed under Rwabugiri, as *alien* privilege.

Hutu and Tutsi changed as identities as did the organization of power in the Rwandan state. At this point, we can identify at least three different periods in this history. More like Siamese twins joined at the hip, or even higher, Hutu and Tutsi most likely had separate early histories. In the *first phase*, during the founding period of the state of Rwanda sometime in the fifteenth century, Tutsi was most likely an ethnic identity. Hutu, we have seen, was never an ethnic identity; it was rather constructed as a transethnic identity of subjects. Hutu was a political construction, a political umbrella under which were assembled different subjugated groups. In other words, those stigmatized as Hutu only became Hutu with their subjugation to the state of Rwanda. In the *second phase*, Tutsi was recast as an identity of power. Given the ennoblement through intermarriage of prosperous individuals from among the subjugated population, Tutsi also became a transethnic identity. It is in this phase that Hutu was constructed as a subject identity alongside Tutsi as an identity of power. The *third phase* came with the colonial period, when both Hutu and Tutsi were racialized, Tutsi as a nonindigenous identity of (subordinate) power and Hutu as an indigenous identity of (nativized) subjects. To the late nineteenth-century dynamic whereby Tutsi symbolized power and Hutu subject, a new and truly volatile dimension was added. This was the dimension of indigeneity: for the first time in the centuries-long history of the Rwandan state, Tutsi became identified with an alien race and Hutu with the indigenous majority. This is the context in which the expression *Rubanda Nyamwinshi* (ordinary folk) came to have a racialized meaning, becoming identified with only Hutu. The big change was that from being at the top of the *local* hierarchy in the precolonial period, the Tutsi found themselves occupying the bottom rung of a hierarchy of *alien* races in the colonial period.

Chapter Four

The "Social Revolution" of 1959

Decolonization in Africa unfolded along two different trajectories, setting apart the process of decolonization in settler colonies from that in colonies without settler minorities. Where settler minorities vied for political power against both the native majority and the imperial power—as in South Africa during the Boer War, Kenya at the time of Mau Mau, and Zimbabwe following the Unilateral Declaration of Independence (UDI)—it took an internal struggle, always extralegal and usually armed, for natives to win state independence. Where settlers did not exist as a group, or none claimed political power, the colonial power had a larger margin of maneuver and was able to differentiate between moderate and militant nationalism, to play one against the other, and to usher in a mode of independence in line with imperial notions of harmony of interests in postcolonial Africa. The two trajectories of decolonization—one armed, the other nonviolent—were at the same time testimony to different modes of colonization in these places.

I have argued that Rwanda was anything but a standard colony, that it was more of a halfway house between a direct and indirect-rule colony. The mode of decolonization in Rwanda, too, did not clearly follow one of the two patterns I have outlined above. On the one hand, the movement toward decolonization was more like the kind of process in settler colonial contexts, unfolding more through a set of internal convulsions than through a direct confrontation with the colonial power. Precisely because Hutu and Tutsi had, under colonialism, become synonymous with an indigenous majority and an alien minority, decolonization was a direct outgrowth of an internal social movement that empowered the majority constructed as indigenous against the minority constructed as alien. Recall that the majority declaration was called "the Bahutu Manifesto," not "the Rwandan Manifesto." It claimed that "the conflict between Hutu and Hamites—i.e., foreign-Tutsi" was the heart of the Rwandan problem and called for a double liberation of the Hutu: "from both the 'Hamites' and 'Bazungu' (white) colonization." As in settler colonies, political independence with majority rule would require a "revolution" at the local level.

On the other hand, this revolution did not have to be violent. Three developments testified to this possibility. The first was that state independence was not just a Hutu demand; it was also made by Tutsi elites. The distinction between the two was not that one called for state independence and the other opposed it, but the perspective each had on the society that would follow colonialism. The second was that, in spite of the divide between Hutu/Tutsi political elites, one could identify political tendencies cutting across the same elites. The third was that most of the violence in 1959–63 occurred not at the time of the revolution of 1959 but in response to subsequent attempts at restoration.

The year 1959 saw the first major political change in colonial Rwanda. Ushered in by political violence, it led to the routing and dismantling of Tutsi power at the local administration level. It also triggered broader constitutional and political developments that led to a transfer of governmental power from a Tutsi to a Hutu elite. In a study that aimed to reflect on "long-term transformations as they related to Rwandan Revolution," Catharine Newbury provided an influential defense of "the Hutu revolution," arguing that "ultimately, an appeal to Hutu solidarity became, for Hutu leaders, the most effective rallying point for revolutionary activity."[1] In writings of this period, 1959 was celebrated as a "revolution." In a major political analysis of the revolution, René Lemarchand compared 1959 Rwanda to 1789 France, and the Hutu revolutionaries to French Jacobins.[2] Lemarchand saw the problems of the revolution not in terms of what it had accomplished, but in terms of what remained to be done: "Now that the initial phase has been completed, there remains the more fundamental task of social and economic reform. . . . Until this is done, the Rwandese revolution must be regarded, in Marx's terms, as 'a partial, merely political revolution, which leaves the pillars of the building standing.' "[3] I shall argue the reverse: the revolution's achievements were more in the economic and the social realm, its problems more political. The Revolution not only left standing, but reinforced, the political identities created by colonialism. In the history of African decolonization, however, 1959 Rwanda most closely resembles 1961 Zanzibar.[4] Both ushered in a transfer of power through political violence. Neither can be dismissed as simply a change of elites. Because 1959 changed the nature of power and had a significant consequence for the mass of the Rwandan people, it needs to be seen as a "revolution." Unlike those who tended to celebrate it, however, I argue that it needs to be problematized.

But before I do so, I find it worthwhile to point out the way in which the political violence that ushered in 1959 marks a significant departure from political violence in the preceding period. The key difference lies in the direction of political violence, in how it demarcated its agents from its target. For the first time in the history of the Rwandan state, the violence demarcated Hutu from Tutsi. The polarization of Hutu and Tutsi in 1959 contrasted dramatically with the presence of Hutu and Tutsi on both sides of the firing line during the Nyabingi revolt only a half century earlier. I argue that this single fact is proof enough that the real turning point in the history of political conflict and political violence was not colonization at the turn of the century, or even the replacement of German by Belgian rule at the beginning of this century, but the reorganization of the colonial state from 1926 to 1936.

To highlight the significance of this shift, we need to recall that the genesis of the Rwandan state can be traced to sometime in the middle of the fifteenth century. In spite of at least four dynastic changes over the next three and a half centuries and no less than ten successions that flouted ritual norms, the fact is that the political elite of Rwanda had been remarkably successful in achieving the raison d'être of any state, that is, to ensure order.[5] One cannot but contrast this outstanding record with the dismal record of the colonial state: in but a handful of decades following the colonial reorganization of 1926–36, Rwanda imploded in a revolution that pitted one section of the population (Hutu) against another (Tutsi). How is one to explain this dramatic shift, from long-term political stability to short-term political breakdown?

The root causes of the 1959 Revolution need to be explored in the changes wrought by colonialism, and not in the precolonial legacy. We have seen that when Mwami Rwabugiri centralized the state toward the close of the nineteenth century, he also made it the custodian of Tutsi privilege. Belgian rule had contradictory consequence for the Tutsi: on the one hand, it branded the Tutsi as not indigenous; on the other hand, it consolidated Tutsi privilege by a double move that affected all strata among the Tutsi. Up above, it made chiefship a Tutsi prerogative with the fused authority of the chief accountable to none but the colonial power; down below, it exempted the *petits* Tutsi from coerced labor. It is precisely because colonialism underwrote Tutsi privilege in law that the Tutsi, beginning with the elite, embraced the racialization of their own identity as nonindigenous. The claim that the Tutsi were nonindigenous Hamites was considered necessary for their privileged treatment in law. Not surprisingly, mainstream Tutsi nationalism presented the colonial construction of custom and customary power—specifically, Tutsi privilege—as authentic "tradition" and demanded that independence be a return to tradition. This was the standard independence rhetoric of nationalism in colonial Rwanda. Unlike in other African colonies, however, standard independence rhetoric, directed only or even mainly at the colonial power, was a marginal phenomenon in colonial Rwanda.

The colonial impetus on Rwanda was contradictory: it tended to stiffen the state while dynamizing society. As an energized society tended to generate new forces, a hardened state structure proved unresponsive to them. These contradictory tendencies led to an escalating and dramatic confrontation between state and society. On the one hand, the state was organized and nurtured as so many localized despotisms. Each of these saw itself as a Tutsi power, lording it over subservient Hutu subjects who were in turn sealed from the world of Tutsi privilege by the requirement to carry an identity card and by the legal impossibility—no matter what their life circumstances—of a ritual rise to Tutsi status. On the other hand, the same colonial power introduced a money economy and school-based education, processes that generated new influences and new opportunities, and in time gave rise to a Hutu elite. Locked into a subordinate status by a legally enforced identity, this socially frustrated group developed—for the first time in the history of Rwanda—into a political counterelite. In the changed context of a post-Second World War Rwanda, the Hutu counterelite was poised to tap the grievances of the Hutu peasantry against local despots who claimed their power was not a colonial imposition but a right by custom.

The Development of a Hutu Counterelite

The Hutu counterelite developed from three social locations. The *first* location was the precolonial elite in the independent non-Rwandan principalities: those elites in the north who were forcibly incorporated into the Rwandan state and subjugated to a Hutu status by the newly forged alliance between German colonialism and the *mwami* (king). The *second* major source was the market economy, in particular the labor market in nearby Congo and Uganda, which made it possible for Hutu peasants to escape the demands of servitude inside Rwanda. The *third* source was school-based education pioneered by the alliance of missionaries and the colonial state.

Precolonial Elite

René Lemarchand has argued that the set of events known as the 1959 Revolution was in reality a confluence of two distinct social processes, one in the north, the other in the center of the country.[6] While "the revolution in central Rwanda was a social revolution in the sense that it developed its dialectic from the social inequities of the caste system," he argues that a more "retrogressive" attitude shaped the revolutionary outlook in the north. The difference was this: "In seeking to evict the Tutsi oligarchy from its position of power the northern Hutu did not aim so much at the creation of a new social order as to revert to the social existence prior to the intrusion of Tutsi conquerors."[7] Lemarchand thus distinguished the key impulse behind the revolution in the north as ethnic, from that in the center as democratic.

"Northern Hutu" refers to the Bakiga, who lived in the former territories of Ruhengeri, Gisenyi, and Byumba. In the already-quoted words of P.T.W. Baxter, their "proud boast," was "that they were never, as a people, subjugated by either Tutsi or Hima."[8] And yet, we need to keep in mind that the fiercely independent spirit of the Bakiga did not always automatically translate into an anti-Tutsi orientation. This orientation was the result of a historical development under specific circumstances.

The context that shaped the "northern Hutu" perspective was marked by at least three features. *First*, there was the historical difference between the incorporation of the north and that of the south and the center in the Rwandan state. Unlike the Hutu of central Rwanda who had been a part of the central court for centuries, and the southern Hutu who were subordinated to central rule before colonialism, even if only in the second half of the nineteenth century, the Bakiga of the north were subjugated to Rwandan state authority only with the onset of Western colonization. *Second*, while it is true that the Bakiga experience of colonial domination was coterminous with their experience of Tutsi domination, it is not true that their opposition to colonial and Tutsi domination automatically translated into an anti-Tutsi hostility. To confirm this, one needs to look at the actual historical revolt of the Bakiga against colonial and Tutsi domination at the onset of colonial rule, one that goes by the name *Nyabingi*. We have seen that this revolt was in reality a coalition of two forces: the section of the Tutsi aristocracy excluded from power at the death of Rwabugiri, and the Bakiga newly subjugated to this hardening Tutsi power. The revolt of the Bakiga was led by members of the Tutsi aristocracy who were bitterly opposed to the usurpation of power by the Abeega clan at the death of

Rwabugiri, the most prominent of these being Muhumusa and Ndun-gutse. Key to its agenda was opposition to forced labor tribute (*ubareetwa*) freshly imposed on the newly colonized Bakiga. *Third*, this protracted rebellion against colonial authority and its Tutsi quislings made for a more arbitrary chiefly authority in the north than was imposed anywhere else in colonial Rwanda.

The outright defeat of the Nyabingi cult created conditions for the emergence of a different type of anticolonial revolt in the north. It was led by an indigenous Bakiga elite that could identify both colonialism and the Tutsi with the arbitrary and oppressive rule of Tutsi chiefs. This elite had roots in those who had controlled access to land in the precolonial period, whether as outright owners of the land (*bakonde*) or as clients (*bagererwa*) who controlled access to it. With colonial repression, both were replaced, the owners by incoming Tutsi and the clients by Bakiga quislings. The language of the day made a distinction between the two groups, referring to the former clients as "traditional *bagererwa*" and the latter as "political *bagererwa*." Colonial repression was never effective enough to erase the claims of the precolonial hierarchy. As a result, the two hierarchies coexisted in a growing tension. According to Lemarchand, the older generation of *bakonde* tended to resort to forms of protest associated with "social banditry." In contrast, the new generation, those "substantially more westernised and better-educated than their predecessors," were able to integrate the traditional claims of the *bakonde* into a modern revolutionary movement, the one that developed in tandem with the revolution of 1959.[9]

It is understandable that the offspring of the precolonial elite would seek to restore a freedom very much real within living memory. For them, the revolution was more of a "national" than a democratic affair. Yet, it seems to me that Lemarchand is so preoccupied with the interests and motivations of this precolonial elite that he tends to ignore those of the ordinary peasants on the ground. Had they not been able to tap the widespread antagonism of Hutu peasants toward Tutsi chiefs, both the traditional *bakonde* and *bagererwa* would have remained isolated and weak forces. For that same reason—that he tends to downplay the tension between peasants and chiefly power—Lemarchand goes too far when he contrasts the perspective of the northern and central Hutu elites in terms that oppose a northern preoccupation with "restoration" with a central commitment to "revolution."[10] If the notion of a north preoccupied with "restoration" sidesteps the perspective of the northern peasants, then that of a south committed to "revolution" errs in the opposite direction: it underplays the point of view and interests of southern elites. To do so is to shortchange the northern initiative and to romanticize the revolutionary thrust in the center. It is generally accepted that the revolution exploded as mainly a hill-level confrontation between Hutu peasants and Tutsi chiefs. At the same time, this tension-ridden relationship cut across the distinction between the north and the south. If anything, chiefly rule in the north was even more arbitrary than in the south—a fact no one has done more to underline than Lemarchand. If we accept that it was the demand for dismantling chiefly despotism that provided the democratic kernel of the revolution, it is difficult to see how anyone can then argue that democracy was a southern demand.

Migrant Labor

Hutu labor migrants in the colonial period found two major destinations. The first was Congo, the second Uganda. Both opportunities opened up in the interwar period. A thriving labor market developed in Congo around the mines in Katanga and the plantations in Kivu. Similar opportunities opened up in Uganda with the growth of a prosperous rich peasant coffee economy in Buganda and sugar plantations in Busoga, followed by the copper mines that were opened in Kilembe after the Second World War. As one would expect, migrants originated mainly from areas adjacent to Congo and Uganda: the west and southwest for those going to Congo and the north and northeast for those heading to Uganda. We have two studies from which to draw general conclusions about the migrant experience. The first is a study of immigrant labor in Buganda, a team effort led by anthropologist Audrey Richards.[11] The second is a study by Mararo Bucyalimwe of land conflicts in Masisi, eastern Congo, following the "transplanting" of peasants from Rwanda.[12] Since these focus mainly on the migrant experience in Uganda and Congo, we shall return to them in the chapters on Uganda and Congo. In this chapter, I shall turn to Catharine Newbury's excellent study of state-society relations in Cyangugu in southwestern Rwanda, the source of most migrants to Congo.[13] Since Newbury's focus was on the home territory from where the migrants originated, and to which they returned, it is a source of fruitful insights into how the migrant experience shaped the anticolonial struggle.

For many of the labor migrants from Cyangugu to Congo, contract work for Europeans was a way of escaping forced labor imposed by Tutsi chiefs and the local authorities at home. Corvée included both *ubureetwa* and *akazi*, the former performed for individual chiefs and the latter for the public authority, which required it mainly for public works projects.

Belgian authorities were quite aware that forced labor for local authorities and low-paid work for European employees were alternatives for the border population. And they worked hard to ensure that Tutsi chiefs not disturb this arrangement by imposing tribute on families of those who had opted to work for Europeans. In 1938, the territorial administrator in Cyangugu wrote three subchiefs under him warning them to keep the whip away from those who worked for the Nyungwe mines: "The chiefs and sub-chiefs have no right to require the workers at Nyungwe to perform forced labour associated with *ubuletwa*." And then: "The chiefs and sub-chiefs do not have the right to require that the wives and children of the workers carry out [obligatory] cultivation as provided for by Regulation 89."[14] Almost a decade later, in 1946, the territorial administrator of Cyangugu made sure to include the same cautionary note in what was otherwise an exhortation to Tutsi subchiefs to ensure that the Hutu peasantry labored according to the following instructions:

> We inform the subchiefs who are present of the results of yesterday's meeting with the settlers and the chiefs. We expect more firm collaboration from the subchiefs so that the indiscipline so evident among the Hutu will cease. It is necessary that the native authorities become aware of the fact that they represent the State, and they must rule those they administer with justice and firmness. And in this regard, they must require from all Hutu [who are] not working for Europeans the completion of all duties with regard to [obligatory] crops, the struggle against erosion, and the maintenance of the roads.[15]

For those who migrated to Uganda from north and the northeast, the turning point was the year 1924, "when Belgian authorities empowered residents to compel natives to carry out the cultivation of food-stuffs and economic crops." The first ten months of 1925 recorded the first large-scale Rwandan emigration into Uganda, being the great majority of the 11,771 laborers recruited by the Labour Department from the southwest of the country. Three years later, Rwanda experienced a prolonged famine; immigration into Uganda reached "formidable proportions" as an estimated 35,000 crossed the border.[16] When asked for reasons they had decided to leave home, the answers highlighted the regime of forced labor and compulsions: "I left because in Rwanda a man and his wife have to work from early morning to late at night for his chief," or "Ordinary men work for their chiefs and when they find they have nothing to wear, they leave their country to look for money." Some complained of beatings: "If

I was not beaten I would never have come to Uganda" or "I left home because I wanted a job without beatings." One man had returned to Rwanda on three successive occasions—1938, 1941, and 1944—to see "if there were still beatings" and had felt it necessary to return to Uganda each time. Others complained that "women as well as men are liable to communal labour." And yet others explained that they had decided to go home and bring their wives to Uganda because, when they were away, their wives were asked to carry out labor obligations of their own, on top of having to make up for the obligations of the absent husband.[17]

The migrant experience was the source of fresh, new insight, often subversive of hierarchy in the existing order. Newbury recorded testimony from numerous respondents, noting "arbitrary action of the powerful as a principal reason they and others went to work for Europeans." She also pointed out that many of the returned migrants provided leadership in the protest that mushroomed over the first postwar decade: "Many of the early leaders of Hutu protest activity in Kinyaga were former wage earners who had taken up trading enterprises of some kind—gaining both economic security and a network of contacts that later proved useful for political party organization."[18]

Educated Youth

Not everything under the colonial political system was hard. Two broad processes were under way: the expansion of a money economy, and school-based Western education. Together, they would erode the social supremacy of the Tutsi while, for a time, leaving intact their political supremacy. Although the cattle-based wealth of the Tutsi aristocracy remained largely uncommercialized, Belgian officialdom made every effort to get the Hutu peasantry to grow cash crops for export. In opening up opportunities for enrichment through other than the ownership of cattle, the money economy weakened the bonds of pastoral servitude that had been the colonial *ubuhake* contract between patron and client. It is in this context that the expanding school system of the 1940s and 1950s provided the structural basis for the emergence of a Hutu counterelite.

The impact of the school system on the few Hutu who managed to enter its corridors was contradictory and explosive. On the one hand, it reproduced the political and social distinction between Tutsi and Hutu at an intellectual level by operating a two-tier system: the Tutsi were introduced into a "civilized" French-medium education, but the Hutu were confined to a "nativized" second-rate Kiswahili-medium education. On the other hand, the same school system was the source of merit-based impulses that could not but generate egalitarian ideas, even if the curriculum included a heavy dose of the Hamitic hypothesis.

We can get an idea of how small were the numbers of Hutu who managed to gain access to secondary education in colonial Rwanda by a second look at the figures for those enrolled at the Groupe Scolaire d'Astrida, the leading secondary school in the country. Students came from the three Belgian colonies of Rwanda, Burundi, and Congo.[19] Until 1945, students from Rwanda and Burundi were registered as a single group, but were identified as Tutsi or Hutu. After 1945, the Hutu were further classified into those from Rwanda and those from Burundi, whereas the Tutsi were still registered as a single group. The figures show that Rwandan Hutu were virtually excluded from the school before 1954: between 1946 and 1954, sixteen Hutu were admitted from Rwanda, as opposed to seventy-one from Burundi. In contrast, 389 Tutsi were admitted from both Rwanda and Burundi during that same period. Only in 1956 did the proportion of Hutu students begin to increase substantially.

Ironically, the first Rwandan student to graduate with a university education was a Hutu, and he graduated from the Centre Universitaire de Kisantu (Congo-Kinshasa) in 1955. Anastase Mukuza was to become a leading figure in the postrevolutionary government of Kayibanda.[20] His example is illustrative of the kind of social frustration that pushed the first generation Hutu elite into the front ranks of 1959 revolutionaries. Mukuza attended the Grand Séminaire de Nyakibanda in Rwanda, and then joined the Centre Universitaire de Kisantu in Congo, where he completed a degree in administrative and political sciences. On return to Rwanda in 1955, he paid a visit to Mwami Mutara to explore the possibility of government employment. His request was turned down. Next, he went to the Institut pour la Recherche en Afrique Centrale (IRSAC) at Astrida, looking to be a research assistant. Here again he was rebuffed. He then went to see the *directeur de l'enseignement* in Bujumbura in Burundi, only to be told that the administration would not recognize his diploma. He ended up as a typist (*candidat commis*) in Kibuye, promoted to administrative assistant in 1957, first in Cyangugu, and then in Kigali. By then, he was a potential revolutionary. Lemarchand's comment is apropos of the significance of this case of the first Rwandan university graduate: "Like other educated Hutu, he derived a burning sense of grievance from the monopoly exercised by the Tutsi caste over all sectors of the administration and the economy; to break the hold of this monopoly became a central objective of the Hutu intellectuals on the eve of the revolution."[21] This point of view was expressed in a popular postwar play. After commiserating aloud on the injustices of *buhake*, one of the Hutu characters in Naigiziki's play, *L'optimiste*, asks his companion, "How long shall we have to wait until our injustices are redressed?" The interlocutor replies, "Until the Hutu no longer has the soul of a serf. For that he must be reborn." The midwife of that rebirth was a political movement of the Hutu counterelite.

Unsurprisingly, most of the leading personalities of the Hutu movement were former seminarians. They had studied for the priesthood, either at Kabgaye or at Nyakibanda. For the Hutu who managed to ascend the Church hierarchy, every climb up the ladder put them in a context dominated by Tutsi priests. The influence of the Western Church—much like that of the Western school system—was contradictory. As an institution, the Church had been the primary force advocating the "civilizing" role of the Tutsi as Hamites. Accordingly, there was preferential entry for Tutsi into the priesthood, at least until after the Second World War. But as an ideology, Christianity was a source of an egalitarian impulse for the Hutu, not just for the masses who entered the Church, but particularly for the few who did manage to enter the priesthood.

The contradiction between Christianity as an ideology and the Church as an institution came to a head in the postwar period as the attitude of the European clergy went through a major shift. With the defeat of Nazism, its collaborators were discredited everywhere in Europe. Most institutions, including the Church, experienced a democratic resurgence. The clergy coming to Rwanda after the war were a changed lot, strongly influenced by antiracist ideological currents. Unlike Monseigneurs Classe or Hirth, early leaders of the Church who were upper-class Flemish men with conservative views, the newcomers were likely to come from *le petit clergé*. Of "relatively humble origins," and with a "previous experience of social and political conditions in the French-speaking provinces of Wallonia," they were "more generally disposed to identify with the plight of the Hutu masses."[22]

The Church was also the location from which the Tutsi intelligentsia defended "racial" privilege. Though its depth went no further than the colonial period, they defended it as a "tradition." Members of the predominantly Tutsi Rwandan clergy were among the first to express public anxiety over the spread of egalitarian ideas among the new Hutu elite. The loudest warning came from Abbé Alexis Kagame, then Rwanda's foremost historian. Without mincing words, Kagame wrote as early as 1945: "Certain egalitarian tendencies are advocated in front of those elements who are sometimes referred to as 'child-like grown-ups', without proper intellectual formation, which are bound to run counter to the common sense principles of most if not all of them." Warning that "the path of progress cannot stray away from our traditional heritage," he went on to champion a type of progress that would not question traditional authority. "Regardless of the type of socio-political system adhered to, one must avoid humiliating traditional authorities, either by disregarding their claims to leadership or casting discredit upon them in front of their subject under the pretext that everybody is equal. The conclusion the masses are likely to draw from all this is that progress, freedom, in short everything, implies contempt for traditional authorities."[23]

When the Hutu graduates of seminaries and of the Groupe Scolaire d'Astrida (now Butare) entered the job market in the mid-'50s and found there were few places open for an educated Hutu, they turned to the Church for opportunities. Literally shut out of jobs in the civil service and the private sector, they looked at their new positions not just as ways of making a living but also as opportunities to articulate their major social grievance: the institutionalized exclusion of Hutu from a Belgian-supported Tutsi monopoly over all avenues of social advancement. With the support of a sympathetic clergy, they took over Church publications—the most important being the Kinyarwanda-language magazine *Kinyamateka*—and began to address whoever would listen sympathetically, mainly Hutu masses below and visiting United Nations Commissions above.

REFORMS AND THEIR LIMITS

Though administered by Belgium after the German defeat in World War I, Rwanda was a UN trust territory. Under UN tutelage, the process of decolonization unfolded as a series of electoral reforms, beginning in 1952. The backdrop to the reform process was a series of UN decolonization missions that were regularly dispatched to its trust territory, at least once every three years, sometimes more often, from 1949.

The first ever visit of a UN decolonization mission coincided with a dramatic reform that promised to abolish the hated *ubuleetwa* and replace it by a mandatory money payment. That was in 1949, yet respondents in Kinyaga told Catharine Newbury that they continued to perform *ubuleetwa* services until the revolution. There was clearly a big difference between the promise of a reform and the fact of its implementation, between the wider propaganda effect of the announcement of a reform and the social impact of its implementation on the ground. The Hutu learned the same lesson when the *mwami* and the Conseil Supérieur (High Council) decided to issue another reform decree to coincide with the visit of the third UN decolonization mission in 1954.[24] The decree provided for the progressive dissolution of *ubuhake* ties and the distribution of cows held under it to former clients. Once again, the impact of the decree fell short of its promise. In the absence of a corresponding reform redistributing grazing land monopolized by Tutsi patrons, it left Hutu owners of cattle dependent on former patrons for access to pasturage. Just as with the previous abolition of *ubuleetwa*, the reform of *ubuhake* did not undo the ties that bound former Hutu clients to Tutsi patrons in a relationship both unequal and coercive. Not surprisingly, peasant protest against the arbitrary use of power by chiefs became the stuff of popular press reports in the postreform period.[25]

It was the taste of reform, and not the absence of reform, that convinced the Hutu intelligentsia that nothing less than radical change was likely to bring an end to the social plight of the Hutu. That taste was developed through an overall encounter with social and political reform. Political reform began with local elections in 1953 and a general election in 1956. The 1953 elections were the result of the decree of 14 July 1952. The elections were wholly indirect: not only was the role of elected councils "advisory," but the electoral choice was limited to "suitable candidates" nominated by chiefs and subchiefs. In a context where the administrative power of Tutsi chiefs was still intact, the result was not an election but an opportunity for subchiefs and chiefs to register their power. Two tendencies testified to this outcome. On the one hand, Tutsi tended to predominate in the councils, more so the higher one went up the administrative ladder. So that whereas 52 percent of council seats at the lowest administrative level were filled by Tutsi, the proportion reached a whopping 90.6 percent when it came to the Conseil Supérieur du Pays, the highest council of the land. On the other hand, when Hutu were nominated to councils, they were inevitably Hutu *abagaragwa* (clients) of Tutsi *shebuja* (patrons).[26]

The final opportunity for reform from above was squandered in 1956 when Mwami Rudahigwa joined the conservative Tutsi tendency to defeat a proposal to provide separate representation for Hutu on the Conseil Supérieur. To appreciate the significance of this proposal, one needs to recall two facts. One, the Conseil Supérieur was the highest advisory body of the state and was expected to become the legislature of an independent Rwanda. Two, in that crucial period from 1956 to 1959, this body included only three Hutu, comprising less than 6 percent of its membership.[27]

The 1956 elections introduced a two-tier system: an all-male universal suffrage at the lowest administrative level, the subchiefdom, while all higher councils continued to be voted indirectly through electoral colleges whose members were nominated by corresponding chiefs. The outcome highlighted the difference in the method employed in each case. There was a clear victory for Hutu candidates at the subchiefdom level, where the vote was direct, but not at higher levels, where the vote was indirect. The contradictory and limited nature of the reform was clear for all to see: it combined *participation* for Hutu at lower levels with guaranteed *power* for Tutsi at higher levels. From the abolition of *ubuleetwa* in 1949 to the general election of 1956, nearly a decade of experience with reform convinced the Hutu political elite that nothing short of political power would crack the Tutsi hold on social, economic, and cultural resources.

THE 1959 REVOLUTION

Two rival documents greeted the visiting UN decolonization mission in 1957. The documents dramatized the growing ideological polarization between Hutu and Tutsi. Anticipating the Mission's visit, the *mwami's* High Council proclaimed an all-Rwandan emancipation program. Called *Mise au Point*, the program called for a rapid transfer of power to the king and his council. This, it argued, was crucial to end racial tensions between blacks and whites.[28] A month later came the Hutu response, in the form of the Bahutu Manifesto. Signed by Kayibanda and eight other Hutu, and originally titled *Notes on the Social Aspect of the Racial Native Problem in Rwanda,* the Bahutu Manifesto maintained that the heart of the problem in Rwanda was "the conflict between Hutu and Hamitic—i.e., foreign— Tutsi."[29] The authors called for a double liberation of the "Hutu from both the 'Hamites' and 'Bazungu' (whites) colonization." It identified the "indigenous racial problem" as the "monopoly which is held by one race, the Tutsi":

> The problem is above all a problem of political monopoly which is held by one race, the Tutsi; political monopoly which, given the totality of current structures becomes an economic and social monopoly; political, economic and social monopoly which, given the *de facto* discrimination in education, ends up being a cultural monopoly, to the great despair of the Hutu who see themselves condemned to remain forever subaltern manual labourers and still worse, in the context of an independence which they will have helped to win without knowing what they are doing.[30]

The difference between the two documents could not have been sharper. And yet, though written from different standpoints, each was a claim for power. Independence first, the view of the Tutsi elite, was the claim that their prerogatives were actually "traditional" (precolonial) and should be restored. Democracy before independence, the view of the Hutu counter-elite, spelled out their demand for power based on the claim that they represented the indigenous majority. One put forth a "nationalist" claim, the other a "subaltern" demand. Out of this subaltern agitation, the Hutu counterelite created a popular nationalism—a nationalism from below, to rival the Tutsi nationalism from above. Both traced economic and social problems among the poor to a "racial" tension. The difference was that while one highlighted the racial contradiction as *only* between foreign black and white, the other underlined it as a contradiction *mainly* between Hamites (Tutsi) and indigenous Bantu (Hutu).

Elections set the context in which the Hutu counterelite forged their consciousness against the Tutsi elite. Such a consciousness emerged from the throes of a political contest. Forged with the creation of the Rwandan state and sharpened with Rwabugiri's centralizing reforms in the late nineteenth century, Tutsi identity had long preceded Hutu identity. In that context, Tutsi consciousness was a consciousness of power, while Hutu consciousness would come to be one of lack of power and of a struggle for power. Like almost everything else about colonialism, colonial power did not erase precolonial realities but added to them: on the one hand, it so sharpened the late nineteenth century contrast between Tutsi power and the Hutu absence of power as to accentuate it as a one-dimensional reality; on the other, it stigmatized Tutsi power as alien rule.

The development of a Hutu consciousness was a protracted affair, stretching from the time of Rwabugiri through the entire span of the colonial period. As late as independence in 1962, the "Hutu" of the northwestern region insisted on being considered Bakiga—like their neighbors in southwestern Uganda—not Hutu. Hutu consciousness developed in phases: before the Second World War, it was a consciousness of subjecthood that transcended all locally anchored identities; in the 1950s it became the consciousness of a people reaching for power. This development required a confluence of two movements: a genuinely popular movement of (Hutu) peasants against the local despotism of (Tutsi) chiefs; and, for the first time in the history of Rwanda, the emergence of a Hutu counterelite. Propelled center stage by a series of electoral contests, this counterelite put forth a program for the Hutu to seize power to overcome their identity as a subject people. Branded with a subject identity—"Hutu"— the counterelite emerging from the ranks of the socially oppressed held it up as a badge of pride: Hutu Power! In turning a chain into a weapon, Spartacus-style, it was neither the first nor would it be the last. One only needs to think of a related example: Black Power.

That consciousness, and the organization it came to wield, was forged in the institutional context of the Church.[31] Both Grégoire Kayibanda, who later became the president of PARMEHUTU, the party of the revolution, and Aloys Munyangaju, initially its vice president and then president of APROSOMA, the party of the alternative Hutu political tendency, achieved prominence as journalists/editors for Catholic periodicals. Besides serving as personal secretary to Monsignor Perraudin, the apostolical vicar of Rwanda, Kayibanda became lay editor of *Kinyamateka*, the Church-owned Kinyarwanda-language paper, in 1955, and then its editor-in-chief in 1956. In December of that year, Church authorities founded a cooperative: Travail, Fidélité, Progrès (TRAFIPRO). Kayibanda became the president of its board of directors. The expanding ground-level organization of TRAFIPRO came to serve as cells for the development of the Hutu movement. It is from this organizational base—the editorship of *Kinyamateka* and the presidency of the board of TRAFIPRO—that Kayibanda launched a cultural association called the Mouvement Social Muhutu (MSM) in June 1957.

The more assertive the Hutu counterelite grew, the more it provoked a shrill reaction from those Tutsi who had swallowed wholesale the venom that was the Hamitic hypothesis and who were bent on defending colonial privilege as a time-tested tradition. The response came in two public letters in May 1958 from fourteen senior Tutsi notables at the mwami's court—called the *mwami*'s clients, the *abagaragwa bakuru b'I bwami*. They claimed there was no question of any fraternity between Hutu and Tutsi since Kigwa, the ancestor of the *Abanyiginya* dynasty, had reduced the Hutu by force. In rejecting the demand for Hutu participation in public affairs, they evoked the tradition of conquest: equal rights were out of question "because our kings conquered the land of the Hutu, killed their 'little' kings and thus subjugated the Hutu: how then can they now pretend to be our brothers?"[32] The second letter rejected the demand that the *ibikingi*, the landed property held by Tutsi lords, be abolished. The letter defended its continuation as "the custom of the country." When Mwami Mutara III Rudahigwa summarized the deliberations of the Conseil Supérieur on 12 June, his response to Hutu agitation was recorded in the minutes as follows: "It is a damaging increasing noisy propaganda spread by a small group acting under foreign influence with communist ideas. Their intention is to divide the country. They would not succeed to

divide a country whose national unity and secular political force organisation has annihilated the most powerful attackers. The country is reunited
to identify, cut down, eradicate, and burn that ill tree which is infecting
its life. Then a motion was voted 'to ask that the colonial government
remove from the official documents the terms Hutu, Tutsi and Twa.' "[33]

The claim that Tutsi power be restored as tradition tended to boomer-
ang in the context of postwar Rwanda: it only succeeded in further mobilizing the Hutu and in discrediting the Tutsi cause. The Hutu response
focused on the prime symbol of Tutsi power, the Kalinga drum. Rather
than its symbolic association with the crown, it was attacked for signifying
a permanent vision of Hutu inferiority: was not the Kalinga drum, after
all, decorated with the sexual organs of defeated Hutu kings? The
frontline Hutu press called for an end to "the idolatry surrounding the
Karinga."[34]

The more the Rwandan polity—and society—began to unravel, the
more room was created for different internal tendencies. We must not be
misled into thinking that the backdrop to the revolution was no more
than a gelling of two polarized tendencies: one Hutu, the other Tutsi.
That it was, but there was also a growing differentiation inside each. While
the revolution was an outcome of the growing polarization between Hutu
and Tutsi in Rwandan society, the outcome of the revolution was shaped
very much by the contest between different points of views within each
camp. To understand the postrevolutionary outcome, we need to go beyond the Hutu/Tutsi polarization to the ideological contest between different tendencies on each side of the Hutu/Tutsi divide.

Historically, the Tutsi political elite was united around the court and
constituted a conservative tendency that equated Tutsi power with tradition. The development of a Hutu counterelite and its growing self-assertiveness brought Tutsi unity under pressure. Those who questioned the
basis of this unity took initiatives to go beyond its narrow and short-term
orientation. In doing so, they both crystallized the plurality of views
within the Tutsi elite and gave it organizational expression. The expanded
arena of Tutsi politics came to be defined by two rival political parties,
Union Nationale Rwandaise (UNAR) and Rassemblement Démocratique
Rwandais (RADER), one conservative, the other reformist. Similarly, it
was the tension between the militantly Hutu PARMEHUTU and APRO-
SOMA's search for a broader constituency that came to define the arena
of Hutu politics. To explore each of these tendencies is to understand
both the limits and the choices—the limited menu—that the revolution
of 1959 placed before the people of Rwanda.

UNAR

Created in August of 1959, the UNAR was a party of monarchists most identified with the "traditionalist" point of view in Rwandan society. Under the nominal presidency of an outspoken Hutu, François Rukeba,[35] it was mainly—but not wholly—a Tutsi party. UNAR's leadership read like a Who's Who of Tutsi high chiefs. The "progressive" tendency in UNAR best expressed its Janus-faced opposition to the Hutu internally and the Belgians externally. Wedded to Tutsi supremacy at home no less than were the conservatives, UNAR progressives championed a nationalism in external policy. In pursuit of this nationalism, they forged several alliances: with militant nationalists like MNC-Lumumba regionally, with the Communist countries in the UN Trusteeship Council, and with the People's Republic of China outside it.

The UNAR's external alliances were not simply another case of the Cold War making for strange bedfellows. UNAR nationalism gave genuine expression to the national grievance that the Tutsi came to feel the most, since their advance was directly blocked by the "racial" privileges of Europeans in the colony. Anticipating the founding of a Hutu party (which indeed came to be three days later), UNAR had distributed a circular on September 16: "Rwandese! Children of Rwanda! Subjects of Kegeri, rise up! Let us unite our strengths! Do not let the blood of Rwanda be spilled in vain. There are no Tutsi, Hutu, Twa. We are all brothers! We are all descendents of Kinyarwanda!"[36]

Because UNAR began to receive money and diplomatic backing from Communist countries in the UN Trusteeship Council, the antagonism between the Tutsi and the Belgian authorities deepened further. During 1959–60, the UNAR leadership-in-exile courted the support of MNC-Lumumba. Rumors spread that local MNC branches in Congo, especially in Goma and Bukavu, were giving financial and military assistance to the Tutsi leadership to fight their way back into the country. The more these suspicions hardened into certainty, the more Belgium became convinced that in keeping UNAR from the reigns of power, it was fighting both feudalism and communism.[37]

RADER

The day after UNAR had held a mass rally in Kigali vowing to "restore customs" and "shake off the yoke of Belgian colonialism," Chief Bwa-nakweri created another Tutsi party with an opposite message: to shake off custom but not the ties with Belgium. RADER was born on 14 September

1959.[38] Its leader, Chief Bwanakweri, came from a small number of Groupe Scolaire graduates who were determined to "avoid the worst by easing the burden of the peasantry through social and constitutional reforms." Chief Bwanakweri not only stood out among his cohorts as a man of his word, but he also stood rather alone. In 1956 he had already gone beyond declarations and dared to translate these aspirations into radical social reforms in his chiefdoms, thereby "filling the Hutu with hope." Though Chief Bwanakweri had significant support among university students, his combined call for internal reform of Tutsi power and a soft line against Belgian power was enough to brand RADER as a pro-Belgium party among the Tutsi.[39] Then came Mwami Mutara's transfer—some would say internal exile—of Bwanakweri to Kibuye, a remote locality in western Rwanda. From then on, RADER, the only organized democratic tendency among Tutsi, was found on the margin of Rwandan politics.

For a while, RADER participated in several preelection meetings jointly with the two major Hutu parties, APROSOMA and PARMEHUTU. In the end, however, RADER had little influence on the outcome of the revolution. Faced with UNAR's dogged determination to uphold Tutsi power, it came to be identified with a moderate tendency—not *any* moderate tendency, but a *moderate Tutsi* tendency. Its fate testified to the narrow social base of Tutsi reformism in 1959 Rwanda.[40]

MDR-PARMEHUTU

The Mouvement Démocratique Rwandais/Parti du Mouvement et de l'Emancipation Hutu was created in October 1959 when Kayibanda transformed the old cultural movement, Mouvement Sociale Muhutu, established in June 1957, into a political party. It is not an accident that while the main Tutsi party claimed to be both "Rwandese" and "nationalist" in name, the main Hutu party claimed to be "Hutu" and "democratic" in the same name. It is also worth noting that PARMEHUTU did not start out as an antimonarchist party. It envisaged the possibility of a constitutional monarchy, but "insisted on a genuine democratisation of all existing institutions before the granting of independence."[41]

APROSOMA

L'Association pour la Promotion Sociale de la Masse distinguished itself from PARMEHUTU, both in name and in program: it claimed to be a party of the "masses" and not just a "Hutu" party. Created in November 1957, APROSOMA was a genuinely populist party whose appeal was aimed at the poor, at Hutu as well as the *petits* Tutsi.[42] In the rapidly polarizing context of Rwanda in 1959, where power was Tutsi and the insurrection Hutu, it could not retain its original identity: "Since most Hutu were poor and the vast majority of poor were Hutu, the party ended up as a primarily Hutu party."[43]

What were the differences between the two Hutu parties? We can identify three, based on the regional basis of their core support, the ideological content of the program each advanced, and the social character of the leadership.

The two Hutu parties had an overlapping yet distinct regional basis. PARMEHUTU derived its strength mainly from two parts of the country: the northern prefectures of Ruhengeri and Gisenyi, and Kayibanda's home region of Gitarama in central Rwanda. APROSOMA's activities were mainly focused in Butera in south-central Rwanda and Kinyaga in southwestern Rwanda. The difference partly reflected the contrasting historical trajectories leading to the incorporation of different regions into the Rwandan state. Whereas APROSOMA focused more on regions like Kinyaga, where Tutsi presence had preceded Tutsi power and thus had a history of Hutu/Tutsi relations preceding the polarization of the colonial period,[44] PARMEHUTU's stronghold was on those parts incorporated into the Rwandan state only on the eve of colonization. But this beginning did not remain a defining feature of PARMEHUTU. The more it became the party of the revolution, the more PARMEHUTU outgrew its regional beginnings and developed into a loose countrywide coalition of different locally based groups.[45]

The two parties differed in the program each advanced, particularly in their definition of who was the enemy. "The only point of divergence among the Hutu," said a petitioner in 1959, "is whether the campaign should be directed against all Tutsi without distinction, against the high aristocracy, or against the specific abuses committed by certain representatives of the Hamitic race. Hence, it is mainly a question of tactics rather than of doctrine."[46] Not surprisingly, this difference in tactics proved key to deciding the future of Rwandan society. The more events highlighted the weakness of a reform tendency among powerful Tutsi, as they did with the internal exile of Chief Bwanakweri to Kibuye in late 1959, the more credible seemed the argument that the question of Tutsi supremacy was the core political problem facing Rwanda on the eve of independence. Beyond the immediate yet stubborn fact of Tutsi supremacy lay a second question of larger and deeper significance: What would be the place of the Tutsi in postrevolutionary Rwanda?

René Lemarchand has argued that behind the difference between the leadership of PARMEHUTU and APROSOMA lay a difference between two categories of intellectuals: the ex-seminarians and the Astridiens.[47] Whereas the Astridiens possessed state skills and could expect to benefit from a constitutional transfer of power, the ex-seminarians did not and could only stake a future in the state through a revolutionary upheaval. The difference between PARMEHUTU and APROSOMA signified more than just a preference in style, the former standing for revolutionary methods and the latter for a constitutional process. In reaching out to unite Hutu and Tutsi poor against Tutsi privilege, the Aristidiens of APROSOMA stood for a popular Rwandan nationalism and held out the possibility of transcending Hutu and Tutsi as colonially constructed political identities. In contrast, PARMEHUTU sought to build on the colonial heritage by organizing the Hutu—all Hutu— against the Tutsi. APROSOMA failed, at least in part, because Tutsi privilege and Tutsi wealth were not the same thing. Although the wealthy were a minority among the Tutsi, Tutsi privilege was a legal/political arrangement that affected *all* Tutsi.

It is a historical tragedy that the conservative Tutsi continued to have the upper hand in court: it triumphed on 28 July 1959, in what has come to be known as the Mwima coup.[48] When the heirless *mwami* died on 25 July, suddenly and mysteriously, the *abiiru* pronounced a 24-year-old half-brother of the deceased the new *mwami*. As a man of poor political judgment, he was an ideal choice for a political figurehead. The appointment was made without any prior arrangement with Belgian authorities in an atmosphere filled with great suspense. This coup set the stage for the chain of events that contemporaries called the social revolution of 1959.

It is in the aftermath of the Mwima coup—and in anticipation of the next round of elections—that PARMEHUTU was created as a Hutu political party out of the old cultural association on 19 October 1959. Almost immediately there followed confrontations between PARMEHUTU militants on one side and militants of the promonarchy Tutsi party UNAR, and Tutsi chiefs in charge of the local state apparatus, on the other. These came to a head in and around Gitarama the next month: when news spread that a group of UNAR militants had attacked the PARMEHUTU leader Dominique Mbonyumutwa, violence spread over the country. The visiting UN Mission of 1960 estimated the killings at two hundred but added that "the number may be even higher since the people preferred to bury their dead silently."[49] The focus of the revolt were the Tutsi chiefs in the local authorities. Some of the chiefs were killed; others were forced to resign. Faced with clear indications that the Tutsi in power were about to unleash repression, Belgium declared a state of emergency and put the country under the command of Colonel B.E.M. Guy Logiest.

Before the first round of violence could swing from a Hutu revolt to a full-scale Tutsi repression, it was checked by emergency military action by the colonial power. But the emergency action did not stop at restoring order. It continued and took on the dimensions of a coup d'état in the local state. Arguing that the presence of Tutsi as subchiefs and chiefs "disturbed the public order," Guy Logiest began to replace Tutsi with Hutu chiefs, thus shepherding a "revolution" against what had hitherto been the colonial power's own local authorities. More than three hundred Hutu chiefs and subchiefs replaced Tutsi incumbents who had been deposed, killed, or had fled what was fast developing into a peasant revolt. The Belgian military decided to go a step further and augment a Hutu administration with an embryonic Hutu-dominated armed force: an indigenous military guard of 650 men was formed in May 1960.[50] It was composed of 85 percent Hutu and 15 percent Tutsi. Without this reconstitution of the local state hierarchy as a Hutu hierarchy, it is difficult to explain the dramatically different outcome of subsequent elections—for it is the local administration that controlled the ballot boxes. Two tendencies gelled, one around PARMEHUTU, the other around UNAR. UNAR boycotted the 1960 communal elections, and was routed: PARMEHUTU, the party of Hutu power, won 70.4 percent of the votes as against 1.7 percent for UNAR, the party of the Tutsi monarchy.

With Hutu chiefs in charge of most local authorities, the newly elected advocates of Hutu power at the center were finally in a position to reorganize the central state. Known in Rwandan history as the coup of Gitarama, this reorganization was carried out on 28 January 1961. On that day, dozens of trucks from all around the country converged on the town of Gitarama, bringing to that destination precisely 3,126 communal councillors and burgomasters. According to Gatwa, another 25,000 people "spontaneously assembled to hear about the unusual event." They were addressed by members of Rwanda's provisional government: the minister of interior, the president of the Provisional Council, and the provisional prime minister. The gathering abolished the monarchy and proclaimed a republic. Then, sitting as a constituent assembly, the councillors and burgomasters proceeded to elect a president of the Republic. The coup was complete when the president called upon Grégoire Kayibanda, as prime minister, to form the future government.[51] Most observers of Rwandan politics have presumed—rightly so, in my view—that such an open reorganization of the central state could not have happened without Belgian support.

How are we to understand the role of the "external" forces that inter-vened on the side of the revolution?[52] Few would deny the internal signifi-cance of three "external" agents: the UN missions, the European clergy, and the colonial government. The triennial UN missions acted as catalysts, each time inviting a regular outpouring of grievances from different quar-ters. The European clergy came to function more or less as a backup force for the Hutu counterelite, providing it with everything from ghostwriters for manifestos and UN petitions to external contacts. On its part, the colo-nial government literally surrendered control over local government to the insurgents. Both the opportunity provided by the triennial UN missions and the support rendered by the European clergy and the colonial govern-ment were real and, at times, even critical. Without that support, there may have been no revolution, only a peasant revolt, joined to middle-class discontent. Yet, none of this made the 1959 Revolution any less real.[53] We shall later see the same explanation surface in hostile accounts of the Rwanda Patriotic Front (RPF) capturing power in 1994: as with Belgium and Guy Logiest in 1959, the role of Uganda and Museveni would be highlighted to explain away both the RPF invasion of October 1990 and its capture of power in 1994 as the outcome of an external conspiracy. While the role of external forces was real in both cases, in neither case can it substitute for an understanding of the internal dynamics of social processes.

The year 1962 saw a change in government in Belgium. The new gov-ernment agreed to cooperate with the UN demand for a fresh general election and a referendum on the monarchy in Rwanda—given UNAR's rejection of the Gitarama coup. When the UN-initiated general election followed, UNAR decided to participate. By now, conditions had changed dramatically: the machinery that organized and oversaw the election was no longer Tutsi. As one would expect, Tutsi power was routed once again: PARMEHUTU won 77.7 percent of the votes against 16.8 percent for UNAR.[54] A referendum held simultaneously led to an equally massive re-jection of the monarchy in favor of a republican system of government.

THE BIRTH OF HUTU POWER

Their political fortunes dramatically reversed, the Tutsi political elite splintered between those who went into political exile and those who re-mained at home. Those who stayed tried to work out a rapprochement with the new power. In contrast, exiles were a mishmash of those deter-mined to return to the old order and those who left because they feared there would be no room for Tutsi in the new political order. At the same time, this division corresponded to an ongoing discussion within the new Hutu political elite: between those determined that the new political community exclude Tutsi, and those exploring ways of going beyond the "racial" divisions inherited from the colonial order. To understand reasons for the shift of opinion on either side, we need to be aware of shifts on both sides.

Even though Hutu Power (in capital letters) emerged as a formal tendency only during the civil war of the early 1990s, I have used the term Hutu power (with "p" in lower case) also to characterize the tendency that stood for the making of a "Hutu Revolution" in the late 1950s—just as I have used the term Tutsi power to speak of those who argued that Tutsi had the traditional right to exercise power, even if they did not use the term themselves. The thread that unites both expressions of Hutu power, the informal and the formal, is an overriding conviction that the Rwandan nation is Hutu and, therefore, power in an independent Rwanda must also be Hutu. Tutsi may live in Rwanda, but only as a resident alien minority, at sufferance of the Hutu nation. For the Hutu who disagreed, Hutu and Tutsi, majority and minority, belonged to a single nation—Rwanda.

Two political tendencies—one accommodationist, the other exclusionist—vied for supremacy between 1959 and 1964. These tendencies did not correspond to the political divide between the Tutsi and the Hutu political elite, or between the revolution and the counterrevolution. Rather, both tendencies could be found on either side. The exclusionists included the adherents of Hutu power as well as the champions of Tutsi power, just as the accommodationists included all those who believed it was possible for Hutu and Tutsi to be part of a common political community. Seen from this point of view, the period from the beginning of the revolution in 1959 to the last exile armed attack in 1964 was marked by several turning points. As the balance of forces shifted, so did the center of gravity of state politics. Like a pendulum, it moved from exclusion in 1959 to accommodation in 1962 and back to exclusion in 1964.

1959 began with a sharp split between Hutu and Tutsi political leaders. Kayibanda, by then the leader of the revolution, called for Hutu power and for the exclusion of the Tutsi from political life. Faced with loss of political power, the Tutsi political elite moved into exile and began preparation for an armed return to power. The ground shifted in 1962 with UN intervention leading to the New York Accord and the formal announcement of state independence that same year. The New York Accord split UNAR into two rival factions: accommodationists and restorationists. As accommodationists returned to Kigali to participate in a coalition government, restorationists persisted with preparations for an armed invasion. The coalition government of the First Republic enjoyed eighteen months of relative peace before the restorationists mounted major armed raids in 1963. Countrywide repression followed in 1964. From 1959 to 1964, the center of gravity of Tutsi politics shifted from home to exile, as did the mode of its opposition from political to armed struggle. At the same time, there was a shift in the Hutu point of view from accommodation to exclusion. The outcome of this double shift was to consolidate Hutu power as the dominant tendency in the state apparatus and to restore Tutsi power as the dominant tendency in exile. To understand the dynamics behind this outcome, we need to look more fully at the developments between 1959 and 1964.

The call for Hutu power came from Grégoire Kayibanda, the leader of the revolution and the future president of the First Republic. Immediately after the November events that came to be known as the 1959 Revolution, he proposed that Hutu and Tutsi be "segregated" into two separate zones as a first step toward a "confederal organisation." Citing Disraeli, he compared Hutu and Tutsi to "two nations in a single state": "Two nations between whom there is no intercourse and no sympathy, who are as ignorant of each other's habits, thoughts and feelings as if they were dwellers of different zones, or inhabitants of different planets."[55] Between the revolution of 1959 and independence in 1962, Kayibanda's exclusionist point of view was moderated in the face of a growing coalition in favor of accommodation.

The outcome of the communal elections of June/July 1960—which UNAR boycotted—seemed to favor the exclusionist point of view. After the elections—in which PARMEHUTU won 70.4 percent of the votes, APROSOMA 7.4 percent, RADER 6.6 percent, and UNAR a paltry 1.79 percent—a provisional assembly of forty-eight members replaced the High Council (Conseil Supérieur) headed by the king. Though Kayibanda formed a "multiracial" provisional cabinet—with nine Europeans, seven Hutu, and three Tutsi[56]—PARMEHUTU was determined to go it alone beyond the formalities of the transition phase. Toward this end, it tried to erode the opposition through the lure of the carrot and the pressure of the stick. The result was a radical shift in the balance of forces within the country over the next three months. Alarmed that PARMEHUTU was willing to use any and all methods to consolidate its hold on power, the opposition joined hands: by November, the leaders of APROSOMA, RADER, and UNAR had come together to form a "Front Commun" in opposition to PARMEHUTU. A spokesperson of the Front Commun denounced the "dictatorial regime" of PARMEHUTU as "racist, racial and anti-democratic." Accusing the regime of "deliberately attempting to crush all other parties through corruption and intimidation," the statement concluded: "This kind of feudalism is worse than the old one."[57]

Cutting across the Hutu/Tutsi divide, opposition unity not only brought pressure on proponents of Hutu power, it also brought important sections of UNAR into the fold of constitutional politics. The result was that when the UN-initiated parliamentary elections were held in September 1961, UNAR agreed to participate. The outcome—with PARMEHUTU gaining 78 percent of the votes and UNAR 17 percent—was polarized, the final result giving more or less a count of Hutu and Tutsi bodies in the country. When the new parliament elected Grégoire Kayibanda as president, UNAR abstained from the vote. Kayibanda, however, appointed a government with members coming from PARMEHUTU, UNAR and APROSOMA.[58] Behind the scenes, discussions continued between the constitutionalist faction in UNAR, and PARMEHUTU. Following the New York Accord of February 1962, the leader of the "progressive" faction in UNAR, Michel Rwagasana, agreed to UNAR participation in a formal coalition government. The coalition took office in May—and remained intact for another eighteen months, until November 1963. UNAR had two ministries: public health and cattle. Rwagasana, its secretary-general, spoke publicly of peace on the hills of Rwanda. He pledged: "Our party can assure you that it will spare no effort in working for the achievement of a genuine understanding between the majority and the opposition, which, by virtue of its entry into the government, can no longer be considered an opposition, but rather a partner."[59] It was the clearest indication that the tide of postrevolutionary politics was turning from exclusion to accommodation.

The countertide also unfolded with the events of November 1959, which, as mentioned above, scattered most of the Tutsi notables into exile. The most complete account available of the period[60] categorizes the exiles into three factions: the monarchists, the progressives, and the activists. The *monarchists* comprised those who had been close to the court in Rwanda. The *progressives* came from the younger, Western-educated Tutsi chiefs, with some attracted to socialist ideas. The *activists* provided the hard-core guerrilla fighters for the armed incursions that began in 1960 and lasted until 1964. Until the February 1962 New York Accord that paved the way for the coalition government of May, "progressives" were in formal control of party affairs. The New York Accord broke the cohesion of the "progressive" faction; some, like the party secretary-general, joined the government coalition, but others remained in exile.

I have characterized the Tutsi political elite as either accommodationist or restorationist. The accommodationists both came to accept the 1959 Revolution as a fait accompli and banked on a peaceful internal political and constitutional process through which to work out their political future in the country. In contrast, the restorationists wished to undo the 1959 Revolution, holding out the prospect of a return to power through armed exile action. As the internal political process gathered momentum—as it did with the formation of the opposition front (the Front Commun) in November 1960, the elections of September 1961, and the coalition government that followed the accord of February 1962—anti-accommodation factions infiltrated small bands of armed guerrillas into border localities. Known as the *inyenzi*, or cockroaches, the armed guerrillas undertook as many as ten known raids into Rwanda.[61] From the outset, the raids targeted the officials of the new power in the local authorities. However low their rank, Hutu officials were considered a legitimate target. But border raids invited cruel repression. And repression, too, began to assume a standard form: it targeted the local Tutsi population as active or potential support for the *inyenzi*. The cumulative outcome was to set in motion a dynamic counter to that of the internal political process.

The worst case of repression took place after the New York Accord of February 1962 but before the coalition government took office in May. Its location was the prefecture of Byumba. Two successive raids in 1962 had led to the death of two policemen in February and one policeman, two civil servants, and an ordinary Hutu in March. The reprisal came the day after the March raid: "Between 1000 and 2000 Tutsi men, women and children were massacred and buried on the spot, their huts burned and pillaged and their property divided among the Hutu population."[62] As the coalition government took office, the Byumba repression came to be an anomaly. But when the life of the coalition ended amid the expanded raids of 1963, the repression of Byumba provided a norm: a raid turned into a signal for the massacre of the local Tutsi population, and for the distribution of their property among those organized as the local self-defense group. Worse than anything that had happened during the revolution, repression joined political violence to redistribution of property, rewarding perpetrators with benefits.

During the first eighteen months of the First Republic, from May 1962 to November 1963, raids were a localized affair, as were the reprisals that followed. Local reprisals went alongside the politics of accommodation at the national level. The balance shifted radically with the *inyenzi* invasions of November and December 1963. Known as the Bugesera invasion, this particular raid reached nearly twenty miles outside of Kigali. The repression was swift, and it was concentrated in the prefecture of Gikongoro, which not only had a very high density of Tutsi, but also contained the former royal residence of Nyanza and was the core area of Tutsi opposition. Available reports indicate both that the killings began at the instigation of the local prefect, backed by higher state authorities, and that they involved enthusiastic popular participation. The prefect, André Nkeramugabe, is reported to have told an improvised meeting of burgomasters and PARMEHUTU propagandists: "We are expected to defend ourselves. The only way to go about [it] is to paralyze the Tutsi. How? They must be killed."[63]

How many were killed? The figures vary widely, depending not only on the source but also on the time of writing. Before the 1990 civil war, estimates of the number killed had ranged from 750 to 5,000. The government officially estimated killings at around 750, but no other source believed it. *Africa Contemporary Record* reported unofficial estimates "nearer 5,000."[64] After the 1994 genocide, estimates tended to be much higher, ranging between 10,000 and 20,000. An international team[65] estimated that between 5,000 and 8,000 were killed in Gikongoro alone, that is, 10–20 percent of the total Tutsi population of the *préfecture*. Catharine and David Newbury estimated that between 10,000 and 14,000 people were killed in the first few years after decolonization.[66] Human Rights Watch put the figure at as many as 20,000.[67]

Many have claimed that the seeds of the genocidal violence that enveloped Rwanda in 1994 lie in the revolution of 1959.[68] But the revolution was not a bloodbath. The highest contemporary estimate from a credible source of Tutsi deaths during the revolution is around two hundred. The fact is that it was not the revolution, but attempted restoration and the repression that followed, that opened the gateway to a blood-soaked political future for Rwanda.

Politically, the invasion gave the upper hand to the Hutu power tendency. And its proponents acted swiftly. Once the invasion was checked militarily, they arrested some twenty leading Tutsi personalities in the country and executed them a week later in the town of Ruhengeri in the northern part of the country. The victims included one of the two UNAR members of government (Etienne Africa), and its president (Rudisitwarane) and secretary-general (Rwagasana) inside the country. It also included the president (Bwanakweri) and vice president (Ndazaro) of RADER. As opponents of Tutsi power who had chosen to return home to work in postrevolutionary Rwanda, they were killed because they were

Tutsi determined to participate in post-1959 politics as Rwandans. The repression meant an end to organized Tutsi politics in Rwanda until the political reforms under the Second Republic. But the real impact of the repression touched both Hutu and Tutsi. By killing leading Tutsi champions of the cause of accommodation and reform, those who had fought restorationists among the Tutsi in a tooth-and-nail struggle, the repression strengthened, at a stroke, the proponents of Hutu power within the country and those of Tutsi power in exile. The former heralded a native postrevolutionary republic in which the Tutsi would be tolerated only so long as they remained outside of the political sphere, whereas the latter held on to the notion that the Tutsi were a civilizing influence with a right to rule precisely because they were different. In reality, these post-colonial twins, Bantu and Hamite, were ideological offspring of Rwanda's poisoned colonial past.

Chapter Five

The Second Republic: Redefining
Tutsi from Race to Ethnicity

L ENIN once chided Rosa Luxemburg about becoming so preoccupied with combating Polish nationalism that she could not see beyond it: he said she risked getting trapped in the world of the cat and the rat. This is a world in which no other animals matter. For the rat, there is no animal bigger than a cat: not lion, nor tiger, nor elephant. For the cat, there is none more delicious than the rat. In the presence of the other, neither has eyes nor ears for any other animal. It is in this sense that the world of the Hutu and the Tutsi was like the world of the rat and the cat. For the subaltern Hutu, as for the nationalist Tutsi, no other political reality was more definitive than that of the other.[1]

The 1959 Revolution was an outcome in the world of the rat and the cat. If you are *not* a rat, then you understand that there are many animals bigger and more dangerous than the cat: the lion is neither as distant nor as benign as it may seem to a rat. But, if you *are* a rat, then the cat *is* truly menacing and dangerous. When rats do triumph against cats, it is at once like the world turning upside down. The danger is that this upside-down world may not change in its relationships. It may still continue to be the *same* world: the world of the rat and the cat. But at second glance, one is not so certain: can the world where rats have belled cats remain quite the same world? How does the nationalism of the rat differ from the nationalism of the cat? How does the nationalism of the majority differ from that of the minority? Even if the majority should in time give rise to a self-interested elite, does not the very process of doing so evoke a difference between nationalism from below as opposed to that from above, between a popular as opposed to an elite nationalism, with different consequences for the society at large?

These questions help illuminate different points of view one finds on the 1959 Revolution in contemporary literature. For all the difference in emphasis, they reflect two standpoints. *First*, both major texts written in the shadow of the revolution take seriously the claims of the revolutionaries. Catharine Newbury highlighted the majoritarian credentials and egalitarian aspirations of those who took power after 1959, as did Lemarchand herald the majoritarian character of the revolution. *Second*, there are those who see 1959 as nothing but the displacement of the Tutsi elite by the Hutu counterelite, with the same world continuing, only upside down, and the revolutionary talk of the insurgent elite as so much opportunist demagoguery. Thus Gérard Prunier concluded his analysis of the 1959 Revolution in a book on the 1994 genocide: "What would later be touted as a 'social revolution' resembled more an ethnic transfer of power."[2] In contrast to Prunier's dismissal of 1959 is the standpoint of Tharcisse Gatwa, a critic of the revolution's *practice* who nonetheless sympathizes with its *perspective*: the revolution, he says, was inspired by "a noble goal."[3] If Catharine Newbury and René Lemarchand fail to *problematize* the revolution, Prunier seems to shake it off a little too easily with a cynical shrug. If the innocent optimism of the former reflected the hopes of a revolutionary dawn, then the pessimism of the latter is cast in the shadow of the genocide. As I stated earlier, I find it important to take the revolution seriously, not to embrace it nor to shake it off, but to understand its limitations in spite of its real gains.

To understand the saving grace of the revolution, one would need to take the majoritarian aspirations of the revolutionaries seriously, and recognize that revolutionaries could not have seized and held power without bringing in at least some changes in response to popular aspirations. Without reform, revolutionaries could not have moved the majority into action. Such an analysis would need to go beyond the cynical observation that all the revolution did was to bring a counterelite to power; it would need to define the consequences of their coming to power to those not in power.[4] The point of view that focuses exclusively on the new elite risks turning into a tautology: since every social order is divided between elite holders of power and the mass subject to that power, this fact is taken as sufficient evidence that no society is different from another. To break out of that cynicism, but without innocently capitulating to revolutionary mythology or demagoguery, one needs both to accent the change in power and to highlight the consequences of the new power for those subject to it.

The revolutionaries made a threefold claim to underline the legitimacy of 1959. They heralded the revolution as national, as democratic, and as the harbinger of social justice. *First*, the mere shift in the identity of power from Tutsi to Hutu, they claimed, was a shift in representation. It was, obviously, a shift from a minority to a majority. More significantly, though, the claim was that the shift identified power with the indigenous Hutu rather than the alien Tutsi. *Second*, 1959 introduced elections at both the local and the national level. After the first direct election of burgomasters and their councils through a secret ballot in 1960, direct popular elections were held in each commune at regular three-year intervals.[5] *Finally*, 1959 carried out a number of social reforms. The revolution abolished *ubureetwa* (forced labor) in 1959, as it did the right of chiefs to have any other kind of forced labor. It also appropriated *igikingi*, land assigned to Tutsi notables as pasturage by the king, and redistributed it to the landless. Unlike colonially appointed Tutsi chiefs who had the power to exact forced labor and personal services from Hutu—in addition meting out severe punishment to recalcitrant subjects—burgomasters and prefects under the First Republic lacked all these powers.

None of these claims were bogus. Yet, each was subject to a critique, more so as time passed. Each set in motion a countertendency that grew in time and led to a growing disenchantment with the new order.

REPRESENTATION AND JUSTICE IN THE HUTU REPUBLIC

Known after the name of his home village as the "Hermit of Gitarama," Grégoire Kayibanda, the president of the First Republic, rarely made public appearances and hardly ever traveled abroad.[6] He was said to be a model of frugality, one who wore shabby clothes and patched shoes. When he was driven, it was in a Volkswagen. The republic he created did not just claim to represent the majority; it claimed to be the republic of the entire nation, that is, the Hutu nation. After 1964, Tutsi presence was forcibly removed from the political arena; the Tutsi were found in education, in business, in the church, even in government employment, but not in the political arena. The political sphere was confined to the Hutu, members of the Hutu nation.

For the postrevolutionary power that was the First Republic, Rwanda was exclusively a Hutu state. The rationale for this was disarmingly simple, disarmingly so because it simply turned upside down the logic of the colonial state: the Hutu were indigenous, the Tutsi were alien. Whereas the Tutsi had been treated preferentially by the colonial state as a nonindigenous civilizing influence, the First Republic considered this claim reason enough to treat them as politically illegitimate. The Tutsi thus continued to be officially defined as a "race," never as an "ethnic group." The implication was crucial. The language of race turned around the distinction "indigenous/alien": a racial difference could only be with foreigners, whereas an ethnic difference was with locals. As "race" was said to distinguish the indigenous from the nonindigenous, "ethnicity" was said to separate different groups among the indigenous. As such, the political distinction between a minority and a majority could only be relevant within the ethnic domain. As a race, the Tutsi were not a political minority; they were politically foreign, as it were, resident aliens. Only the indigenous—ethnic groups—could rightly belong, fully, to both civil and political society. Those classified as nonindigenous would be seen and treated as civil beings, with limitations (discriminations) depending on context, but never as political beings. From this point of view, the view of the First Republic, the Tutsi could expect to participate in civil society, but must not transgress into political society.

The Hutu Republic clearly distinguished between internal and external Tutsi, as one would between resident and nonresident aliens. This was so from the time of the *inyenzi* attacks of 1963–64. Those outside were considered more of a political than a cultural diaspora. Seen as organizing to overthrow the Hutu republic and to establish Tutsi power, they were defined as a permanent threat to the state and were treated as permanent outsiders. In contrast, the internal Tutsi were tolerated as civic, but not political, beings who could aspire to rights within civil society, but not in political society. Once the internal Tutsi parties had been liquidated and their leaders killed, Kayibanda's political ammunition was directed at APROSOMA, the one Hutu-led revolutionary party that had tried to recruit and organize the *petits* Tutsi into its ranks. Between 1964 and 1967, APROSOMA stalwarts were "slowly but surely eased out of any political or administrative responsibility."[7] Thus Kayibanda reorganized the Rwandan state as exclusively a state of the Rwandan nation.

Ironically, the Kayibanda regime faced growing criticism in the 1960s that it had not done enough to advance Hutu representation in civil society. The critique first came from unemployed Hutu school leavers.[8] Many had left primary school for lack of resources and were ploughing urban streets looking for employment. Others, in spite of being degree holders, lacked employment, to which they no doubt felt entitled. The combination created a pool of agitators, ready to be tapped by an ambitious politician with a keen sense of fresh grievances. This pool of educated discontent had grown sufficiently by the mid-1960s to surface publicly. In 1966, the party newspaper *Urmuli rwa Demokrasi* (Light of Democracy) dismissed them summarily as comprising one of four categories: "PARMEHUTU zealots, imbued with the ideas of 1959"; those "conceited and selfish (and) who only seek to accumulate honours, privileges and wealth"; "wind-cocks, who have one foot in PARMEHUTU and the other in the air"; and "those whose only objective is to destroy PARMEHUTU."[9]

The critique focused on government policy in education and employment. It was said that the government was not doing enough to advance Hutu representation in education: while Hutu were the majority in schools, university enrollment in the middle and late 1960s was nearly 90 percent Tutsi.[10] This was so in spite of government policy restricting Tutsi enrollment in postsecondary institutions to 10 percent of the overall figure. The critique no doubt put great pressure on government to take control of the educational system that was mainly under Church control. It is ironic that the political leadership nurtured by the Church in the 1950s established state control over church-directed education in the 1960s and took the initiative to secularize the educational system. To make sense of this, one needs to keep in mind that whereas the political leadership nurtured by the Church in the 1950s was Hutu, the Church leadership in postrevolutionary Rwanda continued to be predominantly Tutsi. The Church was one of the two institutions—the other being business—with a Tutsi preponderance in the postrevolutionary era.

The consequence of the school-leavers' agitation was the law of August 1966, which established state control over education through four key provisions.[11] *First*, it declared as state property all school buildings ever constructed with state subsidies. *Second*, it placed the hiring and firing of all personnel, lay and religious, in all state-subsidized private schools under the supervision and control of the state. *Third*, it removed the admission, promotion, and expulsion of students in these schools from exclusive control of school authorities. *Finally*, it also removed the choice of textbooks and curriculum content from the sole jurisdiction of school authorities. The aim was to bring the entire private—i.e., predominantly Catholic—educational system under state control. It was also the effect. For the Church-educated Hutu leadership of the state, the 1966 law provided an instrument for Hutu-izing control over a Tutsi-dominated educational system.

When it came to employment, critics held that the government's record was even worse. Since there was no official policy requiring adequate Hutu representation in employment, even the modest increase in Hutu school enrollment registered in a few years as a dramatic expansion in the number of unemployed Hutu school leavers. The trend gathered momentum over the years. By early 1970, for example, there were roughly three hundred

Hutu students among the five hundred at the National University. The more Hutu enrollment increased in postsecondary institutions, the more dramatic was the rise in the numbers of educated Hutu who were unemployed. It is this volatile group that triggered the dynamic that led to the coup of July 1973. The context for the crisis was created by the massacre of hundreds of thousands of Hutu by the mostly Tutsi army in neighboring Burundi. Those butchered were mostly school-going youth and were estimated at around 200,000.

The effect was to reignite the "racial" tension in Rwanda's middle class.[12] Hutu students at the National University in Butare began to agitate against their Tutsi colleagues. Lists of "blacklisted" Tutsi students, signed by anonymous and self-appointed Committees of Public Safety, appeared on notice boards at the university, at the National Teacher Training College, and at a secondary school. Among those targeted were children of mixed marriages (*ibyimanyi*) and "cheaters" (*abaguze ubwoko*) who were accused of having changed their "racial" affiliation. The threat was enough to get the bulk of the two hundred Tutsi students at the university to leave. Soon, lists began to proliferate at places of employment—banks, parastatal companies, private businesses—and even at an embassy. Once again, many of the named Tutsi employees left. Radio Rwanda was used to broadcast appeals inciting the Hutu to rise up and avenge themselves. Some extreme proponents of Hutu Power began publicly to call for a "final solution" to the Tutsi question. In the rapidly inflamed situation, a number of Tutsi were murdered. The estimates of the dead ranged anywhere from six to five hundred. The government responded sluggishly. Only after disturbances had gone on for weeks did it move into action. It first warned students to keep protest within "reasonable limits," then threatened to expel unruly students, then warned of "a subversive group which is trying to cause anarchy," and only then did it declare that it would not tolerate "discrimination against individuals because of their race."[13]

The agitation expanded in concentric circles. Just as it had begun in educational institutions and moved into ministries and enterprises, it grew by ripple effect, with each ripple bringing into the fold yet another tension in Rwandan society. The paralysis of power brought to surface the tension both within power and within society: the former between Hutu of the north and those of the south, and the latter between the poor and the rich. The general population began to expand the attack against the Tutsi into an attack on the rich. In the dual context of a popular agitation against deprivation and a student critique of Hutu unemployment, the split in power between the north and the south became the source of imposing a new order from above. Major General Juvénal Habyarimana led the army to carry out a bloodless coup on 5 July 1973. By all accounts, the intervention was received with great relief by all concerned, whether the population at large or the students, whether the business community or officialdom; whether Hutu or Tutsi. Thus was born the Second Republic, which immediately declared itself the custodian of the revolution and the protector of all its children, Hutu as well as Tutsi.

The Second Republic claimed to complete the "national" revolution of 1959 through a "moral" revolution.[14] The key change from the First to the Second Republic—a change that seems to have gone unnoticed by many an observer of Rwandan politics—was a shift in the political identity of the Tutsi from a race to an ethnic group. While the First Republic considered the Tutsi a "race," the Second Republic reconstructed the Tutsi as an "ethnicity" and, therefore, as a group *indigenous* to Rwanda. We have seen that the language of race turned around the distinction indigenous/nonindigenous. The political distinction between a majority and a minority had little relevance within the domain of "race." For, as a race, Tutsi were simply foreign. Their numbers were of little significance. Once reconstructed as an ethnicity, however, the Tutsi became Rwandan and their numbers became significant, just as the minority/majority distinction also became of great relevance. As a "race" under the First Republic, the Tutsi had been confined to the civic sphere and barred from the political sphere; as an "ethnicity" under the Second Republic, however, they were allowed participation in the political sphere, but limited to a scope said to befit their minority status.

The Tutsi faced discrimination, not just in the political sphere, but in the civic sphere, too. From the point of view of the Second Republic, the Tutsi were not just any minority, but a historically privileged one. As a minority defined statutorily and identified legally, its participation in civil and political life was regulated by state policy. The regulation had two purposes: (1) to redistribute through affirmative state action, and (2) to limit political participation. The Second Republic followed a "national" goal and sought to arrive at a balance between two tension-ridden objectives: justice and reconciliation. Reconciliation with the Tutsi was to be in a context of justice for the Hutu. The mode of justice would be through a system of redress within hitherto Tutsi-dominated institutions, particularly the Church, education, and employment. In some instances, as with the Church, this included direct state pressure. Such, for example, was said to be the reason for the "resignation" of Father Muvala a few days before he was to be ordained as bishop of the Catholic diocese of Butare.[15]

In other instances, such as education and employment, it was mainly through state-enforced quotas. The rationale was to redress historical wrongs. As such, this mode of justice was extended not only to the Hutu, but in particular to Hutu from the northern region, who were considered historically the most underprivileged.

The affirmative action program was summed up as "*équitable, ethnique et régional.*" The two moments of the affirmative action program, the "ethnic" and the regional, reflected a tension between the two moments of the program for justice: justice as appropriation, and justice as redistribution. The moment of appropriation targeted the Tutsi, and tended to unite Hutu against Tutsi. The moment of redistribution, however, distinguished between Hutu on the basis of regional affiliation: it thus tended to drive a wedge between Hutu from the north and Hutu from the center and the south. The 1985 law on education captured the unifying character of the politics of appropriation:[16] it stipulated that selection into schools will take into account the "ethnic" affiliation of the child; the Hutu will receive *over* 85 percent of the places, the Tutsi *between* 10 and 15 percent, and the Twa 1 percent. The quota system that defined the parameters for individual appointments to civil service posts—whether by law or by decree—summed up the divisive character of the politics of redistribution.[17] Allocation of posts was to take place, first on a regional basis and then on an "ethnic" basis. In practice, then, 60 percent of posts would be allocated to northerners and 40 percent to southerners. Within each region, allocation would be divided between Hutu and Tutsi/Twa, the former receiving 90 percent and the latter 10 percent.[18]

In practice, the quota system was subject to a number of limitations. Among the small coterie of Rwanda specialists, there is disagreement as to how strictly the quota system was enforced in practice. Citing statistical evidence from L. Uwizeyimana, Fillip Reyntjens maintains that the quota system was not rigorously enforced, as reflected by the fact that the proportion of Tutsi in public, parastatal, and private sector employment greatly exceeded the quotas, which were informal, anyway.[19] Yet, some members of the predominantly Tutsi business community did complain in 1977 that government promotion and hiring practices tended to give disproportionate weight to regional and ethnic qualifications rather than to merit. In response, Habyarimana made it clear that he would not relax his quota policies, arguing that it was important to overcome historical socioeconomic disequilibria in Rwandan society.[20] Finally, the quota system did not apply to the foreign diplomatic and business community in Rwanda, an important source of lucrative employment in the nongovernment sector. On the basis of her observations in Rwanda in the early 1980s, Claudine Vidal reported that a disproportionate number of Tutsi were employed by foreigners in Rwanda.[21]

Even as he pursued an agenda of redress for historical wrongs, Habyarimana was publicly committed to a policy of "reconciliation" between Hutu and Tutsi.[22] The Second Republic marked the day of the coup, 5 July, as "a day of peace and reconciliation."[23] This was not an empty boast or a rhetorical gesture. Although the state had yet to work out a policy of reconciliation toward the Tutsi in exile, it took several concrete steps toward reconciliation between Hutu and Tutsi within Rwanda. Official vocabulary began to speak of Hutu and Tutsi as "ethnicities," no longer as "races." The meaning of the shift was clear: the Tutsi within were there to stay. As opposed to the last year of the First Republic, when many Tutsi were being forced out of their jobs, Tutsi fears were being allayed in the first year of the Second Republic. The new regime rejected the First Republic's "national Hutuism." From being banished from the political sphere under the First Republic, the Tutsi were brought back within the political fold. When Habyarimana announced the formation of his cabinet on June 1, 1974, it included, for the first time since 1964, a Tutsi: André Katabarwa.[24] As astute an observer of Rwandan politics as René Lemarchand ended an analysis of the Second Republic in 1975 with the following conclusion: "If power in Rwanda is still the monopoly of a specific ethnic segment, identified with the Hutu sub-culture, the prospects of a Hutu-Tutsi *rapprochement*, both within and outside Rwanda, have never been brighter since independence."[25]

The distinction was no longer between civil and political rights but between participation and power. As a statutorily defined minority, the Tutsi could have rights, but must give up all thought of any meaningful participation in power. For power must remain Hutu, since Hutu was the identity of the statutorily defined majority. Tutsi participation in politics was regulated, subject to an informal quota, as was Tutsi participation in the formal economy. When speaking to Philippe Decraene of *Le Monde* about relations between Hutu and Tutsi, Habyarimana explained that "hatred cannot dissolve overnight" and clarified his notion of reconciliation: "It is not a question of bringing the Tutsi back to power, which would be equivalent to re-establishing the pre-1959 situation; but each ethnic group has its place in the national fold. There is a Tutsi minister in my government; there are Tutsi senior civil servants in the administration; and Tutsi officers in the army."[26]

Katabarwa remained a member of the cabinet until the reshuffle of January 1979, when he was dropped.[27] The first major internal struggle within the regime took place in 1979–80. Major Théonaste Lizinde, the security chief, was replaced in November 1979 and was accused in April of the following year of plotting a coup d'état. Significantly, Lizinde was also the author of a book entitled *The Discovery of the Kalinga*, an anti-Tutsi tract describing the search for the Karinga drum. The Lizinde faction was "considered to be violently anti-Tutsi and unhappy with Habyarimana's efforts to reconcile the Hutu and the Tutsi."[28] While Habyarimana turned the coup attempt into an opportunity to liquidate physically the southern opposition—literally "the entire generation of revolutionaries from the south"—this did not halt his search for reconciliation between Hutu and Tutsi.[29] In the January 1982 elections for the National Development Council—in effect the national legislature in a single party arrangement—the ruling party, Mouvement Révolutionnaire National pour le Développement (MRND) offered the electorate twice as many candidates as there were seats. It was meant to be an exercise in inner-party democracy. Among the 128 candidates put forth, there were two Tutsi, two Twa, and nine female *militantes*. Concluding his annual survey of Rwanda, René Lemarchand observed: "Rwanda remains one of the very few states in Africa where democracy retains a measure of reality."[30]

Even if limited and qualified, Tutsi participation in the political sphere continued. In October 1990, when the Rwanda Patriotic Front (RPF) invaded Rwanda, there was one Tutsi minister in a nineteen-member cabinet, one Tutsi ambassador, two Tutsi deputies in a seventy-seat national assembly, and two Tutsi in the sixteen-person central committee of the country's only party, MRND.[31] The flip side of the Tutsi presence in the central state was that the Tutsi were carefully kept away from the organs of power: the army and the local state. While there was one Tutsi officer in the army, members of the army were prohibited by regulation from marrying Tutsi women. Similarly, there was an almost total absence of Tutsi from the organs of the local state: there was only one Tutsi prefect, the prefect of Butare who was killed in the genocide, and not a single Tutsi burgomaster.[32] Though the Tutsi were defined as an ethnic minority and integrated as such within the central state, they were denied group recognition and were almost totally excluded from power in the local authority. Here, the gain of the 1959 Revolution—which had replaced Tutsi chiefs by Hutu—held. Tutsi gains under the Second Republic were more in the civic sphere than in the local authority. Its significance can be

grasped from the fact that no major anti-Tutsi political violence was reported from Rwanda between the time Habyarimana came to power in
1973 and the onset of the war with the RPF in 1990. Many thought
Habyarimana popular among the Tutsi of the interior throughout that
period. Popularly, he was considered "the protector of the Tutsi."[33]

Only a Hutu, someone not a Tutsi, would be a "protector of the Tutsi."
The flip side of "protecting" the Tutsi was to keep the Tutsi legally identified as the Tutsi. Thus, Habyarimana defined the prospects and limits of
the Second Republic. The prospect was to rehabilitate the Tutsi to being
Rwandans, alongside the Hutu. The shift was signified both by the change
in the official designation of Tutsi from a "race" to an "ethnicity" and by
lifting the ban on Tutsi participation in the political sphere. The limit was
that Tutsi and Hutu would remain alive as *political* identities. If Habyarimana had the political courage to come to grips with the colonial racial
legacy, he lacked the political foresight to transcend fully the combined
legacy of Rwandan state formation—colonial and pre-colonial—which had
crystallized Hutu and Tutsi into binary political identities.

REVOLUTION AND THE COLONIAL STATE

The processes that gave birth to the First Republic included revolutionary pressures from below. At the same time, the state was reorganized
to make revolution from above. Whereas the revolutionary legacy was best
captured in the *ideology* of the state, the colonial legacy was best reproduced in its *institutions.* The distinction is analytical. In practice, of course,
there was no Chinese Wall dividing ideology from institution and language from practice. Just as there were institutions which claimed a revolutionary legitimacy, there were others that were considered part of an
ongoing tradition and continued to function in a more or less humdrum
manner. In achieving a synthesis of colonial tradition and revolutionary
initiatives, the First Republic had more of a transitional significance. It is
the Second Republic that represented the crowning achievement of the
contradictory construct that was the Hutu Republic.

Rwanda under the First Republic was an *ideological* state, somewhat like
Cuba, North Korea, and Israel, as Prunier says.[34] But Prunier is wrong to
think that this was equally true of the Second Republic. True, when the
Second Republic set up the single party, the party did organize commu-
nity-level displays of loyalty and support, called "animation," with symbols
borrowed from North Korea.[35] But the analogy with North Korea misses
a key shift in the political agenda of the Second Republic, a shift that

made the agenda far less ideological. Unlike the First Republic, the Second Republic accepted the Tutsi within the political sphere, including them in the single party once it was organized.

In the ideological construction of the Hutu Republic, no institution had a greater significance than did the army. Colonial Rwanda—like colonial Somalia—had no army; in times of emergency, order was supposed to be ensured by the Force Publique of colonial Congo. The Rwanda army was built overnight, on the eve of independence, and from scratch, in a context when Belgian policy had shed its pro-Tutsi stance and neighboring Congo, itself on the verge of independence, could not be expected to ensure order in times of crisis. The 650 who formed the core of the Garde Territoriale in May 1960 comprised 85 percent Hutu and 15 percent Tutsi. As the one institution of the state that claimed to be authentically Hutu from birth, the army was both a child and a defender of the revolution. From the outset, the army claimed the mantle of the "nation-in-arms."[36]

While the *ideological* construction of the revolutionary state was most visible in the language of the central state—particularly in the army and the single party—the *institutional* reproduction of the colonial state was clearest in the administrative reorganization of the local state. The politico-administrative apparatus of both the central and the local state was reorganized following a protracted constitutional discussion after the 1973 coup. The discussion led both to the founding of the single party and to the adoption of a new constitution that put a seal of approval on the reorganization of local state administration. The MRND was established as the single party in 1975.[37] Legislative, executive, and judicial powers were exercised through the MRND and were centralized in the hands of the president. At the summit, the president appointed the Central Committee of the party. At the base, the party embraced every Rwandan, since every Rwandan was by law a member of the party, as indeed was the case in neighboring Tanzania and Zaire.

A draft constitution was promulgated in 1977 and was adopted on 17 December 1978. As a complete text, the draft constitution[38] drew on three different experiences: the French constitution for the structure of government, the Belgian model for human rights provisions, and the Tanzanian model for the organization of a single-party state. But the interim discussion focused mainly on which "model" to follow in constructing the party-state: the Zairean or the Tanzanian. While both models involved the building of a party-state, the difference was this: whereas the party controlled the state in the Zairean model, the accent in the Tanzanian model was on the state rather than the party. Habyarimana favored the Tanzanian model and managed to convince his comrades of its virtues.

The Tanzanian influence proved key to defining the character of the *local* state. It provided the model for the communal reform that was initiated in 1960 and completed under the Second Republic. Inspired by the ten-cell system in Tanzania, the reform divided the country into ten *préfectures*, and these into 143 *communes* of about 30,000 persons. Each commune comprised eight *collines* (hills), with each hill divided into *secteurs*, and each sector into two *cellules*. Each cell was to comprise fifty *familles*. As Reyntjens observed in 1985, few African countries could claim to be so well organized administratively as was Rwanda under the Second Republic.[39]

The reorganization both reproduced the administrative structures of the colonial state and built on them. In doing so, it did away with the electoral reforms of the First Republic. Neither the prefect nor the burgomaster, in charge of the prefecture and the commune, respectively, was elected; both were administratively appointed from above. The prefect was like the colonial chief: he decided how many acres of coffee should be cultivated in each commune, and how many people should be put to work on the roads and for how long. He alone was responsible for maintaining public order and tranquility and he had the authority to suspend the execution of ministerial orders when circumstances so required. Granted more or less the powers of the colonial subchief, the burgomaster all too easily tended to reproduce practices familiar in the colonial era: he demanded gifts in return for administrative services, from settling a case to penning a signature.

We shall later see that the administrative machinery of the local state was key to organizing the series of massacres that constituted the genocide of 1994. Between 1973 and 1994, however, this machinery grew on a steady diet of coercive practices, whose means were justified as "customary" and ends as "developmental."

CUSTOM AND THE DEVELOPMENTAL STATE

Postrevolutionary Rwanda could point to important economic achievements. It had come a long way from 1976, when it had a per capita income lower than that of any of its neighbors. By 1990, however, the World Bank estimated that the per capita income of Rwanda was higher than that of any of its neighbors. By 1987, Rwanda had the lowest debt, the lowest inflation rate, and the highest rate of growth of the Gross National Product (GNP) of any country in the region. The share of primary

activities—mainly subsistence agriculture—in the GNP had declined from
80 percent in 1962 to 48 percent in 1986. At the same time, secondary
activities had risen from 8 percent to 21 percent, and services from 12
percent to 31 percent. The rate of mortality was down. Hygiene and medical care indicators were improving. The proportion of children in school
had gone up from 49.5 percent in 1978 to 61.8 percent in 1986. There
had been no political executions since 1982, and there were fewer political
prisoners than in most African countries. The record *was* impressive.[40]

The record was particularly impressive in three sectors: agriculture, reforestation, and infrastructure. Each of these developments was in some
way linked to a set of relationships set in motion by the revolution. The
most benign of these was the development in infrastructure, the result
of a government tapping possibilities opened up by changes in Rwanda's
external relations, mainly the shift from a bilateral colonial relationship
with Belgium to diversified foreign relations. The main roads branching
from Kigali to the country's frontiers were asphalted with the assistance
of foreign aid. This included the road to the Burundi border (European
Development Fund aid), to the Uganda border (World Bank aid), to the
Tanzania border (Chinese aid), and to the Zaire border (West German
aid).[41] Less benign were developments that were triggered mainly by internal changes ushered in by the revolution. New relations, or newly recast
relations, set new energies in motion, underpinning dramatic developments in different sectors. But then each entered a period of crisis either as
the relationship in question turned sour, or as the energies unleashed earlier
got exhausted. The clearest example of this kind of postrevolutionary dynamism is that of agricultural production, which increased through individual effort, and reforestation, which was the result of communal effort.

Agricultural production increased dramatically in the first two decades
and suffered sharply in the following decade. Between the early 1960s
and the early 1980s, Rwanda was one of only three sub-Saharan countries
that succeeded in increasing total food production per capita.[42] This is
extraordinary, especially if one keeps in mind that Rwanda had experienced seventeen years of famine between 1900 and 1950. The Rwandan
population by the middle of the 1980s was roughly five times the average
during the colonial period, over eight million as opposed to between one
and two million; yet, it was better nourished and had been free of famine
for thirty years.[43] How did this happen? It happened mainly through the
expansion of crop area. The 1959 revolution abolished the "customary"
control of Tutsi chiefs over extensive land areas, particularly the *igikingi*
areas that had been reserved as pasture for cattle. This made possible two

developments.[44] First, large numbers of landless and land-poor peasants were brought in from the hills to settle in the drier, low-lying savanna areas in the south-center and southeast of the country. Second, fertile but swampy valley bottomland, previously reserved as dry-season pasture, was drained and brought under cultivation. L. Cambrezy estimates that, in 1978 alone, roughly 800,000 of the population of 4.8 million had been so resettled.[45]

By the close of the 1980s, however, the World Bank was citing Rwanda as one of the three *worst* performing sub-Saharan countries when it came to food production.[46] By then, there was hardly any land left for crop expansion. In the absence of any technological breakthrough, and in the presence of an increase in sheer numbers, soil fertility was decreasing. In response, there was a shift away from cereals and beans toward root crops: the food basket was becoming protein-poor and starch-laden. Yet, there still remained a potentially large area for crop expansion, one that would not be tapped until after 1994. This was the land taken up by the national parks system. Estimated at more than 20 percent of the country's total land mass, it was said to constitute the highest proportion of land mass reserved as park land in any single country on the entire continent of Africa.[47]

If the revolution did away with one kind of custom—a monopoly over land for Tutsi chiefs—it built on another kind of custom: the right of the state to call on corvée from peasants. "Inactivity" was one of the three social evils the Second Republic pledged to eradicate at the very outset.[48] Asked by the Paris daily *Le Monde* to elaborate on his plans for democracy, Habyarimana said: "First the population must get down to work—the Government and myself want to emphasize the value of work on the land. Thus we shall devote each Saturday to tilling the soil with hoes in our hands."[49] Forced labor for the state, usually once a week and usually on Saturday, became an institution, a part of the "custom" initiated by the revolution. Called *umuganda*, it was formally launched by the president in February 1974,[50] and was often explained away in the literature as "co-operative communal labour."[51] This bit of compulsion was used to marshal unpaid labor for public projects, such as planting forests, constructing terraces to fight erosion, and building bridges.

Umuganda went alongside *paysannat*, another standard feature in the agenda of developmental dictatorships that constituted the "radical" path in Africa's postcolonial trajectory. The point about developmental dictatorships was that they seldom claimed to be democracies. Their historical justification for soft-peddling democratic rights was always that they were the best instrument to bring about development. Thus, even when a parliament was created in Rwanda in 1978—not until five years after the closure of the National Assembly—it was called Conseil National de Développement, nothing less and nothing more than a National Council for Development. Both *umuganda* and *paysannat* were justified as developmental initiatives. The difference was this: while *umuganda* marshalled unpaid labor toward public works projects, the *paysannat* was akin to the compulsory villagization that had become standard practice in "radical" states in the region such as Tanzania and Ethiopia. In Rwanda, where the population was relatively concentrated—unlike in Tanzania and parts of Ethiopia where it was not—the *paysannat* was less a way of concentrating population, more a way of bringing wasteland under cultivation.[52]

The radical trajectory in postcolonial Africa tended to reproduce the coercive and enabling aspect of the colonial tradition as "revolution." From this point of view, *umuganda* was really, as Scott Grosse observed in his report to USAID, "a program of forced investment by farmers along the lines of coercive colonial-era conservation policies." Each public works project was a compulsion, and peasants were often doubtful of its social utility, more so as time went by. This much became clear with the onset of "democracy" in 1991 and 1992: farmers revolted against forced communal work, and the government abandoned the *umuganda* system.[53] In some cases, as in the south of the country, peasants even destroyed the communal wood lots they had been coerced into planting and maintaining.[54] The peasants' revolt unmasked official claims that *umuganda* was cooperative communal labor. Ironically, the Rwanda section of the *1993 Human Rights Report* of the U.S. Department of State, issued in February 1994, had this to say on the subject of "forced and compulsory labor": "Forced labor is prohibited by law and is not known to occur in practice."[55]

The Second Republic began to unravel from about the end of the 1980s. The context of that development was both internal and external. The *external dimension* feeding the post-1985 resource crunch in Rwanda accelerated with the multiplication of forces that fed it: coffee prices plummeted from 1989, a Structural Adjustment Programme was imposed from outside in 1990, and military spending rose dramatically following the RPF invasion, also in 1990. Coffee prices dropped by about 50 percent in the summer of 1989. At the same time, a disease affecting coffee trees had begun to spread in some parts of the country. In spite of government regulations banning the cutting down of coffee trees, farmers uprooted an estimated 300,000 such trees in the 1990s.[56] Income from coffee exports fell from $144 million in 1985 to a meager $30 million in 1993.[57] For the coffee farmer, however, the decline in coffee re-

ceipts was the outcome of two factors: not only a decline in the volume
of coffee exported and its international price, but also a sharp devaluation
of Rwandan currency following the imposition of an International Monetary Fund (IMF)-designed Structural Adjustment Programme (SAP) in
1990. When the currency was devalued by 67 percent in 1990, the government was simultaneously able to reduce drastically the *real* price of
coffee to the farmer and to disguise this reduction by limiting the de-
crease in the *nominal* price of coffee. In this context, even a modest
shielding of the coffee growers put the government in conflict with the
IMF. The government thus reduced the nominal price from 125 to 100
Rwandan Franc (RWF) per kilo in 1990 and then unilaterally raised it to
RWF 115 per kilo in 1991, even though the impact on the budget was
adverse. The deficit increased from 12 percent of the Gross Domestic
Product (GDP) in 1990 to 18 percent in 1992 to 19 percent in 1993,
though, the Stabilization Programme had set 5 percent as the target for
a reduced budget deficit in 1993.

Even this modest effort to cushion the impact of sharply declining prices
on the coffee producer exposed the government to the ire of the IMF, and
to the charge that it was in breach of the stabilization agreement. With
two key measures in the Structural Adjustment Programme—eliminating
coffee subsidies and reducing the budget deficit to target—not fully implemented, the Bretton Woods organizations refused to follow the stick of
adjustment with the carrot of financial resources.[58] The World Bank refused to provide the second tranche of structural adjustment credit. Rwanda's resource crunch worsened. According to estimates provided by the
Economist Intelligence Unit, Rwanda's real GDP fell by 5.7 percent in
1989, bringing it below the 1983 level. The slide in GDP continued, by
a further 2 percent in 1990, and another 8 percent in 1993 alone. By then,
Rwanda's debt had rocketed to nearly a billion U.S. dollars—precisely
$941 million—up from $189 million in 1980.[59] The GDP per capita, estimated at $330 in 1985, plummeted to $200 in 1989.[60] It was a 40 percent
fall in only four years. These are, however, averages. For working people,
the consequence was much worse, not only because averages hide internal
disparities between the rich and the poor. To make matters worse, an increasing share of declining resources was diverted to the war after 1990.
Military spending quadrupled from 1989 to 1992, from 1.9 percent to 7.8
percent of GDP. Even before the sharp decline in coffee prices registered in
1989, the south and southwest of Rwanda had already suffered a serious
famine, the first since 1943. As adverse internal and external trends came
together from 1989 onwards, it was as if Rwanda was plunging free fall

into a nightmare. And yet, we need to keep in mind that there was nothing exceptional about the economic crisis that beset Rwanda. It was shared by many an African economy undergoing IMF-supervised structural adjustment. It is not the economic, but the political, crisis that would set Rwanda apart from its neighbors in the decade to come.

FROM REVOLUTIONARY UNITY TO DEMOCRATIC OPPOSITION

To understand the critique of the revolution after 1959, one needs to begin with the revolutionary critique before 1959. Representation and justice were not only the foundation stones of the Hutu revolution and the Hutu republic, they were also the basis of the critique leveled at the postrevolutionary republics. As in other instances, postrevolutionary Rwandan history can be read as one of an unraveling tension between ideals and practice. After all, the claim of the two republics, their raison d'être, was that their core energies had been devoted to translating the principles of 1959 into policies. But implementation inevitably bred its own consequences, not only those intended but also those not. In time, these provided the basis of a critique of the postrevolutionary republic. I shall make a distinction between the internal and the external critique. The internal critique began from within the ranks of the regime; as reform set in, it found other locations within society. In contrast, the external critique came from Tutsi exiles; it gathered momentum with the RPF invasion of October 1990. We shall focus on the internal critique in this chapter, leaving the external critique for the next chapter.

Organizationally, the internal critique was made from a variety of locations, at first from within the ruling party, then from a mushrooming of civil society organizations, and finally, from an ensemble of political parties. The critique came in two different phases. The first phase began with student protests under the First Republic. Critics charged that the government had confined the revolution to the political sphere, failing to end Tutsi privilege and redress Hutu grievances in civil society. After the coup of 1973, this kind of critique led to coup attempts by disaffected members of the Habyarimana government who opposed the redefinition of the Tutsi from a race to an ethnicity as a prelude to their rehabilitation in Rwandan society, claiming that this was evidence that the regime was "pro-Tutsi." The best-known example of this is the Lizinde coup attempt in 1979.

While the first phase of criticism focused on the theme of representation, the second phased focused on the question of justice. The more the beneficiaries of the revolution narrowed into a small and identifiable elite, the more they appeared as its usurpers. The basis of the internal critique was not that 1959 was historically unjustified, but that it had been betrayed and usurped by a narrow elite.

Revolutionary justice was social justice. Key to it was the righting of historical wrongs. As I have argued, the politics of redress involved two contradictory moments. The moment of appropriation targeted the beneficiaries of the old order. In doing so, it tended to unify its victims. In contrast, the moment of redistribution disaggregated this latter group—because it created out of this group the beneficiaries of the new order. Whereas the target of appropriation were the Tutsi in general and its intended beneficiaries all the Hutu, the actual beneficiaries were not all the Hutu. Since the process of redistribution made a distinction between different Hutu, it dissolved the revolutionary unity of the Hutu into postrevolutionary distinctions: such as, for example, a regional distinction between the Hutu of the north and those of the south, and a class distinction between propertied and propertyless Hutu.

The two moments produced two different sets of effects. In distinguishing the new from the old order, the moment of appropriation united the nation against its colonial usurpers. Indigenization was in this case the battle cry of the colonized; against a backdrop of colonial conquest, the demand for justice turned into a demand for indigenization. In this, the politics of the Hutu Republic was no different from that of the regime of Idi Amin in Uganda, or from the politics of indigenization in Nigeria, or from that of "authenticity" in neighboring Congo. In all instances, the demand for indigenization was closely tied to the politics of race as defined through the colonial period: race distinguished those indigenous from those not. The politics of indigenization *was* the politics of deracialization. From the point of view of an Idi Amin or a Grégoire Kayibanda or a Joseph Mobutu, indigenization was not racialism. Rather, it was deracialization.

The moment of redistribution highlighted a different kind of distinction. In distinguishing the beneficiaries of the new order from those who simply identified with it and formed its supporters, it defined the custodians of the new order. Thus, republican austerity gave way to an ethic of consumption, and the myth of the "egalitarian republic" got corroded. The Presidential Instruction of 1975 (no. 556101) gave civil servants permission to do private business without any restrictions, including owning rented houses, purchasing rented vehicles, and having interests in mixed economy or commercial enterprises.[61] The instruction made official that which had been practice for some time. Corruption in and through state office became the subject of more and more writing in the 1980s. By the end of Kayibanda's rule, the locus of corruption had been the cooperative Travail, Fidelité, Progrès (TRAFIPRO). As the national producer/consumer cooperative that had provided the most valued organizing site for revolutionaries of 1959, TRAFIPRO turned into a favored site of accumulation for businessmen and politicians in the First Republic. Its countrywide monopoly was said to strangle other forms of economic enterprise everywhere. Yet, its control was in select southern hands.[62] In the Second Republic, massive corruption came to public light with the dismissal of the governor of the National Bank in April 1985. The new literature referred to the "Zairization of Rwanda," with an isolated urban elite said to be out of touch with the mass of rural population.[63]

The two moments gave rise to two different kinds of literature. The literature that focused on the moment of appropriation tended to be more celebratory: it highlighted the moment of revolutionary transition, of virtuous sacrifice and of intense battle. It put the indigenous identity center stage and celebrated it as the new revolutionary identity. In contrast, the literature that focused on the moment of redistribution tended to highlight the moment of corruption, of déjà vu, of regression—even capitulation—to the ways of old. While the literature of the revolution had a touch of innocence, postrevolutionary literature tended to shade into caricature.

The revolution had defined its beneficiaries as Hutu, but critics implicitly distinguished between beneficiaries and usurpers, whom they defined in regional terms. By identifying the regional identity of key appointments in each period, observers tried to pinpoint both key regional rivalries and the shifting regional focus of the regime. It is in this sense that the center of the First Republic was said to gravitate around a factional competition between two sets of regional elites, from Gitarama prefecture in the center and from Ruhengeri in the northwest. With the coup of 1973, the center of elite competition and control was said to have gravitated to the northwest. By the late 1980s, the political elite of the Second Republic came mainly from two northern perfectures, those of Gisenyi and Ruhengeri[64]—even though they accounted for hardly a fifth of the country's population and exactly a fifth of the ten prefectures in the administrative division of the country.[65] A survey taken in the early 1990s showed that thirty-three of sixty-eight public institutions were under the directorship of individuals coming from either Gisenyi (nineteen posts) or Ruhengeri (fourteen posts). Befitting the home *préfecture* of the president, Gisenyi clearly played the lead role.[66] Rwanda watchers noted that already, by the mid-1980s, nearly a third of the eighty-five most important posts in the republic—as well as almost all the leading positions in the army and the security services—were occupied by individuals from the prefecture of Gisenyi. In Gisenyi itself, Habyarimana's home area, Bushiru, was said to compete favorably with Bugoyi.[67]

The critique that state offices tended to be monopolized by elite groups from a particular region resonated most with elite factions left out in the cold in the competition for office and position. That kind of critique needs to be distinguished from the kind of critique whose target was the single party order identified with the Second Republic, and which for that very reason had a wider audience. The source of this more general and political critique was the small—but influential and growing—number of literate urban people, ranging from professional and salaried middle-class persons to the more articulate workers and artisans in the capital city of Kigali. To be sure, Kigali was hardly more than a medium-sized town, whose population at the time of the 1978 census was around 120,000 in a country of 4.8 million. Yet, as soon as these voices began to express organized discontent with the kind of political order created by the single party, their significance far outstripped their numbers. This was for two reasons, one systemic, the other conjunctural.

The systemic reason had to do with the nature of a political system that held the vast majority of its population—its rural population—in the grip of myriad local authorities whose powers were literally unlimited and un-accountable to any but their superiors. We have seen that this tightfisted dictatorship combined administrative, executive, legislative, and judicial powers. It had been sanctioned as "customary" in the colonial period and then was reformed through elections after 1959. Anointed as "revolution-ary" under the Second Republic, this local authority was without any elec-toral check-and-balance. Instead, it was reorganized and rationalized after the model of the ten-cell system in Tanzania. So long as this dictatorship held—which it did until the pressures of the civil war cracked it—it could only be critiqued from an external vantage point, that of the city. The conjunctural reason was more global. The late 1980s was both a time when Rwanda was becoming more vulnerable to the external environment and a time when winds of change were beginning to blow from without. Just when the collapse of the international coffee price, and even more so of its foreign exchange revenue, was making the Kigali regime more vulnera-ble to external pressures, these pressures began to take on a more political form. While Western creditors—self-described as the donor community—

had been content to push the IMF-designed Structural Adjustment Programme as a standard reform package around the African continent through the decade of the 1980s, the collapse of the Soviet bloc saw demands for political reform take the front seat. It was a context in which any articulate internal critique of single party rule was bound to have a privileged hearing internationally.

This is precisely what happened in the second half of 1989, when critical periodicals and associated human rights NGOs began to surface in Kigali.[68] Peter Uvin, a development administrator in Rwanda at that time, estimates that "by the beginning of the 1990s, Rwanda had one of Africa's highest density of NGOs." He calculates that "there was approximately one farmers' organisation per 35 households, one cooperative per 350 households, and one development NGO per 3,500 households."[69] The internal voices of protest were reinforced by pressures for reform from the outside. These pressures came from two major sources: the assembly of Francophone states and the Vatican. As late as January 1989, Habyarimana considered any political change feasible only within the one-party system; but only a year and a half later, on 5 July 1990, he agreed to the necessity of a separation between the party and the state, possibly within the context of multipartyism. In September 1990, the Catholic archbishop of Rwanda resigned from the Central Committee of the ruling party, for the first time formally dissociating the Catholic Church from the MRND. The occasion was the pope's visit to Rwanda; according to most observers, the resignation came as a result of direct pressure from the Vatican.

In September of 1990, Habyarimana established the Commission Nationale de Synthèse. It was given two years in which to make recommendations for a new democratic national charter. That, however, was before the Rwanda Patriotic Front (RPF) invasion of 1 October 1990, and the civil war that followed. We shall discuss the invasion and the civil war in the next two chapters, but let me make two observations here: (1) the onset of internal political reform in Rwanda preceded the RPF invasion; and (2) the immediate impact of the invasion was to accelerate the reform process. A month after the RPF invasion, Habyarimana spoke to the legislature, declared his support for the establishment of a multiparty system and instructed the National Commission to complete a draft national political charter by the end of the year. In a sharp departure from previous policy, he also acknowledged the right of refugees to return to Rwanda—without conditions, at least in theory. As directed, the commission published its draft in December. Also, as expected, the draft endorsed a multiparty political arrangement. This period also saw a fuller realization of press freedom:

by March 1991, over a dozen newspapers and magazines, mostly critical of the official line, were in circulation. There followed public discussions of the charter's proposals. In another six months, the draft constitution was approved and entered into force. That was in June 1991.

Opposition parties were permitted to register in March 1991. By July, four opposition parties had formed a coalition whose common purpose was to bring down the one-party government. The four-party coalition comprised the MDR, the PSD, the PL, and the PDC.[70] Of these, the Mouvement Démocratique Républicain (MDR), was the first to organize as a party. It was a reformed version of the old MDR-PARMEHUTU. In dropping the appellation PARMEHUTU from its name, the MDR moved away from its old anti-Tutsi affiliation; at the same time, in reestablishing the MDR, the party stressed its affiliation to the central region and its opposition to the northwestern allegiance of the Habyarimana regime. The MDR was rivaled by the Parti Social-Démocrate (PSD). Ideologically positioned on the center-left, the PSD selfconsciously tried to attract an educated stratum that was both Hutu and Tutsi. From this standpoint, the Parti Libéral (PL) was even more interesting: it had no specific geographical base, but it attracted both Tutsi and those of "mixed" parentage who openly scoffed at "ethnic" politics.[71] The last and possibly the least significant of the opposition parties was the Parti Démocrate-Chrétien (PDC), a Christian-Democratic group that had great difficulty establishing its oppositional credentials given the history of close relations between the Church and the single party.

The MRND, too, went through a metamorphosis in this year of change. To begin with, the party took advantage of its extraordinary congress on 28 April 1991 to adapt its statutes to the emerging multiparty context. And then on 5 July—exactly a year after the police had suppressed the strike that had signaled public opposition to single-party rule, and the very day Habyarimana agreed to the separation of the party and the state—the party modified its name. The new name signaled an expansion of its core objectives: it added "democracy" to "development." The MRND was now the MRNDD: the Mouvement Révolutionnaire National pour le Développement et la Démocratie.

To look back at the year of the reform—from 5 July 1990 to 5 July 1991—and to identify the trends it brought to the surface—is to understand the kind of social forces that were being held in check by the single-party closure and were seeking room for expression. The opposition organized along two different lines: regional and ideological. The regional dimension highlighted the demand that power be anchored in a base broader than simply the northwest of the country. Ideologically, the opposition seemed to call for a more liberal arrangement, in both politics and economics. Neither the power nor the opposition was organized along "ethnic" lines. While one of the opposition parties, the Parti Libéral, had a mainly Tutsi leadership, it was not a Tutsi party. By the time of the 1990–91 reform, even in the first year that followed the RPF invasion, the regional question was far more politically volatile than was the "ethnic" question.

Unlike the First Republic—which was more inward-looking and saw itself as a regional exception, a product of Rwanda's distinctive history of "race" relations—the Second Republic tended to situate itself in a regional context defined by two reference models, Tanzania to the left and Zaire to the right. It had borrowed from both and even invited comparisons with one or the other. In its potential capacity to engineer political reform and to charter a peaceful development from single to multiparty rule— while retaining the political initiative—the Second Republic seemed closer to Tanzania than to Zaire. On the eve of the RPF invasion of October 1990, the Rwandan polity was healthier than many others in the region. It had a better record of dealing with the political opposition than did most countries in the region of the Great Lakes, Tanzania being the notable exception. At the same time, there was a demonstrated willingness and capacity to undertake internal political reform. But the fate of the Second Republic turned out to be radically different from that of Tanzania. This was not because the internal critique turned out to be more radical than expected. The unexpected factor, rather, was the critique from without—the critique which stemmed from the RPF and which articulated the aspirations of the mainly Tutsi political diaspora. This, indeed, is where the difference with Tanzania was telling. While Tanzania was the one state in the region that did not drive entire groups into political exile, independent Rwanda was the one state whose very birth was linked to the phenomenon of group exile leading to a mushrooming political diaspora.

The Second Republic's greatest single failure was that it was unable to even pose the question of how to integrate the Tutsi diaspora within the postcolonial polity. To integrate it would require less coming to terms with a political opposition than with the claim that the Tutsi were as much a part of the Rwandan political community as were the Hutu. Its failure was testimony to a past it could not come to terms with, because to do so required nothing less than to shed the presumption of its being a state of the Hutu nation. This single fact distinguished Rwanda from all other states in the region, even Burundi. All these states were organized more or less along the model of cultural pluralism, whose units were called ethnicities in Africa but nations elsewhere. This model presumed that, no matter how dispersed, every ethnicity would have an ethnic home somewhere in the region. That home was not only to be seen as the source of dispersal in the past but also a point of return any time in the future. At the minimum, the existence of the home was said to provide a fallback in times of crisis. Even if this return never happened, its very possibility—the very assurance that everyone had a home, no matter how remote—ensured that no one was orphaned in times of crisis.

It is in this sense that 1959 orphaned the Tutsi who left Rwanda. Even when Habyarimana rehabilitated the internal Tutsi from a nonindigenous "race" to an indigenous "ethnicity," he had no intention of extending this "reconciliation" to the Tutsi diaspora. This created, for the first time, a group that was from the region but not of the region, which was part of the region but without belonging to any particular part of it. The distinctive feature of the Rwandan Tutsi diaspora was that its members were ethnic strangers everywhere; they had no ethnic home. As a group, they had nothing to lose, not even a home. The 1959 Revolution had made of the Rwandan Tutsi diaspora a group akin to the Jews of prewar Europe.

The Rwandan Tutsi diaspora of the sixties may have pined to go home, but their children who were born in exile and grew up in the seventies, away from the ancestral home, were determined to make a home where they were. As events would show, this was the truest of those in Uganda. Faced with a state that was hostile to "strangers," at first racial, and then ethnic, it is in Uganda that the Banyarwanda—for that is how the second-generation exiles and refugees thought of themselves—made the most concerted effort to make a home for themselves by staking nothing less than their lives in the process. That effort was the guerrilla war in the Luwero Triangle of Uganda from 1981 to 1986. The irony was that it was the guerrilla struggle that showed convincingly the limits to which ethnic strangers could make themselves at home in a state that defined "home" as an ancestral—indigenous—abode for "natives," keeping at bay all those considered nonindigenous, no matter what their commitment or predicament, as "settlers." Forced to confront the political fact that in postcolonial Africa one's political home was equated with an ancestral home, and an ancestral home with the precolonial home, the Tutsi diaspora turned to their ancestral home, Rwanda.

Their attempted return was the source of the external critique. This is why the external critique was not really a response to the policies of the Habyarimana regime; its roots were much deeper. It expressed the agony and the predicament, the impossible situation, of those without a political home in postcolonial Africa. This is why we need to look at developments beyond Rwanda, particularly those in Uganda, if we are to understand the nature, the timing, and the strength of that critique. For the RPF invasion was less a response to post-1959 developments in Rwanda than it was an outcome of developments within the region, one that the growing post-1959 Banyarwanda diaspora had crisscrossed and knit together. Only that explained the tenacity with which the RPF invasion persisted, more or less without regard to the tenor or pace of developments within Rwanda, or even whether these developments were moving in the direction of reform or of degeneration.

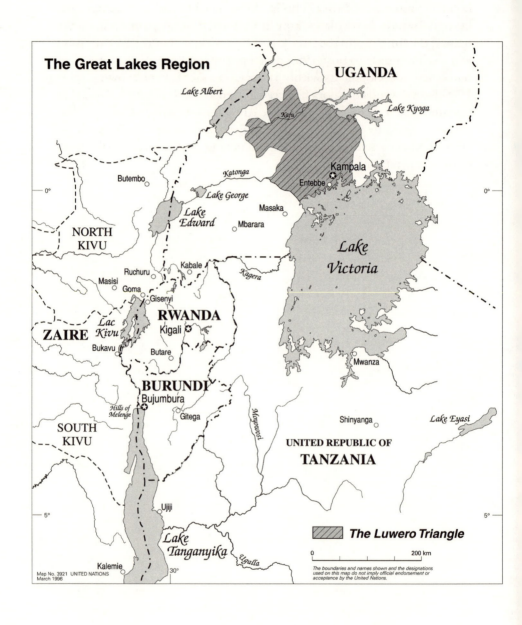

The Great Lakes Region

UGANDA

Lake Albert

Kafu

Lake Kyoga

Kampala ✪

Entebbe

Katonga

Butembo

Lake George

Masaka

NORTH KIVU

Lake Edward

Mbarara

Kabale

Lake Victoria

Ruchuru

Kagera

Masisi

Goma

Gisenyi

RWANDA

ZAIRE

Lac Kivu

Kigali ✿

Bukavu

Butare

Mwanza

BURUNDI

Bujumbura ✪

Hills of Melenge

Gitega

Malagarasi

SOUTH KIVU

Shinyanga

Lake Eyasi

UNITED REPUBLIC OF TANZANIA

0°

5°

30°

Ujiji

Lake Tanganyika

Ugalla

Kalemie

▨▨ **The Luwero Triangle**

0   200 km

The boundaries and names shown and the designations used on this map do not imply official endorsement or acceptance by the United Nations.

Map No. 3921 UNITED NATIONS
March 1996

Chapter Six

The Politics of Indigeneity in Uganda:
Background to the RPF Invasion

THE Rwanda Patriotic Front (RPF) invasion of October 1990 occurred at a time of internal reform—and not repression—in Rwanda. Uganda-Rwanda negotiations on the right of refugees to claim Rwandan nationality had reached an advanced stage by then. An independent survey was to be conducted within Rwandese refugee camps in Uganda to see how many actually wanted to return to Rwanda and how many would prefer to remain in Uganda while claiming Rwandan nationality. On 28 September 1990, only three days before the RPF invasion, President Juvénal Habyarimana addressed the UN General Assembly in New York and announced two key concessions to refugees: Rwanda would grant citizenship and travel documents to those who did not desire naturalization in their countries of asylum, and it would repatriate many of those who wished to return. Supporters of the RPF have preferred to remain silent on this point, while opponents have highlighted it as evidence of the diabolical and power-hungry nature of the RPF. Neither view recognizes that the October invasion was more a response to developments within the region than to those inside Rwanda.

The more the population of Rwanda overflowed its boundaries, the more there developed a political diaspora—besides the earlier and larger cultural diaspora—outside Rwanda. In accepting that some of the 1959 refugees may have a right of return, Habyarimana had acted under pressure. The source of that pressure was not the internal opposition in Rwanda, but the knowledge that a section of the Tutsi political diaspora—that within Uganda—had, even more so than in 1959–63, come to constitute a significant armed and political force. The irony is that both Habyarimana's concession and the RPF invasion that followed need to be understood within the context of developments in Uganda. The October invasion, I will argue, was the outcome of the first major political crisis the National Resistance Army (NRA) faced since coming to power in

Uganda in 1986. At the root of the crisis was the political legacy of the colonial state: that citizenship be defined on the basis of indigeneity. Struggles around postcolonial entitlement had focused on the notion of indigeneity and had led to successive expulsions in independent Uganda. The best known of these was the expulsion of Asians in 1972. But the largest in scale was the expulsion of the Banyarwanda in 1982–83. My point is that it is events within Uganda, and not Rwanda, that set in motion the dynamic that explains both why the Tutsi diaspora in Uganda became a central force in the guerrilla struggle, and why it was marginalized in the conflict about entitlement that followed the victory of the guerrillas. At the root of both developments was the crisis of citizenship and indigeneity. With the invasion of October 1990, the NRA exported its crisis to Rwanda.

Without a regional perspective, it is not possible to understand either the dimensions of the crisis or the intensity it acquired. If the growing pool of refugees in the region can only be explained by internal developments in Rwanda, the organization of the refugees as an armed force and the timing of their armed return in October 1990 can only be explained by developments internal to Uganda. For what has come to be known as the RPF invasion of Rwanda also needs to be understood as an armed repatriation of Banyarwanda refugees from Uganda to Rwanda.

BANYARWANDA REFUGEES IN THE REGION OF THE GREAT LAKES

Tutsi refugees left Rwanda in three different waves: 1959–61, 1963–64, and 1973. The first wave followed the revolution. It involved mainly the Tutsi elite displaced from positions of power. The second wave was triggered by the repression that followed each of the major *inyenzi* attempts to restore Tutsi power through armed attacks. The outflow grew to include broader sections of Tutsi, as the repression expanded beyond perpetrators of the old order to target ordinary Tutsi just in case they may yet support *inyenzi* efforts to restore the old order. The most detailed study of Rwandese refugees in the post-'59 period estimates that between 40 to 70 percent of Tutsi refugees fled Rwanda between 1959 and 1964.[1] After 1964, there was a prolonged period of political stability as armed refugee attacks came to a halt from without and the First Republic came to be stabilized within. The political crisis of 1972–73 triggered a fresh outflow of Tutsi refugees from Rwanda, just as it led to a reconstituted political power within Rwanda. Until the October 1990 RPF invasion from Uganda, there was no further outflow of Tutsi refugees from Rwanda to neighboring countries.

How many Tutsi refugees were there in the region in 1990? Estimates vary radically. Most range between 400,000 and 600,000.[2] Gérard Prunier gives a higher estimate of between 600,000 and 700,000.[3] Captain Eugene M. Haguma of the RPF gives a wildly high estimate of 1.5 million as the number of "Rwandese living in exile" since 1959,[4] thereby reproducing, without any explanation, assumptions widely held in Uganda in the early 1990s about the number of Rwandese refugees in the region. Students of political crisis in contemporary Africa are familiar with the wildly fluctuating estimates of those killed or displaced that tend to accompany reports of political crisis.[5] Often, they are more a reflection of the political orientation of the writer than the nature of the phenomenon being described. At times they reflect a widely held notion that anything goes when it comes to reporting about small, faraway places. Given this, I have tended to give weight to estimates that are accompanied by a credible account of the procedure employed to arrive at figures. From this standpoint, Catherine Watson's estimate of the total number of Banyarwanda refugees in 1990 at "probably about half a million" has a greater credibility than any other I have come across.[6]

If the total number of refugees in the region of the Great Lakes was between 500,000 and 600,000, not all of them were registered as refugees with the United Nations High Commission for Refugees (UNHCR). The registered refugees in the early 1990s numbered a little over two-thirds of this estimate. Most of these were registered in Burundi (266,000), and then in Uganda (82,000), Tanzania (22,000), and Zaire (13,000).[7]

BANYARWANDA IN UGANDA

The Banyarwanda form a distinct cultural group within Uganda. As speakers of the language Kinyarwanda, they constituted the sixth largest ethnic group within Uganda according to the 1959 census, surpassed only by the Baganda, the Itesot, the Banyankole, the Basoga, and the Bakiga. In 1990, the Banyarwanda formed "slightly over 1.3 million of the country's total population of about 18 million."[8] From the standpoint of Rwanda, however, they constituted the Banyarwanda cultural diaspora within Uganda.

The Banyarwanda in Uganda comprised three distinct groups: nationals, migrants, and refugees. *Nationals* were those who were a part of Uganda at the time the country's western borders were defined by the 1910 agreement between Germany and Britain, two colonial powers. *Migrants* crossed that border, mainly during the colonial period, in search of a better livelihood. *Refugees*, in contrast, were mainly those displaced by political crisis in the postcolonial period. Thus, nationals were of precolonial and migrants of colonial vintage, but refugees were solely a postcolonial development. Whereas migrants were mainly economic, refugees were mainly political. All three were part of the Banyarwanda cultural diaspora, but only the refugees constituted a political diaspora.

Nationals

Ugandan Banyarwanda—those I have termed nationals—live mainly in a single county in the western part of the country. Bufumbira County is part of the district of Kabale. Both the Bafumbira whose home is Kisoro district, and the Bakiga in the neighboring Kabale district, were drawn into the Nyabingi movement that constituted the spearhead of the political struggle against the Tutsi aristocracy and German and British colonialism and spanned both sides of the border. The Bafumbira were estimated at roughly 600,000 in the early 1990s. In the period from 1959 to 1990, however, they did not constitute an active political force.

Besides the Bafumbira, who were mostly impoverished cultivators, there was a second group of Banyarwanda nationals in Uganda. These were the nomadic Tutsi who had long been resident in Ankole, and some of whom still roamed the drylands with cattle. Others had bought land and practiced a mixed agriculture, while the rest had scattered, either moving to other pastoral areas to work as cattle keepers or adapting to an urban life. Catharine Watson estimated the Tutsi of Ankole—using this term for the original group that has now adapted to a range of preoccupations, from cattle keeping to mixed agriculture to urban work, whether within or outside Ankole—at roughly 120,000.[9]

Migrants

Migrants constitute about half of the Banyarwanda cultural diaspora within Uganda, numbering between 500,000 and 700,000 in the early 1990s. Labor migrants were mainly Hutu peasants who began flowing across the border in the mid-1920s. But they also included *petits* Tutsi who came to work as cattle keepers for the Baganda in the south and for others in northern and eastern Uganda. Thousands more Tutsi came in the post-Second World War period, in the 1950s and '60s, to work as cane cutters on Asian-owned sugar estates in Basoga and as miners in the Kilembe copper mines. Most labor migrants came in response to a double dynamic, on the one hand a push, on the other a pull. The push came from the tightening regime of forced labor and forced cultivation in Rwanda, identified with the newly appointed Tutsi chiefs who were charged with its implementation.

The pull factor was fresh employment opportunities, which varied over time. In the period between the two world wars, employment could be found on a big scale in two locations: the plantations of Busoga and rich peasant farms in Buganda. In the period after the Second World War, new opportunities came with the opening of the copper mines in Kilembe. "I left home because I wanted a job without beatings," explained one migrant to the anthropologist Audrey Richards.[10] For migrants, unlike for refugees, the move across the border was not a compulsion, but an option. From that starting point, they sought to become a part of the local society, gradually assimilating, taking on local names, clan affiliations, spouses, and even an overall identity. The agricultural Hutu assimilated more easily in the agrarian cultural context in Buganda, just as the pastoral Tutsi assimilated more easily in the context of the cattle-centered culture of the Bahima in Ankole. But the Tutsi assimilation in Ankole came to an end with the influx of large numbers of refugees in 1959.[11]

The preferred destination of agricultural migrants was the rich peasant economy of Buganda. There, they could begin as farm laborers and then aspire to acquire land as tenants, and finally even become land-holding *bakopi* (peasants). Buganda had a total population of 1,302,162 in 1948. Of these, 34 percent were immigrants. By the 1959 census, the total population in Buganda had risen to 1,834,128. Roughly 42 percent of these were immigrants. This means that whereas there was one immigrant for every two "indigenous" Baganda in 1948, there were three immigrants for every four "indigenous" Baganda in 1959.[12] The largest single group of immigrants were from Rwanda. By 1990, many estimated that a quarter of the population in central districts in Buganda—such as Luwero, Mityana, Mpigi, and Mukono—was of Banyarwanda origin.

Migrant relations with indigenous Baganda (nationals) went through three different phases in the period between the heyday of migration after the 1920s and the NRA coming to power in 1986. The first phase closed with the anti-chief and anti-landlord peasant uprisings of 1945 and 1949

in Buganda. Even though half of the tenants in many of the central count-
ies of Buganda were immigrants from Rwanda (and Burundi) by the end
of the Second World War,[13] social relations in rural Buganda did not pit
migrants against residents, but landlords against tenants. The central
trend in Buganda of the 1940s was to join all tenants, indigenous or immigrant, into a common anti-landlord movement called the Bataka Movement. The context for the second phase was set by the combination of
colonial repression and counterreform that followed the peasant uprising
after the Second World War. The point of colonial reform was to reinforce
a landlord initiative set up as an "indigenous" electoral coalition in the
name of the king, Kabaka Yekka (the King Only), to participate in the
coming elections. It was a political initiative designed to draw a sharp
political distinction between all those defined as indigenous, and those
not. It was successful in dismantling the coalition between indigenous
Baganda peasants and migrant Banyarwanda tenants and laborers. This
trend was not reversed until the 1980s, when the NRA reconstituted the
alliance of the indigenous and the immigrants, this time against govern-
ment-installed chiefs and not local landlords, ushering a third phase in
relations between migrants and nationals. Although migrants supported
and joined the NRA, few joined the RPF in the October 1990 invasion of
Rwanda.[14] In contrast, refugees formed the backbone of the RPF.

Refugees

The number of Tutsi who fled to Uganda between 1959 and 1964
were estimated at between 50,000 and 70,000. By 1990, they had swollen
to around 200,000, although only about 82,000 had registered with
UNHCR as refugees.[15] The social destiny of refugees turned out to be
markedly different from that of migrants. For unlike migrants who crossed
the border to take up particular jobs, refugees were destined for camps in
which they lived under a commandant, in circumstances that clearly divided them from the host society. Unlike migrants who were mainly Hutu,
refugees were almost all Tutsi. The political division between the Hutu
and the Tutsi inside Rwanda was reproduced outside Rwanda as a social
difference between migrants and refugees. We shall see that the RPF was
a force socially anchored in refugees more than in migrants.

The lot of the Rwandese refugees in Uganda was arguably the worst in
the region. In Tanzania they could take up citizenship relatively easily, and
the government actually demarcated a separate district for them where
they could even have access to land for livelihood. In Zaire, they were

at times offered citizenship, though—as we shall later see—the offer was withdrawn at other times. By contrast, successive Ugandan governments considered even the children of refugees to be refugees. The closest parallel I can think of to their predicament was that of Palestinian refugees in the Middle East: once a refugee, always a refugee. They were the butt of popular prejudice and official discrimination, the readily available explanation for any situation difficult to explain, from poverty to sabotage. Not surprisingly, a refugee self-consciousness developed first and foremost in response to anti-refugee prejudice promoted by the state and shared by many in the society at large. This is also why the mainly Tutsi refugees in Uganda came to think of themselves as Banyarwanda (Rwandese), and not as Tutsi.

The refugees who crossed the border into Uganda between 1959 and 1964 were settled in seven camps established in western Uganda, with an eighth set up only in 1982. In three of the camps, refugees were able to earn a livelihood by grazing herds on land. In the rest, they were forced to become cultivators. As their numbers multiplied, they overflowed camp boundaries. Those who had remained herders were among the first to leave the camps, moving their cattle to adjacent land. Thus, they entered both Lake Mburu National Park and adjacent ranches. Five square miles on the average, each of these ranches had been demarcated and allocated to bureaucrats in the 1960s as part of the USAID and World Bank–financed Ankole-Masaka Ranching Scheme.[16] Both locations would become flashpoints of political conflict in the 1980s and would bring the Banyarwanda refugee question to the forefront of Ugandan politics, forming the immediate backdrop to the RPF invasion of October 1990.

Whereas the downside of a refugee status lay in its precarious political position, its upside was a consequence of UN recognition. Those recognized by the UN as refugees were entitled to UN aid the way the Ugandan poor were not. The eight refugee camps held mainly first-generation refugees. The only young people to be found in the camps were those poorly educated or those who had opted to stay with their parents and help them tend cattle or cultivate gardens. Most of the younger people had taken advantage of UNHCR scholarships, gone to schools and even to universities, and moved out of camps, mostly to towns like Fort Portal, Mbarara, and Kampala in southern Uganda, or to Nairobi in Kenya, or in some cases even to Europe or North America. The fact of a scholarship bounty that locals considered sure evidence of preferential treatment by UN agencies, and the success it facilitated, bred local resentment against successful refugees. The result was that even when successive generations left the camps, went to schools and some to universities, and came to form an elite educated stratum whose members could be found in the professions, business and the civil service, they could not escape being branded and set apart as refugees. Many had to bribe their way into institutions. Others had to hide their identity and pretend to be what they were not: Banyankole, Baganda, Banyoro. Socially, Banyarwanda refugees came to be distinguished from both Ugandan Banyarwanda (the nationals) and migrants by this single fact: many of their children were educated and successful. But even in the moment of their success, they could not escape the social stigma of being refugees.

THE STATE AND THE REFUGEES: THE POLITICS OF INDIGENEITY

It was the political and not the cultural diaspora, the community of refugees and exiles and not that of migrants and residents, that formed the first Banyarwanda organizations in Uganda.[17] The refugee intelligentsia in Uganda set up the first political refugee organization in the region, the Rwandese Alliance for National Unity (RANU) in Kampala in 1980, openly discussing the question of a return of exiles to Rwanda. RANU was primarily an organization of intellectuals, given largely to debate, discussion, and representation. It was similar to a host of organizations set up in the Banyarwanda cultural diaspora, whether in Nairobi or North America. But in the fast developing situation in Uganda—where every minority defined as nonindigenous was fast becoming the target of state hostility and popular suspicion—RANU was soon to come under great stress.

Indigeneity became a central issue in postcolonial Uganda, as it had in Rwanda in 1959. At its heart, the question of indigeneity was a question of entitlement: Who was entitled to justice in the postcolonial period? Who was the postcolonial subject? The mainstream nationalist response to this question was to turn the colonial world upside down, but without fundamentally changing its terms of reference. If the terms of the colonial world set the indigenous apart from the nonindigenous in a racial sense, and then privileged the nonindigenous in a perverse way, the postcolonial response was to stand this world on its head, so as to privilege the indigenous against the nonindigenous. Even if they had run away from Rwanda, the refugees would find that they had not moved out of the postcolonial world where entitlement was tied to indigeneity.

The question of entitlement became acute at times of political crisis. It is during the political crisis of the late 1960s that the Obote I government began to draw a boundary between nationals and immigrants: to target the latter as trespassers so as to encourage the former to act as gatekeepers—and hope to become beneficiaries—in an independent Uganda. The more it faced opposition, the more the ruling party tried to paint the opposition as illegitimate, claiming that many refugees and migrants were entering the political process as nationals. Such was the rationale behind demands for tighter surveillance over refugees and immigrants. A series of measures followed, each designed to achieve precisely these objectives. To ensure the legal basis of all-around control of refugees, the government passed a bill called the Control of Alien Refugees Act. The legislation made the Rwandese a special class of residents subject to arbitrary questioning or even detention.[18] Among the immigrants, the Rwandese were particularly vulnerable. Those who spoke Kinyarwanda could be found in all three categories: refugee, migrant, and national. This meant both that refugees and migrants could pose as nationals, and that nationals could be dismissed as refugees or migrants. When Obote ordered the removal of all un-skilled foreigners from public employment in 1969, thousands of Banyarwanda were among those affected. That same year, the government issued an invidious order: to conduct a census of all ethnic Banyarwanda. Catherine Watson claims that the objective was to exclude "both citizens and refugees from the political process and possibly even (to) expel(ling) them from Uganda."[19] Before the exercise could be completed, however, Obote was overthrown by his army commander, Idi Amin.

Not surprisingly, many Banyarwanda welcomed the overthrow of Obote—as did many members of the other embattled nonindigenous minority in Uganda, the Asians. Amin reciprocated, bringing the deposed Tutsi king, Mwami Kigeri, from Nairobi to Uganda and allocating a house and a car for his use. Many believed that Amin had promised to help reestablish the monarchy in Rwanda and, in that manner, ensure the return of refugees. Not for the first time in the history of an embattled minority, it sought refuge in a close relationship with an isolated power. A number of Banyarwanda refugees joined Amin's army and secret service. Following Amin's overthrow, there were claims that next to the southern Sudanese the Banyarwanda constituted the biggest number of aliens in his security forces, especially in the dreaded intelligence organization, the State Research Bureau.[20]

If several Banyarwanda refugees joined the Amin regime, there were also others, particularly students, who joined the anti-Amin forces. The most prominent of these was Fred Rwigyema, a teenage secondary-school boy recruited by Yoweri Museveni into the Front for National Salvation (FRONASA) in the mid-1970s. In 1990, Rwigyema would lead the RPF invasion of Rwanda. When FRONASA moved into Uganda behind Tanzanian forces in the anti-Amin war of 1979, Museveni began a mass recruitment that included Banyarwanda. In the post-Amin reorganization of the Ugandan state, FRONASA merged with Obote's Kikosi Maalum (KM) to form the Uganda National Liberation Army (UNLA). Following the rigged election of 1980, which paved the way to the Obote II regime, there were defections from the UNLA as the guerrilla war against the Obote II regime gathered momentum. The Obote regime, in turn, baptized the "Museveni soldiers" as "Banyarwanda." The more the repression of the Banyarwanda was stepped up, the more Banyarwanda soldiers joined Museveni and the NRA in the bush. The regime's claim was fast turning into a reality.[21]

From the point of view of the Obote II regime, the Banyarwanda had sinned twice: not only had they joined the repressive apparatus of the discredited Amin regime, they were now providing the backbone of Museveni's guerrillas in the ongoing bush war. This kind of perspective led to a massive state-organized repression of the Banyarwanda refugees in western Uganda. It all began as an exercise by Ugandan authorities in February 1982 to force Tutsi refugees to return to camps they were said to have left during the Amin period. When the attempt was unsuccessful, the ruling party's regional leadership decided to organize what can only be described as a pogrom. The ensuing repression had a paramilitary and populist flavor about it. Organized by leading members in the Obote regime, it was implemented by chiefs in the local authority and paramilitary youth wingers on the ground, with even a unit of the paramilitary Special Forces joining in. Together, they targeted not only Banyarwanda refugees, but all Banyarwanda, whether nationals or refugees, and even some Bahima and Bakiga—in short, any and all who were ethnically identified with the opposition in the western part of the country. Houses claimed as Banyarwanda-occupied were looted and set aflame, or walls were pushed in and corrugated roofs were stolen. Occupants fled with their cattle and what they could carry. Local authorities tried to broaden popular support for the repression by redistributing confiscated land, cattle, and petty property to followers and promising to expand the circle of beneficiaries through further confiscation. The expulsion, Obote claimed in an interview, was in reality an uprising of Ugandans against Rwandans.[22]

Estimates from the period suggest that some 40,000 had crossed into Rwanda, driving some 25,000 cattle ahead of them. Thousands more preferred to cross into Tanzania. When Rwanda closed its border in November of 1982, another 4,000 were said to be trapped on the Ugandan side of the border, while almost 30,000 were under supervision in camps in Uganda.[23] On a conservative estimate, 40,000 heads of cattle and 16,000 homes were destroyed.[24] Rwanda stated that it recognized only 4,000 persons as entitled to Rwandan nationality and would settle them throughout the country. Uganda said it would take back no more than 1,000. This meant that 35,000 continued to languish in border camps, their future uncertain.[25] In time, they divided into two groups: adults fled to camps, as many a youth headed for the growing army of NRA guerrillas in the bush.

In March 1983, Rwanda and Uganda came to an agreement under international pressure. Rwanda agreed to resettle more than 30,000, and Uganda agreed to set up an additional refugee settlement, Kyaka II, to relieve pressure from overcrowding in the old settlements. In addition, Uganda agreed to a joint screening exercise to determine the citizenship of those displaced and to consider compensation to those who had suffered loss.[26] But there was no compensation. The perpetrators of the violence and the beneficiaries of the looting went unpunished. If anything, the arch of violence broadened. In December 1983, local chiefs and (UPC) youth wingers evicted over 19,000 Banyarwanda from Rakai and Masaka districts. With the Rwanda border closed, half fled into Tanzania, and the other half divided, once again the older ones heading for the security of camps, with the younger lured by the promise of guerrilla ranks. About the same time, "a similar but less calculated attack on the Banyarwanda was taking place" in Teso in the east and Lango in the north, grazing areas where Banyarwanda pastoralists had moved, either in search of grass for cattle, or in search of employment more suited to their skills.[27]

In July 1984, Uganda and Tanzania signed an agreement whereby Uganda agreed to take back 10,000 Banyarwanda refugees who had crossed the border a year earlier.[28] In Uganda, however, the repression of refugees and attack on refugee settlements had become part of the official response to the spreading guerrilla war. In January 1985, the army entered Kyaka II settlement. As the harassment spread, the international staff left the camp and many Banyarwanda followed. It is unclear how many of the more than 30,000 that Rwanda had agreed to settle within its borders were actually so settled. For in mid-November 1985, after the Obote II regime was overthrown and the Lutwa regime was still in power, there was a repatriation, whereby 30,000 refugees expelled from Uganda in 1982 were returned, this time to NRA-controlled areas.[29] One more time, the guerrillas harvested youthful recruits from the victimized refugee population. Two months later, when the victorious NRA entered the city of Kampala to take power in January 1986, roughly a quarter of their ranks of 16,000 were composed of Banyarwanda.

THE GUERRILLAS AND AN ALTERNATIVE POLITICS

The counterpoint to the wave of refugee expulsions was the spreading guerrilla war in the Luwero Triangle. The guerrillas faced more than a military challenge. Their real challenge was political: to define an alternative to the politics of indigeneity. The issue was central both because the state claimed that the guerrillas were a nonindigenous force, a mainly Banyarwanda movement, and because of the very heterogeneous social composition of the Luwero Triangle: between a third and a half of the resident population in the Triangle were non-Baganda migrants. The largest group among the migrants were the Banyarwanda. Unlike the Banyarwanda in the refugee settlements, these were not refugees but residents who had immigrated at different times since the 1920s. As the guerrillas constructed an alternative political power in the areas they controlled, they needed to define the new political subject. Who was to be the bearer of rights and the beneficiary of entitlements under the new political arrangement? It was a question that could not be answered without coming to terms with the dominant mode of state politics in postcolonial Uganda: the politics of indigeneity. For, without a more inclusive alternative, the guerrillas would be faced with a population divided between those indigenous and those not.

The answer evolved over a period of time. It was arrived at through trial and error rather than implemented as a blueprint. As they came to grips with a string of concrete dilemmas, guerrilla leaders evolved an alternative. In contrast to the dominant mode of state politics which drew the line between those indigenous and those not, the NRA's politics turned on the distinction between residents and nonresidents. Whereas the state used descent as the litmus test for defining the political subject, the test for the NRA was that of residence. The effect was to distinguish the political community from the cultural community and the future from the past, no matter what the overlap. If a cultural community was an outcome of historical processes, the political community was defined more with an eye on the future. From this point of view, the members of the political community were not necessarily those who shared a common history, whether defined by biological descent or a common culture. They were, rather, those who labored in the same community and intended to live together under a common political roof, and thus to forge a common future. The question of difference in their circumstances of origin was relegated to a secondary status.

The alternative was never theorized in the course of the guerrilla war, and was only partially theorized by the National Commission of Inquiry into Local Government, set up by the NRA after it came to power in 1986.[30] But the question first arose in the course of establishing organs of local power in areas captured by the guerrillas. Called Resistance Committees, this institutional form really set apart the political community the guerrillas set out to build from the inheritance they intended to set aside. The establishment of the Resistance Committee was key to the reform of chiefship, the institution that symbolized unaccountable power, fused into a single fist by twentieth century indirect-rule colonialism and reproduced by the post-colonial state as "customary" and "traditional." The thrust of the NRA reform was not to replace the agent of power but to reform power itself. It was not to replace one chief by another but to open the fist and to distinguish between different moments of power— the legislative, the executive, the judicial, the administrative—so as to assign each to a different authority. In this arrangement, the Resistance Council, the council of all adults sitting together in an assembly, was to be the holder of legislative power. The question then arose: Who was entitled to sit in the council, to deliberate in it, to vote in it, and to be elected to its executive organ, the Resistance Committee? Any resident adult? Or only the indigenous Baganda?

The truly radical side of the NRA's response was to sublate this colonial inheritance by altering the line that distinguished the political subject from the nonsubject. In doing so, it distinguished politics from culture, and future from history, but without delinking the two. Without ignoring history, it refused to become a prisoner of history. Key to this enterprise to tap the creative potential of politics was the endeavor to redefine the political subject and the political community. By redefining the political subject as the resident, and by considering the historical fact of migration as politically superfluous, the reform moved away from the inherited world of the settler and the native in one single stroke. Yet, the reform was both partial and tentative. The decision to define rights on the basis of residence, and not ancestry, held at the lower levels, being the first two levels of village organization (Resistance Committees 1 and 2), as it did at the highest levels, that of the guerrilla leadership. But it did not hold at the middle level—the level of the district. There, the practice was to invest leadership in only those with an ancestral claim to the land. It was a temporary compromise, an unstable one, sure to be challenged whatever the bigger outcome, defeat or victory. The reform held for the duration of the guerrilla war, but not much longer.

RETURN TO INDIGENEITY

The end of the guerrilla war was not an end to the struggle for power. Mindful that its organization was limited to less than half the country, the NRA gave priority to coalition building after victory; it termed this the creation of a "broad base." Seeking to continue the struggle by other means, the opposition looked to identify the point at which the NRA would be most vulnerable to pressure. The issue it chose was that of entitlement. In demanding that indigenous Ugandans receive priority in the new political order, the opposition brought maximum pressure on the heterogeneity of the NRA, both at the leadership level and at the base. As individuals and factions within the leadership vied against one another for promotions, tensions multiplied at the top. At the same time, social struggles generated tensions at the popular level. The key struggle in this context was that between ranchers and squatters in the southwest of the country. Its larger significance flowed from the fact that while ranchers had been closely identified with every previous regime in the history of the country, squatters had been the source of many a recruit into the ranks of the guerrillas. Those threatened with the possibility of being left out in the cold when it came to jostling for positions and resources highlighted the distinguishing feature of many a squatter recruit into the ranks of the guerrillas: they were Banyarwanda, not indigenous.

Tensions within the NRA

From the very outset, the presence of Rwandese in the guerrilla war was important. Two of the twenty-seven persons who were said to have begun the guerrilla war with the ambush at Kabamba in 1981 were Banyarwanda: Fred Rwigyema and Paul Kagame. They had grown up together in the Kahunge refugee camp in western Uganda, meeting in 1963 and separating in 1972 when they joined different high schools.[31] Both had been active in RANU. When the NRA entered Kampala in 1986, Rwig-

yema was its deputy commander. In 1987, he was appointed deputy minister of defense in Kampala. Paul Kagame became the acting chief of military
intelligence of the NRA. Besides Rwigyema and Kagame, there were others, lesser known but still highly placed. Peter Baingana was head of NRA
medical services. Chris Bunyenyezi was commander of the 306th Brigade.
All in all, six senior officers were part of the senior command of RPF when
it crossed into Rwanda: Lieutenant Colonel Wasswa, and Majors Kagame,
Baingana, Kaka, Bunyenyezi, and Nduguta.[32] And they were just the tip
of the iceberg.

Had they joined the guerrilla struggle in Luwero, as some argue, to
gather skills and weapons, and build an organization, so they could move
to Kigali at the first available opportunity?[33] Or was the move to Kigali a
result of developments that took place after the NRA assumed power in
Kampala, developments that would bring home to refugees a bitter truth:
that in Africa today, once a refugee, always a refugee? To accept the first
proposition is tantamount to assuming that there was a conspiracy to invade Kigali and take power, one that simply took time and effort to hatch.
That would be to ignore the real debate that unfolded within the ranks
of the refugees from the time they joined the NRA. No doubt refugee
ranks included some who were convinced from the outset that there was
no alternative but to return. Just as surely, these ranks could not have
grown without others who had earlier championed naturalization in
Uganda and in the countries of the larger region as the more viable alternative, and later changed their minds.

Initially, the NRA victory strengthened both tendencies. The electric
example of a home-grown guerrilla movement that had defeated an internationally recognized government without substantial external support
was not lost on RPF leaders. As one of them put it, "If the NRM could
liberate Uganda, the RPF began to ask why it could not do the same in
Rwanda."[34] At the same time, precisely because Banyarwanda refugees had
played a vital role in the struggle, there was a radical and sympathetic shift
in the official Ugandan position on naturalizing Banyarwanda refugees.
All along, the Uganda government had insisted on very strict proof of
descent as grounds for citizenship. In the Gabiro Accords of October 1982
with Rwanda, for example, Uganda authorities had insisted that no one
could acquire citizenship without proof that the individual's father,
grandfather, and great-grandfather were born in Uganda.[35] In July 1986,
just six months after coming to power, President Museveni reversed policy
radically: he announced that Banyarwanda who had been resident in

Uganda for more than ten years would automatically be entitled to Uganda citizenship.[36] This meant that all the 1959 refugees would become Uganda citizens. In Rwanda, too, confident that the tide was turning irrevocably in favor of erstwhile refugees being granted citizenship in Uganda, the government was adopting a softer line on the return of Tutsi refugees: it agreed that individual refugees with resources to be self-supporting could return. If one is to go by the resolutions of the conference of Rwandese exiles that met in Washington, D.C., in 1988, the thrust of refugee opinion was also clearly in favor of naturalization in the country of their residence.[37] In another few years, however, the balance of opinion would tilt decisively in the reverse direction. A senior RPA commander put it to me in Kigali in 1995: "You stake your life and at the end of the day you recognize that no amount of contribution can make you what you are not. You can't buy it, not even with blood." What had happened to leave such a bitter aftertaste?

Once guerrillas returned to society from the bush, they returned to a world of citizens and refugees, a world they thought they had forever left behind. Those who had lost the armed struggle, and thus power in the central state, lost no time in applying pressure on what they saw as an unholy power-hungry coalition of indigenous and nonindigenous factions. With hardly any delay, there were further expulsions of Banyarwanda. Though each was the result of a fresh local initiative, it is hard not to conclude that these did not involve some level of central coordination. The most notable of these was the forced eviction of Banyarwanda cattle keepers from Teso in 1986. Yet, the presence of Banyarwanda in the military leadership seemed to be increasing, rather than decreasing, in the first years of NRA rule. In the context of a simmering civil war in the north, their role in the NRA became even more important strategically. While the ratio of Banyarwanda in the army declined sharply—from 3,000 out of 14,000 in 1986 to roughly 4,000 out of a reported 80,000 to a 100,000 in 1989[38]—Banyarwanda veterans formed a rapidly expanding core in the officer corps. The reason for this was simple: a disproportionate number of Banyarwanda had joined the struggle early on and thus had a greater battle experience than most others. The more fighting experience they gathered, the greater were the chances of their being commissioned. The opposition press began to scan the ranks of the NRA for evidence of officers who were Banyarwanda. The issue became politically charged in 1989 when two Banyarwanda officers, Majors Chris Bunyenyezi and Stephen Nduguta, were accused of having committed gross human rights violations during antiguerrilla operations in Teso. More than any other, one fact highlighted the centrality of Banyarwanda refugees in the leadership of the NRA: a Munyarwanda refugee, Major-General Fred Rwigyema, now occupied the position of deputy army commander-in-chief and deputy minister of defense.[39] The only person senior to him in the military hierarchy was the president and minister of defense, Yoweri Museveni.

Soon, when it came to promotions, especially where a Munyarwanda was concerned, descent began to count more than anything else. The NRA tradition of giving preference to residence became distant memory. To Banyarwanda officers and men and women in the NRA, the period after 1986 seemed a betrayal by their former comrades-in-arms. One of the founders of RANU recalled the shifting mood: "The NRA experience was a catalyst in mobilizing the Banyarwanda in NRA. As far as 1983, our position was that people should join the struggle in Uganda voluntarily. It was worthwhile. It was not a deliberate effort to organize an army inside an army. The discrimination and harassment puzzled them, made them look for alternatives. They turned to senior RANU members, like Baingana. The discrimination did mobilize quite a few for us."[40]

The RPF was born of this predicament in 1987.[41] Faced with repression under Obote II, the old RANU had migrated to Nairobi in 1981. Once the NRA took power in Kampala in 1986, the Ugandan capital became the focal point of the political diaspora. RANU held its seventh congress in Kampala in December 1987 and rechristened itself the Rwanda Patriotic Front (RPF). Even though it had a Hutu as its head—ironically, just as had the monarchist UNAR in 1959 and as if to symbolize the nominal character of his presidency—the leadership of the RPF was predominantly Tutsi. More than that, it was predominantly from the "Ugandan" Tutsi, particularly from those who had been part of the NRA. The RPF crystallized two points of consensus: that the leadership of the refugee struggle would come from Banyarwanda in the NRA, and that the return home could only be armed. Unlike the left-leaning ideological tendency that had been RANU, RPF was to be a broad front. Though socially anchored in the broader refugee population and driven by an activist impulse, there was still no agreement within RPF on the future of the refugees—return or naturalization. The issue was at the center of discussions in the 1988 conference of the Banyarwanda political diaspora in Washington, D.C. The outcome of that conference showed that the weight of the opinion in the exile community was still on the side of naturalization in the countries of their residence for those who so wished, and return through peaceful negotiations for the others.

Then came the 1990 debate on ranches. Conducted during a three-day special session of parliament and chaired by none other than President Museveni, the debate followed a squatter uprising in southwestern Uganda. Its consequence, though, went beyond the conflict between squatters and ranch lords to once again placing the question of indigeneity center stage in the politics of Uganda.

The Trigger: Ranchers versus Squatters

The month-long squatter uprising of August to September 1990 took place in Mawogola County in Sembabule subdistrict, Masaka district, in southern Uganda. Classified as public land and grazed by pastoralists through the colonial period, these grasslands were divided and distributed to prospective ranchers by postindependence governments.[42]

The beneficiaries of the process included not only entrepreneurs, but also a combination of businessmen and bureaucrats, politicians and military men. Thus came into being a class that the 1988 Commission of Inquiry into Government Ranching Schemes referred to as "telephone ranchers." The Mawogola ranches had all been allocated in the latter phase when allocation had turned into lucrative political patronage.[43] An anomaly in the arrangement was that while cultivators on the land were guaranteed compensation, pastoralists were not pledged similar treatment since they were not deemed to own property that justified compensation. Deemed squatters, the pastoralists were a mixed lot who had been drawn to these grasslands at different historical periods and in different circumstances. Three different groups traced their arrival in the county to three different periods: the 1920s, 1979–80, and 1983–84. The first were the Bahima settlers who had come to the area as early as the 1920s. Then came migrants who had been displaced from areas bordering northern Tanzania during the 1979 anti-Amin war. Finally, there were mainly Banyarwanda cattle keepers, evicted from their homes and pastures around Lake Mburo in 1982–83, accused of being active supporters of guerrillas.[44] Of the estimated 200,000 squatters, refugees were said to constitute around 80,000.[45]

The combination of absentee proprietors and propertyless squatters made for a flourishing of rental relations. The more squatters moved to idle ranch land to graze their cattle, the more ranchers were able to press home the legal fact of ownership and increase rent. As ranchers upped their demand, rent went from one cow per year to one for every fifty grazed, in addition to labor for digging dams, constructing dips, or clearing thick bush. Rents generally doubled between 1980 and 1984. When a serious drought hit Masaka District in the mid-1980s, a new exploitative relationship—water lordism—was added to this suffocating land lordism: ranchers began to demand rent for water, not just pastures. It was this latter development that broke the proverbial back of the pastoral camel.[46]

Squatters, whether Ugandan or Rwandese, had been an important source of guerrilla recruits for the NRA. When the NRA came to power in January 1986, some of these recruits retired and returned to the pastoral community, bringing to it a capacity to organize, a familiarity with arms, and a sense of self-assertiveness. Others remained within guerrilla ranks, constituting important allies of squatters. That the squatters constituted an important social base for the NRA was clear from one single fact: one of the ten points in the National Resistance Movement (NRM) program explicitly referred to the need to settle displaced peoples. Within the first year of assuming power, the NRA government abolished rent in all ranches, without being specific about the distinction between pasture and water rent. Acknowledging the right of the state to regulate the use of pastures since it was the owner of land, ranchers argued they had the right to charge for water from the dams they had built in the first place. Thus, ranchers suspended pasture rent and hiked up water rent.

In response, the government appointed a commission that recommended that over a quarter (57) of ranches be repossessed by government and reallocated to squatters, and that close to another quarter (50) be repossessed if they fail "to demonstrate (their) ability to develop" in a year.[47] The commission's recommendations were publicly seen as no less than a government-inspired agenda to dispossess swiftly half of the rancher class and empower squatters. Not surprisingly, these recommendations turned out to be a curtain raiser for a fuller conflict between ranchers and squatters, into which were drawn both the political and military leadership of the state. The expectation that they were about to be allocated land precipitated an influx of squatters from neighboring districts, from as far as the Tanzanian border to Masaka, concentrating numbers in the area.[48] In response, the Masaka-based ranchers—being those under the most severe pressure—organized as the Masaka Livestock Farmers Association (MALIFA). They wondered why nineteen ranches were to be repossessed from Masaka but only three from Ankole. The implication was clear: Ankole ranchers must have been protected since they belonged to the president's ethnic group. The wider implication was that the real shift in entitlement under the new order was not from those indigenous to all residents but to the president's ethnic group and their Banyarwanda cousins across the border. MALIFA declared that it considered the government's decision "null and void" and threatened to take the government to court, which precipitated a meeting of the National Executive Council of Parliament. The result was a government declaration upholding the policy to distribute ranch land to squatters.[49] The Mawogola uprising broke out in less than two weeks.

Pushed in a corner, ranchers armed themselves, some bringing armed security guards into ranches. Before government could act to repossess and subdivide ranches among squatters, ranchers began a campaign of terror to get rid of squatters. The state response was immediate and united. Speaking in parliament, President Museveni condemned the killing of squatters as the work of organized terrorists who intended to precipitate a stampede from the county. An army representative alleged that leaflets warning squatters that the area was to become a war zone had been dropped for precisely this purpose. To guarantee their safety and convince the squatters to stay, government deployed a battalion in Mawogola County. The army forbade Resistance Councils, police, and the judiciary—all seen as heavily disposed in favor of ranchers—from intervening in the conflict.[50]

With local organs of the state neutralized, and with an entire battalion deployed in the county to keep ranchers in check, squatters counterattacked. Armed with guns, spears, and machetes, they stormed a number of ranches and seized them by force.[51] The attacks did not simply target individual ranches, but showed a higher degree of coordination and organization: squatters mounted roadblocks closing off all routes by which ranchers could summon armed reinforcement. "The degree of determination, organisation and consistency exhibited by the squatters," wrote Expedit Ddungu after talking to residents in the area, "created much speculation among people in the area that the uprising had been planned well in advance."[52]

The more ranchers were pushed in a corner in the physical confrontation in Mawogola, the more they went on a political offensive. Critics claimed that squatter violence was instigated, and that "instigators" came from the NRA.[53] They accused the government of a double favoritism, siding with both those belonging to the president's ethnicity and their nonindigenous cousins from across the border, the Banyarwanda.[54] In response, those favoring a pro-squatter legislation claimed that the tension in Parliament reflected "nothing but a class struggle," and that the government's proposal was an attempt to rectify a historically perpetrated "social injustice."[55]

Ranchers claimed that governmental power—particularly military power—was bent on favoring nonindigenous Banyarwanda squatters. When an influential group in Parliament echoed the view, it made for the most heated moments of the parliamentary debate. The pro-rancher lobby in Parliament was joined by others determined that the nonindigenous be excluded from entitlement in the new era. Together, they concentrated their fire on Banyarwanda refugees as the core beneficiaries of ranch restructuring. Calling on the House to condemn "destructive or barbarous acts that took place in Mawogola county," the women's representative for Mbarara, Miria Matembe, claimed: "I have been talking to people, they are saying, Mr. Chairman, that these acts were committed by the NRM at the order of officers in this government and, Mr. Chairman, that your government is using this opportunity to bring in foreigners, pushing people in their land." And then she added: "Rumors are saying that your Minister seated there, is behind the whole thing. And they are saying that this is an attempt to bring in foreigners, and you know, Mr. Chairman, the question of citizenship is a crucial matter in this country." Muruli Mukasa, the representative for Nakasongola County in Luwero District, in the heartland of the Luwero Triangle where the NRA had fought the guerrilla war, wanted to know who would be the beneficiaries of ranch restructuring, the Rwandese or the Baruli of Nakasongola: "Mr. Chairman, the issue of citizenship has been highlighted. It has been really a very crucial one particularly in Nakasongola because most of the squatters there, at least, their citizenship is a bit ambiguous. Most of them happen to be from Rwanda and Burundi! So, people are saying okay, if there is this restructuring, it is fine but who are going to be the immediate beneficiaries; the Rwandese and Barundi!" The minister talked of "strong rumors," mainly in Kyaka County, in Kabarole District—based on observations that "numbers within the refugee settlement have reduced from 30,000 to less than 10,000 now"—"that some refugees were undergoing military training." The member for Mawogola County, Mr. Kasiaja, also alleged that squatters in Mawogola were being trained militarily.[56] Later, many an observer would wonder whether these may indeed have been part of RPF ranks that crossed the border on 1 October 1990.

There had been wild allegations outside Parliament, repeated by some within, alleging that the purpose of the newly begun daily bus service from Kigali to Kampala was really to bring Rwandese to live in settlements in Uganda, something the minister of state for defense was compelled to deny in Parliament.[57] Toward the end of the debate, Miria Matembe returned to press home the key point: "Mr. Chairman, we are not complaining of Ugandans to be given land; we are complaining of non-Ugandans—Banyarwanda—those who came as refugees to own land in this country. This is what we are concerned with."[58] She was joined by several others.[59]

Museveni dismissed these allegations as the work of "opportunists," those "always around," always "looking for unprincipled ways of gaining the support." At the same time, he acknowledged that "they are heavily represented in all leadership of Uganda."[60] Though the government denied every charge that it was being partial to nonindigenous Banyarwanda, the opposition had clearly succeeded in placing not only the question of ethnicity, but particularly that of indigeneity, at the center of the political debate. In the process, it had also managed to erode the political cohesion of the government. The clearest evidence of this was that the special three-day parliamentary session convened to discuss the question of the ranches turned into the most heated debate since the NRM had assumed power, pitting the president against his own minister of state for defense. David Tinyefuza, the minister of state for defense, supported squatter action unequivocally and consistently. "There was bound to be an explosion," he argued. "These fellows can organise themselves. They are now more organised because with the fundamental changes in Uganda, the squatter is also the squatter of new mentality. The squatter is no longer the old squatter. He is a new squatter, enlightened, a bit more powerful even because now he has a representation even here which he never had. He is a bit more powerful; a bit armed here and there. (*Laughter*) He is a different squatter. So, this is the crux of the matter."[61]

In a change of tack and direction, President Museveni pinned individual responsibility on his minister of state for defense: "I can give you information because I am also the Minister for Defence and I hold a number of other hats. What the rumours are saying is that Tinyefuza who comes from that area is the one who has been instigating these people. . . . But Tinyefuza I have heard, because there were three boys whom he put there, I have their names, they are army officers and I heard that they were involved in instigating squatters—these boys, the army officers, I ordered that they must leave that area when I heard about it."[62] In recognition of squatter links with many in the army, the battalion was withdrawn and all armed personnel forbidden from staying at the ranches. President Museveni confronted his defense minister: "Would you like to tell the House whether you were inciting the people to fight one another or what?" And then, in an obvious attempt to belittle Major-General Tinyefuza's involvement as that of an individual and distinguish it from that of the state: "But Tinyefuza is not even a military authority in the area. Who made him a military authority there? I am not aware. All I am aware is that Tinyefuza is a Minister here in Kampala and he lives in that area. But in terms of command, he is not in charge of the area. So, how would he be a military authority?"[63] The opposition claims that government policy on ranches had been turned into an instrument of refugee Banyarwanda interests—backed up by governmental, and particularly military, power— seemed to have succeeded in driving a wedge between the political and military leaderships.

Museveni dismissed those who had raised the Banyarwanda issue as "opportunists," but the concessions he made on ranch restructuring had a lasting—and negative—impact on the question of citizenship. In repudiating the political legacy of the guerrilla war, it confirmed the colonial inheritance, yet again. Opening the second day of debate with the observation that while the country had dealt with the citizenship status of resident "Europeans," he insisted that the question of citizenship "is not yet resolved, especially in relation to the Africans who came from neighbouring territories."[64] Though he began the day on a Pan-Africanist note, drawing a basic distinction between two kinds of foreigners[65]—those from outside Africa and those from within—he ended the day confirming the colonial legacy: redrawing the line between Ugandans and foreigners, not simply all foreigners, but particularly foreigners from neighboring areas— nonindigenous Africans. The real outcome of the debate was to strengthen the link between citizenship and indigeneity, and specifically once again to brand the Rwandese as non-Ugandan. Not only the original refugees, but also their offspring were now distinguished from the Ugandan Banyarwanda as nonindigenous.[66] The president took the lead, even against the advice of his attorney general. When a member moved a clause—that "only Ugandan citizens shall be beneficiaries of these ranching schemes"—the attorney general objected that the clause would violate the spirit of Pan-Africanism.[67] But President Museveni disagreed. The clarification, he said, was necessary not only "to undermine this campaign which has been going on but also to make a new beginning." He insisted on a new beginning: "This is our first opportunity—we have never had any opportunity to say anything on this land. In 1900 it was the British and some chiefs; then later on it was all sorts of corrupt people. Now that we have got a chance to say something, why not to say it? . . . (*Applause*)."[68] When another member asked what would happen to Ugandan squatters in the refugee settlements, President Museveni declared that he "would be in favour of the Ugandan cattle squatters in the settlement camps of the refugees be removed to come to these ranches—these lands" and further, that "the Banyarwanda who may be in the ranches be removed to the settlements." That would leave only one question unresolved, added the president: "What do you do with the Banyarwanda who acquired properties outside the ranching scheme?" With no doubt in anyone's mind that the government intended to turn its back on the legacy of the guerrilla war and that entitlements would yet again be linked to descent, the attorney general obliged and moved Clause 8, which he had just opposed: "Mr. Chairman, Clause 8, I beg to move that it reads as follows: 'That only Ugandan citizens shall qualify to benefit from the restructured ranch schemes.' "[69] For the Banyarwanda refugees, the die had been cast.

The debate triggered by the squatter uprising refueled the demand that the nonindigenous—particularly the Banyarwanda—be excluded from citizen entitlement in the postguerrilla political order. An earlier parliamentary decision had called for noncitizens to be identified and dismissed from the army. The shifting fortunes of Banyarwanda in the NRA were reflected in shifts in the fortune of the most respected of their members, Major General Fred Rwigyema. In the very first year of NRM power, he had been transferred from the powerful position of deputy commander of the army to the more ceremonial position of deputy minister of defense. In 1988, he was removed from even this ceremonial position by order of the president as chairman of the High Command.[70] It was a decision that would have far-reaching consequences. With every passing year, the search for noncitizens in the army moved from the rank to the file, from the pinnacles of power to those below, literally turning into a witch-hunt, and was extended to other organs of the state. The consequence of the squatter uprising of August 1990 was to brand Banyarwanda cattle-herders as refugees, not citizens. For a brief period, this episode underlined the common predicament of two otherwise distinct refugee groups: the refugee guerrilla leadership which was being hounded out of the new state, and the refugee squatters who were ruled out as possible beneficiaries in the redistribution of ranching land possessed by the state.[71] The immediate consequence of the squatter uprising was to swing the balance of opinion, among both refugee commoners and refugee leaders, decisively against naturalization in the countries of their residence and tilt it in favor of an armed return to Rwanda.

That armed return was the RPF invasion of October 1990. When he wrote to *Human Rights Watch* to explain the dynamic that led to the invasion, Uganda's new ambassador to the United States, Katenta-Apuli, pinpointed "two fundamental decisions" as relevant: the prohibition against nonindigenous Banyarwanda owning land or holding state positions. "It is believed," he concluded, "that the combination of these two fundamental decisions convinced Rwandese refugees that they did not have a bright future in Uganda and precipitated (both) the mass desertion from the NRA" and the decision to "invade Rwanda to regain their rights in their country of origin."[72] The logic behind the invasion was reinforced by the Uganda government, which declared on the day of the invasion that all Rwandese who had left the NRA to attack Rwanda would be considered deserters under the army's Operational Code of Conduct. "That means," the ambassador clarified, "on conviction by a court martial, they would be punishable by death. This is no incentive for them to cross back into Uganda."

To most Ugandans, the ambassador's claim would seem incredible in retrospect. After all, many in the RPF, particularly in the leadership, did cross back into Uganda at several points during the war, and the RPF enjoyed active support from the Ugandan state. After all, the Banyarwanda in the RPF were no strangers to Ugandan society or the Ugandan state. Some observers even thought of the Rwanda Patriotic Army (RPA) as functioning like an army within an army and the RPF like a state within the state. This point of view stressed that the RPA had already been organized inside the NRA as a separate command answerable to Rwigyema.[73] It is this command structure that was said to have been activated at the time of the invasion, as part of the foreign-funded demobilization exercise within the NRA. The London-based *Economist Intelligence Review* quoted a British East Africa expert: "They demobilized by crossing the border in completely equipped units, taking their insignia off their shoulders as they crossed."[74] Years later, President Museveni told his fellow regional heads of state meeting in Harare that, while the Banyarwanda in the NRA had informed him in advance "of their intention to organise to regain their rights in Rwanda," they had launched the invasion "without prior consultation." Significantly, he continued, even though "faced with [a] *fait accompali* situation by our Rwandan brothers," Uganda decided "to help the Rwandese Patriotic Front (RPF), materially, so that they are not defeated because that would have been detrimental to the Tutsi people of Rwanda and would not have been good for Uganda's stability."[75] It was as candid an admission of complicity as any head of state could have made.

But a qualification needs to be added to this admission: the precondition for official Ugandan support was that there be no return. RPA officers may cross into Uganda as into a rear base, as many times as necessary, but there would be no return to Uganda, no possibility that any of them could define Uganda as home. When the RPF crossed the Uganda-Rwanda border in October 1990, this did not only constitute an armed invasion of Rwanda; it was also an armed repatriation of refugees from Uganda. The condition for Ugandan support, the bottom line, was that the RPF continue to push into Rwanda. The refugee soldiers who formed the core of the RPF—who had been nearly 4,000 of the roughly 14,000 NRA who took Kampala in 1986 and were probably another thousand-plus in 1990—found themselves between the Rwandan devil and the Ugandan deep blue sea. True, the raw material for the refugee crisis that led to the 1990 invasion was the outcome of post-1959 developments in Rwanda, but the crisis itself was very much Ugandan in the making. The dynamic that led to the 1990 invasion was born of the first crisis of the NRA in power. It was a crisis that split its guerrilla leadership and cadre along lines of indigeneity. But it was also a crisis that the NRA leadership, both those who stayed within Uganda and those who crossed the border into Rwanda with the RPF, tried to turn into an opportunity. It was a gamble whose cost would be difficult to tell, even with hindsight.

Chapter Seven

The Civil War and the Genocide

I<small>F</small> R<small>WANDA</small> was the genocide that happened, then South Africa was the genocide that didn't. The contrast was marked by two defining events in the first half of 1994: just as a tidal wave of genocidal violence engulfed Rwanda, South Africa held elections marking the transition to a postapartheid era. More than any other, these twin developments marked the end of innocence for the African intelligentsia. For if some seer had told us in the late 1980s that there would be a genocide in one of these two places, I wonder how many among us would have managed to identify correctly its location. Yet, this failure would also be testimony to the creative—and not just the destructive—side of politics.

To historicize the Rwandan genocide from this vantage point is to begin by identifying key differences between South Africa and Rwanda. From the standpoint of post-1994 Africa, I find one difference telling: if South Africa has millions of beneficiaries and few perpetrators, Rwanda has perpetrators at least in the hundreds of thousands and few beneficiaries. The difference highlights a salient political fact: that the genocide was carried out by subaltern masses, even if organized by state functionaries. I will reflect on this morally troublesome fact in this chapter, and return to think through its significance for postgenocide Rwanda in the conclusion.

T<small>HE</small> C<small>IVIL</small> W<small>AR</small>

The civil war profoundly changed all those who took part in it. The Rwanda Patriotic Front (RPF) went into it as an army of liberation and came out of it as an army of occupation. The Habyarimana regime entered the war pledged to a policy of ethnic reconciliation and came out of it pledged to uphold Hutu Power. From a marginal tendency in the constellation of forces supporting the regime in 1990, the war turned Hutu Power into a central tendency in Hutu politics. With defeat looming on the horizon, the Hutu Power tendency differentiated even further: the genocidal tendency was born of the crisis of Hutu Power.

RPF: From Liberation to Occupation
and Displacement

The trained military cadre of the RPF numbered some 4,000 Banyarwanda who left the National Resistance Army (NRA) barracks in absolute
secrecy in the dark of the night of 30 September 1990, a week before
Uganda's day of independence, 8 October. The initial RPF attack occurred
on 1 October 1990. By any reckoning, it was a failure. From day one,
disagreement over methods and tactics led to infighting among guerrilla
leaders. First, the legendary hero of the NRA guerrilla struggle, Fred Rwigyema, and then Baingana, died in the space of but a few weeks. Once it
recovered from the shock of the initial attack, the Rwandan army was able
to repulse the invasion—with support from French, Belgian, and Zairean
troops. While guerrilla ranks were in great disorder, the RPF attack allowed the Habyarimana regime to put on the mantle of the defender of
the nation in the face of a Tutsi threat. Its legitimacy rose overnight in
ordinary Hutu eyes. This fact, however, had yet to register with the combatants of the RPF.

By the end of November 1990, many RPF soldiers had been killed and
thousands were scattered by the counterassault of the Rwandan army.
About this time, Major Paul Kagame interrupted his military training
course in the United States and took charge of the RPF. Pulling together
some 2,000 men, he withdrew into the cold but heavily forested Virunga
mountains in northwest Rwanda, along the Uganda border. By the middle
of 1991, he had reportedly rebuilt the RPF to a 15,000-strong force. By
the end of the year, the RPF had taken control of a strip of territory along
the Uganda border stretching some 32 kilometers into Rwanda.[1]

It is often said that political movements are shaped more by adversity—
such as Mao's Long March—from which they draw their vital lessons,
than by the dulling effect of success. The political education of the RPF,
however, took place in the context of military victories, not losses. From
the end of 1991, the RPF entered a period in which every military victory
brought home the same bitter lesson about the political realities of
Rwanda. The RPF consistently failed to translate military victory on the
field into political gains within the population. The reason was simple.
Every time the RPF captured a new area and established military control,
the population fled. "Contrary to the expectations of the RPF," wrote
Gérard Prunier in an account otherwise highly sympathetic to the RPF,
"local Hutu peasants showed no enthusiasm for being 'liberated' by
them—they had run away from the area of guerrilla operations."[2] With

every RPF advance, the numbers of the displaced multiplied. From an estimated 80,000 in late 1990 to 350,000 following the Byumba offensive in 1992, the numbers of the displaced swelled to roughly 950,000 after the February 1993 offensive, when the RPF doubled the size of territory under its control.[3] At the peak of the war, when the rebels entered Gitarama in June 1994, the town emptied, as if on cue.

A number of journalists visited RPF-controlled areas in 1992 and 1993. All agree on one thing: that desolate calm prevailed in areas held by the RPF. Interestingly, all of them try to picture this lifeless calm with the same adjective: *eerie*. Writing towards the end of 1992 of the "immense suffering" unleashed by the war in government-controlled Rwanda, Kampala-based journalist Catherine Watson concluded with an observation on the guerrilla-held part of the country: "In contrast, the area under the RPF is eerily calm. One of the most densely populated regions of Africa in peacetime, it now holds a mere 2,600 civilians grouped by the RPF into two 'safe' villages."[4] Visiting after the February 1993 battles, Gérard Prunier also found these places "eerily empty of life." "RPF soldiers had not looted anything and houses could be seen with chairs still set around a table and mouldy food on the plates where people had fled so hurriedly as not to eat their last meal. The RPF admitted that only 1,800 Hutu peasants were left in an area which had had a population of about 800,000 before the war."[5] Roughly at that time, the veteran Ugandan journalist Charles Onyango-Obbo used almost the same words to picture the overall ambiance in guerrilla-held areas: "In RPF-controlled areas of Rwanda, there is an eerie calm." He then gave an additional reason for the exodus of Hutu peasants: "The rebels have asked all civilians to leave, because they don't want the responsibility of caring for them and fear infiltrators. Privately, some officers say they hope that as the number of displaced people swells, pressure will grow on Habyarimana to reach a settlement in the war."[6]

There is no contradiction between some journalist reports that peasants fled as the RPF approached, and other reports, like that of Onyango-Obbo, that the RPF asked peasants to leave. Both are true: peasants left RPF areas both because of their own volition and in response to administrative encouragement from above. Peasant attitudes shifted dramatically with the civil war, for the civil war seemed to have brought to life memories long since buried under the weight of day-to-day concerns. We can get an idea of this from an account by Catharine Newbury and David Newbury. Recalling their search in the late 1980s, they write of "the extraordinary degree to which the Revolution of a generation before seemed

almost to have been removed from the collective historical consciousness." They then follow with an account of conversations with refugees
in camps in Tanzania in July and August of 1994: "But in 1994, time and
again conversation in the refugee camps returned to focus intensely on
the monarchical regime before Independence and the 1959 Revolution.
The RPF was seen by many as the reincarnation of the pre-Revolutionary
power structure."[7] Memories that would have seemed esoteric in the heyday of the second postrevolutionary republic, fitting material for intellectual reflection but no guide for day-to-day endeavors, came alive as the
civil war progressed.

The RPF, too, changed. From recognizing that peasants distrusted
them to a distrust of peasants, a sort of mutual distrust, was but a short
step. For those in the RPF leadership convinced that peasants were anyway
"backward" and "ignorant"—as reported by many a journalist who interviewed leaders in the RPF—this was an easy step to take.[8] From the initial
expectation of a relationship of political tutelage that was meant to translate shared interests into shared perspectives, RPF cadres had to come to
grips with a relationship in which the role of coercion seemed to increase
in direct proportion to military success. Looking back at the record,
Human Rights Watch reported that the RPF had "forcibly moved hundreds, perhaps thousands, of people from Rwanda into Uganda in order
to create free-fire zones." It had also "pillaged and destroyed their property." And finally, it had "recruited boys and men against their will to
serve the RPF as porters and cattle herders." "This abuse," the report
added, "began with the RPF invasion in October 1990. Although it continued on a lesser scale throughout the war, the abuse increased sharply
again with the RPF offensive in February 1993."[9]

If RPF's expectations were based on what the NRA accomplished in the
Luwero Triangle in 1981–85, the reality of the guerrilla struggle in
Rwanda turned out to be dramatically different from that in Uganda. In
sharp contrast to the NRA experience, there were in Rwanda no liberated
zones where alternate modes of governance were introduced under the
benevolent eye of a new administration. There were no Resistance Councils and Committees as in the Luwero Triangle, no effort to reach out to
mobilize peasants politically, so as to transform them into a human resource for the struggle. There was not even an effort to establish administrative structures in the areas over which the RPF had military control.[10]
If anything, there was—unlike in most previous cases—a distrust of the
peasantry, for the peasants were predominantly Hutu and they showed no

enthusiasm at being "liberated."[11] "The RPF's unconventional guerrilla strategy," writes William Cyrus Reed in a euphemistic vein, "was accompanied by the large-scale flight of the peasantry, rather than their politicisation."[12] The object of this kind of liberation was no longer the population, but the territory. Thus, liberation turned out to be a combination of occupation and displacement: occupation of the land and displacement of the people.

Birth of "Hutu Power"

A fringe preoccupation among Rwandan Hutu by the late eighties, Hutu power became a mainstream ideology in the early nineties. The birth of "Hutu Power"—really, Hutu Powa, rather than Hutu Power, which would be an English-language slogan in a francophone milieu—as a formal organized tendency signified a sea change. Its context was the civil war. "Hutu Nation" had been the rallying cry of the 1959 Revolution and the foundation claim of the First Republic of Kayibanda. In contrast, the Second Republic promised "reconciliation" between Hutu and Tutsi. Branded an *alien* minority under the First Republic, the Tutsi were redefined, even rehabilitated, as a *Rwandese* minority under the Second Republic. The more the possibility of Tutsi power receded into a dim history, the less Hutu power had to offer as an organizing ideology, and the bleaker seemed its future.

The 1990 RPF invasion changed this context dramatically. For the first time since the *inyenzi* raids of the early 1960s, the 1990 invasion raised the specter of Tutsi Power inside Rwanda. This, unsurprisingly, is how the Rwandan government portrayed the invasion to the population inside and the world outside. In an address to the foreign diplomatic corps in Kigali, Foreign Minister Casimir Bizimungu accused the invaders of seeking "a reversal of history" which could only mean a return to "forced labour and feudal servitude."[13] And the fact was that many inside the country agreed that RPF rule would mean nothing but the return of Tutsi domination. The irony was that the more successful the RPF was on the battlefield, the more this view came to define the political center stage, bringing Hutu Power back from a fringe preoccupation to the mainstream of respectable politics. Hitherto, the demand that power must remain Hutu had been the rallying cry of those opposed to President Juvénal Habyarimana's line of "ethnic reconciliation" between Hutu and Tutsi. Its last major public assertion had been associated with the failed Lizinde coup of almost a decade ago. Now, its proponents finally had an object worthy of public attention: to prevent the return of Tutsi Power because, surely, no worse calamity could befall Rwanda.

At the core of the ideology of Hutu Power was the conviction that the Tutsi were a *race* alien to Rwanda, and not an indigenous *ethnic group*. The shift in political vocabulary was a return to the vision of the colonial period. That the Tutsi were a race not indigenous to Rwanda was both central to colonial ideology and a key idea that had propelled forward the 1959 Revolution. The same notion had been part of the ideological baggage of the First Republic. This is where the Second Republic made a difference: Habyarimana spoke of the Tutsi as an ethnic group, not a race; as a *Rwandan*, and not an *alien*, minority. The claim that the Hutu constituted a democratic majority because they were the ethnic majority would have made no sense from the point of view of Hutu Power. Because for Hutu Power, the Hutu were not just the majority, *they were the nation*. This is why the birth of Hutu Power as an organized political tendency went alongside a comprehensive propaganda effort discrediting Habyarimana's effort at reconciliation. Hutu Power had to undo Habyarimana's attempt to rehabilitate the Tutsi as an ethnic minority in Rwandan society.

Hutu Power propagandists claimed to be radical nationalist and populist. Yet, in defining the Tutsi as a foreign race, even if without knowing it, they were reaffirming the colonial legacy and construing themselves the same way that Belgian colonialism had construed them prior to independence. At the same time, the emergence of Hutu Power as a radical nationalist tendency in postcolonial Rwanda was evidence enough that the anticolonial struggle did not succeed in reconfiguring Hutu and Tutsi as political identities. The objective of their propaganda effort was to *reracialize* the Tutsi, as they had been in the colonial period, and under the first postrevolutionary republic of Kayibanda from 1961 to 1973. To recast the Tutsi as a race was to confirm that they were aliens in Rwanda. Two propaganda organs were central to this effort: the radio RTLM (Radio et Télévision Libres des Mille Collines) and the newspaper *Kangura*. Funded by members and friends who gathered around the person of the president's wife and constituted a key power group referred to as the *akazu* (little house), RTLM began broadcasting from Kigali only four days after the signing of the Arusha Agreement. Shortly after the RPF invasion, *Kangura* published the widely circulated "Hutu Ten Commandments." The commandments forbade Hutu from entering into a wide range of relations with Tutsi, whether in sex, business, or state affairs. "The Hutu should stop having mercy on the Tutsi," went the eighth commandment.[14]

For Hutu Power propagandists, the Tutsi question was not one of rights, but of power. The growing appeal of Hutu Power propaganda among the Hutu masses was in direct proportion to the spreading conviction that the real aim of the RPF was not rights for all Rwandans, but power for the Tutsi. This is why one needs to recognize that it was not greed—not even hatred—but *fear* which was the reason why the multitude responded to the call of Hutu Power the closer the war came to home. Hutu Power extremists prevailed not because they promised farmers more land if they killed their Tutsi neighbors—which they did—but because they told farmers that the alternative would be to let RPF take their land and return it to the Tutsi who had been expropriated after 1959.[15] Increasingly, the war shaped the context of daily lives. The war, said the government, was about keeping the threat of Tutsi Power at bay. "Defend your rights and rise up against those who want to oppress you," the singer on Radio Libre des Mille Collines repeated as drums beat and guitars strummed a traditional melody. At the receiving end of this message were men and women like Kiruhara, an illiterate twenty-seven-year-old peasant who had spent most of his life cultivating sorghum and sweet potatoes on the steep mountain slopes of Kibunga Prefecture in eastern Rwanda. He had joined the Interahamwe when it was set up in 1992 as a youth militia of the ruling party. The stations "were always telling people that if the RPF, the rebel Rwandan Patriotic Front, comes, it will return Rwanda to feudalism, that it would bring oppression," Kiruhara told his captors in 1994.[16] Interviewed in the Benaco refugee camp in Tanzania, Bénédicte Ndagijimana, a college freshman majoring in English, explained the impact of such a truth on ordinary lives: "They hear over and over that the Tutsis are out to kill them, and that is reality. So they act not out of hate as fear. They think they have only the choice to kill or be killed."[17] We shall later see how others have sought to explain these developments: the economists arguing for a direct link between an increasing resource crunch and the genocide, and the culturalists claiming that the link is really with an ingrained culture of obedience or fear. Both, however, forget the central role that fear—not as a relatively timeless cultural reflex but as a much more time-bound response to a rapidly shifting political and social context—played in providing the ideologues of Hutu Power a mass following for the first time since 1963.

The more credibility Hutu Power ideologues gained among the Hutu multitudes, the more they were able to turn the Tutsi minority inside Rwanda into a hostage population. In the context of the war, there were actually two hostage populations, not one: not only the Tutsi in government-held areas but also the Hutu in RPF-held areas. The difference lies in how each was treated by its captors. While there is evidence of RPF slaughter of Hutu civilians, it suggests select killings that were more in the nature of reprisals or revenge. After a brief summary of these killings, Human Rights Watch concluded in May 1994 that "there is at present no credible evidence that the RPF has engaged in any widespread slaughter of civilian populations, although there are reports of less systematic abuses."[18] But, as we have seen, the RPF did resort to widespread displacement of Hutu civilians, to pillage, and even to conscription for coerced labor. Whereas the RPF resorted to *displacement* of Hutu peasants to pressure the regime into concessions and compromise, proponents of Hutu Power sought to achieve a similar objective through periodic *massacres* directed at ordinary Tutsi citizens.

So the massacres, which had ceased in 1964—once the question of power had been firmly settled—came back to life as the RPF invasion once again brought self-appointed custodians of the Hutu revolution face-to-face with the specter of Tutsi power. Each massacre was carefully timed and deliberately organized to follow a turning point, either in the civil war or in the negotiations that accompanied it. Four massacres occurred in the three and a half years that separated the RPF invasion and the onset of the genocide. The *first* took place in the weeks immediately following the October 1990 invasion, when an estimated three hundred Tutsi were massacred in cold blood in Kibilira. The *second* massacre started in Bugogwe and was a direct response to the January 1991 RPF raid on the town of Ruhengeri. This time at least a thousand Bugogwe cattle herders and their families were slaughtered. The *third* massacre at Bugesera in March 1992 was of a different type. It was less a retaliation than an offensive. The numbers killed were in the hundreds. But this time the killings had been prepared for in advance: the civilian Hutu population was urged and organized to defend itself against an expected massacre by the RPF and its civilian collaborators.[19] The international commission of inquiry that visited Rwanda in January 1993 found evidence that these deaths were carried out by death squads directed by the security services in the office of the president.[20] That same month, on 9 January, a key protocol relating to powersharing was signed in Arusha. The visit of the international commission notwithstanding, the *fourth* massacre followed: some three hundred Tutsi were killed in Gisenyi Prefecture the very next month. It was believed to be a response by Hutu Power to those who championed the call to share power. In all, an estimated 3,000 Tutsi were killed in massacres between 1990 and 1993.

It makes sense to see these pogroms not as projects of the government itself, but of an extremist tendency, Hutu Power, that linked some in the central government with others in local officialdom in different parts of the country. When the first massacre followed the October invasion, the government tried to check it. According to the U.S. State Department's *1990 Human Rights Report*, "The Government, with the help of the Catholic Church, sent troops and teams of clerics to trouble spots in Gisenyi, Gikongoro and Gitarama prefectures and insisted that local officials prevent further violence or face dismissal and punishment."[21] Instigated by a combination of central and local officials, these massacres further cemented an organized link between all those wedded to violence in the pursuit of a political agenda.

Much has been written about a centrally organized apparatus of genocide being in place as early as 1992. Professor Filip Reyntjens organized a press conference at the Belgian Senate in October 1992 giving evidence that a civil-military organization, code-named "Zero Network," indeed functioned as a death squad. It had taken part in the Bugesera massacres of March 1992 and planned various political killings.[22] We have seen that the International Commission of January 1993 also made reference to the existence of a death squad. But a death squad is not quite an apparatus of genocide. Death squads have existed in a variety of contexts, from Latin American rightist dictatorships to apartheid South Africa, but they have not perpetrated anything approaching a genocide. Death squads carry out *individual* assassinations, even group massacres, not the elimination of an entire people.

Later in this chapter, I will return to this question of advance preparation for the genocide. For the moment, however, we need to look at some key features of how the 1990–93 pogroms were organized. While initiated from the center, every massacre was executed locally. Just as it was the apparatus of the local state that had organized the flight of the Tutsi during the pogroms of 1963–64 and 1973, and then redistributed their property, so local authorities also organized the massacres that followed the RPF invasion of October 1990.[23] Over time, a pattern could be discerned. Prefects and burgomasters organized Hutu militants who identified and targeted Tutsi "collaborators," took over the land of those who were killed or fled, and redistributed it to militants. The use of local authorities was not simply a matter of using whatever instrument was available and at hand. There was, rather, a deliberate effort to use the "customary" as opposed to the "civic" apparatus of the state. In my view, the relevant distinction between the two was that while "customary" power highlighted the obligations of those *indigenous* to the land, civic power recognized the rights of all those *resident* on the land. We need to recall that customary power was employed through the colonial and postcolonial periods to enforce obligations on entire communities—such as coerced labor (*umuganda*) and compulsory villagization (*paysannate*)—in the name of observing custom. When it came to pressing ordinary people into a violent political campaign, it was not at all surprising that the *génocidaire* tendency decided on "customary" power as the agency most suited to cleanse the community of threatening alien influences.

The use of the "customary" apparatus went alongside that of the language of "customary" obligation. Right from the first massacre at Kibilira that followed the October 1990 invasion, local officials were instructed to kill Tutsi as part of their communal work obligation. Killings came to be referred to as *umuganda* (communal work), chopping up men as "bush clearing," and slaughtering women and children as "pulling out the roots of the bad weeds."[24] "In one commune," writes Timothy Longman, "a massacre occurred when the burgomaster called the Hutu peasants to gather with machetes for *umuganda*, ostensibly to clear bush, then, with gendarmes present, sent them to kill their Tutsi neighbours."[25] After the slaughter of thousands of Tutsi at the church in Cyahinda in Nyakizu, the burgomaster told local people that burying the dead was required as *umuganda*.[26] The use of the language of "custom" was highly significant. After all, was not customary obligation supposed to distinguish the indigenous from the nonindigenous? With clearing the land of those branded alien considered a "customary" obligation, the genocide would ultimately be presented as a community project.

Two trends gathered over time. One accelerated the element of spontaneity, the other reinforced organization. The spread of massacres gave free reign to forces of banditry and pillage. As banditry and pillage grew, so did random killings. Yet, while there were reports of the poor attacking the well-off, the killings remained directed in the main at those identified as the political enemy, not the class enemy.[27] As it developed, the genocide was undoubtedly the outcome of an interaction between dynamics that were both central and local. As in 1973, there were developments in several localities that tended to turn the focus of the conflict away from Hutu against Tutsi to poor against rich. At the same time, we know from the outcome that the predominant tendency in most localities was to target the Tutsi as the enemy.

The enemy was, first, the Tutsi, all of them, with the RPF considered the spearhead of Tutsi power, and then it was those Hutu branded as their accomplices. That the enemy was defined in the context of a war situation gave the massacres a degree of coherence they would otherwise have lacked. The more the war grew in scale, and the closer it got to Kigali, the more the country was put on a war footing. Everyone had to contribute, at first to the war effort, then to the war itself. The leaders of Hutu Power decreed that the war was everywhere, since the Tutsi—the enemy—were everywhere. "Everyone was asked to keep guard—to go to the barricades," explained a Hutu resident of Kigali to a *Christian Science Monitor* reporter. "If you stayed at home, you risked being labeled an accomplice."[28] As in any war, but particularly in this one, there could be no neutrality. No wonder perpetrators who defend the genocide usually explain the massacres as inevitable excesses in a war situation.

If we are to understand the context of the mass killings that together constitute the hundred-days genocide, we need to move away from an assumption of the genocide as simply a conspiracy from above to an understanding of how perceptions could radically shift in response to an equally radical change in forces and circumstances—by making the genocide thinkable. I will try and make this point with reference to two key participants in the leadership of the genocide. The first is Léon Mugesera, a leading ideologue of the genocidal tendency in Hutu Power. The second is Stanislas Mbonampeka, a leading member of the Parti Libéral (PL) and an outspoken opponent of Léon Mugesera in 1992.

A Canadian-educated linguist, Mugesera was reportedly the first to air publicly the notion of eliminating the Tutsi physically as a final solution to the question of Tutsi Power. "We the people are obliged to take responsibility ourselves and wipe out this scum. No matter what you do, do not let them get away," Mugesera invoked in a notorious 1992 speech in northwestern Rwanda, one that has been taken as the clarion call for the genocide that followed two years later. He went on to advise that the Tutsi be returned to Ethiopia, from where they had come anyway, but this time by "the river route," specifically by way of the Nyabarongo River, which feeds into the Nile.[29]

By then, Rwanda had a coalition government. Mbonampeka, the minister of justice, came from the Parti Libéral, a critic of the government. He issued a warrant for the arrest of Mugesera, but was unable to carry it out because Mugesera fled to a military camp where he remained hidden until he escaped from the country. Fed up with what he understood as political vacillation on the part of President Habyarimana, Mbonampeka resigned as minister of justice. From then on, his position shifted radically, as radically as did the constellation of circumstances and forces in Rwanda. From one who was ready to arrest Mugesera in December 1992, Mbonampeka moved to a partisan anti-RPF position as the war advanced, and then to a defense of the genocide, finally emerging in the rump post-1994 government in exile as *its* minister of justice.[30] Philip Gourevitch interviewed him in Goma, eastern Zaire, in June 1995. Mbonampeka explained the genocide as violence that inevitably accompanies war. "In a war, you can't be neutral. If you are not for your country, are you not for its attackers?" He passed off the genocide as crimes of war committed in the course of civil defense. "This was not a conventional war. The enemies were everywhere. It wasn't genocide. Personally, I don't believe in the genocide. There were massacres within which there were crimes against humanity or crimes of war. But the Tutsis were not killed as Tutsis, only as sympathizers of the RPF. 90% of Tutsis were pro-RPF." To drive the point home, he added: "Think about it. When the Germans attacked France, France defended itself against Germany. They understood that all Germans were the enemy. The Germans killed women and children, so you do, too." In a space of but two years, Mbonampeka had moved from issuing a warrant of arrest for the prime ideologue of Hutu Power to appearing on a government of Kigali list of 414 "suspected commanders, organizers and authors of genocide."[31] It is this shift, and not the premeditated conspiracy of a Léon Mugesera which can provide a clue to the question: Why did hundreds of thousands, and perhaps more, of Hutu respond to the call of Hutu Power?

ALTERNATIVE EXPLANATIONS

To explain the mass involvement in the genocide, writers have accentuated one of two factors: the economic and the cultural. Without necessarily denying the significance of either, I shall shift accent away from both to the *political* aspect of the genocide. Hegel once said that humans are distinguished from animals by the fact that they are willing *to give life* for a reason higher than life. He should have added that humans, unlike animals, are also willing *to take life* for a reason they consider higher than life. In both cases, there is a demarcation between life that is considered worth taking (or giving) and life considered worth preserving (or enriching). When the life in question is that of groups, involving large numbers, the decision is inevitably political. Though it may be taken under the pressure of necessity (economy) or the force of habit (culture), we need to highlight the decision as conscious, as the result of a deliberation. If not, we risk losing sight of any difference between humans and animals. My critique of those who tend to accent the economic or the cultural in the understanding of the genocide is that their explanation obscures the moment of decision, of choice, as if human action, even—or, shall I say, particularly—at its most dastardly or heroic, can be explained by necessity alone. Though we need to take into account circumstances that constrain or facilitate—that is, necessity—we must resist the temptation to present necessity as choice and thereby strip human action of both the dimension of possibility and that of responsibility.

A Resource Crunch

Two kinds of explanations highlight the world of necessity. For economists, necessity is a resource crunch. For culturalists, it is a closure of the mind. When it comes to writings on the genocide of 1994, both have figured, though the economic has tended to predominate. The economic standpoint highlights internally and externally generated constraints closing in on ordinary people in the decade before the genocide, like a growing sense of claustrophobia in a crowded commuter train. The resource crunch was said to be a result of rapidly increasing numbers of people having to look for a piece of cultivable land from a relatively stagnant pool. A postgenocide study on population growth and agricultural change commissioned by USAID—titled "More People, More Trouble"— pointed out that average farm holdings in Rwanda had shrunk by 12 percent from 1984 to 1989.[32] Another evaluation, this one following the genocide, pointed out that 57 percent of rural households were already having to farm less than one hectare of land in 1984, while 25 percent of these had less than half a hectare. At the same time, these shrinking land parcels had to feed an average family of five people. Prevailing inheritance practices required that a family divide land among all sons. The result was not only diminishing but fragmented parcels: "Thus, in the beginning of the 1990s, the average Rwandese household farmed at least five plots of land."[33] These studies point at land conflict as the inevitable result of increasing human pressure on a fixed pool of land. The USAID-commissioned study summarizes existing research thus: "Land scarcity in Rwanda has resulted in intense rivalry and conflict among neighbors, with frequent fights and lawsuits over disputed land and frequent thefts from fields." The conclusion: "Disputes over land are reported to have been a major motivation for Rwandans to denounce neighbors during the ethnic conflicts of 1994."[34]

If land conflict was one outcome of land scarcity, diminishing food production was its other consequence. Food production declined after 1985: postgenocide research pointed out that kilocalories produced by Rwandan farmers had dropped from 2,055 per person per day to 1,509 over the period 1984–91. Even the "severe and moderate malnutrition (which) remained stable up to 1993" increased dramatically thereafter.[35] The link between rising numbers, worsening poverty, and political extremism was made by Tipper Gore, the wife of the U.S. vice-president, Al Gore, at the Cairo World Population Conference in 1994: "Rwanda is a tragedy and a warning. It is a warning about the way in which extremists can manipulate the fears of a population threatened by its own numbers and by its massive poverty."[36]

No matter how depressing these facts may seem, we need to keep in mind that there is no *necessary* connection between a drastic reduction in resources and deadly human conflict. One only needs to read the social history of natural disasters—be it drought, flood, or hurricanes—to recognize that countries have suffered a worse crunch than did Rwanda between 1989 and 1993 without the population turning in on itself, with one part devouring another. The connection between the constraints under which we live and the choices we do make is mediated through how we understand and explain these constraints and the resources we can muster to change them. As always, humans shape their world based on human consciousness and human capacities.

A Closure of the Mind

Few have dared to argue that the Holocaust was linked to a resource crunch in Germany. In contrast, there have been many explorations into German culture and psychology. In a well-known study, Shulamit Volkov deemed "anti-Semitism" a "cultural code," created in the first decade of the German Reich as a convenient abbreviation for a broad "cluster of ideas, values and norms" that opposed "liberal, capitalist, democratic, and internationalist currents associated with the nineteenth century emancipation of Jews" in the name of "militant nationalism, imperial expansion, racism, anti-socialism, militarism, and support for a strong authoritarian government." Arguing that the existence of an anti-Semitic tradition did not "require" the murder of Jews, Michael Marrus observed: "In the end it was Hitler, and his own determination to realize his anti-Semetic fantasies, that made the difference; in brief, 'No Hitler, No Holocaust.' " This is precisely why, he argued, "for historians of the Holocaust, the greatest challenge has not been making sense of Hitler, but rather understanding why so many followed him down his murderous path."[37]

If an understanding of what motivated functionaries to participate in the Holocaust has puzzled its historians, the riddle is perhaps even greater for those trying to make sense of mass participation in the Rwandan genocide. The final report of the Kigali conference observed: "The massive participation of the population in the Rwandan genocide is virtually without historical precedent."[38] What, indeed, explains the participation of vast masses, neighbors, coworkers, friends, even family members in the slaughter of those they knew well only yesterday? The response of those who write of the genocide divides into two: one focuses on society, the other on the state. Society-based explanations stress the historical legacy of racism in the Hutu population of the country, but without grounding racial perspectives in institutions, or distinguishing race from ethnicity as political identities, or even appreciating the historical dynamic making for the shift from one to the other. In an article that tries to understand the link between "demographic entrapment" and the genocide, Peter Uvin writes: "The most profound factor fueling the transmission of genocidal ideology from the regime to the masses, however, was the longstanding and deeply ingrained racism of Rwandan society." He then continues: "For decades, Rwandan society had been profoundly racist. The image of the Tutsi as inherently evil and exploitative was, and still is, deeply rooted in the psyche of most Rwandans; this image was a founding pillar of the genocide to come. Although ethnic peace had prevailed during most of the regime, the racist nature of Rwandan society had not changed."[39]

The second explanation shifts attention from society to the state as the lead actor and the active agent in the genocide. It focuses on the dead weight of cultural traditions that demand conformity to power. The proverb cited most often to sum up the cultural compulsion ordinary people felt to obey authority goes as follows: an order is as heavy as a stone. Gérard Prunier speaks of a "Rwandese political tradition" through the ages, before, during and after colonialism, as "one of systematic, centralised and unconditional obedience to authority." Then he adds: "Most people were illiterate. Given their authoritarian tradition, they tended to believe what the authorities told them."[40] The idea that tradition and illiteracy make for a powerful mix is not uncommon: the more illiterate the population, the more it is said to be held within the grip of a mindless tradition. The implicit identification is of literacy with reason and tradition with unreason.[41]

In articles for the *New Yorker*, Philip Gourevitch let survivors of the genocide, both Tutsi and Hutu, speak for themselves. Laurent Nkongoli, a Tutsi survivor who became the vice-president of the National Assembly in the post-1994 RPF government, reflected on why the Tutsi were re-signed to death. "There were four thousand Tutsis killed here at Kacyiru. The soldiers brought them here and told them to sit down because they were going to throw grenades. And they sat. . . . Rwandan culture is a culture of fear." For François-Xavier Nkurunziza, a Hutu lawyer, the di-lemma was how so many Hutu had allowed themselves to kill. "Conformity is deep, very developed here. In Rwandan culture, everyone obeys author-ity. People revere power, and there isn't enough education. You take a poor, ignorant population, and give them arms, and say, 'It's yours. Kill.' They'll obey."[42] Fear and obedience are like flip sides of a single coin: common to them is the claim that the person involved has ceased to think. When he got to talk to the leaders of the RPF, Gourevitch described their take on the genocide "as a crime committed by masterminds and slave bodies."[43]

To believe that ordinary Rwandans killed, in their hundreds and thou-sands, and perhaps more, because of a congenital transhistorical condi-tion—"a culture of fear" or of "deep conformity"—would require stretch-ing one's sense of credibility. For the period under discussion, the early years of the 1990s, was precisely when these very multitudes responded to a democratic opening with a growing defiance of authority, by uproot-ing coffee trees and refusing to perform compulsory communal labor. Yet, we need to remember that the culture of conformity is not an original construction of Gourevitch; it is, rather, Gourevitch the reporter quoting Rwandan respondents, both Hutu and Tutsi. Could it be that these Rwan-dan respondents were regurgitating as truisms "the mythical imagery of racism": in the words of Peter Uvin, "the old myths of the Hutu as obedi-ent and docile and the Tutsi as commandeering and cunning"?[44]

The notion of an unthinking participant, whether killer or victim, whether caught in the grip of fear or tradition, does not rule out the notion of a calculating individual, but one who calculates without reason-ing, whose response to stimuli is predictable. From this point of view, calculation is short term, understandable under the circumstances because it is an adaptation to circumstances, but hardly reasonable since it also suggests a capitulation to the force of circumstance. This, then, is how the two kinds of explanations of the *mass* nature of genocidal violence are brought together without contradiction: the Rwandese peasant is por-trayed as capable of both obedience to authority and calculated self-inter-est. This is more or less how Prunier sums up his exploration into the "mechanics of the genocide": "unquestioning obedience to authority, fear of the Tutsi devils and the hope of grabbing something for oneself in the general confusion."[45]

Without caricaturing this point of view or dismissing it outright, I want to point out its limits. The observation that ordinary participants in the genocide hoped to gain from it has been made by many a source, usually citing perpetrators of violence. Reporting in January 1994 on sporadic massacres that predated the systematic killing of Tutsi, Human Rights Watch noted that combat operations by the Rwanda army were often accompanied by civilian atrocities: "Civilian groups, composed of majority Hutu, committed widespread acts of ethnic violence against Tutsi. These rampaging crowds were incited and led by local administrators and by militia attached to Rwanda's longtime ruling political party, the National Republican Movement for Democracy and Development (MRNDD). They destroyed crops, stole food, slaughtered cattle, burned homes and attacked their neighbours using machetes, spears and clubs."[46] Alison Des Forges of Human Rights Watch/Africa explained how those in authority could convince "those reluctant to kill" to join the killing spree anyway: "They also offered attractive incentives to people who are very poor, giving license to loot and promising them the land and businesses of the victims. In some cases, local officials even decided ahead of time the disposition of the most attractive items of movable property. Everyone knew who had a refrigerator, a plush sofa, a radio, and assailants were guaranteed their rewards before attacking."[47] Rakia Omaar, the director of Africa Rights, which provided detailed accounts by witnesses and survivors pointing accusing fingers at members of the educated Hutu elite, agreed: "The motive was often to secure a coveted job or property."[48] A Tutsi who survived because he had been away at a conference in Uganda, but who returned to find his wife and two children murdered, had this to say: "It was politics. Politicians told the people: kill, and you will get your neighbours' goods and land."[49]

After all, had there not been precedents to vindicate the expectation that a pogrom would enrich its participants? None would deny that the mass exodus triggered by the killings of Tutsi in 1959–63 had opened up vast tracts of land for landless Hutu. The link between political violence and social redistribution has been key to revolutionary politics everywhere. What distinguishes social redistribution from individual greed and theft is precisely the difference between two kinds of action: one social, the other individual; one political and extralegal, the other apolitical and illegal. Precisely this difference has been at the root of another distinction, one between two kinds of violence: revolutionary and criminal, the former an instrument of justice but the latter a source of injustice. The connection between political violence and social redistribution has been central to radical discourse and practice of justice in postcolonial African politics. It is the connection to justice that explains a range of reactions to revolutionary violence, from ambivalence to enthusiasm and romance. Since it involved large masses of people in common action, and not small groups or individuals in a conspiracy, the violence needs to be understood as political, and not criminal. At the same time, this violence did not pit the poor against the rich. If anything, it divided the poor—as it did the rich—into antagonistic groups: Hutu against Tutsi. It had little to do with either revolutionary violence or class struggle.

Neither does the reverse argument, that the violence was some kind of a desperate bid for survival in a resource-impoverished environment, hold. The crudest formulation I have seen of this argument was in a submission to the United Nations tribunal in Rwanda. It argued that those who killed "were engaged in a desperate scramble for survival at each other's expense, of a kind that is all too familiar in the economic wastelands of Africa."[50] But the genocide was not a collapse of power and authority, a free-for-all in which everyone turned against their neighbor, with all thrown into some sort of a Hobbesian state of nature where life had turned "nasty, brutish and short." The target of the genocide was clearly defined: not anyone, only the Tutsi. The truly disturbing aspect of the genocide is that the definition of the enemy appeared credible to many ordinary Hutu. To explain why this was so, we need to understand the violence of the genocide as a *political* violence born of the civil war that was a struggle for power within an elite once again fractured between Hutu and Tutsi. In many ways, the civil war of 1990–94 was a repeat of 1959–63, with one difference: this time, it is the Hutu political elite that was internally fractured, while its Tutsi counterpart showed greater political and ideological cohesion. To understand the circumstances that shaped the political violence and its genocidal magnitude, we need to join our historical discussion of political identities in Rwanda to an understanding of how the war reshaped these political identities. For the 1990–94 civil war changed not only those who directly participated in it but also those who suffered its consequences. It changed not only the political elite but also ordinary working people, both Hutu and Tutsi.

THE CONTEXT OF THE GENOCIDE

The genocide was born of civil war but it also marked a rupture in the civil war. Its perpetrators understood the multiple massacres that ultimately added up to genocide as a continuation of the civil war. Without keeping this fact in mind, it will be difficult either to understand the dynamic that propelled Rwanda into its darkest hour ever, or to explore ways out of it.

The war is crucial for several reasons. Its consequences for the civilian population were drastic. Coming at the end of a decade of economic decline, the war disrupted agricultural production, the infrastructure of communication, and thus the distribution and availability of food. It created widespread hunger and starvation. In addition, the war also displaced a substantial minority, so large that it came to include *one out of every seven Rwandans.* To this group were added Hutu refugees from Burundi. Living in camps scattered around the country, the internally displaced and the refugees were like so many bundles of dry tinderwood, awaiting but a spark to light a conflagration.

The civil war not only generated the raw material for the coming conflagration, it also provided the spark that would light it. To begin with, the government lost the civil war. The war discredited the army, fragmented the political class, and divided it into two hostile sections, each blaming the other for losing the war. Every major political party divided into two: those supporting a power-sharing deal with the RPF, and those opposed to it. Major opposition parties—the Mouvement Démocratique Républicain (MDR), the Parti-Libéral (PL), and the Parti Social-Démocrate (PSD)—were not immune from this trend. Each split into two factions, one called "power" and the other called "moderate"; one identified with the defense of Hutu Power, the other with power sharing. Each held the other responsible for defeat. Defeat discredited the army. Its leadership, in turn, held the political opposition responsible for dressing up defeat as power sharing and disguising national betrayal as democratic opposition. But the army too split in the face of defeat and disgrace at the battlefront. The erosion of the army's esprit de corps, and the cohesion of its leadership, set the context in which the president's plane was brought down. The hour had struck for the most ardent champions of Hutu Power—for those whose patriotic zeal knew no limits—to call the nation to arms against those they considered to have betrayed it. The enemy within were the Tutsi and their objective accomplices, the Hutu political opposition; in a word, the *inyenzi* and their *abeyitso.* We shall see that the killing of the *abeyitso,* the Hutu opposition that was branded as having betrayed the nation, was the curtain-raiser to the genocide.

The Displaced and the Refugees

For the civilian population, the war translated, first and foremost, into day-to-day hardships. It became that much more difficult to find bare means of daily survival. When the RPF attacked the most fertile part of the country in January and February 1993, the supply of agricultural produce

reaching markets dropped by a drastic 15 percent.[51] The second consequence for the civilian population was displacement. Every time the RPF
scored a military victory and gained territory, another group of Hutu
peasants and civilians was flushed out of the "liberated" areas. They
flooded refugee camps that in turn mushroomed like so many sore and
poisonous outgrowths around the capital city. The growth in their numbers was dramatic: from 80,000 in late 1990 to 350,000 in May 1992 to
950,000 after the February 1993 offensive. In its *1993 Human Rights
Report*, the U.S. State Department estimated that 650,000 of them were
displaced for the first time but 350,000 were "re-displaced, some for the
fourth time."[52] Other sources gave higher estimates of the numbers displaced, at 1.1 million, reaching beyond 15 percent of the total population
of the country.[53] The United Nations Information Center reported in August 1993 that most of the displaced "were living in and around 30 camps
where serious malnutrition and disease were prevalent."[54]

The liberalization of political activity drew two volatile constituencies
into the political arena: the unemployed youth and those displaced by the
civil war. Starting with the ruling party, one by one, political parties began
reaching out to this constituency, incorporating it into its youth wing.
The ruling party created its own youth wing in early 1992. It was called
the *Interahamwe,* variously translated as "those who work together" or
"those who attack together." Once it had formed its own political party,
the Coalition pour la Défense de la République (CDR), the extreme Hutu
Power tendency followed by organizing their own youth wing. This was
the Impuzamugambi ("those who have the same goal"). Its leader, Robert
Kajuka, was a Tutsi.[55] In the context of the civil war, unarmed youth wings
rapidly transformed into so many armed militia. *Africa Rights* notes that
the arming of the militia intensified following the February 1993 RPF
offensive.[56] The U.S. State Department noted in its *1993 Human Rights
Report* that armed militias were involved in the massacre that followed the
RPF offensive.[57]

To the growing pool of internally displaced and unemployed youth was
added a third volatile influence. This was the stream of Hutu refugees
from Burundi, also victims of political violence. The flow of refugees from
Burundi into Rwanda, as from Rwanda into Burundi, had a long history,
in the case of Rwanda stretching to the 1959 Revolution, in the case of
Burundi beginning with the massacres of 1972. Refugees from Burundi
were mainly Hutu fleeing army-perpetrated massacres after each major political crisis. Of these, three were key: 1972, 1988, and 1993. As each wave
of refugees subsided, and as the political situation at home returned to

normal and realities of a normal refugee existence began to sink in, many returned home. But each time a minority would remain, holding on to bitter memories of home while nurturing sharp night-and-day type of distinctions between good and evil. Nineteen thousand such refugees from 1972 remained in Rwanda in 1990. They were joined by between 47,000 (U.S. Department of State) and 55,000 (U.N.) others in mid-1988. But unlike the 1972 group, they were refused refugee status by the Rwanda government, which granted them temporary asylum, insisting that they return to Burundi by the end of the year. By 1990, approximately one thousand had refused to return and remained within Rwanda.[58]

The last wave of Barundi refugees entering Rwanda was, however, also the biggest ever. It was a consequence of the violence that spread in the wake of the assassination of President Ndadaye of Burundi in October 1993. When conditions in Rwanda began to turn nasty in April 1994, about 200,000 people were in refugee camps in southern Rwanda. As the slaughter grew in magnitude, the violence taking on the force of a tornado, many fled to Tanzania or even returned home. Human Rights Watch estimated in May 1994 that "as many as 80,000 may still be left in Rwanda." Other estimates were much higher, even as high as 400,000.[59] Soon after their arrival into Rwanda, many were recruited into the Interahamwe. The UNHCR complained, but with little effect.[60]

Many an account speaks of the catalytic role of the Barundi in starting massacres in south-central Rwanda, a part of the country considered a stronghold of the opposition and difficult terrain for Hutu Power ideologues. Here, the long history of Hutu/Tutsi relations predated by centuries the bipolar racial mold in which colonialism came to cast it. Hutu/Tutsi intermarriage had not only predated the colonial period, it had also flourished in the postcolonial period. This kind of history tended to give rise to a plurality of notions about how Hutu and Tutsi may live together, in turn generating ambivalence toward ideas associated with proponents of Hutu Power. While this ambivalence tended to dissolve in the crucible of civil war, it never really vanished completely. In contrast, the historical memory of the refugees was sharp and simple. For them, the Tutsi were responsible for their continuing misfortune. Even those who believed in coexistence with the Tutsi would not tolerate any thought of sharing power. Not only did many of the Barundi refugees take an active part in the political violence of 1994, those who did were also responsible for some of the most gruesome tortures that marked the genocide. When I talked to survivors at the Church in Ntarama in 1995, I was told of the "Barundi torture" as the most cruel: beginning with the heel, a part of the body would be cut daily, a process that usually took a week as the victim bled to death. It is as if they were settling old scores, even if across the border.

A Defeated Army

The Rwandan army grew in size dramatically, from 5,000 to more than 30,000 in the course of a few years of civil war. New recruits were poorly trained and badly disciplined. At the same time, small arms were easily and cheaply available in local open-air markets.[61] Following the model of many radical regimes in the region, the Habyarimana government in 1991 began a program to arm civilians and create "self-defense" forces. The program began as a pilot project, confined to the four border communes of Muvumba, Ngarama, Muhura, and Bwisige. Its aim was to provide a gun for every administrative unit of ten households, and to train the civilians who would be expected to handle the gun as part of "self-defense." After February 1993, when the RPF doubled the size of territories under its control, the program was extended from border communes to interior communes. It is these "self-defense units," found in every commune and village, that formed the civilian core of the machinery that came to carry out the genocide. They killed in response to orders from above because most believed in the moral rightness of obeying one's government, particularly in a war situation, that is, when confronting an "enemy." While an integral part of the machinery that carried out the genocide, it is most unlikely that they were created in the first place as machinery to execute a genocide. Rather, like much of the administrative innovation under the Second Republic, they were initially borrowed from the experience of regimes in the region, and only later adapted in response to changing circumstances.

The government responded to battlefield losses with a strategy to expand the army and to train and arm the civilian population following the ten-cell strategy made popular in Tanzania. The state initiative to create armed civil units for self-defense was different from the initiative of the ruling party and its allies in CDR. We have seen how political parties created youth militias, which began to take on paramilitary functions as the civil war expanded. An easily available anchor for frustrated and unemployed youth, the militia began to proliferate throughout the country. By early 1994, some 30,000 to 50,000 youth were estimated to belong to militias.[62] From becoming active participants in the political process that expanded as the democratic opening broadened, they soon turned into perpetrators of the violence that began to consume that same political process.

Crucial to this souring of reform, to its turning inside-out from a democratic opening to open political violence, was the specter of defeat. Here, it may be useful to note a comparison between Rwanda and Somalia. Neither Rwanda nor Somalia had a military in the colonial period.[63] In both countries, the army was a child of revolution: in Rwanda, of the 1959 Revolution, and in Somalia, of the 1969 revolutionary coup. No wonder the army came to consider itself not only the child but also the privileged *custodian* of the *national* revolution. Military defeat not only demoralized the army; it disgraced the army and fragmented it. After defeat in the Ogaden, the Somali army ceased to have a national project. From a project of pan-Somali nationalism, the fragments of the Somali political leadership—including Siad Barre—embraced the fragment of the nation, the clan, as the vehicle for their political ambitions, in the process turning in on the nation. Not surprisingly, the leadership for each clan militia that contended for supremacy a decade later came, not from outside the army, but from one or another commander of the army defeated in the Ogaden.[64]

In Rwanda, too, as defeat disgraced it, the army exploded, as if into so many fragments of a cluster bomb. Rather than simply deflate the esprit de corps and the sense of mission of the army, defeat seemed to energize its parts, such as the Presidential Guard, and its attachments, such as the Interahamwe and the Impuzamugambi. From confronting the enemy that seemed to advance relentlessly on the battlefield or on the diplomatic frontier, they turned around to face the enemy within. Rather than forsaking the nation for an object worthy of its diminished capacity, as did the army in Somalia, the Rwandan army and its paramilitary attachments went on to purify the nation and rid it of all impurities that detracted from its strength. Even then, we shall see that this was not the project of the entire army, but of a fragment. This fragment was the *génocidaire* tendency. Born of defeat in the civil war, this fragment re-created a sense of national unity—unity of the Hutu Nation—and lived its moment of national glory through a shadowy "struggle" in which it locked defenseless civilians into a deadly embrace. For the perpetrators of the genocide, the enemy within were the Tutsi and the Hutu political opposition, accomplices who had betrayed the national cause in the name of democracy. It is in this sense that the genocide was both a continuation of the civil war and marked a rupture with it.

Political Democracy as National Betrayal

The great paradox of Rwanda of the 1990s is that democratic reforms blossomed at the same time as the civil war raged. The former fed aspirations for individual and group freedom, the latter gave rise to demands for loyalty to the nation. The two processes could not continue side by side, except through generating great tension. As war intensified and defeat loomed on the horizon, more and more of those in power, and even those in the population, came to see dissent not only as a luxury but, at a time of national crisis, as betrayal. Defeat in civil war spelled an end to both the democratic opening and to the democratic movement and its torchbearers. After the fires of war had consumed democracy, its burning ashes extinguished life itself.

Though political party activity predated the beginning of the civil war, political parties were only legalized in July 1991. In the opening phase, opposition parties demanded a recasting of political life along plural lines: some wanted a national conference, as in Benin or Congo, others wanted elections. To dramatize the extent of public support behind the demand for continuing reform, the three major opposition parties formed a coalition and organized a series of public demonstrations. The first was held in November 1991, to highlight the demand for a national conference when Habyarimana named a man from his own party as prime minister. It drew 13,000 persons. The second followed a month later, when the new prime minister named a cabinet in which all positions but one were held by members of the ruling party. This time, the attendance was estimated at 50,000. The government agreed to a Church-mediated negotiation. A few months later, in March 1992, President Habyarimana appointed a prime minister from the largest opposition party, the MDR, being the successor to Kayibanda's PARMEHUTU.[65]

It is unlikely that the introduction of multiparty reform was wholly or even mainly a government response to opposition activity on the streets. Though the level of opposition organization had reached noticeable proportions, oppositional activity was still mainly an urban affair in a predominantly rural country. It is far more likely that official reform was a response to a combination of factors, internal and external. At a time when the Rwandan economy was fragile and deeply indebted, and things were getting even worse, the most significant of these factors must have been direct pressure from key creditors, including France. It is this which provides a clue to the great paradox of 1990: that a government drawn into civil war would respond, not as most governments in similar situations would, by curtailing civil liberties and declaring a national emergency, but by ushering in the dawn of multiparty democracy.

"Multiparty competition at a time of civil war put Rwanda in a state of permanent tension," the head of the Parti Libéral (PL), one of the three main opposition parties, told me in Kigali in 1995. Its immediate effect was to strain unity in the ruling party. Those who believed that the nation deserved loyalty and not dissent in the hour of its need began to organize publicly and separately. To organize against reform, they left the ruling Mouvement Révolutionnaire National pour le Développement (MRND) to form a new party on the right, the Coalition pour le Défense de la République (CDR). From an ideological tendency inside the ruling party, Hutu Power was rapidly beginning to create its own institutions—at first a radio/television (Radio-Télévision Libres des Mille Collines) and a newspaper (*Kangura*), then a political party (CDR) and its youth militia (Impuzamugambi). At the same time, it battled to take over existing institutions of power: the media of the ruling party and its youth militia (Interahamwe).

Ironically, the first phase of the democratic opposition gave Hutu Power the legal space to organize its own institutions and to develop the capacity for independent political initiative. Not surprisingly, the first phase also came to an end once Hutu Power got organized as an independent force. Henceforth, every time the reform tendency registered its presence publicly—such as at the time of the March 1992 negotiations for a multiparty government or the December 1992/January 1993 negotiations between the multiparty government and the RPF—the institutions of Hutu Power responded with organized massacres of Tutsi. From the time a genuine coalition government was organized in March 1992 and Hutu Power responded by organizing its own institutions, there began a struggle between these two tendencies for political leadership. In July 1992, a former minister of information from the president's home region and one of his closest associates, Christophe Mfizi, resigned from the MRND. In a public letter explaining his resignation, he accused the government of coming "under the control of a narrow group of extremists who [now] dominated all aspects of Rwanda's public life for their personal gain and were fighting to protect their hold on power."[66] As the civil war progressed, the middle ground—that defined by Habyarimana's project of "ethnic reconciliation"—eroded. As Hutu and Tutsi once again polarized as political identities, the battle for popular support was lost by the democratic opposition and won by the proponents of Hutu Power.

The Arusha Talks

A month after the inauguration of the first real coalition government in Kigali, talks were held between three opposition parties (MDR, PSD, and PL) and the Rwanda Patriotic Front (RPF) in Paris. The May–June 1992 discussions led to an agreement to start peace negotiations at a formal and governmental level. The Arusha talks began on 10 August 1992.[67]

The first thing to note about the Arusha negotiations was the *process* itself. The government delegation comprised at least three different tendencies, each responding to a separate center of power: the opposition parties in the power-sharing arrangement in Kigali took their orders from the prime minister, a member of the opposition MDR; others "were more clearly Habyarimana's men," with "still other delegates representing Hutu extremist groups in Kigali."[68] The most notorious of the last group was Colonel Théoneste Bagosora, a senior member of the extremist CDR who would later emerge as the key coordinator of the genocide.

It was not difficult for the Hutu Power tendency to portray the Arusha negotiations as talks between the internal opposition and the RPF, that is, between the RPF and its internal Hutu accomplices. Based on personal interviews in Rwanda in 1992–93, Timothy Longman observed: "Portraying the opposition parties as sympathetic to the RPF effectively served to discredit them with a large portion of the population."[69] For this reason, the Arusha talks were doomed from the outset. They unfolded in two phases: the first was led by the minister of foreign affairs and cooperation, Boniface Ngulinzaire of the main opposition party, MDR; and the second by the minister of national defense, James Gasana of Habyarimana's party, the MRNDD.[70] Shortly after the signing of the accord in 1993, James Gasana had to run for his life to Switzerland, but the unfortunate Boniface Ngulinzaire stayed behind and was among the first to be slaughtered in April 1994.[71]

Hutu Power claims were vindicated by an outcome suggesting that the RPF had won at the conference table what it had yet to win on the battlefield. Three parts to the final agreement fed this conclusion.[72] The *first* was the provision on merging the two armies: these stipulated that the RPF would provide 40 percent of the soldiers in the new national army, but 50 percent of the officer corps. When the army had ballooned into six times its original size in four years of civil war, and when the country was plagued with massive unemployment, this was literally like serving an unemployment notice to young recruits in the army. The *second* was that the RPF was given charge of the important Ministry of the Interior. Together, these provisions gave the RPF decisive control over forces of coercion in the new state, especially at the leadership level. *Third*, while the RPF was to have eleven of seventy seats in parliament and five of twenty-one ministries, the power-sharing agreement excluded the organized Hutu Power tendency, CDR, from taking any seats in Parliament. A *fourth* relevant part of the peace agreement was the provision that recognized the right of return of all refugees. This was the fodder that Hutu Power media used to convince the population that the opposition had in fact sold the nation, and that all the gains of the 1959 Revolution—particularly land to the tiller and power to the Hutu—were now in imminent danger.[73] The irony is that while Arusha was central to the opposition claim that it held the key to end the civil war and usher in the dawn of national reconciliation and peace, Arusha in reality confirmed the Hutu Power claim that the opposition had betrayed the nation. In doing so, Arusha sealed the political fate of the opposition.

Arusha was the reason why the first coalition government fell, and the reason why the second coalition government never really got established. The first coalition government fell in July 1993 when Prime Minister Dismas Nsengiyarmye strongly and publicly criticized President Habyarimana for his resistance to a negotiated settlement. In response, the president dismissed him and appointed a new prime minister, also a member of the MDR, but one considered less sympathetic to the RPF and closer to the political center. It is when the main opposition parties refused to support Agathe Uwilingiyimana's appointment as prime minister that each split into two factions over the next two months, one called "power," the other "moderate." One called for a defense of Hutu Power, the other for a negotiated settlement with the RPF.

The Arusha Agreement was signed stillborn, mainly because it failed to take account of the extremist CDR, either by including it or by containing it. Instead, the peace agreement wholly excluded the CDR, even from the transitional government. Strong in both the government and the army, the extremists faced a double loss: of the government to the opposition and of the army to the RPF. Not surprisingly, when the opportunity presented itself, the extremists struck out viciously—at both. Nor was this outcome quite unforeseen by others at the Arusha talks. According to close observers, "All of the major third parties involved in the Arusha process"—the Tanzanians, the Americans, and even its principal regional support, the Ugandans—warned the RPF against "winning pyrrhic victories at the negotiating table," and particularly against excluding the CDR from power and splitting the army disproportionately in its favor. The

Tanzanians and the Americans were even said to share a metaphor: "If the hardliners weren't brought into the tent, they would burn the tent down." Some put it in a more colorful version: that it was "better to have the hardliners inside the tent, pissing out, than outside of the tent, pissing in."[74] One recalls the more sober advice offered by a wise old Tutsi man to a young RPF fighter who had come to "liberate" him in Ruhengeri in January 1991: "You want power? You will get it. But here we will all die. Is it worth it to you?"[75]

The Arusha Agreement was signed on 3 August 1993. Because the Uwilingiyimana government was unable to form a coalition government, the peace accord could never be implemented. While the "moderate" factions of the opposition refused to support a prime minister and a government not wholly behind the power-sharing agreement, the "power" factions of the same parties—now rapidly getting absorbed in a fast expanding movement to defend and assert Hutu Power—went on the offensive. The newspaper *Kangura*, set up by Hassan Ngeze in 1990, had already broadcast genocide as a political solution in its January 1994 issue. Three months before the mass killings began, *Kangura* reported: "We will begin by getting rid of the enemies inside the country. The Tutsi 'cockroaches' should know what will happen, they will disappear."[76] Three months later, when precisely that agenda unfolded, Radio Mille Collines began calling for the assassination of those who had betrayed the nation. Its chilling broadcasts invited listeners to join in the killing, as if this were an appeal to patriotism: "The grave is only half-full. Who will help us fill it?"[77] It would then caution its listeners to do a thorough cleanup: this time—as opposed to the last time, 1961–63—even the children should not be spared.

The war provided the context in which the Interahamwe transformed, from a youth organization at its founding in 1990 to a vigilante group in 1991–92, and ultimately into a death squad whose members led the house-to-house search for identifying and killing Tutsi in 1994. Robert Kajuga, a founding member and by 1994 the national president of Interahamwe, was born of a multiethnic family. His father was a Hutu, an Anglican priest, and his mother a Tutsi. Interviewed by an English journalist at the height of the genocide, Kajuga's defense of violence was simple: "It's a war against the Tutsis because they want to take power, and we Hutus are more numerous. Most Tutsis support the RPF, so they fight and they kill. We have to defend our country. The government authorises us. We go in behind the army. We watch them and learn."[78] The coalescence of civil war and a democratic opening put Rwanda "in a state of permanent tension." The surest sign of it was the fast-eroding middle ground.

Having subjected Rwanda to a series of conditions throughout the course of the four-year civil war, the West sensed that the end of the regime was fast approaching and prepared to leave. The arrival of a 1,000-strong UN peacekeeping force in November was followed by the departure of French forces the next month. It signaled the complete isolation of the government in Kigali. That same month, the UN contingent escorted an RPF battalion into UN premises in Kigali. Meanwhile, Prime Minister Uwilingiyimana was still failing to put together the transitional government: it was less a sign of lack of will, then of mounting tension on the verge of defeat in the civil war.

The more the paralysis of government continued, the more tension increased, incredibly and palpably. Killing, burning, and looting spread through Kigali in the last weeks of February 1994. Many were killed right in front of UN troops, who just stood by and let it happen. The slaughter of the prime minister and ten Belgian soldiers sent to protect her, right inside the UN compound,[79] presented the UN with a clear choice: either increase the size of the United Nations Assistance Mission to Rwanda (UNAMIR) force and change its mandate, or pull out. The UN chose to all but pull out. The Security Council met on 21 April. While the secretary-general requested more than a doubling of the size of the contingent, from the original 2,500 to 5,500, the major powers hesitated: led by the United States, the Security Council decided to leave behind a derisory force of only 270 soldiers. The message to the government was clear: implement the Arusha Agreement or else the UN will pull out and the RPF take power. By putting in place the final squeeze, the UN had succeeded in fully polarizing the situation.[80]

Could the UN have done otherwise and thus prevented the genocide? Opinions varied. Mr. J. Brian Atwood of USAID, in a press comment after the genocide, maintained "it would have been virtually impossible" to do anything under the circumstances, especially given that planned attacks were augmented by "irrational forces at work." General Roméo Dallaire, the Canadian commander in charge of UN forces in Rwanda, had thought otherwise. On 11 January 1994, he sent a cable to the office of the secretary-general, concluding on the basis of the testimony of an informant in the Interahamwe: "Principle aim of the Interahamwe in the past was to protect Kigali from RPF. Since UNAMIR mandate he has been ordered to register all Tutsi in Kigali. He suspects it is for their extermination.

Example he gave was that in 20 minutes his personnel could kill up to 1000 Tutsis."[81] A high-ranking UN official in New York also disagreed with USAID.[82] We may never know the answer to the question: Could the UN have prevented the genocide? What we do know is that the UN took no action indicating that it took a serious view of the shedding of African blood. If anything, it gave the opposite message. When the slaughter began in April, a story familiar to African ears played itself out again. Belgian and French paratroopers swooped in to repatriate those who were least in danger: their own nationals and those from other rich countries who wanted to leave. They categorically refused to consider evacuating any Rwandans unless, of course, they were married to Europeans.[83] When the French did return to Rwanda, it was toward the end of the genocide, as benefactors of a UN-sanctioned "humanitarian" intervention called Opération Turquoise. Ostensibly undertaken to save the remnants of the Tutsi population running for their lives, it also turned out to be a protective umbrella for those in the leadership of the genocide running for cover.

Let us return to consider the fate of the democratic opposition. If we are to go by the threefold increase in those joining opposition public demonstrations in a single month in late 1991, the democratic opposition seemed to be enjoying a groundswell of urban support at the time. But in the aftermath of the signing of the Arusha Agreement, precisely when it may have hoped to reap the harvest of popular support, the opposition was instead thrown to the margins. In my view, this outcome was the result of a confluence of three forces: a reckless internal opposition, an irresponsible donor community, and a naive RPF. The internal opposition was reckless because it acted without a sense of the balance of forces within the country. Had it taken the balance of forces into account, it would have moderated both the nature of its demands and the pace of its momentum. It did not because of a false confidence that it derived from the backing of donors whom it knew the government could not ignore because of dire financial need. The donor community force-fed Rwanda a reform agenda out of a textbook, without regard to the situation on the ground and secure in the knowledge that they would not have to suffer the consequences of their actions. Joined to immunity, power bred a reckless irresponsibility. The RPF had even less contact with the situation on the ground than did the internal opposition or the donors. The naivité of the RPF was fed by leaders who were mostly born outside the country and whose sense of possibilities was shaped by their experiences in Uganda, and not in Rwanda.

Prelude to Genocide

Neither political assassinations nor massacres make for genocide. It will also not help to equate Hutu Power as a whole with a genocidal tendency. The genocidal tendency arose out of a double crisis, of both the democratic opposition and of Hutu Power. Faced with a military defeat that seemed to sound the very death knell of Hutu Power, the *génocidaires* chose to embrace death itself as an alternative to life without power. Turning away from the enemy on the battlefield—the enemy it could not defeat—it looked for an enemy within. There were two turning points in defining the shift of focus from an armed target on the battlefield to unarmed and defenseless civilians within. The *first* was the assassination of the first Hutu president in neighboring Burundi, Melchior Ndadaye. The *second* was the assassination of Rwanda's own Hutu president, Juvénal Habyarimana, and the murder of the prime minister, Agathe Uwilingiyimana. If Ndadaye's death was taken as a prophetic lesson that the only alternative for the Hutu was between power and servitude, that there could be no power sharing between Hutu and Tutsi, Habyarimana's death was a signal that the hour to choose between power and servitude had indeed struck. Finally, the death of the president and the killing of the prime minister removed precisely those leaders who had publicly championed an agenda for an "ethnic reconciliation" between Hutu and Tutsi.

In spite of a history that presented a milder version of Tutsi power and Hutu servitude, Burundi had come to be seen by Rwandan Hutu and Tutsi alike as some sort of an accursed Siamese twin.[84] For Hutu in post-1959 Rwanda, Burundi presented a real life portrayal of what it would be like for Hutu to continue to live under Tutsi power. The mass killing of Hutu schoolchildren and intellectuals in 1972—estimated at around two hundred thousand—gave the Great Lakes region the first sight of a genocidal wave of killing. That was until the political reform under President Pierre Buyoya, which brought universal franchise with one-person–one-vote in a system of multi-party competition. In the ensuing election of 1993, Melchior Ndadaye was elected president. For the first time in its postindependence history, Burundi had a Hutu as president and, even more incredibly, a Hutu-dominated government with a nearly all-Tutsi army. But only two months after the signing of the Arusha Agreement—on 21 October 1993—the promise of the Burundi reform turned into a nightmare when elements from the all-Tutsi army murdered the Hutu president. Political violence swept the country and some 200,000 panic-struck Hutu crossed the border into Rwanda. The core message of Hutu Power began to sound credible to ordinary Hutu ears in Rwanda: power sharing was just another name for political suicide. History had ruled out political coexistence between Hutu and Tutsi.[85]

As tension mounted, arms proliferated and training in the use of arms became open and prevalent. Every organized political tendency, and not just the advocates of Hutu Power, felt it necessary to have an armed militia attached to it. If the ruling party had the Interahamwe and the CDR its own Impuzamugambi (those with a single purpose), then the MDR had the Inkuba (thunder) and the PSD its Abakombozi (the liberators).[86] It came to be accepted that only armed politics was credible politics. A pastoral letter issued in December 1993 by the Catholic bishop of Nyundo, the diocese where Habyarimana's home was located, also the diocese where a number of massacres had been carried out between 1900 and 1993, criticized the distribution of arms to youth militia. But the level of political violence continued to escalate. In March 1994, the head of one of the three main opposition parties, the PSD, was assassinated. The next day, a mob of PSD supporters lynched the head of CDR.[87]

The last major signpost of "ethnic reconciliation" in Rwanda—even in the context of Hutu Power—was in the person of President Habyarimana himself, and of his prime minister, Agathe Uwilingiyimana.[88] Representing the "power" wing of the largest opposition party, the MDR, Uwilingiyimana had been appointed prime minister a year before by Habyarimana in place of a moderate-opposition prime minister who appeared to be too closely identified to the RPF. Though defenders of Hutu Power, Habyarimana and Uwilingiyimana defined the middle ground that the *génocidaire* tendency needed to clear if it was to assume power. With the shooting down of Habyarimana's plane on 6 April and the brutal killing of his prime minister that same day, the agenda of "ethnic reconciliation" ceased to exist. The genocidal tendency was now in a position to take over the reigns of political power. The *génocidaires* were not synonymous with the army, but with a faction that cut across the army, the political, and the civil elite. They were different from other defenders of Hutu Power in the means they advocated: for the *génocidaires* were the faction who advocated genocide as the only effective—and remaining—way of defending power.

One needs to exercise the same caution when it comes to an understanding of what has been called "the institutional machinery of genocide": the Presidential Guard in the army, the youth militia Interahamwe and the Impuzamugambi, the local-level ten-cell civil defense units, and the machinery of local government and "customary" rule. "By 1992, the institutional apparatus of genocide was already in place," wrote René Lemarchand.[89] Just as the *génocidaires* were a political tendency born of civil war—and not simply one that had marked time awaiting a suitable opportunity—so were none of the instruments used to perpetrate genocide not *created* for that purpose from the outset, but were *turned* to that purpose in the face of defeat in the civil war. The Presidential Guard had been created in 1992 to wage war, not genocide. The administrative ten-cell groups were created as units for civil defense. The youth wing of each political party was created to expand political participation in the course of multiparty competition. And the machinery of local administration, which was built in the colonial period and had preceded all others, was created to enable colonial government, to give it teeth, while masking this project as customary. Though they perpetrated the worst political violence in the history of Rwanda, none of these had been created for that purpose. To understand how their original purpose came to be subverted, one needs to understand—as I have argued—the consequences of civil war and defeat.

By portraying opponents as potential perpetrators and ourselves as potential victims, war tends to demonize opponents and sanctify aggression as protective and defensive. The Rwandan genocide was carried out by two different groups. The first were actual victims of the RPF war and of the massacres that followed Ndadaye's assassination in Burundi, the former displaced from territories RPF captured in the northeast of Rwanda and the latter refugees from Burundi. The second were those who were convinced that they would surely, even if potentially, be victims if Tutsi Power won. They included two classes of beneficiaries of the 1959 Revolution, one prosperous but the other poor, the former members of the post-1959 Hutu middle class, and the latter ordinary peasants who would not have had access to land but for the land reform that followed 1959.

The president's death and the prime minister's murder presented the *génocidaires* with an opportunity for a coup d'état. It is said that the head of the Presidential Guard, Colonel Théoneste Bagosora, and his circle, tried to take power in their own right, but failed to secure the support of "a number of officers as well as ranking representatives of the UN in Rwanda." Their next move was "to install a regime of extremists" other than themselves; the move was successful.[90] Without their hands on the levers of power, they could have carried on with political massacres in different areas, but they could not have unleashed a countrywide terror whose object was to annihilate the entire community of Tutsi so as to remove any trace of a Tutsi presence from the soil of Rwanda. Only from a position of state power could they put the stamp of law and authority on a genocidal design. To consolidate that grip, they began with the physical elimination of all Hutu in public life who were identified with the middle ground. The elimination of moderate Hutu, estimated to number 50,000, cleared the ground of any significant group that could mount a challenge to the tidal wave of violence that was about to follow.

INSIDE THE GENOCIDE

A Central Design

The *génocidaires'* tendency had to do more than simply capture power to implement its design. To embark on an agenda calling for the total physical elimination of the Tutsi and of the "moderate" Hutu political and civil elite—those branded as "accomplices" because they were likely to stand in the way of such a gruesome "solution" to civil war—they needed a reliable machinery. To do that, they had to ensure the loyalty of both the political machinery of "customary" power that would direct the violence, and the coercive machinery, mainly the Presidential Guard and the youth militias, that would enforce it. The first step was to remove those with suspect loyalties from positions of power. The presidential plane was shot down on 6 April. Public appeals were made to a meeting of prefects on 11 April and on the radio the next day, to the effect that partisan interests must be set aside to fight the common enemy, the Tutsi. All this while, the Presidential Guard was busy identifying and eliminating members of the political opposition. On 16 and 17 April, they replaced "the military Chief of Staff and the prefects best known for opposing the killings." This included "one who was murdered with his family" and another who "was later imprisoned and executed." Also slain were "three burgomasters and a number of other officials who sought to stop the killings."[91]

The pivotal role of a centrally-coordinated plan for the unfolding of ground-level violence—as well as its limits—comes out most clearly where popular participation was absent, or was too weak to provide the necessary deadly force. Legendary in accounts of the genocide is the case of Butare, whose local authority actually *refused* to carry out the orders to kill the internal "enemy". This extraordinary courage came from its prefect, Jean-Baptiste Habyarimana, the only Tutsi prefect in the country. For two weeks, Butare remained a calm oasis while a storm raged in the rest of the country. At that point, the president of the interim government, himself a Butare man, came to rebuke the population for "sleeping" through the war, and appointed a new prefect whose enthusiasm would equal the demands of the situation. He came to town with soldiers of the Presidential Guard and with militia members from Kiaka Cooperative in Gisenyi in the far north of the country. As the town population gathered to witness the investiture of the new prefect, the former prefect and his family were murdered by the Presidential Guard. For those harboring moral ambivalence about the new direction of the "war," the signal was clear: any wavering in the face of orders from above would mean certain death. Fear could silence opposition, but it could not generate enthusiasm. To sustain the killing in Butare, the new officials had to bring in armed groups from the outside and unemployed youth from the hills.[92]

The role of outside forces in triggering the violence appears to have been the greatest in the prefectures of Butare and Gitarama, both at the center of the old Rwanda kingdom. This is where there had been the highest incidence of intermarriage, especially among the elites, and where the colonial history of more or less unaccountable Tutsi power in the local authority was but an interlude in a centuries-old history.[93] It is in this region that the presence of a substantial number of Hutu refugees who had fled violence in Burundi the previous year made the job easier: "Angry about being forced to flee their own homes by Tutsi in Burundi and concentrated in a camp where they had nothing to do with their time and energy, the people from Burundi (known as Barundi) offered the ideal recruits for launching an attack on the Tutsi of Nyakizu."[94]

No matter how prominent and predominant the role of external forces in particular locations, their presence should not detract from the decisive role of locals in the genocide. To understand the variety of local responses, we need to make a number of distinctions. The first is regional. The genocide, we must remember, took place mainly in central and southern Rwanda, and hardly in the north. After the first RPF attack in 1990, Tutsi in the north were killed. Not only were the Tutsi in post-1990 Rwanda resident mainly in the center and south of the country, so were the parties that comprised the internal political opposition and that had allied with the RPF at Arusha. The genocide thus divided the southern Hutu more than it did the northern Hutu into two sharply opposed groups: those who joined the massacres and those who got massacred. The two extremes were joined by middling reactions that tried to combine moral extremes. The predicament of ordinary Hutu is clear from a single fact: it is not only the political opposition that got massacred in the days that followed the president's assassination. As they grew in scope, the massacres targeted anyone, peasant or professional, who refused to join in the mélée. Kodjo Ankrah of Church World Action recounted to me what happened when soldiers entered a church in Ruhengeri and asked that Hutu step on one side, and Tutsi on another: "People refused; when they said, Tutsis this side, all moved. When they said Hutus that side, all moved. Eventually, soldiers killed them all, 200 to 300 people in all."[95] Professionals who refused to join in the killing also met the same fate. Take, for example, the parents of François Nsansuwera, deputy attorney general under Habyarimana, later appointed to the same post under the RPF. Nsansuwera's father was a retired army officer. When thirty Hutu and Tutsi gathered to seek shelter at their house, the militia called in the army; all thirty, including his parents and father-in-law, were killed. Of his family of nine, Nsansuwera said only two survived, himself and a younger brother who had gone through Burundi to join the RPF.[96]

The Hutu who were slaughtered in the opening days of the genocide—either because they were identified with the political opposition or because they simply refused to join in the killing—were the first of three groups among the southern Hutu. The second were Hutu who not only saved their Tutsi neighbors, but also got away with it. Some were indeed textbooklike heroes, such as the retired soldier-turned-policeman I met at the church in Ntarama. He hid eleven people in different locations: from ceilings up above to pits down below. When I asked him whether he knew of anyone else who had helped people by hiding them, he said "no." When I asked why he thought there had not been others like him in the area, he simply said: "People don't have the same mind."

Later on, I heard of a different kind of response from Faustin, my guide during my 1995 visit. This ambivalent response illustrates the third type. He narrated an account he had heard from a survivor from Kibuye, on the eastern shores of Lake Kivu. As in several other places, there too the attack against the Tutsi began with the arrival of a group of Interahamwe from outside. This time though, the entire community—Tutsi, Hutu, and Twa—got together and fought them with stones. The Interahamwe retreated, tried again on a second day, and failed yet again. On the third day, the Interahamwe sent political cadres, one by one, to approach local Hutu and promised not only that their lives would be spared if they didn't join Tutsi in the fight, but also that they would benefit from the distribution of Tutsi property. The next time the Interahamwe attacked, the Tutsi found themselves isolated. Some 20,000, they retreated into the ridges, up in the hills. There they fought for two months, with the fighting taking on a regular daily pattern: from 8:00 in the morning till 12:30, when the Interahamwe would descend the valley for lunch, and from 2:00 in the afternoon until 5:00 or 6:00. The hours of sleeping, shooting, and eating were known to all. So were the means of defense: the Interahamwe shot, whereas the Tutsi simply ducked bullets by running around the hill in concentric circles, at most throwing stones. By the time French paratroopers arrived and stopped the massacre, two months had passed and nearly 19,000 were dead and two hundred injured, with some eight hundred still alive. If in this instance the Hutu deserted their Tutsi neighbors, leaving them to face Interahamwe rifles alone, at least they did not join the Interahamwe in massacring the Tutsi.[97]

The most ambivalent stories of the genocide I heard from survivors were about the Hutu who saved a friend or a colleague in one place, only to go and join the killings in another. A lecturer at the University of Butare rescued the child of a Tutsi colleague, and then ran for shelter in the Zone Turquoise, only to find herself accused upon return of having participated in the genocide. Whereas she was released after four months in prison, her husband was not. When I spoke to her in July 1995, she told me her husband was not alone but languished in jail with ten other lecturers, all accused of participation in the genocide.[98] I never did find out the truth of the allegations against them. But I did often wonder: How could the same person risk his or her own life to save another at one time in one place, and yet take life at another time in another place? As I heard more and similar stories, I posed the same question to those I met, and mulled over it myself. As so often happens in postgenocide Rwanda, I usually got two answers to the question, one Hutu and the other Tutsi, depending on the respondent. The Hutu answer was that these were stories made up by Tutsi survivors reluctant to recognize any Hutu savior, and the Tutsi answer was that the act of mercy lacked sincerity and was more an alibi for the future. Over the next year, as I regularly perused discussions on Rwandanet, an email listserve, I realized that these cases were not solitary. Many had combined saving in one place with killing in another. Could they have killed under duress—knowing that if they refused or even appeared reluctant, they would surely be killed—and saved a life when the opportunity presented itself? Was this not more representative of humanity in the ordinary? They were less than heroic under stress, yet humane in ordinary circumstances—perhaps one reason their experiences are not be celebrated in the open and without reservation.

Mectilde's Story

The ambiguity of responses in the real world of the genocide comes together in the experience of a single Tutsi survivor, Mectilde.[99] I met Mectilde during my second visit to postgenocide Rwanda, in December

1995. She was working with a UN agency and was engaged to be married. At the time of the genocide, Mectilde was a typist with an international company in Kigali. She lived in Kiyovu Joc, a youth hostel for Catholic women workers which housed sixty women. "On 6 April, I went to study computer at Ministry of Planning during the morning, returned to the office in the afternoon, and went home at five with a colleague. About 8:30 P.M., we heard bangs. My neighbor said it was the plane of President Habyarimana exploding. I closed my door. I had a one-room apartment and was alone. I turned my radio on at 9 P.M. Radio RTLM gave news of the president's death." The first group she turned to for support were neighbors. "I invited them to come to my room. We waited for the news, heard it together, and decided to search where to go that night." The next morning, the Presidential Guard entered the hostel. "They killed four with guns. My other neighbors asked me not to stay there, but come with us to a priest. Our neighbors were mixed, Hutu and Tutsi. But at that time, no one was thinking of ethnie. We were thinking only of the death of the president."

"On the second day, they began to kill Tutsi." She then turned to a Canadian priest, spending two nights in his compound, along with three hundred others, until the priest suggested they leave. "He said we should go out because he had heard that the Interahamwe had killed all priests and refugees at another center. He said, pray, and you die, God will receive you."

Her next refuge was with two girlfriends, "one mixed with a Hutu father and a Tutsi mother, and the second a Hutu." They spent four days in the hostel, living on tea and rice. On the morning of the fifth day, the president of the Catholic Workers Youth, a Hutu, came to her room and broke the news that she was number three on the list of those to be killed that day. She and her girlfriends decided to go to the town of Gitarama. The problem was that whereas her girl friends had Hutu ID cards, she didn't. The Youth Association president said he would help pass her through the roadblocks if she went with his younger brother, who was in the military. She agreed. But when the brother arrived, he refused. "He said no, I was very very Tutsi and he could not help; they will kill us both. I said OK, go. The president said no, you come. They said, take nothing, try and be as a peasant. I went with a trouser and slippers. I put out my glasses. I wrote my name on a paper saying I am a wife of a military staying in Gisenyi. They said I should wait in Gitarama for the other girls while they continued to Gisenyi."

She took a taxi jammed with passengers, negotiating roadblocks, first at Kiyovu, then at Muhima. "When I arrived at Muhima, near the workshop, I met a woman with a gun. She asked me to leave the car and said she saw me once at CMD [the military camp of 600 RPF soldiers near Kigali]. I said it was not me. She insisted, said the car could go without me. I pleaded. She said no, but then allowed me to go."

The next roadblock was manned by Interahamwe. "They said I must be a Tutsi because I had no card. They took me out. The military (in the taxi) said no, it is a mistake, for this is the wife of our colleague who is in Gisenyi and came without an ID. They took out their machete. Someone with a gun said he will do it. The military said you can't kill someone with us; if you kill her, we will kill you. They said, OK, you are *Ikotanyi*. In our army, there are some, we know. But we know you can't pass the roadblock of Nyabarongo, manned by the Presidential Guard. The driver said, now, we will pass the next roadblock and we won't discuss with them, because if we do, they will kill us all. So just pray. When we arrived, the Presidential Guard asked where we were going. We said Gisenyi. They said you can pass, without any discussion. I had passed the last step of death."

The taxi dropped her at Gitarama, where she had to pass the night before meeting up with her friends. "It was 4 P.M. when they left me on the road. I had 2,000 francs only in my pocket. I had a Fanta and returned to the road. I saw someone who was working near my office. He said, why are you here? What have you done to be here? I said I had no idea where to go. He invited me to his apartment. There were forty-two people, three families, inside the apartment. They were both Hutu and Tutsi." She spent the night in the apartment and returned to the road the next day. "I waited until 2 P.M., when I saw a taxi with my two friends. Their families were in Gitarama in a neighboring commune. We were the first to arrive from Kigali since the war began. I went with my friend who had a Tutsi mother and a Hutu father. I thought I wouldn't have a big problem since the mother was a Tutsi, better than going into a Hutu family. I arrived there. They took us as survivors. We received many visitors who asked news of Kigali. We spent a week without any problem."

The following week, a neighbor reported that they had begun to kill Tutsi in the commune. The family also had a daughter married to a Tutsi. "They went to see if he [her husband] was alive. Now we were two who were a problem to the family, the son-in-law and me. They decided to dig a hole in the kraal. We would spend the whole night in that hole, with the cows there also. During the night, about one or two, they would put us out, and give us something to drink after a bath. We would go to bed for one or two hours and return to our hole."

The hole-in-the-ground routine went on for three weeks. "Then the son-in-law said, it's enough for me. I don't want to cause trouble for this family. He told his father-in-law that he preferred to be killed as a man who respects himself. They said, where can you pass with your ID card? They took the son's ID card, put the photo of the man, and tried to draw a stamp. Then they gave him the ID. He took it. He passed three communes and arrived in Butare without any trouble. He spent a month there. Once he went out and met his former student who was a military. He asked for his ID, and when he saw it he accused him of lying and killed him with a gun."

Mectilde continued to stay in her hole, but not for too long. On 27 April, the *Ikotanyi* came and took them to the refugee camp at Musamo. There, they spent a month and then returned to Gitarama. Another month there, and the *préfet* said she could go home. "When I arrived in Kigali, I saw so many people. We passed the night at my girlfriend's place. The second day, I went to town to see if my brother was still alive. He had gone to Bujumbura. Our house was empty. My brother said my father, mother, younger brother, all were killed. Only the three sisters are alive. He gave me 20,000 francs." Mectilde returned to work. "Before I used to be a senior personnel officer, but I was asked to be a receptionist because it was very difficult to think, to make a report."

I asked Mectilde if many Hutu had helped Tutsi. She said, "ten percent helped. A Hutu can help you in Kigali, but in Butare he can begin to kill Tutsi. Take the president of Catholic Workers Youth we went with to Gitarama. When he arrived in Butare, he killed people. I don't know why." I asked her, what about the remaining 90% Hutu? She gave me a rough count: "Ten percent helped; 30 percent were forced to kill; 20 percent killed reluctantly; 40 percent killed enthusiastically." It is the 40 percent, those who "killed enthusiastically," who represent the real moral and political dilemma of the Rwandan genocide. Mectilde is, of course, one person. My purpose in citing her estimates of how many were killed—whether enthusiastically, reluctantly, or under duress—is not to give these a stamp of approval. Later, we shall see that some of the most responsible leaders in the RPF also estimate the killers in the millions. I will later discuss the political uses to which such estimates can be put and which in turn can lead to inflated estimates. Here, I want to make two different points. One, from the point of view of the minority in postgenocide

Rwanda, the majority is guilty, either of killing, or condoning, or just looking elsewhere while the killing happened. Second, even if we can never know the numbers of those who killed, there is no escaping the disturbing fact that many did enthusiastically join in the killing. The genocide was not simply a state project. Had the killing been the work of state functionaries and those bribed by them, it would have translated into no more than a string of massacres perpetrated by death squads. Without massacres by machete-wielding civilian mobs, in the hundreds and thousands, there would have been no genocide. We now turn to the social underbelly of the genocide: the participation of those who killed with a purpose, for whom the violence of the genocide and its target held meaning.

Women Killers and Child Accomplices

By September 1995, several hundred of the 10,000 inmates in Kigali's sweltering central prison were women. Rakiya Omaar of African Rights told an Associated Press journalist that some "were actively involved, killing with machetes and guns" while others "acted in support roles—allowing murder squads access to hospitals and homes, cheering on male killers, stripping the dead and looting their houses."[100] Calixte, the survivor I talked with at the church in Ntarama, gave a ground-level view of female agency in the massacres. "Women killed a few, but mainly waited for Tutsi women crossing the river with a kid on the back, so they would take the kid and throw it in water. Or they did espionage, reporting on who was hiding where."[101] Aloysius Inyumba, the RPF minister in charge of women's affairs in 1995, gave me a more global picture. "I have 838 women in prison. One woman said to me, I have only killed eight; there are people who have killed many and are free."[102] Alongside women there were children, eight hundred according to one report. Their ages ranged from seven to seventeen years. The vast majority of the older children "were charged with genocide."[103]

Killings Sanctified

Just as the killing in Rwanda was not done by shadowy death squads but by mobs of ordinary people guided by armed militia and trained infantrymen, the killing also did not happen in secluded but in public places. Most often, the killings happened in places of worship. Contrary to Gérard Prunier's contention that "the bystanders were mostly the churches,"[104] the church was a direct participant in the genocide. Rather than a passive mirror reflecting tensions, the Church was more of an epicenter radiating tensions.

Like the middle class of which they were a prominent part, priests were also divided between those who were targeted in the killings and those who led or facilitated the killings. Here, too, there was hardly any middle ground. A Lutheran minister recalled what the gangs told him: "You can have religion afterwards." Explaining why he walked around with a club, the minister told a reporter: "Everyone had to participate. To prove that you weren't RPF, you had to walk around with a club. Being a pastor was not an excuse."[105] Priests who had condemned the government's use of ethnic quotas in education and the civil service were among the first victims of the massacres. In all, 105 priests and 120 nuns, "at least a quarter of the clergy," are believed to have been killed. But priests were not only among those killed, they were also among the killers. Investigators with the UN Center for Human Rights claimed "strong evidence" that "about a dozen priests actually killed." Others were accused of "supervising gangs of young killers."[106] Hugh McCullum, a former editor of the *United Church Observer* and author of *The Angels Have Left Us*, told *The Toronto Star* that two-thirds of Rwanda's Catholic priests either died during the genocide or ran into exile after the genocide. He said the figures were similar for the Protestant churches.[107] Twenty-seven of the priests in Goma sent a letter to the pope on 2 August 1994, claiming that the massacres in Rwanda were "the result of the provocation and of the harassment of the Rwandese people by the R.P.F." They continued in the same vein: "We dare even to confirm that the number of Hutu civilians killed by the army of the R.P.F. exceeds by far the Tutsi victims of the ethnic troubles."[108] At a press conference in Nairobi in early June, more than two months into the genocide, the Anglican archbishop refused unequivocally to denounce the interim government. The Catholic archbishop even moved with the interim government from Kigali to Gitarama.[109]

How low the moral terpitude of the clergy had sunk is illustrated by a story Jean Carbonnarre, honorary president of the Paris-based NGO Survie, narrated to correspondents of the Inter-Press Service: "André Karamaga, president of the Anglican Church in Rwanda, told me that he went to the Taba commune near Kigali to settle a dispute between two priests quarreling over who should run the parish. The first priest told Karamaga that he was more deserving because the second priest had killed 15 people. When Karamaga challenged the second priest, he admitted the killings, but still maintained that he deserved to run the parish as, he said, the other priest had killed even more."[110] Father Wenceslas Munyashyaka, the curate of Sainte-Famille church, sheltered eight thousand refugees but provided the militia members with lists of those he alleged had expressed sympathy for the RPF and agreed to let them come and pick off those they wanted. Wearing a flak jacket and toting a pistol during the massacres, he fled to Goma with the interim government and was one of the twenty-seven who wrote to the pope defending the Rwanda army and blaming the RPF for massacres.[111] In an open letter to His Holiness, Pope John Paul II, Rakiya Omaar, director of African Rights, listed the most shocking instances of clergy organizing massacres, and summed up participation of the Church in the genocide: "Christians who slay other Christians before the alter, bishops who remain silent in the fact of genocide and fail to protect their own clergy, priests who participate in the murder of their parishioners and nuns who hand people over to be killed cannot leave the Church indifferent."[112]

How could it be that most major massacres of the genocide took place in churches? How could all those institutions that we associate with nurturing life—not only churches, but schools and even hospitals—be turned into places where life was taken with impunity and facility? Médecins sans Frontières, a medical charity, pulled out of the University Hospital in Kigali after its patients kept disappearing. *The British Medical Journal* quoted the testimony of Dr. Claude-Emile Rwagasonza: "The extremist doctors were also asking patients for their identity cards before treating them. They refused to treat sick Tutsis. Also, many people were coming to the hospital to hide. The extremist doctors prevented many of these people from hiding in the hospital." A medical doctor, a member of the hospital staff, directed the militia into the hospital in Kibeho and shut off the power supply so that the massacre may proceed in darkness. Some of "the most horrific massacres occurred in maternity clinics, where people gathered in the belief that no one would kill mothers and new-born babies."[113] "The percentage of doctors who became 'killers par excellence' was very high," concluded African Rights on the basis of extensive investigations. They included persons as highly qualified as Dr. Sosthène Munyemana, a gynecologist at the University Hospital of Butare, Rwanda's principal teaching hospital. "A huge number of the most qualified and experienced doctors in the country, men as well as women—including surgeons, physicians, paediatricians, gynaecologists, anaesthetists, public health specialists and hospital administrators—participated in the murder of their own Tutsi colleagues, patients, the wounded and terrified refugees who had sought shelter in their hospitals, as well as their neighbours and strangers." In a sector as small as Tumba, three doctors played a central part. Of these, one was a doctor at Groupe Scolaire Hospital, and the other, her husband, was the health director for Butare. "Two of the most active assassins in Tumba" were a medical assistant and his wife, a nurse.[114]

Close on the heels of priests and doctors as prime enthusiasts of the genocide were teachers, and even some human rights activists. When I visited the National University at Butare in 1995, I was told of Hutu staff and students who betrayed their Tutsi colleagues and joined in their physical elimination. Teachers commonly denounced students to the militia or killed students themselves. A Hutu teacher told a French journalist without any seeming compunction: "A lot of people got killed here. I myself killed some of the children. . . . We had eighty kids in the first year. There are twenty-five left. All the others, we killed them or they have run away."[115] African Rights compiled a fifty-nine-page dossier charging Innocent Mazimpaka, who was in April 1994 the chairman of the League for the Promotion and Defence of Human Rights in Rwanda (LI-PRODHOR) and simultaneously an employee of a Dutch aid organization, SNV, with responsibility for the genocide. Along with his younger brother, the *burgomaster* of Gatare commune, he was charged with the slaughter of all but twenty-one of Gatare's Tutsi population of 12,263.[116] Rakiya Omaar pointed out that "several members of human rights groups are now known to have participated" in the killings, refuting "the notion that an independent civil society—of which the educated and the political opposition were the backbone—resisted the project of genocide."[117]

That victims looking for a sanctuary should seek out churches, schools and hospitals as places for shelter is totally understandable. But that they should be killed without any let or hindrance—even lured to these places for that purpose—is not at all understandable. As places of shelter turned into slaughterhouses, those pledged to heal or nurture life set about extinguishing it methodically and deliberately. That the professions most closely associated with valuing life—doctors and nurses, priests and teachers, human rights activists—got embroiled in taking it is probably the most troubling question of the Rwandan genocide.

One could go on narrating atrocity stories ad infinitum, and indeed some have.[118] The point of such an exercise may be to show how base human nature can be, or it may be, I fear, more self-serving: to show how base is the nature of some humans, usually some others, not us. This is not my purpose, nor do I wish to shut my eyes to atrocity when atrocities have indeed been perpetrated. My point, though, is that atrocity cannot be its own explanation. Violence cannot be allowed to speak for itself, for violence is not its own meaning. To be made thinkable, it needs to be *historicized*. My preoccupation is not with the universal character of evil, with describing acts of cruelty to underline the fact that people—or some people—are capable of unspeakable cruelty. It is, rather, with trying to understand the *political* nature of violence—that its targets are those defined as public enemy by perpetrators who see themselves as the people— and thus with the process that leads to it and the specific conditions that make this possible.

This study has located the genesis of Hutu/Tutsi violence in the colonial period, specifically around the 1959 Revolution and its recurrence at times when Hutu and Tutsi emerged as identities of groups contending for power, as in 1959–63 and 1990–94. True, elements of Tutsi Power began to gel over a long period, from the sixteenth century onwards, but the identity "Tutsi" became associated with privilege only in the reign of Rwabugiri toward the end of nineteenth century. Yet, it was not until Belgian colonialism that the local state structures were fully Tutsified, and that Tutsi hardened into a category signifying local privilege. From being a transethnic distinction of local significance, Belgian colonialism inserted Tutsi and Hutu into the world of *races* and *indigeneity.* Key to the political impact of Belgian colonialism is the opposite ways in which it constructed Tutsi and Hutu—Hutu as indigenous and Tutsi as alien—thereby racializing the difference between them. Unlike at any time in Rwanda's history, the Tutsi were presented as both a nonindigenous and a civilizing influence, as Caucasians of a lesser breed. The identities "Tutsi" and "Hutu" were politically enforced through state-issued identity cards. The educational system separated Tutsi from Hutu—and not just chiefs from commoners, as in other colonies—and nurtured its beneficiaries in notions of the Hamitic hypothesis. Hutu were effectively excluded from recruitment in local government and in the priesthood, both of which were completely Tutsified. More than ever in the history of Rwanda, the colonial world effectively sealed the Hutu into a servile status: while the mass of Hutu were compelled to do forced labor (*ubureetwa*) for Tutsi chiefs, the few who would have been ritually ennobled in a previous era were also branded into a servile condition. Their only salvation lay in politics.

The Hutu middle class had a different history from that of the Tutsi middle class. This different history was also adversarial: it made of them a counterelite. While many Tutsi could date their climb to a middle-class status to educational opportunity and civil service appointment in the colonial period, few Hutu could put forth such a claim. Their history was more likely one of individuals whose aspirations had been frustrated by the racialized structure of colonial Rwanda. Unlike their Tutsi counterparts, most members of the Hutu middle class dated their genesis from the 1959 Revolution, and not from the colonial period. They not only provided the leadership of the 1959 Revolution, they were also its main beneficiaries. The Hutu middle class was both the child of the 1959 Revolution and its proud inheritor. In time, many came to criticize postrevolutionary power, but hardly any voiced criticism of the revolution. When youthful members of this class began calling for democratic rights toward the end of the 1980s, they presumed a context where the gains of the revolution were secure. The civil war that began with the RPF invasion of 1990 removed this certainty. It put the Hutu middle class in a state of crisis, and it hurled them yet again into a world where Hutu and Tutsi were names of corporate groups contending for political power. It was a world in which democratic opposition came to be synonymous with treason.

POWER struggles in the bipolar world of Hutu and Tutsi are marked by a truism: not only are members of the middle class the main beneficiaries of every victory, they are also the core victims in every defeat. And since victory for one is defeat for the other, every struggle bears the hallmark of a life-and-death tussle. Three events in recent history bear testimony to this truism: 1959 in Rwanda, and 1972 and 1993 in Burundi. Few Rwandans could have been unaware that when the Tutsi army in neighboring Burundi unleashed terror on Hutu in 1972 and killed nearly 200,000, it did not go for the lives of ordinary Hutu but for those of school-going youth. The objective was to crush the flower from which would come tomorrow's intelligentsia. Anyone who had come out of the colonial period understood that the existence of an intelligentsia was the prerequisite for initiative, independence, and leadership.

The 1972 massacre of Hutu school youth in Burundi stirred demands in Rwanda. Critics said that while the Hutu revolution of 1959 had managed to transform the state, its impact on society had been superficial. While Hutu had gained political supremacy, they had yet to win social supremacy, whether in education or in the marketplace. This unrest was the context of the emergence of the Second Republic, a fact all the more remarkable since it was the Second Republic under President Habyarimana that began the process of deracializing the Tutsi and of reintegrating them into the Rwandan polity as an ethnicity. From one based on the distinction between two races, one indigenous and the other alien, the political discourse in the Second Republic turned around the distinction between majority and minority. From a nonindigenous race, the Tutsi became an indigenous minority. As an ethnic group, they could aspire to rights like other Rwandans; but as a minority, they would have to give up any claim to power.

The life of the Second Republic was cut short by the RPF invasion of 1990. The invasion literally reversed the dynamic of the Second Republic. By highlighting the distinction between the struggle for *rights* and the pursuit of *power*, it once again *polarized* Hutu and Tutsi as political identities. Key to this shift, this repolarization of Hutu and Tutsi as political identities, was the growing realization that the real objective of the RPF invasion was not rights but power—specifically Tutsi Power. The assassination of the newly elected Hutu president, Melchior Ndadaye, in Burundi in 1993 by a Tutsi army merely confirmed this realization as a truism. It is, after all, defeat in the civil war, and the specter of Tutsi Power, that provided the context in which a tendency born of Hutu Power—the *génocidaire*—chose to embrace death in preference to life. For the Hutu from Rwanda's postrevolutionary middle class, and those from other sectors, who followed the lead of the *génocidaires*, the true stake in the civil war was the key gain of the 1959 Revolution. That gain was a future for the Hutu, synonymous with the existence and expansion of a Hutu middle class. While the existence of the middle class could be said to be of direct interest to its members only, its expansion surely interested all those of humble origin, peasants or artisans, who looked with hope to their children and to the future. This point of view begins to make some sense of why so many hundreds and thousands who had never before killed participated in the genocide; why they included not only the victims of Hutu/Tutsi civil wars (the displaced and the refugees), but many more yet to be touched by the expanding civil war; why they thought of massacres of neighbors not only as a continuation and culmination of the civil war but also as a defense of the gains of the revolution; and why so many of these came disproportionately from Rwanda's Hutu middle class.

One needs to remember that the Tutsi were killed as Hamites, not as Tutsi. Whereas the Tutsi of precolonial vintage never claimed political privilege because they came from elsewhere, the Hamites of colonial vintage were said to be "a civilizing influence" for no other reason than that they were said to have come from elsewhere. Whereas ethnicized Tutsi existed before colonialism, the racialized Hamites were creatures of colonialism. As a political identity, ethnicity marked an internal difference, whereas race signified an external difference. Ethnic conflict does not breed genocide; at most, it can give rise to massacres. The difference is that only with genocide is there an attempt to obliterate the other physically and totally. When it comes to ethnicities, there is no question about the legitimacy of their presence in the political arena: as indigenous groups they belong, all of them. The points of conflict concern borderline issues, matters of excess. It is only with racialized groups, those constructed as nonindigenous, that their very presence in the political arena is considered illegitimate. And the racialization of the Tutsi, we must not forget, was the joint work of the state and the Church.

Herein lies the clue as to why the violence was marked by a greater fury in the Church than in any other institution in Rwandan society. The Church was the original ethnographer of Rwanda. It was the original author of the Hamitic hypothesis. The Church provided the lay personnel that permeated every local community and helped distinguish Hutu from Tutsi in every neighborhood: without the Church, there would have been no "racial" census in Rwanda. At the same time, the Church was the womb that nurtured the leadership of the insurgent Hutu movement. It provided the intellectual and organizational backup for this movement, from talent as ghostwriters to funding for the cooperative movement which oiled the tentacles that ran through Rwandan society like so many arteries through a body politic. It is from the ranks of the Church-connected movement that the leadership of the 1959 Revolution was drawn. On the morrow of the revolution, that same leadership used the power of the state to establish control over church education, both in terms of its content and its personnel. The fusion of the Church and the state, both in personnel and in vision, was symbolized by the fact that the archbishop of Rwanda sat as a formal member of the Central Committee of the ruling party until he was forced to resign in the early 1990s, on the eve of the pope's visit to Rwanda.

But the Church also differed from every other state-connected institution in Rwanda. While Hutu came to occupy the top echelons of the Church hierarchy, its middle level continued to include a substantial number of Tutsi. The civil war brought the power struggle in the Church to a climax. In the Church, there could be no middle ground, no sanctuary. Rather than a place of healing, the Church turned into a battleground for settling scores.

"A religious community which wages wars," wrote Carl Schmitt, "is already more than a religious community; it is a political entity."[119] So indeed was the Church in Rwanda. Let us recall that there was no single institutional home, no mortuary, bigger than the Church for the multiple massacres that marked the Rwandan horror. After all, but for the army and the Church, the two prime movers, the two organizing and leading forces, one located in the state and the other in society, there would have been no genocide.

If it is the struggle for power that explains the motivation of those who crafted the genocide, then it is the combined fear of a return to servitude and of reprisals thereafter that energized the foot soldiers of the genocide. The irony is that—whether in the Church, in hospitals, or in human rights groups, as in fields and homes—the perpetrators of the genocide saw themselves as the true victims of an ongoing political drama, victims of yesterday who may yet be victims again. That moral certainty explains the easy transition from yesterday's victims to killers the morning after.

Chapter Eight

Tutsi Power in Rwanda
and the Citizenship Crisis
in Eastern Congo

Conventional wisdom in Goma and Bukavu has it that Kivu Province in eastern Congo is where losers in Rwanda traditionally end up, and it is from Kivu that they prepare to return to power in Rwanda.[1] A civil society activist in Bukavu explained to me the long-term effect of Rwandan conflicts that tend to "spill over into our country": "These ethnic conflicts are cyclic with each ethnic group taking turn in power and misfortune. The fate of one today is the fate of the other tomorrow. The consequence for us are the refugees of the conflict. Another consequence of cyclical fortunes is that when they return, not everyone returns, some remain. Those who remain become Congolese."[2]

The RPF victory set off a massive exodus of Hutu from Rwanda. Like everything else about Rwanda those days, the rate and extent of the exodus was without precedent: over two million crossed Rwanda's borders in a week, dividing roughly between Congo and Tanzania. Over a million spilled over into Congo, mainly into North and South Kivu, a region that hosted most of the Kinyarwanda-speaking population in Congo. As they crossed the Congo-Rwanda border in mid-1994, the million-plus refugees literally brought the trauma of postgenocide Rwanda to the region of Kivu. The impact was volcanic, and its effects have yet to ebb. The escalating crisis in Rwanda introduced a double tension in Kivu, both external and internal, both a tension between Kivu and the power in Rwanda and a tension within Kivu society. This tension grew in intensity as the Kinyarwanda-speaking refugee and exile population in Kivu grew in size, increasing the weight of refugees and exiles while blurring the distinction between them and earlier immigrants. In turn, this fed the tendency on the part of many "indigenous" Congolese to refuse to distinguish between Kinyarwanda-speaking Congolese and the mix of refugees and exiles from Rwanda. If the 1990 RPF invasion of Rwanda from Uganda was born of the confluence of citizenship crisis on both sides of the Uganda-

Rwanda border, the RPF invasion of Congo in 1996 needs to be understood as an outcome of a similar confluence, except that this time it joined the citizenship crisis on the Rwanda and the Congo sides of the border. To explain this is the first purpose of the chapter.

The Banyarwanda of Congo, who then numbered fewer than a million, were already in the political limelight by the early 1990s. Historically, the Congolese Banyarwanda were divided between those in North Kivu and the rest in South Kivu, the former mainly Hutu and the latter mainly Tutsi. There was also a political difference between the two parts of Kivu. North Kivu had been home to a long-simmering citizenship crisis, stemming from the fact that the Banyarwanda of Masisi, previously recognized as indigenous, had been systematically disenfranchised over the three decades beginning on the eve of independence. In South Kivu, though, the crisis of citizenship had been late in coming, and did not really surface until the expectation of elections in the early 1990s. When they organized to defend their citizenship rights, the Banyarwanda of Congo tended to come together on a linguistic and regional basis, seldom as Hutu or Tutsi. The shift in political identity from Kinyarwanda speakers of a particular locale to Hutu and Tutsi across different locales is a distinct development of the 1990s. To understand that development is a second purpose of this chapter.

Not surprisingly, when the RPF connected with Banyarwanda across the border, it was with those in South Kivu, and not with Kinyarwanda speakers in North Kivu, in spite of the fact that the citizenship crisis in the north had been brewing for much longer than in the south. This was proof enough that the RPF had already begun to think of itself as Tutsi and the power in Rwanda as Hutu, for the simple fact about Kivu was that the Banyarwanda of the south were predominantly Tutsi, whereas those of the north were predominantly Hutu. But for anyone taking a longer view of things, there was a great historical irony in this. We shall later see that the Tutsi influx into South Kivu had been prompted by two late-nineteenth-century developments: the centralization of kinship in Rwanda at the expense of independent Tutsi aristocratic families, and the bitter factional struggle in the Tutsi elite on the death of Rwabugiri. The Tutsi who left did so voluntarily. For them, Rwanda was no subject for a romantic construction of home. Rather, it signified the suffocating tentacles of a centralizing power, something from which to stay away. This negative historical memory was reinforced by later developments. Since the 1959 Revolution, and especially since the 1972 massacres in Burundi, the Tutsi of South Kivu had made great attempts to distance themselves from the explosive world of Hutu and Tutsi in Rwanda and Burundi, instead seeking to define their place in the ethnic kaleidoscope called Congo. Like their counterparts in Uganda, the Tutsi in Congo also attempted to change from a descent-based to a territorially based political identity: from being Banyarwanda, those ancestrally belonging to Rwanda, they had tried to become Banyamulenge, those living in the hills of Mulenge in South Kivu. But this attempt boomeranged, as had the Ugandan reform, testifying to the regional character of the crisis of citizenship.

Finally, this chapter should allow the reader to compare the nature of political identity in Congo with that in Uganda, and contrast both with the nature of political identity in Rwanda. The difference arises from the history of state formation in the colonial period. The Congolese state—like the Ugandan state—distinguished between those Banyarwanda who had been on Congolese territory when it was first colonized and those who came later. The former were considered *nationals*, but the latter were divided into colonial-era *migrants* and postcolonial *refugees*. The nationals were presumed to have a right to their own Native Authority, whereas migrants and refugees were regarded as ethnic strangers and were denied the group right to a "customary" home and a Native Authority. The divide between ethnic and civic dimensions of citizenship obtained in Congo and Uganda, but it did not in Rwanda. Whereas the Native Authority in Uganda and Congo was ethnically defined, the Native Authority in Rwanda was simply demarcated territorially, as a local authority, but without an ethnic identity. This difference, of course, stemmed from the defining feature of the Rwandan state, that it recognized only races, and not ethnic groups, as political identities.

ETHNIC STRANGERS

To understand the impact of the million-plus refugees who streamed into North and South Kivu from postgenocide Rwanda, we need to sketch the contours of ethnic relations in North and South Kivu on the eve of the genocide. As in Uganda, the Banyarwanda of Congo comprised three distinct groups: nationals, migrants, and refugees. *Nationals* could claim the greatest historical depth: they were already resident in the territory that Belgian colonialism demarcated as Congo in the late nineteenth century. *Migrants* crossed the border at different times during the colonial era, either voluntarily in search of a livelihood or under compulsion. *Refugees*, in contrast, were wholly a postindependence phenomenon. They testified to the mercurial instability of postcolonial politics in the region.

Whereas refugees were part of a volatile political diaspora, nationals and migrants were part of a more stable cultural diaspora. Before the great overflow of Hutu refugees in 1994, nationals and migrants far outnumbered refugees. But after 1994 the relationship was reversed. As the numbers of refugees began to exceed those of nationals and migrants, the political diaspora came to dominate and define the life circumstances of the cultural diaspora.

The predicament of the Banyarwanda in Congo flowed directly from the political arrangement put in place by Belgian colonialism in the colonial period. As elsewhere in colonial Africa, the law distinguished between the indigenous (natives) and the nonindigenous (nonnatives). But this is where the similarity between Rwanda and Congo ended. Whereas political identities in Rwanda tended to correspond to those under direct-rule colonialism (such as in preapartheid South Africa), those in Congo were more characteristic of indirect-rule colonialism. We have seen that group identity in Rwanda was racialized for all: the Tutsi as Hamites and the Hutu as Bantu. In contrast, group identity in Congo was both racialized and ethnicized: unlike in Rwanda where the majority defined as indigenous was pressed into a racialized identity called Bantu, single and homogenized, this majority in Congo was further divided into multiple ethnicities, each with its own "customary" home, "customary" law, and a "customary" authority to enforce it.

The Banyarwanda of Congo thus fell between the stools of the bifurcated world created by indirect-rule colonialism. Racially considered the same as native Congolese—"Africans"—those who had come to Congo after its conquest by Belgians were set apart ethnically as being nonindigenous to Congo. This historical circumstance left them without a claim to a Native Authority in Congo. Without an ethnic patch of their own on Congolese soil, they were treated as ethnic strangers in every Native Authority. This dilemma became even more acute after independence.

The world of the racialized citizen and the ethnicized native changed after independence. All postindependence regimes were determined, to one degree or another, to do away with the stigma of race that they associated with colonial rule. The tendency of the postcolonial state was to deracialize civic identity. Civic citizenship ceased to recognize any difference based on race or place of origin. That is where similarities ended and differences sprouted among different kinds of post-colonial reform agendas. The conservative variant of the postcolonial state—to which belong the experiences of Congo and Uganda—continued to reproduce the native identity as ethnic. The irony was that deracialization without deethnicization continued to reproduce a bifurcated citizenship since not every civic citizen, a citizen of the state of Congo, could claim ethnic membership of a Native Authority. Even if the civic sphere ceased to make a distinction between citizens who were indigenous and those who were not, the ethnic sphere continued to reproduce this distinction. To be recognized as ethnically indigenous meant to have an ethnic home (a "Native Area") governed by an ethnic administration (a "Native Administration"). To understand the practical significance of being a civic but not an ethnic citizen, it is worth exploring further the distinction between civic and ethnic dimensions of citizenship.

Civic citizenship is a consequence of membership of the central state. Both the qualifications for citizenship and the rights that are its entitlement are specified in the constitution. Under deracialized civic law, these rights are mainly individual and are located in the political and civic domain. In contrast, ethnic citizenship is a result of membership in the Native Authority. It is the source of a different category of rights, mainly social and economic. Further, these rights are not accessed individually but by virtue of group membership, the group being the ethnic community. The key socioeconomic right is the right to use land as a source of livelihood. Herein lies the material basis of ethnic belonging, particularly for the ethnic poor. The immediate practical consequence of being defined a citizen of nonindigenous origin is this: nonindigenous citizens are denied "customary" access to land since they do not have their own Native Authority. To access land in "customary" areas, they are compelled to pay tribute to "customary" authorities in these areas. To understand why "nonindigenous" citizens in rural areas should persistently call for a Native Authority of their own, we need to begin with a fuller understanding of the Native Authority in Kivu.

The Native Authority in Kivu is three tiered. At the lowest level is the chief of the *locality*. Then comes the second-level chief, the *chef de groupement*, and then finally the *mwami* of the *collectivité*. Those considered nonindigenous and living in rural areas may, and usually do, have a chief of the lowest order from among their own ranks, one who is answerable to the higher authority for their immediate governance. Only those considered indigenous, however, have the right to a chief of the second and third tier from one of their own. The distinction is crucial for customary power really rests at the level of the *chef de groupement* and the *mwami*. They have the power to confirm ethnic belonging and to issue identity cards, oversee administration, allocate customary land for livelihood, hold tribunals through which customary justice is meted out, run local markets, and so on.[3]

To understand the growing dilemma of the Kinyarwanda-speaking minority in Kivu, we need to understand their changing relationship to the Native Authority system. That *nationals* could claim a precolonial tie with the land, *migrants* a connection that went to the colonial period, and *refugees* only a postcolonial link turned out to be a fact of not just historical but also great political significance. The key term differentiating civic from ethnic citizens, indigeneity, was defined wholly in reference to the colonial experience: the indigenous were those who could demonstrate a tie to the land predating colonial occupation. This distinction also divided the Banyarwanda residents of Congo into two: those considered indigenous to Congo and those not. For reasons of history, the balance between the two groups was different in North from South Kivu.

The Kinyarwanda-speaking minority in Kivu consists of three territorially distinct groups, the Banyarutshuru and the Banyamasisi in the north, and the Banyamulenge in the south. As we shall see, the Banyarutshuru and the Banyamasisi are predominantly Hutu, whereas the Banyamulenge are Tutsi. Furthermore, because their presence on Congolese soil preceded its demarcation as a Belgian colony in the 1880s, the Hutu of Rutshuru are considered "indigenous" and so are entitled to a Native Authority of their own.[4] Matters, however, are not as straightforward with the Banyamasisi of North Kivu or the Banyamulenge of South Kivu, the two groups on whom we shall focus.

THE BANYAMASISI OF NORTH KIVU

The neat division between nationals of precolonial vintage and colonial migrants, the former indigenous and the latter not, tended to break down in Congo because two entire groups seemed to fall between the cracks. The first of these were the Banyamasisi of North Kivu, and the second were the Banyamulenge of South Kivu. The claim of the Banyamasisi to Congolese citizenship became a bone of contention in the decades that followed independence. The contention stemmed from the difference between two types of colonial migrations, separating "labor migrants" of an earlier period (1926 to 1937) from those "transplanted" after 1937.

Labor migrants were a response to the arrival of Belgian settlers in Kivu. The Kivu highlands had fertile land, a mild climate, and no tse-tse flies, an ideal location for white settlement. To prepare the highlands for just that fate, the fundamental law of 1908 made a distinction between "indigenous" and "state" land: all land actually cultivated by "natives" was declared "indigenous" and the rest was declared "vacant" and seized by the state. It did not matter that this "vacant" land was actually used for grazing, or hunting or foraging, as was the forest around Masisi by the local Bahunde people. Then, companies—three of them—were granted land in millions of hectares. These generous grants were periodically reviewed and reduced if the company concerned did not show sufficient evidence of putting the land to use. After two such reviews, a single company, CNKI, was granted the overall authority to parcel out land to individual white settlers as and when they arrived and asked for land. From 58 in 1928, the number of settler families increased to 330 in 1949.[5]

The corollary of white settlement was a labor problem. The local Bahunde were given to a hunting and foraging life. As the land was divided and the forest cleared, hunting and foraging entered a period of crisis. To force the Bahunde into an alternative, colonial authorities passed a 1917 ordinance that required them to grow food and crops. Following that, forced labor practices were "generalized in Masisi," specifically between 1914 and 1928. The response of the Bahunde was to run from encroaching administrative authorities.[6] In this context of incoming white settlers and fleeing locals, Belgium turned to the more thickly populated colony of Rwanda for labor. A decree of 19 July 1926 authorized Rwandans to seek employment freely outside their country and legally opened the country to labor recruiters from the outside. Three types of recruiters came into Rwanda: Union Minière, the mining conglomerate (1925–31); CNKI, the plantation oligopoly (1928–32); and individual settlers.

But this solution did not fully work. The hitch was that labor migrants had an option between Belgian-dominated Congo and the British colonies in East Africa. Figures told that the preference was for the latter: in 1931, for example, 6,869 men worked in Uganda and Tanganyika, but only 4,170 in Kivu.[7] Thus began the era of "transplantation." The idea was to go beyond encouraging the migration of individual laborers whose options were limited by the thought of returning one distant day. The new approach was to get entire families to move, with no thought of return. To achieve this goal, Belgian administration decided to manipulate the "push factors," in particular a combination of overpopulation and famine: the more famine spread, the more transplantation could be put forth as a humanitarian response to a growing tragedy. Though the immigration was supposedly voluntary, Catharine Newbury's research in Kinyaga suggests that a measure of force was involved: Gishari in Kivu, one respondent told her, is "the place where chiefs sent the people they didn't like."[8] The immigrants were a trickle in 1937—only 691. The big increase was the result of the big Rwanda-wide famine (*nyirahuku*), which stimulated an increase from 8,492 in 1942 to 24,448 in 1945.[9] Even though Gishari was declared saturated in 1945, the Mission d'Immigration Banyarwanda (MIB) was created in 1948 to transplant immigrants to other parts of Masisi. The population of Masisi territory increased threefold between 1936 and 1969, and rose further from 273,920 in 1970 to 482,007 in 1983.[10]

Whereas labor migrants were presumed to have a home away from where they were resident, those "transplanted" were not. The whole idea was that they were uprooted from home, and had to make another. In line with this thinking, the transplanted Banyarwanda were granted their own Native Authority in Gishari in Masisi. This made for a tension with the local population. To begin with, the Bahunde had been opposed to the influx because they saw it as increasing competition for land. Local chiefs, on the other hand, were happy to see more coming in: given that ethnic strangers would have to give the chief an extra payment in return for the temporary right to use land, every new immigrant meant an additional source of tribute. To escape that very tribute, post-1936 immigrants insisted on having their own Native Authority, which they got.[11] This single development brought Bahunde peasants and Bahunde chiefs together on an "indigenous" basis. The more the numbers of the Bahunde shrunk in proportion to those of the transplanted—by 1990, the Bahunde were but 15 percent of the population of Masisi[12]—the more they asserted the one political right that the colonial state recognized as a native prerogative: ethnic belonging as custom. The Collectivité Gishari was established in 1938 and disestablished in 1957, just as the colonial power prepared to turn the corner to independence. This dissolution set the stage for the postindependence crisis of citizenship.

THE DIALECTIC BETWEEN ETHNIC AND CIVIC CONFLICT

When Collectivité Gishari ceased to be a Kinyarwanda-speaking Native Authority in 1957, the Banyarwanda in Masisi lost any ethnic space to express their political preference. With the coming independence of Congo, however, an alternate political space began to open up for natives. The opening of civic space was marked by oncoming provincial and municipal elections. Being the majority, the Banyarwanda in Masisi won the collegial elections of 1958. The response of the Bahunde elite was to use their ethnic prerogative as the population "indigenous" to the *collectivité* to hound most Banyarwanda from positions of influence in the local state: "They systematically removed Rwandan immigrants from important positions they held in local administration and maintained only a few loyalists in minor positions." This practice became "common elsewhere in the former MIB zones by 1960," so much so that "it became common to see, in each locality, only one Hunde family, that which had been brought in to rule over the Rwandan immigrants."[13] Outside the political sphere, the indigenous prerogative translated into an assertion of "customary" control over all land designated as "indigenous" so that only those immigrants paying tribute to "traditional" authorities were allowed to continue to till customary land. The widespread slogan *udongo ya baba* (literally, earth of the father, or fatherland) summed up the point of view that the Hunde were landowners and the immigrant Banyarwanda tenants. It is the acceleration of these trends that led to the eruption of armed conflict in Masisi in 1963–64. Called "La Guerre du Banyarwanda," this conflict was in reality a popular Banyarwanda uprising against abuse by Bahunde chiefs.

So sensitive was the nationality status of the Kinyarwanda-speaking minority as independence approached that even the Roundtable Independence Conference in Brussels was unable to fix the juridical status of this minority. This was in spite of the fact that conference participants included representatives of the Banyarwanda from Masisi. The Fundamental Law left the citizenship status of the minority unresolved, stating that the Congolese people will themselves decide this issue. Even though Mobutu Sese Seko abrogated the Fundamental Law when he usurped power in 1965, the Brussels outcome came to introduce an element of insecurity in the juridical status of the Kinyarwanda-speaking minority.

In the three decades that stretched from the end of La Guerre du Bayarwanda in 1963–64 to the beginning of the Rwandan genocide in 1994, a complex of processes unfolded in Kivu. In retrospect, one can see how this dynamic produced the environment that incubated the post-1994 crisis of Kivu. The more they felt blocked at the local level, the more the Kinyarwanda-speaking minority looked to the civic sphere—both the market and the central state—for alternate strategies, economic as well as political. Unable to access land as did the "indigenous" Congolese, as a "customary" right, those with resources devoted them to purchasing as much land as possible through the market. Frustrated from exercising power locally by the ethnic character of the local authority, they made every effort to access positions at higher provincial and national levels, whether through elections or through connections. This, in turn, provoked a response from among the "indigenous" majority. Afraid that the Banyarwanda would use national representation to acquire power locally, "indigenous" Congolese came to oppose citizenship rights for them. When their citizenship was questioned and their right to run for office denied, the Kinyarwanda-speaking minority—particularly the Tutsi, a minority within the minority, without a "home" anywhere in the region, one they could count on as a fallback in times of crisis—developed a strategy of entry into organs of the state, particularly the security apparatus.

Three key decisions marked the course of the spiraling crisis of citizenship that fed the insecurity of the Kinyarwanda-speaking minority. Each had a vital impact on the future of this minority. The first was Mobutu's 1972 Citizenship Decree. The second was the 1981 Citizenship Law passed by an elected Parliament, and the third was a resolution by the 1991 Sovereign National Conference upholding the provisions of the 1981 law. To understand the nature of the movement from 1972 to 1981 to 1991, we need to grasp the changing political context over these decades.

The 1972 Citizenship Decree

The context of the 1972 Citizenship Decree was the first major post-independence crisis of regional proportions that sent thousands of refugees streaming into Kivu. This development took place as the aftermath of the massacre of about 200,000 Hutu in Burundi in 1972. Faced with a growing refugee influx, the local population began to see themselves as an imperiled "indigenous" majority. This, in turn, made the position of the Kinyarwanda-speaking minority even more insecure. As the "indigenous" majority responded with pressure on the Kinyarwanda speakers, the minority looked to the central state for adequate protection. This was the context in which the Mobutu regime extended citizenship to those who had come as refugees from Rwanda in 1959–63. This measure was introduced as the 1972 Citizenship decree. Its effect, though, was to alarm the local majority who saw the decree as a direct outcome of growing Tutsi influence within the state apparatus. Many believed that Mobutu had signed the decree under the influence of Bisengimana, his *chef de cabinet* who was himself said to be a 1959 Tutsi refugee.

The following year, 1973, the Mobutu government passed the General Property Law. A measure similar to that passed by the Amin regime in Uganda, it nationalized all land, including both the land under the control of "traditional" authorities in the rural areas and land controlled by white settlers. While the state was unable to implement the provision with regard to rural land under "customary" control, it was able to transfer settler-controlled land to Zairean citizens. The result was to usher in "a newly formed class of rural Congolese capitalists." This is the context in which the more prosperous among the Kinyarwanda-speaking population cashed in on their newly acquired civic citizenship to gain property rights. Soon, some of the biggest plantations in North Kivu passed into the hands of Banyarwanda and were turned into ranches. A study conducted in 1991 showed the long-term result in Masisi: 512 families—of which 502 were Banyarwanda—controlled about 58 percent of the available land. Of these 502 Banyarwanda families, most were Tutsi-Banyarwanda.[14] To many in Kivu Province, the 1972 Citizenship Decree came to symbolize not simply an inclusive citizenship policy but one so undiscriminating that, if followed in practice, it would surely turn Kivu into an open sanctuary for the surplus population from Rwanda and Burundi. "What can't be accepted," a prominent civil-society leader concluded in a conversation on citizenship in 1997, "is an order whereby every immigrant who comes in is granted citizenship automatically—a practice that came in with Bisengimana becoming Chief of Staff to Mobutu."

The 1981 Citizenship Law

It is not until the legislative elections of 1977 that the "indigenous" majority developed a strategy equal to countering the minority strategy of penetrating the security and party apparatus of the Mobutist party-state. The prospect of election brought home the realization that sheer numbers could be translated into political power, so that the majority could get access to power even if it was shut out of appointments in the state party, the Mouvement Populaire Révolutionnaire (MPR). The "indigenous" majority followed a single guideline: better not elect another Tutsi if you want to balance out against them. When one was elected— as was Gisaru, a Munyamulenge, as deputy of Uvira in South Kivu—the response of the local majority was to accuse him of having manipulated the election. Not surprisingly, the parliament that came out of the 1977 elections passed a new citizenship law hostile to the Kinyarwanda-speaking minority. The 1981 law was said to have been passed under strong pressure from Nande and Hunde politicians from North Kivu:[15] it stipulated that only those persons who could demonstrate an ancestral connection to the population residing in 1885 in the territory then demarcated as Congo would qualify to be citizens of Congo.

It was one thing to pass the law, quite another to implement it. By the time of the 1985 provincial assembly elections, the question of citizenship was still unsettled, though the 1981 law remained on the books. In this context, the "indigenous" majority improvised a solution: the Kinyarwanda-speaking population may vote in the elections, but none of its members may run for office. The solution seemed to compound the problem; for the first time, all Kinyarwanda speakers were lumped together into a single group, regardless of how long different sections had been on Congolese soil. The response of the Kinyarwanda-speaking minority, particularly the Tutsi, was to smash ballot boxes. As a result, no provincial assemblies were elected in North or South Kivu.

The Sovereign National Conference (Conférence Nationale Souveraine, CNS) and the Resolution on Citizenship, 1991

The Sovereign National Conference marked a turning point in the political history of postcolonial Congo. Countrywide, the CNS heralded the coming together of an internal opposition to the Mobutist party-state. In Kivu, however, it had a double significance: it also marked an important step in the constitution of a self-conscious political majority. Though this majority transcended ethnic lines, it constituted more of an interethnic rather than a nonethnic majority, seeing itself as an "indigenous" majority threatened by a "nonindigenous" minority growing through the periodic influx of refugees.

The CNS took place at a time when the Banyarwanda minority was once again gripped by anxiety about their citizenship status. Following the RPF attack on Rwanda in October 1990, many young Tutsi in Kivu decided to cross the border into Uganda and join the RPF. The Mobutu regime responded with Mission d'Identification de Zaïrois au Kivu, authorized to carry out an on-the-ground verification of who among the Kinyarwanda speakers was Zairean and who was not—because their families had come after the Berlin Conference. As a result, many Hutu and Tutsi from 1936 were not verified as Zaireans. This in turn increased the flow of Tutsi youth crossing into Uganda to join the RPF. By the time the CNS met in 1991, citizenship had become a hot issue, particularly in the region of Kivu. Not surprisingly, the delegations from North and South Kivu urged the CNS to give priority to the citizenship issue. In response, the Haut Conseil de la République, an organ of the CNS, adopted the 1981 Citizenship Law.

To understand why a majority constituted through the democratic process would appear as a threat to the minority, we need to take a brief look at the history of the internal opposition. The history of organized peaceful opposition goes back to the formation of the Union pour la Démocratie et le Progrès Social (UDPS) in 1982. This formation was the result of several impulses, including calls for reform from thirteen parliamentarians in 1980. Whereas the tendency before 1980 was for opponents of the regime to flee into exile, the tendency after 1980 favored the growth of a peaceful internal opposition. Combined with the reform wave that followed the end of the Cold War, the gradual development of this internal opposition led to Mobutu's "opening up" speech of 24 April 1990. In that speech, he promised political reform. As a first step, Mobutu promised to relinquish the presidency of the MPR and thereby ensure the separation of the party and the state. In the two weeks before he took that promise back, the idea of holding the Sovereign National Conference had caught the imagination of the political opposition. The CNS opened officially on 7 August 1991.

The proceedings of the CNS were televised throughout urban Congo. It was enough to inspire further initiatives. There was a mushrooming of civil society organizations, thickening the texture of the internal political opposition.[16] The overall thrust of the CNS was to deepen and to coordinate the internal opposition to the Mobutist state. At the same time, the CNS impacted on the provinces in different ways. In the region of Kivu, it tended to crystallize two related trends, one in the "indigenous" majority, the other in the Kinyarwanda-speaking minority. It accelerated the majority tendency to differentiate Tutsi from Hutu and to lump together all Tutsi, regardless of the depth of their presence on Congolese soil, into a single group. The tendency to use the term "Banyamulenge" as a generic term for all Congolese Tutsi really gathered momentum with the CNS. Correspondingly, it was during the CNS that the Banyamulenge found out that, even though they had moved to Congo in the nineteenth century—much earlier than the post-1959 Tutsi immigrants to North Kivu—their situation was not very different from that of the Tutsi of Masisi and Goma in North Kivu.

The Sovereign National Conference brought several contradictory political tendencies to a head in Kivu. While the Kinyarwanda-speaking minority—particularly the Tutsi—continued to look to organs of the state party, including its security organs, for protection against the "indigenous" majority, the majority continued to invest in representative processes both as protection from the arbitrary rule of the party-state, and as guarantee that they would prevail against the minority. The very democracy that tended to create a majority across ethnic lines tended to pit a self-consciously "indigenous" majority against what many increasingly came to think of as a "nonindigenous" minority, one they saw as not only

Kinyarwanda-speaking but also owing political allegiance to Rwanda. Within the Kinyarwanda-speaking minority, the Hutu began to differentiate themselves as "indigenous" from Tutsi as "nonindigenous." It testified to a double development: the growth of politics of indigeneity in Congo, and growing Hutu/Tutsi tensions in the region. This is why it should not be surprising that the very fact that the CNS began to discuss the question of citizenship raised a fear in the minority—particularly the Tutsi—that it was about to lose its citizenship status. The CNS also marks the point after which the course of ethnic developments in South Kivu began to converge with those in North Kivu, particularly Masisi.

THE BANYAMULENGE OF SOUTH KIVU

The minority question in South Kivu is less complex than that in the north. Whereas the situation in North Kivu has a longer history and is intimately affected by what happens in Rwanda, the situation in South Kivu is of more recent origin but is influenced by developments in both Rwanda and Burundi. The long-standing immigrant minority in South Kivu originates more from Burundi than from Rwanda. North Kivu has always had a Banyarwanda Native Authority in Bwisha, and one in Gishari from 1938 to 1957, but South Kivu has never had a Banyarwanda Native Authority. Those living in South Kivu and Burundi have tended to shift back and forth between two adjacent valleys: the Imbo Valley in Burundi and the Ruzizi Valley in South Kivu. Today, the population of both valleys is Kirundi speaking. Thus, the Kirundi-speaking population in South Kivu is considered "indigenous" to the region. Like the Banyarwanda in Rutshuru in North Kivu, the Barundi in Ruzizi Valley have also had their own customary chief, in a *collectivité* named Barundi.[17]

The Banyamulenge are mainly Tutsi. It is said that their arrival in South Kivu dates to the 1880s, when Rwabugiri ruled the central kingdom of Rwanda. Two explanations are advanced for the movement of Tutsi away from the kingdom. The first relates to Rwabugiri's determination to gather more tribute from the rich, the second to the bitter conflict of succession that took place at his death, an event named after the place where he was buried, called Rucunshu. In Rwanda and Burundi, an aging king does not publicly proclaim his successor. The result is a struggle for succession at the king's death. When the conflict is particularly bloody, those who lose are compelled to move away. The two explanations do not rule out the possibility that both may be true.[18]

The claims about when and why the Banyamulenge moved are many and have multiplied as the political crisis has intensified. After the original migration of the Banyamulenge—whether during the reign of Rwabugiri or as an aftermath of the succession conflict at his death—there were successive migrations. Labor migrants followed in the colonial period. The impetus began with labor recruitment in Ruanda-Urundi by the Union Minière du Haut Katanga, which began in 1925 and continued to 1929. More than seven thousand workers are said to have been recruited in that five-year period. Government reports note the steady trickle of labor migrants from Rwanda to South Kivu, particularly Bukavu, from the 1930s.[19] The next big influx was that of Tutsi refugees in 1959–60. Unlike the bulk of the Banyamulenge who lived on the high plains and were pastoralists, both the labor migrants of the colonial era and the 1959–60 refugees tended to live in urban areas or in refugee camps, such as Kalonge near the airport.

Unlike the Barundi, however, the Banyamulenge have never had their own Native Authority. Banyamulenge chiefs were confined to the first level, the chief of the locality. For access to land, they paid homage to existing chiefs where they settled. The area in which the Banyamulenge resided covered three territorial administrations: (a) the *territoire* of Mwenga inhabited by the Balega, (b) the *territoire* of Fizi inhabited by the Babemba, and (c) the *territoire* of Uvira inhabited by the Bavira and the Bafuliro. The *territoire* is a fourth level of administration, after the *localité*, the *groupement*, and the *collectivité*; it comprises several *collectivités*. The *territoire* of Uvira thus comprises three *collectivités*, called the Bavira, the Barundi, and the Bafuliro. The name of each *collectivité* is taken from the name of the ethnicity considered "indigenous" to it.

Unlike in North Kivu, the Banyamulenge in South Kivu were seen as one among many ethnicities, and not as a nonindigenous minority set apart from the indigenous majority—at least until the holding of CNS in 1991 raised expectations about forthcoming elections. We need to recall that the politics of indigeneity in Masisi developed locally, in a context shaped by two factors: the macro factor of colonial legislation which made a clear distinction between those indigenous and those not, and the appropriation of land from the Bahunde whose very mode of livelihood was destroyed at the local level. In South Kivu, the Banyarwanda migration preceded the establishment of colonial authority and proceeded on the basis of mutuality between different groups. As the colonial period came to a close and the politics of Rwanda took on explosive dimensions, the Banyarwanda immigrants in the hills of Mulenge began to distance themselves from their ancestral world and define their identity and thus their future more in line with their new home. Thus was born the identity "Banyamulenge."

There is no agreement on when the term "Banyamulenge" came into general usage and why. Some historians I spoke with in South Kivu said the triggering event was really the genocidal killing of Hutu in Burundi in 1972; after it, the Tutsi became very unpopular in the entire area, that is why the Congolese Tutsi began to distance themselves from Rwanda.[20] To the colonial construction of political identity tied to ethnic origin, was counterposed a radically different notion of political identity, this time tied to territorial residence. To understand the nature of the shift, we need to begin with the understanding that the point of political identity is to claim (or to deny) political rights. From the point of view of an immigrant population stigmatized as "nonindigenous," the fact that power is identified in ethnic terms—say, as Bafuliro—means that rights are also restricted to those who belong ethnically, in this instance to the Bafuliro, thereby disenfranchising all others considered immigrants. The claim to shift identity from the ethnic (the Banyarwanda) to the territorial (the Banyamulenge) must, in this context, be seen as an attempt to define a more inclusive basis of rights, based on residence rather than ethnicity.

This shift did not become contentious until after 1991, when the CNS passed the 1981 Citizenship Bill. Before that, group relations in South Kivu were defined more along ethnic lines, less along a divide defined by the notion of indigeneity. Unlike in Masisi, the politics of indigeneity in South Kivu was more of an import—at first from the central government and then from the democratic movement—than a local construction. The central government's contribution was summed up as the principle of *géopolitique*, whereby the Mobutu government argued that "all positions of authority could only be awarded to those indigenous to the region concerned."[21] Faced with the prospect of democratic elections in 1991, local authorities launched a campaign to identify Zairean nationals. Local politicians, too, got converted in the face of elections as they also began to discover the political uses of indigeneity.

More than any other, one single shift marked this change in context. When Congolese Tutsi tried to distance themselves from the socially explosive world of Tutsi and Hutu in Rwanda and Burundi, this suggested a deeper and more sinister agenda to "indigenous" ears. Why otherwise, many asked, would immigrants seek to hide their "real" identity? It is precisely the creative side of the Tutsi initiative—that a change from a descent-based to a residence-based political identity would mean a radical shift in the definition of the subject of rights—which sounded sinister to "indigenous" ears. The consequence, an indigenous politician pointed out to his growing audience, would allow all local residents without exception, even those ethnically not indigenous, to claim rights. Later, the Bafuliro would point out that Mulenge is the name of the place, the *groupement*, where the Tutsi were first allowed to settle by the Bafuliro. In 1924 they had asked for permission from the colonial power to occupy the high plateau farther south. When permission was granted, they moved south, which is why some claim the Banyamulenge really arrived in 1924. The term may seem innocent on the surface, but the Bafuliro claim it is not, for it really sums up the Tutsi claim to "own" Mulenge, which actually was "owned" by Bafuliro. From this point of view, the Tutsi have developed a disturbing tendency to call themselves by the name of the place where they have settled. The more the Tutsi move, the more they seem to sprout place-based identities such as the Banya-tulambo, and Banya-minembwe, and so on. To "indigenous" ears, then, immigrant claim to a place-based identity really masks an immigrant strategy to lay claim to local land. Why else, many ask, would the Banyamulenge seek to distinguish themselves from the Banyarwanda, except to mask their history, the fact that they came from Rwanda? To tolerate this, they point out, is to encourage any Kinyarwanda-speaking person to follow the same strategy and claim to be a Munyamulenge, and thus a Congolese, no matter how shallow their presence on Congolese soil.

Indeed, the citizenship status of the Kinyarwanda-speaking minority was a matter of lively debate among civil society leaders in Kivu when I was there in 1997. Who should be a citizen and who not? Should the Mobutu/Bisengimana Decree of 1972, allowing all refugees of 1959 to become Congolese citizens, prevail? Or should there be an affirmation of the 1981 law, passed by Parliament and affirmed a decade later by the Sovereign National Conference, that only those with a proven connection to an ancestor resident in the territory demarcated as Congo in 1885 be verified as Congolese? Or should all those currently resident in Congo who pledge political allegiance exclusively to the Congolese state be considered Congolese—regardless of their parentage, place of birth, or duration of stay in Congo?

Interviews with civil society leaders in 1997 brought two strong convictions to light. The first related to civic citizenship, the second to ethnic citizenship. The more one pressed home the link between the mounting political crisis in Kivu and the citizenship question, the more civic leaders tended to agree that the more inclusive option may also be the more prudent. The other side to this growing consensus—that all those resident in Congo before the Rwanda genocide of 1994 be recognized as its citizens, meaning *civic* citizens—was an equally firm consensus that ethnic citizenship must be restricted only to "indigenous" Congolese. While the first tendency was a source of hope, it is the "indigenous" consensus reflected in the second that gives real insight into the crisis of citizenship in contemporary Kivu.

TWO CROSS-CUTTING TENSIONS

For the decade and a half that stretched from the end of La Guerre du Banyarwanda to the Citizenship Law of 1981, the nationality conflict in North Kivu revolved around two pivots. The first pitted the "indigenous" majority against the Kinyarwanda-speaking minority, whether immigrant or not. We have seen that the more this tension grew, the more it tended to blur all historical distinctions among different groups of Banyarwanda: between immigrants and nonimmigrants, and between different groups that had come at different times. As a consequence, all Kinyarwanda speakers came to be considered nonindigenous. The second pivot of conflict was internal to the Banyarwanda; it pit Tutsi against Hutu. As the tension between Hutu and Tutsi increased in Rwanda, it also did in North Kivu. This is clear from the impact of the 1959 "social" revolution in Rwanda. As the group that came in 1959–63 began to organize to return to power in Rwanda, relations began to sour, both with the "indigenous" majority, and between Hutu and Tutsi in the Kinyarwanda-speaking minority. When articulated with the first, there was a tendency for the Hutu, who had either been there before the colonial period or came during its heyday, to claim an indigenous status against the Tutsi, most of whom arrived in North Kivu after 1959.

The shift from a mainly Banyarwanda immigrant identity to an identity highlighting the difference between Hutu and Tutsi is reflected in the breakup of Umoja, a common Banyarwanda organization, into two separate bodies, one Hutu, the other Tutsi, in the 1980s. Umoja was formed as a Banyarwanda organization in the aftermath of the 1981 Citizenship Law, which classified as noncitizen all Banyarwanda who came to Congo after its colonial boundaries were drawn up in 1885. Its second president, Senzeyi Ryamukuru, claimed that Umoja was formed at the behest of Bisukero, the first president of the Provincial Assembly of Kivu.[22] After a consultation between Bisukero and Ryamukuru, two young men, one a Hutu (Sekimonyo Cosmos) and the other a Tutsi (Munyamakuo David), were given the task of bringing local Hutu and Tutsi together in a single organization. Umoja was born as an organization of all Congolese Banyarwanda from Goma, Rutshuru, and Masisi. Sekimonyo became its first president in 1983. In 1985, Sekimonyo (a Hutu) became the president of the Regional Assembly, and Ryamukuru (a Tutsi) became president of Umoja. In another few years, however, Umoja was no more.

Umoja disintegrated in 1988 and was replaced by separate Hutu and Tutsi organizations. With the direct financial support of President Habyarimana of Rwanda and the political support of President Mobutu of Congo, the Hutu in Rutshuru built links with the Hutu in Masisi and formed a common organization of Hutu in North Kivu called Maghrivi (Mutualité des Agriculteurs du Vironga). It was said that part of Mobutu's electoral strategy was to identify "indigenous" Hutu through Maghrivi so as to grant them citizenship. The main message of Maghrivi was that there are no "indigenous" Tutsi in Congo. The proof, it was said, was the Native Authority, which was Hunde in Masisi and Hutu in Rutshuru. Maghrivi called for elections of all chiefs. It figured that an electoral strategy would both neutralize the Bahunde claim to be "indigenous" and translate the numerical majority of the Hutu into local political supremacy over both the Bahunde and the Tutsi. In response, the Tutsi leaders of Umoja founded SIDER (Syndicat d'Initiative pour le Développement de la Zone de Rutshuru) as an exclusively Tutsi organization. SIDER was later absorbed into the ADP, the Alliance Démocratique des Peuples; the difference, according to Sekimonyo, was that ADP was an organization of all Congolese Tutsi. By the middle of the 1990s, not only were Hutu and Tutsi organized across localities in Congo, but Hutu and Tutsi associations crossed state boundaries and began to function as regional networks.

Class and Ethnic Conflict in Masisi

At the heart of the conflict was the question of land. Pitting poor against rich Hutu from the outset, the land conflict soon turned into an ethnic confrontation between Hutu and Bahunde in Masisi. To understand the shift from one to the other, we need to focus yet again on the two ways of acquiring land under the system inherited from colonialism. One is through a market transaction, a way that by its very nature is open only to the well-off, those with means to register a preference on the market. The other is by asserting one's "customary" right as a member of a Native Authority. This is the more political way, and it is the only one open to the poor. The land conflict in North Kivu began in Masisi in 1993 as a class conflict among the Hutu, and then turned into an ethnic conflict between the Hutu and the Bahunde over whether the former should have the right to their own Native Authority. At the outset, the Tutsi joined the "indigenous" Bahunde (and the Banyanga) against the Hutu. By the end of the year, however, as the conflict came to focus on the question of who was entitled to a customary right to land through a customary authority, it pitted the "indigenous" (the Bahunde and the Banyanga) against the "nonindigenous" (the Hutu and the Tutsi).

Masisi is an area with a Hutu immigrant majority, said to be around 75 percent of the population by the early 1990s. The conflict began when rich absentee Hutu (and Tutsi) landlords began taking over the lands of mostly poor Hutu (and some Bahunde) in Masisi. The displaced poor, said to be around one thousand, fled to Walikali, where they demanded the right to elect their own ethnic leaders. Since the Wanyanga held that this "customary" right could be exercised only by those indigenous to the soil, the claim led to a clash between the one thousand Hutu and the Wanyanga in Walikali. The poor one thousand then returned to Masisi, where they made the same "democratic" claim, except that this time they also had the backing of their richer kin, the rich Hutu, and the general Kinyarwanda-speaking population. The claim led to a conflict with the Bahunde in Masisi. According to leaders of the civil-society-based Peace Campaign in Goma, the emerging Hutu point of view was strongly shaped by the Hutu organization Maghrivi.[23]

The response of the Mobutist state to growing conflict in Masisi was to send in units of the DSP and the Garde Civile. Neither, however, was provided with means of sustenance. All were forced to live off the local population, which they did. The difference was that while the DSP lived off the more prosperous Hutu, the Guard Civile lived off both the Bahunde and the ordinary Hutu. The army ended up protecting the land claims of the "nonindigenous" (mainly the Hutu) against the "indigenous" (mainly the Bahunde) population, while the conflict grew into a bloody affair. When asked to give an idea of the intensity of the conflict, a Xavérien Father in Bukavu estimated that between 10,000 and 20,000 were killed, while some 200,000 Bahunde, Hutu, and Tutsi must have run away in the process.[24] This was the context in which a million-plus refugees streamed from Rwanda into North and South Kivu.

POSTGENOCIDE RWANDA COMES TO KIVU

The numbers of Kinyarwanda-speaking people in Kivu Province exploded with the genocide of 1994 in Rwanda. In North Kivu, in particular, their arrival coincided with a rapidly escalating ethnic conflict. To understand fully their impact on the local situation, we need to bear in mind that the refugee question actually mediated a relationship between three different factors. These were: the local conflict in Kivu; the explosive dynamic of the Hutu/Tutsi conflict in Rwanda; and the pernicious role played by major foreign powers, particularly France and the UN.

The first set of refugees actually came before the Rwandan genocide began: from Burundi into South Kivu in late 1993 and early 1994. These were mainly Hutu fleeing the terror of the army after the assassination of Ndadaye in October 1993. They numbered roughly 50,000 and were unarmed. Not so, however, the million or so Hutu refugees who poured in from Rwanda in mid-1994. They lived in armed camps, controlled by the ex-FAR (the Rwandese National Army, or Forces Armées Rwandaises) and the Interahamwe, who continued to be supplied militarily by the French. The armed soldiers and militia were said to number some 20,000 in Bukavu and 30,000 to 40,000 in Goma. According to a local priest working with the Catholic Relief Services (Caritas) in Bukavu, there was agreement between the French and Mobutu that the Congolese forces will not disarm soldiers of the defeated Rwandan army. The refugee question allowed a crisis-plagued Mobutu to resurface politically by posing as the protector of refugees in central Africa.

Both the UN system and U.S.-based NGOs, however, continued to treat these armed camps as exclusively refugee settlements. Along with mainly Northern-funded international NGOs, the UNHCR continued to provide daily provisions for the inhabitants of these camps, advertising this as a humane and charitable act. Asked who he thought bore moral responsibility for that situation, the Congolese priest who worked with Caritas, also the local partner of UNHCR in providing assistance to refugees, answered categorically. The responsibility, he said, lay with UNHCR since it had a real choice in late 1994. That choice was to ask member states to disarm the camps so as not to have to feed what was fast turning into an army. The contrast with Tanzania, which also had to shoulder the burden of a million-plus refugees, makes this clear. Unlike Tanzania, which had a functioning central state and army, Zaire did not. In the absence of a functioning central state in Mobutu's Zaire, it was clear that only the international community was in a position to impose a solution on Mobutu.

From this point of view, the larger responsibility lay with France and with the UN. The French had deliberately and effectively used humanitarianism as a cloak for the defense of narrow state interests. Through Opération Turquoise, France had gone out of its way to create a protective corridor to save those politically responsible for the genocide in Rwanda. The UN had watched the unfolding of the genocide in Rwanda without so much as lifting a finger. In similar fashion, they watched with complacency as refugee camps were established in the vicinity of international borders, and then as they were turned into camps to arm and train refugees.

The setting up of armed camps of Hutu refugees made life hell for the Tutsi in North and South Kivu. Already, the threat of being declared non-citizens by the 1991 Mission d'Identification de Zaïrois au Kivu had increased the cross-border movement of young Congolese Tutsi going to join the RPF for military training. This movement lent credibility to the notion spread by some "indigenous" organizations, including Maghrivi, that the Congolese Tutsi were really Rwandese, not just culturally but also in their political allegiance. Yet, the fact was that the vast majority of Congolese Tutsi had stayed behind in spite of the bloody fighting in Masisi in North Kivu for the simple reason that they had everything to lose and little to gain by moving. That period came to an end in 1994. On the one hand, the Tutsi of Kivu felt physically endangered by the influx of over a million Hutu in armed camps; on the other, they felt a vacuum in Rwanda, to which they could retreat in safety. Even then, not all left willingly. While the 1959 refugees hoped to reacquire their properties upon return, Rwanda held little promise for earlier immigrants who showed little desire to return. When they left, they did so because they felt they had to, because everyone seemed to want them to leave. As if to underline this development, the High Command of the Republic (HCR)—the Parliament of transition—sent a member of Parliament, Mambweni Vangu, to review the situation in Kivu following the genocide of 1994. The Vangu Commission was stacked with anti-Banyarwanda extremists. All Kinyarwanda-speaking people, Hutu or Tutsi, are refugees and must return home—such was the verdict of the commission. Anzuluni Mbembe, the co-speaker of Parliament, joined the chorus when in April 1995 he signed an HCR resolution branding the Banyamulenge as recent refugees and including a list of Banyamulenge to be expelled from Congo.[25] The situation in North Kivu reached a climax between March and May 1996, when the remaining Tutsi from Masisi and Rutshuru were identified and taken to the border. They were chased out, not killed. They moved into refugee camps in the Rwandan border town of Gisenyi. In these same camps, one also found the Bahunde, because the Hutu had decided to go after *all* their enemies: the Banyanga, the Tutsi, the Bahunde. This was the peak of the crisis. It is also when the First Rebellion broke out, leading to the end of the Mobutu regime.

In contrast to North Kivu, the citizenship problem in South Kivu seemed forced until the 1994 refugees came in. Only then did the local administration begin to appropriate Tutsi property in the valley, openly supported by Anzuluni Mbembe. Under pressure from armed Hutu in the camps and from soldiers of the Congolese army, the Banyamulenge began to forge links with the RPF to acquire arms. Many in the valley population blamed Gapangwa, the bishop of Uvira, for colluding in the arming of the Banyamulenge population. A similar split occurred in the Protestant Church, and even in the NGO population. An academic sympathetic to the plight of the Banyamulenge recalled that period: "For anybody in the NGO world, to be publicly sympathetic to the Banyamulenge was to court death. The rationale was: how can you sympathise with those arming when the opposition is unarmed?"[26] The reference to being unarmed was to the Congolese opposition, not to the Interahamwe in the armed refugee camps, nor to the Congolese army.

The insertion of a million-plus refugees in camps that were armed and resourced from the outside had a devastating effect on civilian life in Kivu. First, it led to the *dollarization* of the economy. This bitter truth is best conveyed in the words of the Bukavu-based priest who participated in this humanitarian effort. "One talks of all the humanitarian organisations that came here but one doesn't talk of how they ruined our economy through its dollarization, its rents going up, local Zairois finding life increasingly beyond their reach. In short, amazing resources were deployed in an unreachable endeavour, one which did not correspond to our vision."[27] To talk to civil society leaders in Kivu about the experience of hosting a million-plus refugees resourced through international NGOs was to listen to a litany of troubles—criminality, ill health, increased prices, lowered production, mounting insecurity—all traced to that single experience.

The second effect of armed refugee camps was to accelerate the tendency to *militarize* ordinary life. From Kivu, the genocide in Rwanda loomed like a volcanic eruption. As the spillover into Kivu translated into armed refugee camps, the people of Kivu began to experience the violence of Hutu/Tutsi antagonism directly. Subjected to a regime of terror by armed Interahamwe based in refugee camps, more and more Congolese Tutsi crossed the border into Rwanda. In response, the RPF trained and armed Congolese Tutsi. As the Interahamwe roamed the countryside, they began collaborating with the Congolese army. In response, more and more Native Authorities created their own militia. The anatomy of political life in Kivu began to resemble that in Rwanda. As in Rwanda, where every political party had come to have its own militia by the genocide of 1994, so in Kivu every Native Authority began to acquire its own militia in the postgenocide period.

The origin of the militia phenomenon lies in the Mulelist rebellion against the Mobutist coup of the early 1960s, when the militia from around Fizi and Uvira joined the Mulelists. The commander of the Rwanda force in Congo, James Kabarebe, traced the militia operating in Kivu to the remnants of the "Mulele wars":

> When Mulelists were defeated, the leadership fled to Europe, and peasants retreated into the countryside to defend themselves. They added more weapons to theirs, but failed to forge a political organisation. When they are asked to sing, they sing about Lumumba. When you tell them about Kabila, they ask, "'*Nani Kabila? Huyu ni mtoto wa Lumumba?*'" ("'Who is Kabila? Is he the son of Lumumba?'") When you say yes, they dance with joy.[28]

The original militia tended to have a number of factors in common. First, faced with superior military technology, they tended to rely on supernatural resources. How else could men and women with no more than bows and arrows overcome guns and bullets, except with the help of a pantheon of spirits that would transform lethal bullets into harmless raindrops? Just as in the Mayi Mayi resistance in pre–World War I Tanganyika and many a rebellion thereafter, so in the Mulelist uprising in Congo of the 1960s magic turned out to be a key component of rebellion. Rebel forces marching into battle chanted "*Mulele Mai! Mulele Mai!*" evoking the power of Mulele the leader to turn bullets into Mai, literally, water.[29] Second, the militia tended to combine "a very strict military code" with frequent "experiments with more egalitarian forms of social organisation for self-help and protection."[30] Though every militia developed in tandem with ethnically defined Native Authorities, it also functioned at an arm's length from the Native Authority. Stemming from the old order, they seemed to reach out to define possibilities of a new one.

The land conflict in Masisi was another important turning point in the development of local militias. The Congolese head of the First Rebellion, Laurent Kabila, traced the development of an "ethnic militia" in North Kivu—unlike in South Kivu—to the formation of Maghrivi by Hutu partisans.[31] Gradually, the nature of the militias changed to favor youthful members. The more that fighting turned into a mode of earning livelihood, the more militia membership became a refuge for many a marginalized youngster and school dropout. It is in this period that, faced with an "indigenous" militia, the Hutu developed their own countermilitia, called Les Combattants. After 1994, it collaborated freely with the Interahamwe. In a parallel movement, the Tutsi, concentrated in South Kivu, consolidated their organizations under a single umbrella, the ADP, in November 1996. The ADP, as already pointed out, was an organization of the Congolese Tutsi.

While the biggest of the militias in Kivu were those of the Congolese Hutu and Tutsi, at least four militias operated on an "indigenous" basis in North Kivu by 1997. The first of these, the Mayi Mayi,[32] was said to be based in the central area of Masisi and Walikali. Its recruits came mainly from two ethnicities, the Bahunde and the Batembo. The second was the Ngilima. Based in the northern areas of Lubero and Beni, it drew members mainly from the Banande. The Banande were also the main force in the third militia, the Kasingien. The difference was that the Kasingien was a cross-border militia, its members coming from Congolese living on both sides of the Uganda-Congo border. With its headquarters at the foot of Mount Ruwenzori, the Kasingien freely cooperated with the Ngilima. Like the Ngilima, the Kasingien also claimed to have found a mystical antidote that would render humans safe against bullets. The last militia to organize by 1997 was Katuko. With mainly young Banyanga recruits, it operated in the area stretching from Kale in the south to Walikali in the north.

Just as the term "Banyamulenge" has become a generic term for all Congolese Tutsi, so the term "Mayi Mayi" became a generic term for all militias in Kivu Province linked to "indigenous" Native Authorities. The forces that mounted the first rebellion against Mobutu were a coalition of recruits from various ethnic militias, both "indigenous" and "nonindigenous"—on the one hand the Mayi Mayi, on the other the Banyamulenge. In an interview at the height of the First Rebellion, when he was trying to downplay the numbers of the Banyamulenge among his forces, Laurent Kabila said, "The Banyamulenge are no more than 4,000 in our forces, which are more than 15,000."[33] One was struck by the almost exact parallel with the numbers of the Banyarwanda among the National Resistance Army (NRA) as it took Kampala almost a decade ago. There was also a second parallel. If it was the disenfranchisement of the Banyarwanda in the NRA that created the immediate context of the RPF invasion of Rwanda in 1990, it was more or less a similar threat to the Banyamulenge in the new Congo army that would bring Rwanda to back a Second Rebellion, this time against the government of Laurent Kabila. The Second Rebellion found the various "indigenous" Mayi Mayi and the "nonindigenous" Banyamulenge on opposite sides.

The Mayi Mayi joined the First Rebellion in Congo, the rebellion against Mobutu, but opposed the rebellion when it came to power. The reason is simple. They joined it when the rebellion targeted the Interahamwe and the allied Congolese army. And they opposed the rebellion when they saw it turn into the spearhead of a likely Rwandese occupation. Most civil-society leaders in Kivu shared this fear. To explain it, they cited two developments. The first was that the commander of the Rwandese army was formally appointed the commander of the Congolese National Army. Second, this army had begun to intervene directly in Congolese affairs, actively supporting demands by the Congolese Tutsi: that the Banyamulenge be given a separate Native Authority in South Kivu, and that the Hutu head of the Native Authority in Rutshuru (North Kivu) be replaced by a Tutsi, so as to return the situation to what it had been before 1918. From the point of view of "indigenous" ethnicities in Kivu, the postgenocide Rwandese army was an armed expression of Tutsi power that would be used to give teeth to Tutsi claims for an "indigenous" status in Congo or, worse still, to annex Kivu to Rwanda.

The ethnic situation in Kivu went from bad to worse with the success of the First Rebellion against Mobutu. The opportunity for removing a long-standing dictatorship in Kinshasa was turned into revenge-seeking in Kivu. No sooner had the war begun than revenge killings started to happen in Goma (North Kivu). The first half of 1997 was marked by lots of killings—with even more people displaced—particularly in Masisi as the Tutsi of North Kivu settled accounts with the Hutu in Maghrivi. A prominent civil-society leader claimed that approximately six thousand Hutu must have been killed in Goma alone in the short space of a week.

The situation in South Kivu was worse. The "Banyamulenge"—I put the term in quotes since we don't really know who these were—entered the Ruzizi Valley in September 1996. A prominent Bukavu-based intellectual, otherwise sympathetic to the citizenship claims of the Banyamulenge, described the situation in words that one would have dismissed as an exaggeration had they come from a stranger.

> The Banyamulenge conquered their rights by arms but the rift between them and the local population has grown. The attitude of the Tutsi soldiers—the Rwandese and the Banyamulenge—during and after the war has made them more detested by the population due to killings, torture. For example, they will go into the village, raid all the cattle,

tell the population—since when have you learned to keep cattle; we are cattle; we know cattle. In Bukavu, they went into and stole from houses. Not so much in Goma. The result is the population is increasingly getting concerned over the question of the Tutsi presence.

Two tendencies seemed to be coming together in this assault on the "indigenous" population. For the Congolese Tutsi, it seemed an opportunity to settle scores with local opponents. The Rwandese Tutsi, however, seemed to have generalized their hatred of the *génocidaires*, first to all Hutu and then to the "indigenous" population in Kivu, seeing it as a willing host to armed camps of the *génocidaires*. But their actions fed wild fears in the local population, creating an incredibly tense situation. Some thought that Tutsi power in Rwanda was trying to annex Kivu and turn it into a homeland for Hutu. Others were convinced that a plan was afoot to kill the "indigenous" elite, such as intellectuals and business people, and that lists had already been compiled for that purpose. Several dates were in circulation. Bukavu seemed in a state of grand panic in September 1997. "Today," a highly respected academic claimed, "it is being said that Ugandan and Rwandan soldiers are digging trenches all around the city, with guns aimed at the city. Everybody is preoccupied with security, not with how to improve relations with one another."

The more the crisis grew, the more it gave rise to stereotypes which, in turn, nourished the crisis. When asked to reflect on possible solutions to the conflict, a peace activist in Goma mused: "One needs to ask the indigenous whether they can chase away all the Rwandese, and ask the Rwandese whether they can kill all the *autochtones*."[34] Unwittingly, he had thrown light on the kinds of fears that fed popular stereotypes: the Rwandese fear that they may be chased away by the "indigenous," and the "indigenous" fear that they may be killed by the Rwandese.

Militarization spread two tendencies in Kivu, indeed as it had in Rwanda. First, the link forged between militarization and genocidal tendencies inside Rwanda spread across its borders. The First Rebellion led to an indiscriminate slaughter of Interahamwe, of unarmed Hutu refugees, of the Hutu in Maghrivi, and even of those Hutu not connected to Maghrivi. Those responsible for that slaughter became part of the post-Mobutu government and were part of the forces that opposed a UN inquiry into the matter. Those who carried out indiscriminate massacres of Hutu in Kivu are today a part of the military forces of the Second Rebellion. The Second Rebellion, in turn, evoked from the Kabila government an exhortation to the "indigenous" population in Kivu to slaughter indiscriminately not only invading forces from Rwanda, but also the Congolese Banyamulenge in the rebellion, and even all Congolese Tutsi civilians. While Rwanda armed the Congolese Tutsi to beef up the Second Rebellion, the Kabila government armed Congolese Hutu as a countermeasure. Each seemed determined to liquidate the other—physically.

The second effect of militarization was to reduce all credible politics to armed politics. The result was to undermine politics as a civil activity. Once again, this tendency developed in a consolidated form in pregenocide Rwanda, where each political party felt compelled to organize its own militia as a matter of self-defense. As in postgenocide Rwanda, those in power tend to demonize all oppositional politics—regardless of its political character—as *génocidaire*, and, as if on cue, opposition takes on an armed character.

CUSTOMARY SPHERE AND ETHNIC CONFLICT

The depth of the crisis in eastern Congo cannot be understood unless we see it as the result of a confluence of two distinct processes: the social crisis of postgenocide Rwanda and the citizenship crisis in the entire region. The genocide has given rise to a diasporic state, Rwanda. Two convictions underline the diasporic character of postgenocide power in Rwanda. The first is an overwhelming sense of moral responsibility for the very survival of all remaining Tutsi, globally. The result is that postgenocide power is defined by a diasporic, rather than a territorial, notion of political obligation and political community. The second—also a direct outcome of the experience of genocide—is the conviction that power is the condition of Tutsi survival. As the Congolese Tutsi legal adviser to the secretary-general of the Alliance put it, "In Rwanda, the Tutsi have reached a conclusion that power is the only guarantee for their right to life, otherwise they will be killed by Hutu."[35] The newly appointed Rwandese commander of the Congolese army echoed that same thought: "The Tutsi are just a scared group, from 1959, 1973, 1994. They will feel no assurance until they are protected by Tutsi themselves. That is natural."[36]

The crisis in Kivu was immediately triggered by the spillover of the Rwandese genocide across the border into eastern Congo. For that reason, its external aspect has been more dramatic. Yet, the internal aspect of the crisis, generated by the partial and incomplete reform of the colonial state, is the more salient. While the reform deracialized the civic sphere, it left the ethnic character of the customary sphere intact. The rationale was that this would preserve the authenticity of Congolese custom. The consequence, though, was to contaminate the deracialized civic sphere with conflict generated in the ethnic sphere. So long as the customary sphere distinguished between citizens on the basis of whether they were ethnically indigenous or ethnic strangers, it continued to generate conflict in ethnic terms. Those denied rights in the customary sphere on ethnic grounds turned to the civic sphere to marshal resources to establish customary claims—just as those considered ethnically indigenous sought to turn customary prerogatives into an advantage in the civic sphere. So long as the customary sphere is not deethnicized as part of a broader reform, deracialization of the civic sphere will only lead to a spillover—even to an explosion—of ethnic conflict in the civic realm.

We can now see the location of the political problem called ethnic. Whereas "customary" power—the power at the level of the *collectivité*—is defined monoethnically, the population resident on the ground is multiethnic. Thus, for example, while the power and the locality were defined as Bafuliro, the resident population included both "indigenous" Bafuliro and Banyarwanda immigrants. I have suggested that it is the struggle of the Banyarwanda immigrants in this area to change from a descent-based (Banya-rwanda: those from Rwanda) to a residence-based (Banya-mulenge: those from Mulenge) political identity that illuminates the nature of this dilemma. And further, that it is the reasons for the failure of this initiative in the context of a rapidly regionalizing crisis that may suggest ways out of this conflict.

In attempting to change from indigeneity to residence as the basis of rights, the Banyamulenge tried to undo an important legacy of colonialism. Their initiative paralleled that of the NRA in the Luwero Triangle in Uganda. Though there is no proof of any contact between the two, both responses were born of similar postcolonial state histories. But there was also a difference. In the Ugandan context, the initiative came from a leadership of both migrant and "indigenous" origins. Locked in a civil war against a despotic state, this majority tried to construct a political umbrella under which they could mobilize all residents, indigenous and nonindigenous. In the Congolese case, however, the initiative came exclusively from those considered not indigenous as part of their effort to find accommodation as residents. Without a further initiative underlining a broader commonality of interests among residents, however, this initiative appeared as a "nonindigenous" attempt to usurp "indigenous" resources. The civil war in Congo thus took a turn very different from the earlier civil war in Uganda: instead of a coalition of all residents against a despotic state, as was the earlier tendency in the Luwero Triangle in Uganda, the war in

Congo pit the "indigenous" majority against a divided nonindigenous minority, with the Congolese Tutsi allied to the postgenocide state in Rwanda and the Congolese Hutu opposed to it just as firmly. The war in Congo thus crystallized two volatile regional diasporas—one Hutu, the other Tutsi—each determined to set the region on fire if the demands it considered legitimate were not met.

Conclusion

Political Reform after Genocide

I BEGAN this book with a discussion on the need to distinguish between three different kinds of identities: cultural, market based, and political. By highlighting Hutu and Tutsi as political identities, I distanced
myself from alternate views that see Hutu and Tutsi as either cultural or
market-based identities. Both points of view tend to gloss over the existence of specifically political identities: one does it by subordinating the
political to the cultural, the other by presuming that political identities
are nothing but a version of market-based identities.

I pointed out that prominent among those who see culture as the basis
of politics are the core theorists of the nation-state. For nation-state theorists, the "self" in the notion of self-determination is a cultural self. This
core premise came to be shared by most theorists across the ideological
spectrum of nineteenth-century Europe, from Max Weber to V. I. Lenin.
The doctrine of self-determination proclaims the right of every "nation"—defined variously as a group with a common culture—to its own
state. It translates cultural into political identities, innocently and unprob-
lematically. Where the identities are explicitly political, as with Hutu and
Tutsi, it assumes them to be cultural.

Those who still think consistently along "nation-state" lines call for a
separation of present-day Rwanda into two political entities, one a Hutuland, the other a Tutsiland—or some version of this proposal.[1] The proposal will not solve the problem of a minority in the context of a nation-
state. It will only ensure a balance by reproducing the problem. Since it
will produce two states out of one—a Hutuland with a Tutsi minority
and a Tutsiland with a Hutu minority—it will allow each identity to be a
permanent majority in one state while being held hostage as a permanent
minority in the other. The idea is that the majority which wishes fair treatment for its cultural brethren who are a minority in another state will have
no choice but to treat fairly cultural others who are a minority within its
own borders. By institutionalizing Hutu and Tutsi as political identities
in the state, the solution makes permanent the civil war between them.

Those who would give political primacy to market-based identities also think of the state as a state of the majority or minority, except that in this case the majority or the minority in question is identified with classes gelled through market-based relationships or, occasionally, with occupational groups such as pastoralists or agriculturalists. As with nation-state theorists, the market-state theorists too do not see political majorities and minorities as outcomes of distinct political processes, but of prior processes. For both, then, the political process is simply a litmus test that confirms vital prepolitical identities, either cultural or market based. From this point of view, politics appears as fundamentally a noncreative activity. Instead of being seen as outcomes of political processes, political majorities and minorities are seen as permanent features of political life introduced into it from the outside. Neither point of view has methodological room for a serious reflection on the question of political reform.

Anyone interested in the question of political reform after the genocide will need to keep in mind three salient features of the Rwandan situation: first, its starting point, the genocide; second, the consequence of the genocide, a tension-ridden polity and society; and third, that these consequences have overflowed the boundaries of Rwanda, making it the epicenter of the crisis of the African Great Lakes. The starting point of reform in Rwanda, the genocide, is radically different from that in any other country in the region. Like molten lava, the genocide has imparted to the Rwandan polity, and particularly to Hutu/Tutsi relations, tensions that are volcanic in nature. To contain these tensions will not only require a drawn-out cooling-off period and an approach that puts reform in Rwanda in the context of a regional reform agenda; it will also require a commitment and a responsibility that is international, not just regional. Whatever the nature and the length of this transition period, this custodianship, its direction will be shaped by its end goal. Will Rwanda follow the example of Israel and create a separate political community of Tutsi, alongside another of Hutu? Will it follow the example of Zanzibar and merge in a larger union with the tendency to dissolve bipolar political identities— Arab and African in Zanzibar, Tutsi and Hutu in Rwanda—in a wider arena with multiple political identities? Or will it charter a third course— without a wider merger and without creating a Tutsiland, a course we have come to associate with postapartheid South Africa—by trying to forge a political identity that transcends Hutu and Tutsi? Whatever course of action Rwanda chooses, its people will have to begin by making one basic choice: between political union and political divorce.

A Reconciliation with History

Postgenocide Rwanda presents a sharp contrast to postapartheid South Africa. In the white population in Apartheid South Africa, there were few perpetrators but many beneficiaries. Among the Hutu in Rwanda of the genocide, there were fewer beneficiaries and many more perpetrators. If it is true that hundreds of thousands of Hutu participated directly in the killings, then reconciliation presents a dilemma, morally and politically. Even a cursory visit to postgenocide Rwanda brings one face-to-face with this dilemma. Every time I visited postgenocide Rwanda, I would ask responsible state officials—sometimes a minister—as to how many ordinary civilians they thought had participated in the genocide. Every time, the answer was in the millions. Even more troubling, the estimate grew with each visit. The first time I went, a minister suggested a practical way to apportion blame and mete out justice: "Categorize according to responsibility. Let those with responsibility be shot in the national stadium. Then go ahead and say that for all those who participated, the three to four million, let them say we did the wrong thing."[2] From "three to four million" in 1995, the figure had grown to "four to five million" in 1997, when another minister told me that "80 percent of those [Hutu] alive had participated in the killing."[3] What was the point of these growing estimates? Was it an attempt by those in power to underscore that the majority of Hutu in Rwanda are guilty of genocide? Or, was it also a claim that this guilty majority be deprived of political rights as punishment for its crimes? I am concerned less with the truth of the claim than with its political significance. Rwanda's key dilemma is how to build a democracy that can incorporate a *guilty majority* alongside an aggrieved and *fearful minority* in a single political community.

The Rwandan state generally avoids the use of Hutu and Tutsi as political identities. But it has adopted a "genocide framework" from which to categorize the population politically, meaning that "the 1994 genocide is singled out as an event producing the only politically correct categories for identification and guidelines" for state policy.[4] The state language in Rwanda, the language one hears from all officials, and also from many who are not, divides the population into five categories: returnees, refugees, victims, survivors, and perpetrators. The *returnees* are, first and foremost, the mainly Tutsi (and some Hutu) exiles who returned with the Rwanda Patriotic Front (RPF). The *refugees* are divided into two: the "old case load" refers to mainly Tutsi pregenocide refugees, whereas the "new case load" refers to the wholly Hutu postgenocide refugees. The terminology is also used by UN and NGO circles. The *victims* are said to be both Tutsi and Hutu—the latter victims of the massacres of the internal political opposition. But when it comes to identifying living victims, this identification is limited to the "Tutsi genocide survivors" and "old caseload refugees"; "new caseload are not considered victims and as such are often not entitled to assistance for the construction of homes."[5] Finally, *survivor* is a term applied only to Tutsi. This is because the genocide was aimed at only the Tutsi, I was told. From this point of view, the "survivor" is a Tutsi who had been in the country at the time of the genocide and who is alive today. The word is not used for any Hutu then in the country. The assumption is that every Hutu who opposed the genocide was killed. The flip side of this assumption is that every living Hutu was either an active participant or a passive onlooker in the genocide. Morally, if not legally, both are culpable. The dilemma is that to be a Hutu in contemporary Rwanda is to be presumed a *perpetrator*.

Associated with this is another obvious fact: that political violence in the Rwandan genocide had an open, mass, and perversely popular character, as opposed to the secret, cloak-and-dagger nature of political violence in South Africa. Killings in Rwanda were not done by shadowy death squads, but by mobs of machete-wielding citizens. Killings did not happen under cover of darkness, with hardly a witness in sight, and with every effort to destroy the evidence. Instead, they happened in broad daylight, for all to see, and with no effort to destroy the evidence. In a nutshell, while the identity of the perpetrator was not always known in South Africa, it *is* known in Rwanda.

True, there are many more perpetrators than there are beneficiaries in Rwanda, unlike in South Africa, and their identity also tends to be more public. And yet, neither the identity of the perpetrator nor that of the survivor is as transparent in Rwanda as these differences would lead one to think. This is because the identification of both perpetrator and survivor is contingent on one's historical perspective. This is why it is not possible to think of reconciliation between Hutu and Tutsi in Rwanda without a prior reconciliation with history. In a 1996 visit to Kigali, I requested to be taken to a school so I could talk to a history teacher. My host, an aide to the vice-president, said this would be difficult since history teaching in schools had stopped. I asked why. Because there is no agreement on what should be taught as history, was the reply. History in Rwanda comes in two versions: Hutu and Tutsi. Ever since the colonial period, the cycle of violence has been fed by a victim psychology on both sides. Every round of perpetrators has justified the use of violence as the only effective guarantee against being victimized yet again. For the unreconciled victim of yesterday's violence, the struggle continues. The continuing tragedy of Rwanda is that each round of violence gives us yet another set of victims-turned-perpetrators.

To break the stranglehold of Hutu Power and Tutsi Power on Rwanda's politics, one also needs to break their stranglehold on Rwanda's history writing, and thus history making. This exercise requires putting the truth of the genocide, the truth of mass killings, in a historical context. To find a way out of this cycle, it is necessary to link political outcomes more to political institutions and less to political agency. The tendency has been the opposite: indeed, to so individualize and decontextualize the truth of the genocide—South Africa-style—that it escapes comprehension. What would it mean to contextualize the truth? It would be, *first of all*, to connect it to the civil war. This means to avoid two pitfalls: neither to merge and dissolve the genocide in the civil war, in which case it would cease to exist analytically, nor to sever it so completely from the civil war that the act of killing would become devoid of motivation. To see the genocide as one outcome of defeat in the civil war would be to see it as *political* violence, an outcome of a power struggle between Hutu and Tutsi elites. That would mean both to recognize Hutu and Tutsi as political identities and to recognize that the problem of Rwanda is first and foremost one of political power. There can be no reconciliation without a reorganization of power.

The *second* consequence of contextualizing the truth would be to understand the civil war in Rwanda as the development of a regional dynamic. I have argued that the critical impetus behind the RPF crossing the border in October 1990 was the confluence of a citizenship crisis in Uganda with that in Rwanda. The invasion was at the same time an armed repatriation from Uganda and an armed return home. Having embraced the Banyarwanda refugees as "comrades-in-arms" during their hour of need in the Luwero Triangle, Ugandan guerrillas-turned-government did not hesitate to "solve" their first major crisis in power by dispensing with the same comrades. The combination of loss of state positions for the elite and refusal to give grazing land to ordinary pastoralists highlighted the continuing homelessness of the generation born of 1959 Tutsi exiles. This same development also dramatically underscored the limits of Habyarimana's internal reform. Thus the Museveni government exported Uganda's internal crisis to Rwanda.

The *third* consequence of contextualizing the truth would be to put the question of power in a historical context. It would be to trace the genesis of Tutsi Power to two moments in Rwanda's recent history. The first is

Rwabugiri's reforms at the turn of the century, which mark the starting point of a process with two related outcomes, the degradation of the Hutu and the genesis of Tutsi privilege. The second is the colonial reforms of 1926–36 that racialized the Tutsi identity and hardened Tutsi privilege into a crust, giving it an apartheid-like quality. It would undercut both the Tutsi version of Rwanda's history that Tutsi privilege was exclusively a colonial creation, and the Hutu version that Tutsi privilege is as old as the presence of Tutsi on Rwandan soil.

The *fourth* consequence of contextualizing the truth would be to reflect on the complicity between the imperial project in twentieth-century Rwanda and history writing in and about Rwanda. In racializing Rwandan society and polity, the imperial project also racialized the parameters within which most historians pursued knowledge most of the time. If the colonial state underscored racial origins as a key attribute of citizenship and rights, historians became preoccupied with *the search for origins.* If official racism presumed that migration was central to the spread of civilization, particularly statecraft, historians seemed content to center their scholarly pursuits on the question of migration. And finally, if the colonial state defined the subject population as Hutu and Tutsi (and Twa)—regardless of the extent of intermarriage—historians presumed an equally *unproblematized* link between ancestral Hutu and Tutsi and those contemporarily so identified. Historians preoccupied with the search for origins read cultural differences from facts of migration and translated cultural into political difference. To differentiate cultural from political identity, and thereby to depoliticize historical facts of migration, it seems to me, is a prerequisite to rethinking the question of citizenship in post-genocide Rwanda.

The *fifth* consequence of contextualizing the truth would be to problematize both the 1959 Revolution and the ideology born of it, Hutu Power. To do so would be to recognize both the *historical legitimacy* of the revolution and its *historical limitation.* The 1959 Revolution was the antidote to Tutsi privilege that had crystallized between the time of Rwabugiri and the end of the colonial period, just as Hutu Power was the antidote to the Hamitic hypothesis that provided the civilizational rationale for Tutsi Power. Hutu Power had undertones of a subaltern ideology, similar to Black Power in the United States, Black Consciousness in South Africa, or Dalit Power in India. The obvious difference was that by the time Hutu Power was formulated as ideology, its proponents were already in power. Theirs was a call to defend power, not to take it. Yet, like its counterparts elsewhere, Hutu Power needs to be understood as a contradictory possibility. An outcome of struggle in the world of the rat and the cat, it had not only the potential of liberating the rat from the terror of the cat, but also of locking the rat forever in a world driven by fear of the cat. That world is one in which there are no other—and bigger—dangers or possibilities. To be locked into the claustrophobia of intimate differences, and to be blind to larger possibilities, is the historical limitation of Hutu Power. The historical failure of Hutu Power was that it failed to transform the political legacy of colonialism. Instead, it built on the very racialized political identities generated by colonial rule: of Hutu as Bantu and Tutsi as Hamites.

The *sixth* consequence of contextualizing the truth would be to distinguish between Hutu Power and *génocidaire*, as ideology and as political tendency. While Hutu Power was a broad and contradictory tendency born of the hope of the 1959 Revolution, *génocidaire* is a narrow tendency coalesced by the desperation of defeat in the civil war. True, the latter is born of the former, of its negative side. Yet, this child of adversity cannot be confused with the parent. While Hutu Power reconciled itself to living in the bipolar world of Hutu and Tutsi by a political struggle with Tutsi Power so as to acquire political supremacy over it, the *génocidaires* looked for a final solution to this bipolarity in the physical elimination of the Tutsi.

The *final* advantage of contextualizing the truth would be to recognize that Rwanda is once again at a historical crossroads where its political leadership is faced by two clear options. The first is a continuation of the civil war, as those defeated in the last round prepare for battle in the next; the second is its termination through a political reconciliation that rejects both victory and defeat and looks for a third and more viable possibility. Each of these possibilities is linked to a different form of justice and a different form of the state. The first is victor's justice, the second survivor's justice.

TWO FORMS OF JUSTICE

Victor's Justice

To pursue victor's justice would be to follow the example of Israel. It would be to build a Zionist-type state on the ashes of the genocide. This is indeed what is happening in contemporary Rwanda. Three convictions underline the character of postgenocide power in Rwanda. The first is an overwhelming sense of moral responsibility for the very survival of all remaining Tutsi, globally. This gives postgenocide power its first distinguishing characteristic: it is defined by a diasporic, rather than a territorial, notion of political obligation and political community. The second conviction—also a direct outcome of the experience of the genocide—is that Tutsi Power is the minimum condition for Tutsi survival. Tutsi will only be protected if they have a state of their own. I found this conviction shared by both the Congolese Tutsi legal adviser to the secretary-general of the Alliance of Democratic Forces in Kabila's Congo, and the newly appointed Rwandese commander of the Congolese national army in 1997. This point of view marks postgenocide power with yet a third conviction: that the only peace possible between Tutsi and Hutu is an armed peace. It also lends credibility to those in the opposition who argue that the Hutu must be armed if they are not to return to the servile condition of pre-1959 Rwanda.

Thus, even the moderate opposition to the RPF complains that not only are structures of power in Rwanda being Tutsified, civic organizations—from the media to nongovernmental organizations—are being cleansed of any but a nominal Hutu presence.[6] On its part, postgenocide power is determined to remove from the soil of Rwanda any trace of conditions that could possibly lead to a repeat of the genocide. Its unswerving motto recalls the claim that made post-Holocaust power in Israel immune to any moral doubts when it came to atrocities against Palestinians: NEVER AGAIN. Ironically, the conviction that Tutsi Power is the precondition for Tutsi survival means that life itself can be subordinated to this supreme goal, the survival of Tutsi Power.

The founding ideology of Tutsi Power in postgenocide Rwanda is the memory of the genocide and the moral compulsion never to let it happen again. The pursuit of the *génocidaires* is the raison d'être of the postgenocide state, the one permanent part of its agenda. In the real world of state politics, however, the word *génocidaire* may be used to label any Hutu seen as an opponent, or even a critic, of Tutsi Power. Arrests can be made on the basis of denunciation, not investigation. Even if the crowded jails of Rwanda take a daily toll on the lives of those incarcerated within, this does not disturb moral sensibilities.[7] The moral certainty about preventing another genocide imparts a moral justification to the pursuit of power with impunity.

Most recognize that the precondition for victor's justice is, clearly, victory. Few, however, recognize its price. The victor must remain on constant guard, lest the spoils of victory be snatched yet again. Just as a jailer comes to be tied to the jail as much as is the prisoner, so a victor must live in anticipation and fear of the next round of battle, why adversaries often tend to get locked into a single cycle more securely than do friends. The price of victor's justice is either a continuing civil war or a permanent divorce. It is worth remembering that it is not simply German defeat in the Second World War that made Nuremburg possible, but also the effective divorce between Gentiles and Jews in Germany, since most surviving German Jews departed for either America or Israel. In the absence of this effective divorce, anything resembling Zionist power in Germany would have been a recipe for triggering a civil war. In this sense, we need to bear in mind that while the RPF won the war, there has been no divorce between Tutsi and Hutu in Rwanda. The price of victor's justice, in Rwanda, must thus be yet another round of a continuing civil war.

It is also worth remembering a second difference between the Nazi Holocaust and the Rwandan genocide. Though both were designed from above, from within the state, the genocide alone unfolded as wave upon wave of mass killings, where not only victims but perpetrators too were drawn from civil society. As a state project that was carried out by many in society, the Rwandan genocide resembles apartheid more than it does the Holocaust. This is why victor's justice—the Tutsification of state institutions—cannot be an effective guarantee against a repeat of genocidal violence in Rwandan society. If anything, it will keep alive the specter of yet another round of genocidal violence.

Survivor's Justice

The form of justice flows from the form of power. If victor's justice requires victor's power, then is not victor's justice simply revenge masquerading as justice? To get away from this dilemma, we need to explore answers to two questions. Is a form of justice possible that is not at the same time victor's justice? Is a form of reconciliation possible that is not at the same time an absence of justice, and thus an embrace of evil? These questions provide a clue to finding a way out of the dialectic of civil war. That way has to be anchored in an alternative form of justice that I will call *survivor's justice*.

The prerequisite for survivor's justice, as for victor's justice, may also be victory. For victory presents alternatives to the victor, which it does not to the vanquished. Only the victor has the choice of reaching out to the vanquished on terms that have the potential of transcending an earlier opposition between the two, by defining both as survivors of the civil war. To transcend the terms of the earlier opposition is to forge a new community of survivors of the civil war. From this point of view, the term "survivor" does not refer to surviving victims—which, as I have pointed out, is how it is used in contemporary Rwanda—but to all those who continue to be blessed with life in the aftermath of the civil war.[8] The notion of survivor seeks to transcend the bipolar notions of victim and perpetrator.

The difference between victor's justice and survivor's justice is clear if we look at the two major postwar paradigms of justice: de-Nazification and de-Sovietization. The former came into being at the onset of the Cold War. The latter marked the end of the Cold War. Simply put, the logic of de-Nazification is to blame the agent, that of de-Sovietization is to blame the system; de-nazification requires identifying both victims and perpetrators. De-Sovietization is anchored first and foremost in the identity of survivors; it acknowledges victims, but not perpetrators. From this point of view, to identify individuals as perpetrators would be to demonize them. To pursue the logic of de-Nazification in contemporary Rwanda would be to identify the leadership of the genocide so as to hold it accountable. Such, indeed, is the purpose of the international court in Arusha and the local courts inside Rwanda. To pursue the logic of de-Sovietization would be to put emphasis, first and foremost, on the institutions of rule in Rwanda. Where survivors—victims and perpetrators from an earlier round of struggle—must learn to live together, ways must be found to reconcile the logic of reconciliation with that of justice.

Survivor's justice is different from revolutionary justice. It makes sense only in contexts where there have been few beneficiaries in the preceding civil war. I have already commented on the difference between South Africa and Rwanda on this score: one is struck by how few were the perpetrators of apartheid, and how many its beneficiaries, and conversely, how many were the perpetrators in Rwanda's genocide and how few its beneficiaries. Where beneficiaries are many, reconciliation has to be social to be durable, which is the same thing as saying there can be no durable reconciliation without some form of social justice.[9] But where beneficiaries are few, the key to reconciliation is political reconciliation. The prime requirement of political reconciliation is neither criminal justice nor social justice, but *political justice*. It requires not only shifting the primary focus of reform from individuals to institutions, but also recognizing that the key to institutional reform is the reform of institutions of rule. Thus the question: What would it mean to reform institutions of rule so as to give survivors of the genocide another chance?

RECONCILING JUSTICE TO DEMOCRACY

The genocide retrenched Hutu and Tutsi as salient political identities. The dilemma of postgenocide Rwanda lies in the chasm that divides Hutu as a political majority from Tutsi as a political minority. While the minority demands justice, the majority calls for democracy. The two demands appear as irreconcilable, for the minority sees democracy as an agenda for completing the genocide, and the majority sees justice as a self-serving mask for fortifying minority power. To break out of this logjam, I suggest we link both political justice and political democracy to a reform of institutions of rule.

Justice

The question of political justice goes beyond holding the perpetrators of the genocide accountable. Ultimately, it is about the definition of political identities. I have argued that European colonialism in twentieth-century Africa turned indigeneity into the litmus test of rights. Every postindependence regime vowed to change the political world of the settler and the native. Every one of them pledged to deracialize civic rights by making them available to all citizens regardless of color. That is where similarities ended.

While everyone agreed that the settler's prerogative had to go, not everyone was agreed that the native too was a colonial construct that needed to be reformed just as urgently. Could the political identity "settler" be done away with when its bipolar twin "native" was embraced? Anticolonial nationalism was divided on this question. Radical nationalism—as championed by Julius Nyerere, for example—was determined to reform citizenship consistently, both to deracialize and to deethnicize it. From this point of view, it was not enough to do away with just the settler's prerogative; all prerogatives, racial as well as ethnic, would need to be abolished. The predominant trend in African postcolonialism was otherwise: for conservative nationalism, the point of independence was precisely to replace the settler's prerogative by the native's prerogative.

Even though the political prerogative was transferred to the native, the continued legal representation of the indigenous population as *natives* showed that the colonial political legacy had yet to be fully transcended. Where colonial rule had been indirect, as in Uganda and Congo, the native prerogative was defined as ethnic. But where colonialism had imposed a version of direct rule—a halfway house, as I have said, in the case of Rwanda—the prerogative was racial. The 1959 Revolution in Rwanda against the Tutsi, like the 1964 Revolution in Zanzibar against Arabs and the 1972 expulsion of Asians in Uganda, belongs to this second category. Targeted in 1959 as an alien race, the Tutsi were recognized as an indigenous ethnicity by the Second Republic after 1973, but reconstructed as an alien race by the *génocidaires* after the coup of April 1994. As in the 1959 Revolution, so in the 1994 genocide too, the Tutsi were targeted as an alien race. Political justice for the Tutsi cannot mean simply identifying and holding the perpetrators of massacres accountable. By itself, that would return them to the world of the rat and the cat. It also requires a juridical and institutional reform that ceases to make a distinction between two kinds of citizens: one indigenous, the other not.

In contrast to colonial Rwanda, where race was the salient political identity, Congo and Uganda were indirect-rule colonies where *both* race and ethnicity defined political identity. If the settler identity was *racialized*, the native identity was *ethnicized*. Did it not follow that, in indirect-rule colonies such as Uganda and Congo, decolonization would require a combination of deracialization and deethnicization, as indeed Nyerere had championed in Tanzania? On this question, too, nationalism was differentiated. The mainstream—conservative—view was that the world of the "customary" as defined by colonialism was indeed the world of African tradition, and so the conviction that it must be preserved.[10] A reform executed from this point of view did two things. While civic law and civic authority were deracialized in the name of a universal rights culture, an ethnically defined "customary" law and an authority to enforce it were retained as *particular* to the tradition of those indigenous to Africa. Independent governments also vowed to end the perversion of colonialism by restoring the political prerogative of those indigenous over strangers. The result was to reproduce the bifurcated world created by colonialism: the distinction between indigenous and non-indigenous, abolished in the civic sphere, remained in the ethnic sphere. Even if turned upside down, the political world remained as designed by the settler.

The antidote to the embrace of colonially constructed custom as authentic African tradition came from among the postindependence oppositional political movements that had to contend with the rights of ethnic strangers. As one would expect, the most promising initiatives came from those that stood to lose the most from an uncritical reproduction of the colonial legacy. Not surprisingly, the most creative departures have come from those movements strongly influenced by Rwandan Tutsi: the Banyamulenge in Congo, and the National Resistance Army in Uganda. Of the two, we have seen that the most radical solution to this dilemma came from the latter, born of the guerrilla struggle in the Luwero Triangle. Luwero had an extremely heterogeneous population: anywhere from a third to a half of its residents had immigrated from outside the area. To continue to define rights on the basis of indigeneity in such a socially heterogeneous context was bound to be politically explosive and disruptive—regardless of whether one leaned in favor of those indigenous or those not. Welding an alliance between locals and migrants required a political identity that could encompass both. The National Resistance Army found this identity in the criterion of resident. When it came to deciding who would be a member of a village council and who could run for office on the ten-person village committee, what mattered was residence, not the circumstances of one's birth or ethnic belonging.

To leave the test of indigeneity for one of residence as the basis for political identity and political rights is to take leave of the world of the rat and the cat, of ethnicity and race, of the native and the settler, as political identities. This, in turn, would require making a clear distinction between cultural and political identities so as to redress the dialectic between the past and the future. To ground political rights in cultural identities is to accent the past—of which a shared culture is one outcome—as a guide to limiting future possibilities. To differentiate political from cultural identities, however, is to accent the commitment to live under a common roof over the recognition of a common history—no matter what the overlap between them—as the real basis for a shared future.

Democracy

Just as the question of political justice goes beyond holding the perpetrators of the genocide accountable, so the question of democracy goes beyond that of *who* should govern to deciding *how* they should govern—through what kinds of institutions. To address the institutional basis of rule is to address a dual and combined legacy. To the colonial legacy of administering local communities through despotic forms of power, nationalism has added the legacy of equating democratic rule with unqualified majority rule, in a setup in which the winner takes all and power is the prized and unchecked possession of the majority.

I have restated here with reference to Uganda and Congo—and, with qualifications, to Rwanda—the argument that I elaborated in an earlier book with reference to indirect-rule colonialism in twentieth-century Africa: the true seat of colonial despotism was not the central state and civic law which limited the regime of rights to races, but the local state wherein an unaccountable authority called "customary" enforced an authoritarian version of custom as "customary" law.[11] The conquest state removed any trace of democratic accountability to those below, and reinforced every sign of bureaucratic accountability to those above. In Rwanda of 1959, this "customary" authority was totally discredited since it was identified with Tutsi Power and Tutsi privilege. The revolution not only replaced Tutsi with Hutu chiefs, it also made the Hutu functionaries accountable to a popular mandate through regular elections, but without disaggregating the despotic power—legislative, executive, judicial, administrative—that these agents exercised. The Second Republic eliminated local elections and re-created the despotic local state constructed under colonialism—this time, though, as not only "customary" but also "revolutionary." Power and authority defined as "customary" in the colonial period have not only been at the center of coercive day-to-day practices in much of postindependence Africa, they have also—in the context of a racialized bipolar difference as in Rwanda—orchestrated and organized the mass slaughter that led to the genocide.

To this, some may say: Why not just go ahead and junk custom? My argument is that when a particular version of history (custom) is found wanting, in this case because it builds on the authoritarian strand as if it were the entire past, this surely cannot be reason to junk the very notion of history. From a reified language fortifying a despotic authority, custom needs to be rethought as a thread of life, not only one that makes us but also one that we make. To smash one version of the past as a prison dressed in the language of custom, one needs to turn that very past—the entire treasure house called custom, and not simply the authoritarian strands in it that colonial power welded into a "customary" law—into a plural resource for more open futures. There has been little effort at a comprehensive and critical rethinking of custom and its relationship to law, and it is not the purpose of this book to do so.

The region of the African Great Lakes, provides one important clue, by way of experience, to dismantling the local machinery of despotism that went by the name of Native Authority. We have seen that the guerrilla struggle in the Luwero Triangle recognized local power by disaggregating the moments of power that had been fused into one. The chief thus ceased to have the right to pass a by-law; instead, this legislative power became a prerogative of popular local councils, from the village at the lowest level to the district at the highest. Similarly, judicial and executive power was also transferred from the chief to other organs. Where the chief remained, he retained only administrative power as a paid agent of the state. Whether for the Hutu majority or for the entire people, democracy has to mean first of all an institutional reform that unravels this armed fist and separates each moment in this fused power (executive, legislative, judicial, administrative) and makes it accountable.

Both in forging a majority and in waging a struggle for unqualified majority power, the region offers two lessons to postgenocide Rwanda. The first comes from indirect-rule colonies; the second from colonies with more of a legacy of direct rule. The distinctive feature of the indirect-rule state, such as in Uganda and Congo, was that it fractured the identity of the colonized majority into so many ethnicities, each a minority. It was thus said that, unlike with nations in Europe, there were no natural majorities in African colonies; everyone was said naturally to belong to a minority. The statement contained an element of truth: everyone did belong to a minority, except that the minorities were not natural; ethnic identity was a political artifact of state power. In such a context, democracy was likely to be a recipe for instability, and there was a strong temptation to see a benevolent dictator as the only realistic source of stability, even for rule of law. To forge a political majority in this context would require dismantling the ethnically organized apparatus of indirect rule. Before that could be done—indeed, so that it may be done—a way had to be found to put together a *transitional* majority.

In the political vocabulary current in the region of the African Great Lakes, the search for an agency of rule that can bring stability to a post–civil war context has come to be known as the search for "a broad base." Where no political movement could marshal a consensus and where there was a history of bitter fragmentation, as in Uganda, the practice of coalition government came to be seen as necessary to ensuring a sufficiently broad base for rule in a period of transition. The practice of the "broad base" made a clear distinction between means and ends. All political tendencies—whether monarchist or "tribalist," even when identified with as brutal a dictatorship as that of Amin—were welcomed into the broad base provided they gave up violence as a means for attaining their objectives.

The lesson for postgenocide Rwanda is indeed radical. It would mean making a distinction between proponents of Hutu Power and perpetrators of the genocide. This would mean making a distinction between ends and means, politics and ideology, and thus between those proponents of Hutu Power willing to give up violence as a means and those not willing to do so: the former would be invited into the "broad base," the latter would be left out of it. This, indeed, is also the lesson of Rwanda's political history. The last attempt to put an end to the cycle of civil wars in Rwanda was the Arusha Agreement. Its key lesson is that one cannot put an end to the civil war by excluding one party to it, especially the party most entrenched in its partisan ideology. The lesson is to be inclusive, to recognize the right of all ideological currents—without exception—to compete in the marketplace of ideas, leaving out in the cold only those unwilling to disarm as a precondition to gaining entry to the reform process.

In colonies with more of a tradition of direct rule, as in Rwanda, the majority classified as indigenous was literally panel-beated by the apparatus of rule into a single, racialized mass. This is why in instances like Rwanda, Zanzibar, and preapartheid South Africa, the "Hutu," the "African," or the "Bantu" appeared as *natural*, prepolitical, majorities. It is also in these very countries that privileged but vulnerable minorities—such as Arabs in Zanzibar or whites in South Africa—concluded that power was indeed their only guarantee for life, liberty, and, indeed, property. Does this not echo the central conclusion that the RPF seems to have drawn from the history of postindependence Rwanda: that the Tutsi cannot survive without power? But, here too, the weight of experience seems to point in a different direction. Rather than think that power is the precondition for survival, the Tutsi will sooner or later have to consider the opposite possibility: that the prerequisite to cohabitation, to reconciliation, and a common political future may indeed be to give up the monopoly of power. Like the Arabs of Zanzibar, and even the whites of South Africa, the Tutsi of Rwanda may also have to learn that, so long as Hutu and Tutsi remain alive as political identities, giving up political power may be a surer guarantee of survival than holding on to it.

Yet, we cannot ignore the one fact that must weigh like a nightmare on the minds of Tutsi survivors: neither the Arabs of Zanzibar nor the whites of South Africa have gone through the experience of genocidal violence as have the Tutsi of Rwanda. To find historical parallels to this situation, where an imperiled minority fears to come under the thumb of a guilty majority yet again—even if the thumb print reads "democracy"—we have to take leave of the boundaries of Africa for the New World. Only in the erstwhile settler colonies of the New World do we have a comparable history of violence that has rendered the majority guilty in the eyes of victimized minorities. Such, indeed, has been the aftermath of genocide and slavery: the genocide of indigenous populations in the Americas, Australia, and New Zealand, and the slavery of Africans in the Americas.

If we are to go by these experiences, we have to admit both that the attainment of self-enlightenment by guilty majorities has been a painfully gradual process, and that even the little progress made along that road has been as much a result of international pressure as it has been of internal struggle. Rwanda is different from the New World in one important respect: the cycle of violence has alternated positions between victims and perpetrators. The internal pressure in Rwanda is now joined to a regional dynamic as two diasporas—one Hutu, the other Tutsi—confront each other in a life-and-death encounter. Both diasporas are animated, not simply by the cycle of revenge in Rwanda but also by the common regional inheritance that has been translated into a mode of citizenship that denies full citizenship to residents it brands as ethnic strangers. Not surprisingly, Rwanda has become the epicenter of the wider crisis in the African Great Lakes. Tied together by the thread of a common colonial legacy—one that politicized indigeneity as a basis for rights—the region has little choice but to address the Rwandan dilemma, if only to address its own dilemma. To do so will mean, first of all, to reform the state and citizenship within their own borders so that power recognizes equal citizenship rights for all based on a single criterion: residence.

To reform Rwanda, the epicenter of the crisis, will require a regional approach through a regional agenda that approaches the center as fire-fighters would approach the heart of a raging fire, from the outside in. If a regional reform of citizenship needs to be its first step, its second step may have to focus on Rwanda's splitting political image, Burundi. Precisely because Rwanda and Burundi read developments in each other's backyard as prophetic signs of their common fate, reform in Burundi can serve as a compelling example for Rwanda. For that reason if for no other, it is in Burundi that the regional and international community would be wise to invest physical resources alongside political guarantees to bring a political reform. For without a reform in power, one that recognizes both the importance of a majority in politics and the need for fearful minorities to participate in the exercise of power, there can be no sustained reconciliation between Hutu and Tutsi. To do so will be to recognize that neither the tragedy of Rwanda nor its possible salvation can be exclusively, or even mainly, a Rwandan responsibility.

ONE needs to close with a sense of real political obstacles that will face any attempt to democratize public life in postgenocide Rwanda. Where there is an uneasy coexistence between guilty majorities and fearful minorities, the possibility of a democratic transition is likely to appear more as a threat than a promise to the minorities concerned—why vulnerable minorities tend to fear rather than welcome democracy. The experience of the Tutsi, too, is likely to reinforce an ambivalent attitude to democracy. Were not the Tutsi liberators inside Uganda's NRA sidelined on the morrow of the guerilla victory precisely because they came from a vulnerable minority? Did not the dawn of democracy in Zaire, signified by the coming together of a National Conference of civil and political society in the early 1990s, complete the process leading to the disenfranchising of the Banyarwanda minority? Was not the Rwandan genocide driven forward by the energy of popular mobs mobilized to defend Hutu Power? By itself, majority rule provides no guarantee for minorities that fear majority domination. My point is that if we go by the experience of Banyarwanda—and more specifically Tutsi Banyarwanda—in the African Great Lakes, majority rule can be turned into a bedrock for domination over fragile minorities.

How to foreclose the possibility of a *democratic despotism* remains our toughest challenge yet. While this question is not directly the subject of this book, I believe its subject does bring us a step closer to addressing this question. I began the book with the claim that, even when they mimic preexisting identities—whether cultural or market based—political identities need to be understood as a product of the political process. From this point of view, Hutu and Tutsi need to be understood both as *historical* identities and as *political* identities. As majority and minority, Hutu and Tutsi are not natural identities brought into the political realm; they are political artifacts of a particular form of the state.

If the immediate challenge in Rwanda is to undercut Hutu and Tutsi as political identities, I have argued that this will not happen so long as the minority monopolizes power. If anything, it will be the surest way of locking the Banyarwanda into the world of the rat and the cat, and giving these identities a longer lease on life. The region provides us two examples of how a minority may give up power. The first is Zanzibar, the second South Africa. For a minority gripped by the fear of extinction, the Zanzibari example is likely to have greater resonance, for at least one reason: it involved longer-term political concessions by both the minority and the majority. Not only did the "Arab" minority cede power, the "African" majority in Zanzibar also ceded full claim on power as the country merged with mainland Tanganyika to form a wider union, Tanzania. The union set in motion a new dynamic tending to dissolve the identities "Arab" and "African" in a wider crucible, over time generating a "Zanzibar" identity. Is a dynamic possible that may undercut the legacy of Hutu and Tutsi as binary political identities, dissolving them in the crucible of a larger Banyarwanda identity in the short run and, other identities we may not imagine today, in the medium run? If yes, it will require us to question the hitherto presumed equation of the democratic project with the national project. Indeed, if it is to be, it will need to draw on energies that go beyond any national assertion. Such a dynamic will need to be the result of a regional initiative, backed up by international support, which in turn needs to be driven by the urgent need to defuse a simmering volcano before it blows up yet again, this time engulfing the wider region.

Notes

INTRODUCTION
THINKING ABOUT GENOCIDE

1. The lower estimate comes from the UN Commission of Experts. The figure of a million is often heard of in the media and in RPF statements. Gérard Prunier gave the figure as "between 800,000 and 850,000" or roughly 11 percent of the population in his 1995 book. The 1997 multinational, multidonor evaluation team scaled the numbers down, writing that "an estimated five to eight hundred thousand" were killed "as a result of civil war and genocide" over three months in 1994. The final estimate has come from the 1999 book jointly published by Human Rights Watch and Fédération Internationale des Ligues des Droits de l'Homme. The book opens with the lower estimate: "In the 13 weeks after April 6, 1994, at least half a million people perished in the Rwandan genocide." However, it then goes on to cite the demographer William Seltzer's estimate of 657,000 dead, a figure extrapolated from 1991 census data, which in turn are accepted as problematic by some authorities. See "UN Commission of Experts Established Pursuant to Security Council Resolution 935 (1994) on Rwanda," *Final Report*, Geneva, 25 November 1994 (check); Gérard Prunier, *The Rwanda Crisis: History of a Genocide, 1959–1994* (London: Hurst & Co., 1995), p. 265; Tor Sellstom and Lennart Wohlgemuth, *The International Response to Conflict and Genocide: Lessons from the Rwanda Experience*, Study 1, *Historical Perspective: Some Explanatory Factors* (Uppsala, Sweden: The Nordic Africa Institute, 1997), p. 1; Human Rights Watch and Fédération Internationale des Ligues des Droits de l'Homme, "Leave None to Tell the Story: Genocide in Rwanda" (London and New York: Human Rights Watch; and Paris: Fédération Internationale des Ligues des Droits de l'Homme, 1999), pp. 1 and 15.

2. Many Jewish scholars here insisted that it was the Nazi intention to eliminate Jews as a people—and not the numbers of Jews killed—that marked the Holocaust as different from any other mass killing in history. As we shall see, others, like Hannah Arendt, disagreed and pointed out that genocide too has a history. Michael R. Marrus, *The Holocaust in History* (New York: Meridian Penguin, 1987), pp. 24–28.

3. Patrick Mazimpaka, Interview, Kigali, 11 July 1997.

4. Opening speech by H. E. Pasteur Bizimungu, president of the Republic of Rwanda, International Conference on Genocide, Impunity and Accountability, Kigali, 1–5 November, 1995, mimeo, pp. 1–2, 3.

5. See, for example, the articles submitted at the CODESRIA conference on the Rwandan genocide, held in Arusha in March 1995, and the articles in the special edition on the Rwandan genocide in the official magazine of the African Studies Association of USA, Issues 23/2 (1995).

6. Numbers, chapter 31:9–10, Old Testament. I am indebted to Ian Shapiro for guiding me to the Old Testament.

7. For details, see Jan-Bart Gewald, *Herero Heroes: A Socio-Political History of the Herero of Namibia, 1890–1923* (Oxford: James Currey, 1999) chapters 5 and 6, pp. 141–230; Tilman Dedering, " 'A Certain Rigorous Treatment of all Parts of the Nation': The Annihilation of the Herero in German South West Africa, 1904," in Mark Levene and Penny Roberts, *The Massacre in History* (New York: Berghahn Books, 1999), pp. 204–222; Regina Jere-Malanda, "The Tribe Germany Wants to Forget," *New African* (London), no. 383 (March 2000): 16–21; Horst Drechsler, *"Let Us Die Fighting": The Struggle of the Herero and the Nama against German Imperialism (1884—1915)* (London: Zed Press, 1980).

8. Cited in Jan-Bart Gewald, *Herero Heroes: A Socio-Political History of the Herero of Namibia, 1890–1923* (Oxford: James Currey, 1999), p. 173.

9. Jan Cloete, who had acted as a guide for the Germans, deposed the following oath: "I was present when the Herero were defeated in a battle at Hamakiri in the vicinity of Waterberg. After the battle all men, women and children who fell into German hands, wounded or otherwise, were mercilessly put to death. Then the Germans set off in pursuit of the rest, and all those found by the wayside and in the sandveld were shot down and bayoneted to death. The mass of the Herero men were unarmed and thus unable to offer resistance. They were just trying to get away with their cattle." Drechsler, *"Let Us Die Fighting,"* p. 157.

10. Dedering, " 'A Certain Rigorous Treatment,' " p. 213.

11. Cited in Gewald, *Herero Heroes*, p. 174.

12. Later relieved of his duties because he failed to defeat the Herero militarily, Governor Leutwein wrote: "I do not concur with those fanatics who want to see the Herero destroyed altogether. Apart from the fact that a people of 60,000 to 70,000 is not easy to annihilate, I would consider such a move a grave mistake from an economic point of view. We need the Herero as cattle breeders, though on a small scale, and especially as labourers. It will be quite sufficient if they are politically dead." Cited in Gewald, *Herero Heroes*, p. 169.

13. Dedering, " 'A Certain Rigorous Treatment,' " p. 213.

14. Jere-Malanda, "The Tribe Germany Wants to Forget," p. 20.

15. Frantz Fanon, *The Wretched of the Earth* (London: Penguin, 1967), p. 33.

16. Ibid., p. 66.

17. Ibid., p. 68.

18. Ibid., p. 73.

19. A notable exception is Leo Kuper, *The Pity of It All: Polarization of Racial and Ethnic Relations* (Minneapolis: University of Minnesota Press, 1977).

CHAPTER ONE
DEFINING THE CRISIS OF POSTCOLONIAL CITIZENSHIP

1. The best-known theorist of underdevelopment in Africa was Samir Amin. See Samir Amin, *Accumulation on a World Scale* (New York: Monthly Review Press, 1974).

2. Immanuel Wallerstein, "The Uses of Racism," *London Review of Books* 22, no. 10 (18 May 2000): 11–14.

3. See, for example, Samuel Huntington, *The Clash of Civilizations and the Remaking of World Order* (New York: Simon and Schuster, 1996).

4. "The political," writes Carl Schmitt, "can derive its energy from the most varied human endeavours, from the religious, economic, moral, and other antitheses." Carl Schmitt, *The Concept of the Political*, trans. and with an introduction by George Schwab (Chicago: University of Chicago Press, 1996), p. 38.

5. Among the most suggestive earlier works are Schmitt, *The Concept of the Political*, and Mao Tse-tung, "Analysis of the Classes in Chinese Society," in *Selected Works of Mao Tse-tung*, vol. 1 (Beijing: Foreign Language Press, 1967). Carl Schmitt writes: "The specific political distinction to which political actions and motives can be reduced is that between friend and enemy" (p. 26), and then, "For as long as a people exists in the political sphere, this people must . . . determine by itself the distinction of friend and enemy" (p. 49). Mao begins his essay: "Who are our enemies? Who are our friends? This is a question of the first importance for the revolution" (p. 13). For some of the more recent works that grapple with the question of political identity, see Robert Meister, *Political Identity: Thinking through Marx* (New York: Blackwell, 1991); Ernesto Laclau, *The Making of Political Identities* (London: Verso, 1994); Aletta J. Norval, *The Deconstructing Apartheid Discourse* (New York: Verso, 1996); Partha Chatterjee, "Nationalist Thought and the Colonial World: The Nation and Its Fragments" and "A Possible India," in *The Partha Chatterjee Omnibus* (Delhi: Oxford University Press, 1999); and David Scott, *Refashioning Futures* (Princeton: Princeton University Press, 1998).

6. For the left tendency in African Studies, see Issa Shivji, *Silent Class Struggle* and *Class Struggles in Tanzania* (Dar-es-Salaam: Tanzania Publishing House, 1973 and 1976); Colin Leys, *Under-development in Kenya* (London: Heinemann, 1974); Mahmood Mamdani, *Politics and Class Formation in Uganda* (New York: Monthly Review Press, 1976); Archie Mafeje, "The Ideology of Tribalism," *Journal of Modern African Studies* 9, no. 2 (1971).

7. The entire literature on "tribalism" and "ethnicity" in Africa shared the presumption that "tribe" was a cultural identity that got translated into a political identity. For a more recent statement that Africa's political problems stem from the late-nineteenth-century partition that drew state boundaries cutting across "natural" ethnic communities, thereby making it difficult to create "nation-states" in Africa, see Basil Davidson, *The Black Man's Burden: Africa and the Curse of the Nation-State* (New York: Times Books, 1992).

8. Joseph Stalin, "Marxism and the National Question" (1913), in *The Essential Stalin*, ed. Bruce Franklin (London: Croom Helm, 1973).

9. For a theoretical discussion on the modern state, law and rights, see G.F.W. Hegel, *The Philosophy of Right* (Amherst, N.Y.: Prometheus Books, 1996).

10. See Mahmood Mamdani, *Citizen and Subject: Contemporary Africa and the Legacy of Late Colonialism* (Princeton: Princeton University Press, 1996).

11. No doubt, the terms of that incorporation were never a given and always had to be fought for. Nonetheless, even where the "civilized" minority successfully won rights, up to self-determination, the resulting civil society was demarcated racially, as in every settler colony that became independent.

12. Mahmood Mamdani, "When Does a Settler Become a Native? Reflections on the Colonial Roots of Citizenship in Equatorial and South Africa," Inaugural Lecture, University of Cape Town, New Series No. 208, 13 May 1998.

13. Nyerere was joined by Abdul Rehman Babu, a Zanzibari "Arab" who broke away from the party of Arab privilege, the Zanzibar Nationalist Party, to form Umma, an "Afro-Arab" party pledged to fighting privilege in all its forms. For anyone probing why postrevolutionary Zanzibar has been able to avoid the tragic fate of postrevolutionary Rwanda, a fruitful beginning would be to examine the contribution of the two political leaders, Nyerere and Babu. For an appreciation of Babu, see Mahmood Mamdani, "Babu: A Personal Tribute," *Review of African Political Economy* (London), no. 19 (1996).

14. A later regional contrast to Hutu Power was the Black Consciousness Movement in South Africa; the latter stretched the notion of "black" to include all those oppressed by apartheid, whereas the former made a bid for power in the name of natives only.

15. Literally referring to the right of the indigenous majority. I am thankful to David Himbara for help with translation of the term.

CHAPTER TWO
THE ORIGINS OF HUTU AND TUTSI

1. Dominique Franche, "There's Only One Ethnic Group in Rwanda: Rwandan," *Le Monde Diplomatique/Guardian Weekly*, 24 November 1996, p. 14.

2. Jean Hiernaux, *The People of Africa* (New York: Charles Scribner's Sons, 1974), p. 60.

3. Walter Rodney, *How Europe Underdeveloped Africa* (Dar-es-Salaam: Tanzania Publishing House, 1971), p. 138.

4. Captain Eugene M. Haguma, "The Rwandese Crisis: A Political Economy of Genocide," Symposium on Interface, Dialogue and Co-Operation between Government and NGO's for Popular Participation in National Reconstruction, Conflict and Psycho-social Trauma Management, organized jointly by Africa Humanitarian Action and the UN Economic Commission for Africa, Kigali, 28 February 1995, mimeo, p. 4.

5. Franche, "There's Only One Ethnic Group in Rwanda," p. 14. It is difficult to ignore that Dominique Franche argues on the basis of a historical analogy, and not a historical analysis. True, a difference in physique does not necessarily prove a difference in ancestry. Yet, it remains equally true that a difference in physique *can* provide a clue to different histories.

6. Laurent Excoffier, Beatrice Pellegrini, Alicia Sanchez-Mazas, Christian Simon, and André Langaney, "Genetics and History of Sub-Saharan Africa," *Yearbook of Physical Anthropology* 30 (1987): 151–194, see p. 183.

7. Cited in Scott Grosse, "The Roots of Conflict and State Failure in Rwanda: The Political Exacerbation of Social Cleavages in a Context of Growing Resource Scarcity," School of Public Health, University of Michigan, Ann Arbor, mimeo, 15 November 1994.

8. Numerous studies in industrialized countries have established that this ability in adults is strictly inherited and is not influenced by current or even recent milk consumption practices. Certain global populations, such as those in northwestern Europe or the Sahara and the Arabian peninsula, show a high ability to digest lactose. The hypothesis that accounts for this difference suggests that this characteristic favored reproductive survival of pastoral populations living in harsh desert environments. In other words, where there is an absence of vegetation during much of the year, the complete digestion of lactose makes more of the milk nutrients available for absorption. Only a limited number of groups in Africa are said to possess such an ability in substantial numbers. These groups include the Beja of eastern Sudan, the Tuareg and the Fulani of West Africa, and the Tutsi of Rwanda and Burundi. Summing up the available literature, Scott Grosse argues that one relevant thread links them together: their ancestors were pastoralists "for probably thousands of years," for "millennia were needed for the natural selection process to produce a high frequency of lactose persistence under these conditions." The relevant literature includes G. Flatz, "Genetics of Lactose Digestion in Humans," *Advances in Human Genetics* 1 (1987): 1–77; R.A.L. Bayoumi, N. Saha, A. S. Salih, A. E. Bekkar, and G. Flatz, "Distribution of the Lactose Phenotype in the Population of the Democratic Republic of the Sudan," *Human Genetics* 57 (1981): 279–281; R.A.L. Bayoumi, S. D. Flatz, W. Kuhnow, and G. Flatz, "Beja and Nilotes: Nomadic Pastoralist Groups in the Sudan with Opposite Distributions of the Adult Lactose Phenotypes," *American Journal of Physical Anthropology* 58 (1982): 173–178; and D. Brasseur, Goyens, and H. L. Vis, "Some Aspects of Protein-Energy Malnutrition in the Highlands of Central Africa," in R. E. Eeckels, O. Ransome-Kuti, and C. C. Kroonenberg, eds., *Child Health in the Tropics* (The Hague: Martinus Nijhoff Publishers, 1985), pp. 167–178; and Grosse, "The Roots of Conflict and State Failure in Rwanda."

9. Flatz, "Genetics of Lactose Digestion in Humans."

10. Archie Mafeje, *The Theory and Ethnography of African Social Formations: The Case of the Intralacustrine Kingdoms* (Dakar: CODESRIA, 1991), pp. 19, 26, 21, 20.

11. C. Wrigley did, however, dismiss it as outright fiction. To accept that there were Chwezi kings in a fifteenth-century kingdom in the intralacustrine region, because myth and cult claim so, would be, he argued, tantamount to believing that Odin and Freya were kings of ancient Sweden because the *Ynglinga Saga* says so. Writing the chapter on the Great Lakes Region from the twelfth to the six-

teenth centuries, the Kenyan historian Bethwell Ogot disagreed: "In this chapter, we accept the historicity of the Bachwezi. We therefore proceed to discuss the major developments which took place in the Kitara complex from 1350 to 1500 as part of East African history, and not as an aspect of East African mythology." See C. Wrigley, "Some Thoughts on the Bachwezi," *Uganda Journal* 22, no. 1 (1958): 11–21; B. A. Ogot, "The Great Lakes Region," in *UNESCO General History of Africa*, vol. 4, D. T. Niane (London: Heinemann, 1984), p. 503.

12. Ibid.

13. "In the development of a number of body proportions with age, which appears to be largely determined by heredity, the Tutsi are more different from Europeans than the Hutu," Hiernaux wrote in *La Croissance des Ecoliers Rwandais* (Brussels: Académie Royale des Sciences d'Outre-Mer, 1965).

14. Hiernaux, *The People of Africa*, pp. 62, 81, 82–83.

15. Hiernaux, "Heredity and Environment: Their Influence on Human Morphology. A Comparison of Two Independent Lines of Study," *American Journal of Physical Anthropology* 21 (1963): 579–590. All other quotes from Hiernaux, *The People of Africa*.

16. Disputing the assumptions of "a dramatic turning-point" implied in earlier explanations of migrations following the spread of the agricultural revolution—either as a result of a population explosion (Merrick Posnansky) or of conquest (C. C. Wrigley)—the body of the article concluded: "The expansion of the Bantu did not assume the dimensions of an exodus from one area to another. It was most probably a movement of small numbers of people from one village to the next and sometimes back again, a process that was repeated over and over again until successive generations reached all parts of sub-equatorial Africa, perhaps over the space of a thousand or more years. It should not be imagined that the Bantu migrations took the form of a linear progression, unidirectional, in a perpetual forward movement. On the contrary, over thousands of years, movements must have occurred in all directions." See S. L. Lwanga-Lunyigo and J. Vansina, "The Bantu-Speaking Peoples and Their Expansion," in *UNESCO General History of Africa*, vol. 3, ed. M. El Fasi (Oxford: Heinemann, 1988), p. 151.

17. Around that same time (1987), the prevailing academic view was put forth in a survey article on "Genetics and History in Sub-Saharan Africa": "Bantu-speaking populations, extending from sub-Saharan Central Africa to southern Africa, appear genetically quite homogeneous. This fact suggests that their expansion was quite recent and rapid, as is suggested by linguists. Bantu speakers are often found genetically close to western Africans. This is in concordance with their linguistic affiliation and the assumed Bantu homeland located on the Nigeria/Cameroon border (Greenberg, 1964)." See Lwanga-Lunyigo and Vansina, "The Bantu-Speaking Peoples and Their Expansion," p. 161 for the appended note; Excoffier et al., "Genetics and History of Sub-Saharan Africa," p. 182.

18. J. K. Rennie, "The Precolonial Kingdom of Rwanda: A Reinterpretation," *Transafrican Journal of History* 2, no. 2 (1972): 15, 24–25.

19. "Instead of having a single exotic origin, pastoralism had many different centers of innovation, which built on a more general fund of pastoral knowledge innovated by the earliest groups of Bantu speakers to settle in the area, groups that had enjoyed long-term contacts with non-Bantu herders. There were correlates to development of cattle-as-wealth in the banana gardens of Buganda and Buhaya." See David Lee Schoenbrun, *A Green Place, A Good Place: Agrarian Change, Gender, and Social Identity in the Great Lakes Region to the 15th Century* (Kampala: Fountain, 1998), p. 79. See also David Lee Schoenbrun, "Cattle Herds and Banana Gardens: The Historical Geography of the Western Great Lakes Region," *African Archaeology Review* (1993), pp. 23, 41–75.

20. A 1956 colonial report, for example, spoke of Batutsi "small cattle owners who are at the same time cultivators." See Catharine Newbury, *The Cohesion of Oppression: Clientship and Ethnicity in Rwanda, 1860–1960* (New York: Columbia University Press, 1989), p. 206.

21. Mafeje observes that "as in Nkore," there was in Rwanda too "a conscious effort to deny non-Batutsi access to cattle in general." See *The Theory and Ethnography of African Social Formations*, p. 60.

22. For a detailed discussion, see David Newbury, "The Invention of Rwanda: The Alchemy of Ethnicity," mimeo, University of North Carolina–Chapel Hill, pp. 14–17.

23. "The Politics of language aside, nearly twenty million people speak Rwanda, Rundi, Ha, Shuubi, Haangaza and Vinza in the Western Highland region. These communities could draw on the mutual intelligibility of their dialects and languages to form a regional tongue to rival the prominence of Swahili elsewhere in East Africa." See Schoenbrun, *A Green Place, A Good Place*, pp. 22–23.

24. Tor Sellstom and Lennart Wohlgemuth, *The International Response to Conflict and Genocide: Lessons from the Rwanda Experience*, Study 1, *Historical Perspective: Some Explanatory Factors* (Uppsala, Sweden: The Nordic Africa Institute, 1997), p. 56.

25. I say "more or less the same culture" because there were cultural variations within this single linguistic community. Besides regional variations, there were also important variations in work-style and life-style between (mainly Hutu) agriculturalists and (mainly Tutsi) pastoralists.

26. Jacques Maquet wrote in his 1961 study: "Inter-caste marriage was not prohibited between Hutu and Tutsi. Hutu informants say it happened frequently, Tutsi informants claim that such marriages were very rare, but that Tutsi often had Hutu concubines. This discrepancy shows clearly that for a Tutsi to take a Hutu wife in a primary marriage entailed a loss of prestige. It was resorted to mainly because of poverty. Bride-wealth was lower in these inter-caste unions. . . . A prosperous Hutu could marry a Tutsi girl, but then the bride-wealth was often

greater than that for a Tutsi (three cows instead of one). It happened also that a Tutsi cattle-lord (*shebuja*) would grant a daughter to one of his Hutu clients." Jacques J. Maquet, *The Premise of Inequality in Rwanda: A Study of Political Relations in a Central African Kingdom* (London: Oxford University Press, 1961), pp. 65–66.

27. Yet, in the 1994 genocide, Tutsi women married to Hutu men were identified as Tutsi and killed.

28. Jacques Maquet observed that his Banyarwanda respondents held a "biological basis to the patrilineage principle of descent": "According to their theories, the man's participation in conception was more important than the woman's. The analogy with the sowing of seeds in a field is commonly used by informants. It was pointed out to me that if it is indeed necessary for the seed to be buried in the soil, strength and vitality are unquestionably in the seed rather than in the passive ground." See Maquet, *The Premise of Inequality in Rwanda*, p. 83.

29. Francis M. Deng, "An African Reflects on Race and Ethnicity," *Brookings Review* 13, no. 3 (1995).

30. Neil Fleming, "Rwanda and Burundi—Africa's Northern Ireland?" United Press International, BC Cycle, Internet, 7 October 1990.

31. See Maquet, *The Premise of Inequality in Rwanda*, pp. 30, 33–35, 46.

32. Ibid., p. 46

33. David S. Newbury, "The Clans of Rwanda: An Historical Hypothesis," *Africa* 50, no. 4 (1980): 390–399.

34. Ibid., p. 398.

35. The class-difference point of view is popular in progressive RPF circles. Textually, it is identified with the writings of Walter Rodney (see note 3). It has most recently been put forth by two authors, first by Tharcisse Gatwa in an otherwise excellent historical analysis of church-state relations in Rwanda, and then by Shinichi Takeuchi, who has argued that the notion of "Tutsi" as developed in the central court in the kingdom of Rwanda be thought of as a "ruling class." Its earliest employment, to my knowledge, was by d'Hertefelt, who argued that Maquet's use of the term "caste" to describe the Hutu/Tutsi difference had static implications, and instead proposed that the difference be thought of as one of "social class."

Writing the chapter on the Great Lakes in the *UNESCO General History* (1988), the Kenyan historian Bethwell Ogot tended to see the difference as both a class and an occupational difference, making nothing of the distinction between the two:

We hope to show in this chapter that state formation among the agriculturalists in this region antedates the advent of most pastoralists. We also hope to show that for a long time there was peaceful existence between agriculturalists and pastoralists prior to the major state formation processes of the fifteenth century, which to a large extent were responsible for the creation of social classes or castes in this region. In this connection, it is important to emphasize that the terms 'pastoralists' and 'agriculturalists' are occupational and not ethnic terms. The interlacustrine traditions reveal that when pastoralists lost their cattle and were unable to recoup their losses, they became cultivators; and when cultivators acquired cattle, they became pastoralists. This change of occupation was continually occurring in the region, both at the individual and the group levels. (Karugire, 1971)

See Tharcisse Gatwa, "The Churches and Ethnic Ideology in the Rwandan Crises (1900–1994)," Ph.D. diss., University of Edinburgh, 1998; Shinichi Takeuchi, "Hutu and Tutsi: A Note on Group Formation in Pre-colonial Rwanda," in Didier Goyvaerts, ed., *Conflict and Ethnicity in Central Africa* (Tokyo: Institute for the Study of Languages and Cultures of Africa and Asia, Tokyo University of Foreign Studies, 2000); M. d'Hertefelt, *Les Clans du Rwanda Ancien* (Tervuren: MRAC, 1971); Ogot, "The Great Lakes," pp. 498–499.

36. This was the view taken by a multinational, multidonor evaluation that arose out of a consultative meeting of international agencies and NGOs in Copenhagen in November 1994. According to its report: "In large part, during the colonial period or before the 19th century, Tutsi, Hutu and Twa roughly corresponded to occupational categories. Cattle-herders, soldiers and administrators were roughly Tutsi, while Hutu were farmers. Twa were marginalised and often mistreated by the others." See Sellstrom and Wohlgemuth, *The International Response to Conflict and Genocide*, p. 19. A similar view was attributed to Alex de Waal, the codirector of the human rights group Africa Rights: "It is difficult to define a tribe, but tribal peoples do have a distinct language, a distinct territory and a distinct culture. This is not the case with these groups. *The differences tend to be occupational.* Traditionally, it was more like the caste system in the Indian sense" (italics mine). See Martin Bright, "Rwanda: Blurred Roots of Conflict," *The Guardian* (London), 9 May 1994, p. E13. Finally, even an author as careful about historical changes as J. K. Rennie shared this view: "The Rwandan state comprised three classes (sometimes called castes): a ruling aristocracy of primarily pastoral Tutsi; a lower class of Hutu agriculturalists making up the bulk of the population; and a tiny minority of intermediate Twa who engaged in specialized or 'unclean' tasks such as pot-making or hunting." See Rennie, "The Precolonial Kingdom of Rwanda," p. 15.

Writing in the aftermath of the genocide, the social geographer Dominique Franche disagrees: "The word 'caste' doesn't apply either, because it presupposes an economic polarisation that has never existed and a notion of purity that is utterly foreign to the traditional Rwandan or Burundian mind-set." See Franche, "There's Only One Ethnic Group in Rwanda," p. 14. Roughly this same view is repeated by des Forges, *Leave None to Tell the Story,* as it is by Alex de Waal of African Rights in "The Genocidal State," *Times Literary Supplement,* 1 July 1994, pp. 3–4.

37. It was in this vein that Filip Reyntjens wrote: "The ethnic groups existed in the 19th century and in virtue of the principle of patrilineal transmission, each one knows whether he is Hutu, Tutsi or Twa." To this statement, he added a

footnote (16): "The fact that a certain social mobility permitted the passage from one ethnic group to the other does not take anything away from this principle." Filip Reyntjens, *L'Afrique des Grands Lacs en Crise: Rwanda, Burundi, 1988–1994* (Paris: Karthala, 1994). Passage translated by Scott Grosse, selected notes on Reyntjens's *L'Afrique des Grands Lacs en Crise*, e-mail communication, 22 November 1995.

38. David Newbury has flatly rejected the migration hypothesis on the grounds that "we have no data on these migrations, and little information on the interaction of these groups in historical terms." In a personal communication, however, he makes a distinction between "migration" and "mobility," one that "removes the primacy of cultural interpretation from these histories" and "accounts for the presence of many physical stocks in the region" without "an interpretation that relies on racial determinism or ethnic reification." See David Newbury, "The Invention of Rwanda: The Alchemy of Ethnicity," University of North Carolina–Chapel Hill, mimeo, November 1995, p. 1; also, personal communication, 24 May 2000.

In contrast, Gérard Prunier has few scruples, either in accepting the migration hypothesis or a linear connection between Tutsi migrants of centuries ago and contemporary Tutsi. Prunier puts forth as follows: "This is a delicate point and we will not try to fudge the dangerous issue of the theories concerning Tutsi origins. Yes, *our feeling* [my emphasis] is that the Tutsi have come from outside the Great Lakes area and that it is possible they were initially of a distinct racial stock. They of course did not come from Tibet or from Ancient Egypt, but their distinct physical features probably point to a Cushitic origin, i.e. somewhere in the Horn, probably southern Ethiopia where the Oromo have long proved to be both mobile and adventurous. The physical evidence seems plain enough when one has lived in the area and the whole accumulated weight of observations since the 1860s cannot be entirely baseless." And then he adds in a footnote: "Just as the 'different race hypothesis' has caused much crankish writing during the past hundred years, some modern authors have gone to great lengths in the other direction to try to refute this theory and to prove that Tutsi and Hutu belonged to the same basic racial stock." Gérard Prunier, *The Rwanda Crisis: History of a Genocide, 1959–1994* (London: Hurst & Co., 1995), pp. 16–17.

39. The notion "cultivators" here does not necessarily refer to those without cattle. Pastoralists and cultivators refers, rather, to incoming cattle keepers looking for grazing land and resident cultivators, whether with or without cattle, but with land.

40. Jan Vansina, *L'évolution du royaume Rwanda des origines à 1900* (New York: Johnson Reprint, 1968), quoted in Rennie, "The Precolonial Kingdom of Rwanda," pp. 23–24.

41. See Franche, "There's Only One Ethnic Group in Rwanda," p. 14.

42. Vansina, *L'évolution du royame Rwanda des origines à 1900*. For an appreciation, see Rennie, "The Precolonial Kingdom of Rwanda," pp. 12–13.

43. See René Lemarchand, *Rwanda and Burundi* (New York: Praeger, 1970), p. 18.

44. Vansina, *L'evolution du royaume Rwanda des origines à 1900;* Rennie, "The Precolonial Kingdom of Rwanda," pp. 11–64; and Ogot, "The Great Lakes," pp. 498–554. The following two paragraphs sum up the argument in the *UNESCO General History*, pp. 515–518.

45. This period coincides with the chronology of kings of Rwanda, as proposed by different historians, basing themselves on oral history. The chronology was first proposed by the Rwandan historian, Alexis Kagame in the colonial period. Subsequent scholarly opinion has held that six of the first seven names on Kagame's list were mythical, not historical.

The first to rely systematically on Rwandan oral literature, Kagame concluded that the Ruganza Bwimba, now accepted as the first king, had started ruling in 1312. Vansina dated the start of kingship in 1482, Rennie in 1532, Nkurikiyimfura in 1468. Following Kagame, all used the enthronement of Mibambwe Seentaabyo as the benchmark year, followed by the genealogy of twenty-one accepted kings as given. Their differences were based on two disagreements. First, each dated the starting point, being the occurrence according to Rwandan oral tradition of a solar eclipse during the year Seentaabyo ascended to the throne, differently. For Kagame, this was in 1741. Vansina, however, took into account other historical material and insisted on 1792 as the true date. Rennie and Kurikiyimfura followed Vansina. Second, while each followed the practice of subtracting a fixed number of years to account for the rule of each king in the genealogy, they disagreed on the average length of rule, and thus on how many years specifically to subtract for each king. Kagame subtracted 33 years, Vansina 24, Rennie 27, and Nkurikiyimfura 23. The result is a difference of more than 200 years, ranging between 1312 (Kagame) and 1532 (Rennie) as the earliest and the latest founding dates proposed for the kingdom.

In a recent article, David Newbury suggested that the genealogy may not be all that sacrosanct. Arguing that part of it may have been repeated simply to extend it and thereby add to the legitimacy of the kingdom, he has cast doubt on the existence of five kings between the well-known rulers, Ruganza Ndoori and Cyilima Rujugira. This means that although the founding date has generally been given as in the fourteenth (Kagame) or the fifteenth (Vansina) century, it may be even later. For this reason, I have generally followed the chronology suggested by Rennie, who dates the founding of the kingdom the latest, in 1532. See David Newbury, "Trick Cyclists? Recontextualizing Rwandan Domestic Chronology," *History in Africa* 21 (1994): 191–217; for the discussion on the genealogy of kings in different writers, see Shinichi Takeuchi, "Hutu and Tutsi: A Note on Group Formation in Pre-colonial Rwanda," in Didier Goyvaerts, ed., *Conflict and Ethnicity in Central Africa* (Tokyo: Institute for the Study of Languages and Cultures of Asia and Africa, Tokyo University of Foreign Studies, 2000), pp. 190–191, appendix 1.

46. Rennie, "The Precolonial Kingdom of Rwanda," pp. 23, 15.

47. Louis de Lacger, *Ruanda* (Kabgayi, 1959), p. 88, cited in Prunier, *The Rwanda Crisis*, p. 17.

48. David Newbury, " 'Bunyabungo': The Western Rwandan Frontier, c. 1750–1850," in Igor Kopytoff, ed., *The African Frontier: The Reproduction of Traditional African Societies* (Bloomington: Indiana University Press, 1987), p. 167.

49. Rennie, "The Precolonial Kingdom of Rwanda," pp. 34–38.

50. Ibid., pp. 31–32.

51. Newbury, *The Cohesion of Oppression*, pp. 134–35, 75–76.

52. Shinichi Takeuchi pens an interesting note to his discussion of changes in land tenure and clientship in precolonial Rwanda: "It should be emphasized that in this case we do not know whether the 'non-Tutsi', once appointed chief, would hold on to his Hutu identity, or to what extent this Hutu identity was deemed important" (p. 18). See Takeuchi, "Hutu and Tutsi," p. 194, fn. 28. Takeuchi gives the number of *igikingi* according to region (c. 1900) in appendix II.

53. Newbury, *The Cohesion of Oppression*, pp. 108, 111, 115; also see Newbury, "Ubureetwa and Thangata: Catalysts to Peasant Political Consciousness in Rwanda and Malawi," *Canadian Journal of African Studies* 14, no. 1 (1980): 97–111.

54. Sellstom and Wohlgemuth, *The International Response to Conflict and Genocide*, p. 5.

55. Newbury, " 'Bunyabungo': The Western Rwandan Frontier," pp. 167–169.

56. Newbury, *The Cohesion of Oppression*, p. 43.

57. Maquet, *The Premise of Inequality in Ruanda*, p.120; unless otherwise indicated, the information in this paragraph is culled from pp. 109–124.

58. De Lacger, *Ruanda*, p. 142, as cited in Prunier, *The Rwanda Crisis*, p. 15.

59. The information in the next two paragraphs is culled from the following sources: Maquet, *The Premise of Inequality in Ruanda*, pp. 101–102, 105–106, 124–125; Lemarchand, *Rwanda and Burundi*, p. 27; Newbury, *The Cohesion of Oppression*, pp. 40–43, 46–47; Antoine Lema, *Africa Divided: The Creation of "Ethnic Groups"* (Lund, Sweden: Lund University Press, Lund Dissertations in Sociology 6, 1993), pp. 51, 54.

60. Sellstom and Wohlgemuth, *The International Response to Conflict and Genocide*, p. 20.

61. Newbury, *The Cohesion of Oppression*, pp. 10–11, 51–52; M. C. Newbury, "Ethnicity in Rwanda: The Case of Kinyage," *Africa* 48, no. 1 (1978): 17–21; see also Elizabeth Hopkins, review of Catharine Newbury, *The Cohesion of Oppression*, in *Contemporary Sociology* 20, no. 1–3 (1991): 365–366; René Lemarchand, review of Catharine Newbury, *The Cohesion of Oppression*, in *Canadian Journal of African Studies* 24 (1990): 473–475.

62. L. Dorsey, *Historical Dictionary of Rwanda* (London: Scarecrow Press, 1994); D. Waller, *Rwanda: Which Way Now* (Oxford: Oxfam, 1993), cited in Sellstrom and Wohlgemuth, *The International Response to Conflict and Genocide*, pp. 19–20.

63. Captain Eugene M. Haguma of the RPF writes: "The serfs called HUTUS could move up the social ladder, in what was called KWIHUTURA, thanks to their acquisition of cattle . . . a symbol of wealth in ancient Rwanda. On the other hand being a Tutsi was no guarantee of wealth and influence in the social, economic and political establishment of the nation. Loss of property meant loss of status as a Tutsi. The kinyarwanda word 'GUCUPIRA' meant just that." See Captain Eugene M. Haguma, "The Rwandese Crisis: A Political Economy of Genocide," Symposium on Interface, Dialogue and Co-Operation between Government and NGO's for Popular Participation in National Reconstruction, Conflict and Psycho-social Trauma Management, organized jointly by Africa Humanitarian Action and the UN Economic Commission for Africa, Kigali, 28 February 1995, mimeo, p. 4. The process of ennoblement and of its loss is discussed in Maquet, *The Premise of Inequality in Ruanda*, pp. 65–66, 135–36; Lemarchand, *Rwanda and Burundi*, pp. 38, 98; Newbury, *The Cohesion of Oppression*, pp. 12–13; Prunier, *The Rwanda Crisis*, pp. 14, 21–22.

64. Jean-Népomucène Nkurikiyimfura, *Le gros bétail et la société Rwandaise: Evolution historique des XIIe–XIVe siècles à 1958* (Paris: L'Harmattan, 1994), pp. 96–97; cited in Prunier, *The Rwanda Crisis*, p. 22.

65. Two traditions persist. In one version, the cult is said to have been "introduced into Rwanda during the last half of the 19th century by two Rwandan cattle traders returning from Uzinza, a kingdom to the southeast." In the second version, Nyabingi is said to be a historical figure "who ruled Ndorwa-Kajara before the formation of Mpororo" and who even after death "continued to issue her decrees through the mouth of her Bagirwa (lit. 'those who initiate') who were almost invariably women." See Elizabeth Hopkins, "The Nyabingi Cult of Southwestern Uganda," in Robert I. Rotberg, ed., *Rebellion in Black Africa* (London: Oxford University Press, 1971), pp. 63–64.

66. Alison L. Des Forges, " 'The Drum Is Greater than the Shout': The 1912 Rebellion in Northern Rwanda," in Donald Crummey, ed., *Banditry, Rebellion and Social Protest in Africa* (London: James Currey, 1986), p. 313.

67. Hopkins, "The Nyabingi Cult of Southwestern Uganda," p. 60. As late as 1920, a British District Commissioner in Kigezi, on the Ugandan side of the border, wrote: " 'Nyabingi' is indestructible: thus the breakup of the agitation and the arrest of those practicing it would not convince anyone of the futility of the practitioners' claims but would only point to the ill-luck of the chosen media and to the fact that the 'Nyabingi' had left them to settle elsewhere." Cited in Murindwa Rutanga, "The Agrarian Crisis and Peasant Struggles in Kigezi, 1910–1995," Ph.D. diss., Jadavpur University, Calcutta, 1999, p. 57.

68. Des Forges, " 'The Drum Is Greater than the Shout," pp. 317–318.

69. Cited in Lemarchand, *Rwanda and Burundi*, pp. 57–60, 100–101; see also M. J. Bessell, "Nyabingi," *Uganda Journal* 6 (1938–39): 73–86. Alison des Forges argues that Muhumusa was not the historical wife of Rwabugiri but a medium who after 1905 "decided to tap the legitimacy provided by the Rwandan royal tradition" by claiming the identity of "Muserekande, the wife of Rwabugiri and rival of Kanjugera, who had led an uprising to put her son in power a decade before." In a similar vein, Elizabeth Hopkins points out two different traditions with regard to Ndungutsi, that "Ugandan sources regarded him to be no more than an influential lieutenant of Muhumusa" whereas Rwandan sources "view him as one of Muhumusa's sons, by Mibambwe IV, Rwabugiri's successor, who had been killed within a year of his succession." No matter which version we take, my point remains: in the popular imagination, Nyabingi linked popular grievances of the Bahutu to the claims of reformist elements in the Rwandan court. See Des Forges, " 'The Drum Is Greater than the Shout," p. 318; Hopkins, "The Nyabingi Cult of Southwestern Uganda," p. 76.

70. J.E.T. Philips, "The Nyabingi: An Anti-European Secret Society in Africa," *Congo* 1 (1928): 318; cited in Lemarchand, *Rwanda and Burundi*, p. 100.

71. Cited in Lemarchand, *Rwanda and Burundi*, p. 99.

72. An early and partial formulation of our hypothesis can be found in several authors. I find two particularly worth citing. The first is an observation from the 1972 essay of J. K. Rennie, which both surveyed the existing literature masterfully and came to several original conclusions.

> The terms "Tutsi" and "Hutu" seem to me therefore to be historically applicable only when the two groups of pastoralists and cultivators have entered into intimate social and economic relations. "Tutsi" and "Hutu" existed within the state of Rwanda as it grew and expanded, but not outside it. Within the state, the three classes of Tutsi, Hutu and Twa represented ascribed status, defined supposedly by way of life and ethnic origin. Tutsi were rulers, warriors and herders; Hutu were subjects, cultivators, labourers and taxpayers; and the hunting Twa were incorporated as personal retainers, court jesters, executioners and potters. Twa ties to the Tutsi rulers were personal and not mediated through the vassalage arrangements. . . . Nor did they enter blood brotherhood with Tutsi.

One notices that Rennie saw the Hutu/Tutsi distinction not only as a political division between rulers and subject, but also as a division of labor between cultivators and herders. See Rennie, "The Precolonial Kingdom of Rwanda," p. 32.

An epoch separates the first from the second formulation. In a reflection on the genocide that draws on their considerable research on Rwanda, Catharine Newbury and David Newbury have this to say: "The nature of Hutu and Tutsi identity changed not only across time; it also varied across regions. Indeed the two identities each have their own separate histories, such that in the context of Rwandan state-building, a collective Tutsi identity emerged before a collective Hutu identity did." And yet, the authors continue to consider the Hutu/Tutsi distinction as ethnic throughout this reflection, the main reason why this work fails to break with ethnic accounts of the genocide in spite of its being pregnant with several insights. See Catharine Newbury and David Newbury, "Was the Genocide in Rwanda an Ethnic Struggle?" mimeo, University of North Carolina–Chapel Hill, p. 33.

73. In my view, Jacques Maquet erred in tending to diminish the significance of social mobility through ennoblement on the grounds that the numbers involved were small: "It is certain that the number of Hutu and Twa assimilated to Tutsi because of their holding of political offices or because of their wealth, has always been tiny." See Maquet, *The Premise of Inequality in Ruanda*, p. 150.

CHAPTER THREE
RACIALIZATION OF THE HUTU/TUTSI DIFFERENCE UNDER COLONIALISM

1. Hannah Arendt, *The Origins of Totalitarianism* (New York: Harcourt Brace, 1975), p. 207. At the beginning of the chapter, she begins with a different and contradictory statement: "Both discoveries were actually made on the Dark Continent" (p. 185).

2. Ibid., p. 185.

3. Hannah Arendt makes a useful distinction between two kinds of race doctrines in nineteenth-century Europe: one sought to explain decadence, the fall of cultures, while the other focused on progress, the rise of cultures or civilizations. Doctrines of decadence were epitomized by the Comte de Gobineau, who is credited with the discovery "that the fall of civilizations is due to a degeneration of race and the decay of race is due to a mixture of blood." Gobineau's doctrines, however, did not fit in with the progress theory, that of "the survival of the fittest," so popular in the ruling circles of nineteenth-century Europe. Hannah Arendt explains the reasons of that popularity thus: "The liberal optimism of the victorious bourgeoisie wanted a new edition of the might-right theory, not the key to history or the proof of inevitable decay." Ibid., pp. 170–75, 162–164.

4. G.F.W. Hegel, *Lectures on the Philosophy of World History, Introduction: Reason in History*, trans. from the German edition of Johannes Hoffmeister by H. B. Nisbet (London: Cambridge University Press, 1975) (Hegel's second draft is dated 1830) pp. 173–177, and *The Philosophy of History*, trans. J. Sibree (New York: Dover Publications, 1956), pp. 95–99. The section on Africa in *The Lectures* is the more elaborate while *The Philosophy* repeats the same speculation, but in brief.

5. "Africa must be divided into three parts: one is that which lies south of the desert of Sahara—Africa proper—the Upland almost entirely unknown to us, with narrow coast—tracts along the sea; the second is that to the north of the desert—European African (if we may so call it)—a coastland; the third is the river region of the Nile, the only valley land of Africa, and which is in connection with Asia." Hegel, *The Philosophy of History*, p. 91.

6. According to Hegel:

The northern region stretches across to Egypt. . . . It includes the countries of Morocco, Fas (not Faz), Algeria, Tunis and Tripoli. It could be said that this whole region does not really belong to Africa but forms a single unit with Spain, for both are part of one and the same basin. With this in mind, the prolific French writer and politician de Pradt has said that, in Spain, one is already in Africa. The northern region is the non-independent portion of Africa, for it has always been subject to foreign influences; it is not itself a theatre of world-histori-cal events, and has always been dependent on revolutions of a wider scope. . . . It is a country which merely shares the fortunes of great events enacted else-where, but which has not determinate character of its own. This portion of Af-rica, like the near East, is oriented towards Europe; it should and must be brought into the European sphere of influence, as the French have successfully attempted in recent times.

Hegel, "Introduction: Reason in History," in *Lectures on the Philosophy of World History*, pp. 173–174.

7. See Hegel, *The Philosophy of History*, p. 91. And, yet again, at the end of the section in *The Philosophy of History* (pp. 91–99) that deals with Africa: "At this point we leave Africa, not to mention it again. For it is no historical part of the world; it has no movement or development to exhibit. Historical movement in it— that is, in its northern part—belongs to the Asiatic or European world. Carthage displayed there an important transitionary phase of civilization; but, as a Phoeni-cian colony, it belongs to Asia. Egypt will be considered in reference to the passage of the human mind from its Eastern to its Western phase, but it does not belong to the African Spirit. What we properly understood by Africa, is the unhistorical, Undeveloped Spirit, still involved in the conditions of mere nature, and which had to be presented here only as on the threshold of the world's History" (p. 99).

8. Pagès (1933, p. 491), cited in J. J. Maquet, *The Premise of Inequality in Ruanda* (London: Oxford University Press, 1961), p. 108.

9. This and the third myth are from P. Loupais, "Tradition et légende des Tutsi sur la création du monde et leur établissement au Ruanda," *Anthropos* 3, no. 9 (1908): 1–33; cited in Antoine Lema, *Africa Divided* (Lund, Sweden: Lund Uni-versity Press, 1993), pp. 43, 47.

10. Edith R. Sanders, "The Hamitic Hypothesis: Its Origin and Functions in Time Perspective," *Journal of African History* 10, no. 4 (1969). This paragraph draws from pp. 521–522.

11. "In the Talmud there are several contradictory legends concerning Ham— one that God forbade anyone to have sexual relations while on the Ark and Ham disobeyed this command. Another story is that Ham was cursed with blackness because he resented the fact that his father desired to have a fourth son. To prevent the birth of a rival heir, Ham is said to have castrated his father. Elsewhere in the Talmud, Ham's descendents are depicted as being led into captivity with their buttocks uncovered as a sign of their degradation." T. F. Gossett, *Race—the His-tory of an Idea in America* (New York: Oxford University Press, 1997), p. 5.

12. R. Graves and R. Patai, *Hebrew Myths: The Book of Genesis* (New York: Doubleday, 1964), p. 121.

13. The stakes in the debate that Greene titles "Are All Human Beings Born of One Biological Species?" were high and inclusive: theological, political, and scientific. "Theologically, it bore upon the Christian doctrine of the spiritual unity of mankind in their common descent from Adam. Politically it coloured conceptions of the white man's rights and duties with respect to the inhabitants of those regions of the earth which were being subjected to his control. Scientifically, it involved the distinction, enormous in the eyes of eighteenth-century naturalists, between a species and a variety. If the various types of human beings were separate species, the task of the natural historian was to classify them according to their specific characters, accepting these as permanent and divinely ordained. But if human races were but varieties of a single species, science must account for their peculiarities by natural causes." J. Greene, "The American Debate on the Negro's Place in Nature, 1780–1815," *Journal of History of Ideas* 15 (1954): 384. Also see Sanders, "The Hamitic Hypothesis," p. 524.

14. According to Gossett:

In 1591, Bruno asserted that no thinking person would imagine that the Ethiopians had the same ancestry as the Jews. . . . Lucilio Vanini argued in 1691 that the Ethiopians must have had apes for ancestors because they were the same colour as apes. Undoubtedly, he added, the Ethiopians had once walked on all fours.

In 1655, Isaac de la Peyrère, a French Protestant, published a book in which he argued that there had been two separate creations of human beings. In the first chapter of Genesis, a man and a woman are given dominion over every living thing, but it is not until the second chapter that anything is said of the creation of Adam and Eve. Therefore, argued Peyrère, a race of men must have existed before Adam. It was from this race that Cain had chosen his wife when he was cast off by his own people for the murder of Abel. It was the pre-Adamite races from whom the natives of Africa, Asia and the New World were descended. . . . Vanini and Bruno were burned at the stake for their various heresies. Peyrère was imprisoned for six months and released only on condition that he retract his heretical beliefs, among them his belief in pre-Adamite races.

Gossett, *Race—the History of an Idea in America*, p. 15.

15. V. Denon, *Travels in Upper and Lower Egypt* (London, 1903), cited in Sanders, "The Hamitic Hypothesis," p. 525.

16. Volney, *Travels through Syria and Egypt 1783–1784–1785* (1787, p. 83), cited in ibid.

17. Comte de Gobineau's thoughts are summarized in Martin Bernal, *Black Athena: The Afroasiatic Roots of Classical Civilization*, vol. 1: *The Fabrication of Ancient Greece, 1785–1985* (New York: Vintage, 1991), pp. 339, 343, 353–355, 361.

18. Ibid., pp. 269, 261, 230.

19. Ibid., pp. 241–246.

20. Ironically, this same notion would later be advanced in Cheikh Anta Diop's claim that the decline of ancient Egypt led to the dispersal of its population—an Egyptian diaspora, as it were—in turn leading to "the peopling of Africa."

21. Ibid., p. 9.

22. J. H. Speke, *Journal of the Discovery of the Source of the Nile* (New York: Harper and Brothers, 1864), p. xvii.

23. Here is how Speke began his elaborate speculation on the subject:

The reader has now had my experience of several of the minor states, and has presently to be introduced to Uganda, the most powerful state in the ancient but divided kingdom of Kitara. . . . Before entering on it, I propose to state my theory of the ethnology of that part of Africa inhabited by the people collectively styled Wahuma, otherwise Gallas or Abyssinians. My theory is founded on the traditions of several nations, as checked by my own observation of what I saw when passing through them. It appears impossible to believe, judging from the physical appearance of the Wahuma, that they can be of any other race than the semi-Shem-Hamitic of Ethiopia. . . .

In these countries the government is in the hands of foreigners, who had invaded and taken possession of them, leaving the agricultural aborigines to till the ground, while the junior members of the usurping clans herded cattle—just as in Abyssinia, or wherever the Abyssinians or Gallas have shown themselves. There a pastoral clan from the Asiatic side took the government of Abyssinia from its people and have ruled over them ever since, changing, by inter-marriage with the Africans, the texture of their hair and colour to a certain extent, but still maintaining a high stamp of Asiatic feature, of which a marked characteristic is a bridged instead of a bridgeless nose.

Speke claimed that the Tutsi (Watutsi in Kiswahili) were none other than the Wahuma: "How or when their name became changed from Wahuma to Watusi no one is able to explain; but, again deducing the past from the present, we cannot help suspecting that, in the same way as this change has taken place, the name Galla may have been changed from Habshi, and Wahuma from Gallas." The problem, he admitted, was that "the confusion of travellers . . . is increased by the Wahuma habit of conforming to the regulations of the countries they adopt." Nonetheless, he concluded: "We are thus left only one very distinguishing mark, the physical appearance of this remarkable race, partaking even more of the phlegmatic nature of the Shemitic father than the nervous, boisterous temperament of the Hamitic mother, as a *certain* clue to their Shem-Hamitic origin." Speke, *Journal of the Discovery of the Source of the Nile*, pp. 241–242, 244–245.

24. Writing in 1850, a Protestant theologian by the name of August Knobel of Giessen University wrote that "the Hamitic peoples, judging from their physical characteristics, belong, with the Jephites and Semites to the same race of human beings categorised by the naturalists as the Caucasian branch." Twenty years later, in 1870, sixty-eight fathers of the Catholic Church gathered in the Vatican I Council, appealed for a missionary vocation toward Central Africa, more or less

as a rescue operation for "hapless Hamites caught amidst Negroes," so as to allevi-
ate "the antique malediction weighing on the shoulders of the misfortunate Hamites inhabiting the hopeless Nigricy." J. P. Chrétien, "Burundi," *Histoire Retrouvée*
25, and *Le Métier d'Historien en Afrique* (Paris: Karthala, 1993), pp. 336, 339;
both cited in Tharcisse Gatwa, "The Churches and Ethnic Ideology in the Rwandan Crises (1900–1994)," Ph.D. diss., University of Edinburgh, 1998, p. 106.

25. Charles Gabriel Seligman, *Races of Africa* (London: Oxford University
Press, 1966), 4th ed., p. 61. Seligman went on to explain "the mechanism" by
which the "incoming Hamites"—"pastoral 'Europeans,' " he called them—arrived "wave after wave . . . better armed as well as quicker witted than the dark
agricultural Negroes," leading to "the origin of the Negro-Hamitic peoples":

> Diagrammatically the process may be described as follows. At first the Hamites,
> or at least their aristocracy, would endeavour to marry Hamitic women, but it
> cannot have been long before a series of peoples combining Negro and Hamitic
> blood arose; these, superior to the pure Negro, would be regarded with disdain
> by the next incoming wave of Hamites and be pushed farther inland to play the
> part of an incoming aristocracy vis-à-vis the Negroes on whom they impinged.
> And this process was repeated with minor modifications over a long period of
> time, the pastoralists always asserting their superiority over the agriculturalists,
> who constantly tended to leave their own mode of life in favour of pastoralism
> or at least to combine it with the latter. The end result of one series of such
> combinations is to be seen in the Zulu, of another in the Ganda, while an even
> more striking result is offered by the symbiosis, to use a biological term, of the
> Huma of Ankole and the Iru. The Huma, a tall cattle-owning aristocracy with
> narrow noses and faces, so unlike the Negro (though they always have Negro
> hair) that Johnston when he first saw them thought they were Egyptian soldiers
> left behind by Emin Pasha, live in the country of the shorter, broader-faced
> Negro Iru; the latter normally provide them with grain, and no doubt in the past
> there has been inter-marriage (witnessed the spiralled hair of even the Huma
> aristocracy), though at the present time each group is said to keep to itself.

Seligman, *Races of Africa*, pp. 100–101.

26. "The missionaries who were the first ethnologists of Rwanda concluded
that the Tutsi pastoralists with their slender figures and clear pigmentation belonged to a superior race, the Hamites, whereas the Hutu peasants were representatives of a supposed inferior Bantu race." Luc de Heusch, "Rwanda: Responsibilities
for Genocide," *Anthropology Today* 11, no. 4 (August 1995): 4.

27. According to Father Léon Classe, "Les Tutsi sont des hommes superbes,
aux traits fins et réguliers, avec quelque chose du type aryen et du type sémitique"
("The Tutsi are great men, with fine and regular traits, with something of the
Aryan and Semitic type"). For Father Menard, the "Tutsi est un Européen sous
une peau noire" ("the Tutsi is a European under black skin"). The predisposition
of the Church was fully backed two years later by the Belgian minister of colonies,
J. Frank, in his first ever visit to Rwanda: "Il ne s'agit pas, sous prétexte d'égalité,

de toucher aux bases de l'institution politique; nous trouvons les 'Watutzi' établis d'ancienne date; intelligents et capables; nous respectons cette situation" ("It is not, under the pretext of equality, to touch the bases of the political institution. We find the 'Watuzi,' who are established for a long time, intelligent and capable; we respect this situation"). L. Classe, "Missions d'Afrique des Pères Blancs" (September 1902, p. 385); F. Menard, "Les Barundi," Archives des Pères Blancs, Rome, par Gahama, J., *Le Burundi sous Administration Belge* (Paris, 1983, p. 275); both quoted in Chrétien, 1985, p. 138; J. Rumiya, p. 138; all sources cited in Gatwa, "The Churches and Ethnic Ideology in the Rwandan Crises (1900–1994)," pp. 109–110.

28. J. Rumiya, p. 133, cited in Gatwa, "The Churches and Ethnic Ideology in the Rwandan Crises (1900–1994)," p. 83.

29. The 1925 report stated: "Les Tutsi sont un autre peuple. Physiquement ils n'ont aucune ressemblance avec les Hutu, sauf évidemment quelques déclassés dont le sang n'est plus pur. Mais le Tutsi de bonne race n'a, à part la couleur, rien de nègre. Les caractéristiques physiques "rappellent de façon troublante le profil de la momie de Ramsés II. Les Tutsi étaient destines à régner. . . . D'ou viennent ces conquérants? Ils ne sont pas Bantu, cela est bien certain. Mais leur langue est celle du pays, nettement bantoue, sans trace d'infiltration quant à leur origine." (Translation: "The Tutsi are another people. Physically, they have a resemblance to the Hutu, except, evidently, some 'declassés' whose blood isn't pure anymore. But the Tutsi of good race has, apart from color, nothing of a negro. The physical characteristics remind one in a troubling way of the profile of the mummy of Ramses II. The Tutsi were destined to rule. . . . Where are these conquerers coming from? They are not Bantu, this is quite certain. But their language is the one of the country, clearly Bantu, without any trace of infiltration regarding their origin,") Administration Coloniale, Ruanda-Urundi (Brussels: Report Administration, 1925), pp. 34–35; cited in Gatwa, "The Churches and Ethnic Ideology in the Rwandan Crises (1900–1994)," p. 81.

30. A. Pagès, *Au Rwanda, sur le bord du Lac Kivu (Congo Belge). Un royaume Hamite au centre de l'Afrique* (Brussels: IRCB, 1933). L. de Lacger, *Ruanda* (Kabgayi, 1939, 1961); Luc de Heusch, *Rwanda: Tableau d'une monarchie féodale* (Brussels, 1954; film produced in cooperation with Maquet; all cited in Gatwa, "The Churches and Ethnic Ideology in the Rwandan Crises (1900–1994)," p. 48.

31. Gatwa, "The Churches and Ethnic Ideology in the Rwandan Crises (1900–1994)," p. 44. I am thankful to David Himbara for a translation of the phrase.

32. The next two paragraphs are based on Gatwa, "The Churches and Ethnic Ideology in the Rwandan Crises (1900–1994)," pp. 123–126; I. Linden, *Church and Revolution in Rwanda* (Manchester: Manchester University Press, 1977), pp. 135, 152, 161; Buluda Itandala, "Ethnicity versus Nationalism in Rwanda," paper presented at the conference on Academic Freedom, Social Research and Conflict Resolution in the Countries of the Great Lakes, organized by CODESRIA in col-

laboration with the University of Dar-es-Salaam and the Centre for Basic Research (Kampala), Arusha, Tanzania, 4–7 September 1995, pp. 17–18.

33. The Groupe Scolaire d' Astrida, the top school for the Belgian colonies of Rwanda and Burundi, had no Rwandan Hutu enrolled up to 1945, as opposed to 3 Hutu from Burundi and 46 Tutsi from both territories. As we shall see, the entry of Hutu increased after the Second World War following an antiracist shift in the worldview of the European clergy. By 1954, 3 Rwandan Hutu, 16 Barundi Hutu, 3 Congolese, and 63 Tutsi (from both Rwanda and Burundi) were registered as students at the Groupe Scolaire. See Lemarchand, *Rwanda and Burundi*, p. 138.

34. Antoine Lema, *Africa Divided*, p. 59.

35. Lemarchand, *Rwanda and Burundi*, pp. 119–120. "By destroying the pre-existing balance of forces on the hills, the 1926 reform prepared the ground for the emergence of a more starkly authoritarian system, centered on the rule of a single and virtually omnipotent chief." Ibid., p. 72.

36. In his words: "A revolution of that nature would lead the entire state directly into anarchy and to bitter anti-European Communism. Far from furthering progress, it would nullify the government's actions by depriving it of auxilliaries who are, by birth, capable of understanding and following it. This is the view and the firm belief of all superiors of the Ruanda mission, without exception. Generally speaking, we have no chiefs who are better qualified, more intelligent, more active, more capable of appreciating progress and more fully accepted by the people than the Tutsi." Cited in ibid., p. 73.

37. "In fact, these tribunals became the instruments through which the ruling Tutsi oligarchy not only retained but abused its privileges. Their function was not so much to dispense justice as to legitimize abuses and wrong-doings. Since they were in every case headed by Tutsi chiefs it is difficult to imagine how they could have served a different purpose." See ibid., p. 76.

38. The next two paragraphs are based on Itandala, "Ethnicity versus Nationalism in Rwanda," pp. 14–17; Gatwa, "The Churches and Ethnic Ideology in the Rwandan Crises (1900–1994)," p. 127; Alison des Forges, "Kings without Crowns: The White Fathers in Rwanda," in D. F. McCall, N. R. Bennett, and J. Butler, eds., *Eastern African History* (New York: Praeger, 1969), pp. 178–180; M. d'Hertefelt, "The Rwanda of Rwanda," in J. L. Gibbs, ed., *Peoples of Africa* (New York: Holt, Reinhart and Winston, 1965), p. 406.

39. See Tharcisse Gatwa, "The Churches and Ethnic Ideology in the Rwandan Crises (1900–1994)," p. 127.

40. The text of the bill signed by Mwami Musinga read: "Moi Musinga, mwami du Rwanda, je décide qu'à dater de ce jour, tout sujet de mon royaume sera libre de pratiquer la religion vers laquelle il se sent incliné. Tout chef ou sous-chef qui défendra à ses subordonnés, à ses sujets et aux enfants de ceux-ci de pratiquer le culte de leur choix ou de suivre les leçons des écoles pour y recevoir l'instruction, sera puni, selon la coutume, comme tout chef qui oublie qu'il me doit respect et obéissance, de 1 à 30 jours de réclusion." (Translation: "I Musinga, mwami of

Rwanda, decide that as of today every subject of my kingdom will be free to practice the religion toward which he feels himself inclined. Every chief or subchief who will forbid his subjects and their children to practice the faith of their choice, or to follow the school lessons where they receive instruction, will be punished according to the custom—just like every chief who forgets that he owes me respect and obedience—from one to 30 days of reclusion.") In F. Muvala, *Introduction à l'Histoire de l'Evangélisation* (Kigali: Pallotti Presse, 1990), p. 16; cited in Gatwa, "The Churches and Ethnic Ideology in the Rwandan Crises (1900–1994)," p. 127.

41. "The 1927 colonial administration report shows that those among the chiefs who would not convert, were considered as sorcerers, diviners and superstitious and were deposed." *Report Administration Coloniale Ruanda-Urundi*, 1927, p. 38; cited in ibid., p. 129.

42. Lemarchand, *Rwanda and Burundi*, p. 67.

43. Ibid., p. 70.

44. "The Banyarwanda called the movement *Irivuze Mwami*, what the king has said you must follow. According to many views, the King never gave such an order, but those concerned, the missionaries and the King let the confusion persist so as to harvest a religious and political benefit." Gatwa, "The Churches and Ethnic Ideology in the Rwandan Crises (1900–1994)," p. 128.

45. "*Kiliziya yakuye Kirazira*. This is a popular Kinyarwanda saying literally meaning that the church preaching replaced the culture." Captain Eugene M. Haguma, "The Rwandese Crisis: A Political Economy of Genocide," Symposium on Interface, Dialogue and Co-Operation between Government and NGO's for Popular Participation in National Reconstruction, Conflict and Psycho-Social Trauma Management, Organized Jointly by Africa Humanitarian Action and the UN Economic Commission for Africa, Kigali, 28 February 1995, mimeo, p. 8.

46. The two decrees are cited in Lema, *Africa Divided*, p. 59.

47. Catharine Newbury, *The Cohesion of Oppression: Clientship and Ethnicity in Rwanda, 1860–1960* (New York: Columbia University Press, 1989), p. 167.

48. Haguma, "The Rwanda Crisis: A Political Economy of Genocide," p. 2.

49. Kagame, *Abrégé*, vol. 2, 205; cited in Newbury, *The Cohesion of Oppression*, p. 157.

50. Cited in Catherine Watson, *Exile from Rwanda: Background to an Invasion*, Issue Paper (Washington, D.C.: U.S. Committee for Refugees, February 1991), p. 4.

51. Newbury, *The Cohesion of Oppression*, pp. 153–155.

52. S. Martin, "Boserup Revisited: Population and Technology in Tropical African Agriculture, 1900–1940," *Journal of Imperial and Commonwealth History* 16 (October 1987): 109–123.

53. Cited in Roger Botte, "Rwanda and Burundi, 1889–1930: Chronology of a Slow Assassination, Part 1," *International Journal of African Historical Studies* 18, no. 1 (1985): 86.

54. Cited in Roger Botte, "Rwanda and Burundi, 1889–1930: Chronology of a Slow Assassination, Part 2," *International Journal of African Historical Studies* 18, no. 2 (1985): 313–314.

55. An official note from May 1919 is clear that government tax levies favor exactions on the part of the chiefs: "nice opportunity for chiefs and sub-chiefs to gather cows, goats, hoes, etc." Cited in ibid., p. 305.

56. Cited in Newbury, *The Cohesion of Oppression*, p. 132.

57. Watson, *Exile from Rwanda*, p. 4.

58. Mgr. Classe in 1916, quoted in Lemarchand, *Rwanda and Burundi*, p. 122. For further examples, see pp. 121–124.

59. Catharine Newbury, "Ubureetwa and Thangata: Catalysts to Peasant Political Consciousness in Rwanda and Malawi," *Canadian Journal of African Studies* 14, no. 1 (1980): 97–111.

60. Catharine Newbury, *The Cohesion of Oppression*, p. 112.

61. Take, for examples, the following assorted comments about official tyranny from peasants in the southwest of the country, compiled by Catharine Newbury from various sources:

That man [hill chief at nyamavugo] commanded like the others; when someone didn't have beans to give as prestations, he expelled him from his land, and likewise for someone who didn't have mats to give.

In fact, there was no recourse to the courts; a chief could take someone's goods and could chase him away or have him "killed" by another chief.

They would come to take your cow on the pretext that you were a rebel, and you couldn't say anything. . . . You would let your cow go, for at the least resistance you would be put in chains or sometimes killed. And in such a case you could not introduce a court case to claim your rights on the cow.

After the cows of Gisazi [Chief of the Bugarama region] had perished in the Iragara epidemic (1920–21) he went around seizing cattle from people, both those who were clients and those who were not. The informant's lineage lost a cow in this manner.

See Catharine Newbury, *The Cohesion of Oppression*, p. 133.

62. Filip Reyntjens, for example, has traced a 1917 circular from the Resident which identifies Tutsi as lords and Hutu as subjects, and Tutsi as cattle owners and Hutu as agriculturalists. F. Reyntjens (1985, p. 131), cited in Gatwa, "The Churches and Ethnic Ideology in the Rwandan Crises (1900–1994)," p. 66.

63. See, for example, African Rights, *Rwanda: Death, Despair and Defiance* (London, 1995), rev. ed., pp. 11–12: "Despite the emphasis on height and straight noses, such was the slender basis of the racial categorization that, during the 1933–34 census, the Belgians were obliged to use ownership of cows as the key criterion for determining which group an individual belonged to. Those with ten or more cows were Tutsi—along with all their descendents in the male line—and those with less were Hutu. Those 'recognized as Twa' at the time of the census were

given the status of Twa." Also see Haguma, "The Rwandese Crisis: A Political Economy of Genocide," p. 3.

64. Scott Grosse, communication on Rwandanet, 22 January 1996. Grosse goes on to say:

I think I may have found in Prunier's book the origin of the myth of the 10-cow rule. On p. 29, Prunier cites Jean-Népomucène Nkurikiyimfura, an historian murdered in 1994, as reporting that the administrative reforms of 1926–31 allowed anyone owning 10 cows or more to claim private ownership of Ibikingi grazing land, which had previously been collectively held. It appears that only a small number of individuals qualified for this. The vast majority of "petits Tutsis" as the colonial administrators referred to them, were no more well-off than their Hutu neighbours. A survey conducted by Leurquin in the 1950s revealed that the average family income of Tutsi families in Rwanda, excluding the aristocracy and chiefly families, was only 5% higher than that of Hutu families. These survey results have been reported by Linden, DDD, Prunier (p. 50), among others. These data put the lie to the claim that all, or even most Tutsis as officially defined by the Belgians owned large amounts of wealth, as 10 cows certainly would constitute.

65. Gatwa, "The Churches and Ethnic Ideology in the Rwandan Crises (1900–1994)," p. 84.

66. And then added in parentheses: "There is a third racial group—the pygmoid Twa hunters—but they number about 1% of the population and play no part in the political situation." The Belgian Congo and Ruanda-Urandi Information and Public Relations Office, *Ruanda Urundi* 60, no. 4 (September 195): 5.

CHAPTER FOUR
THE "SOCIAL REVOLUTION" OF 1959

1. Catharine Newbury, *The Cohesion of Oppression: Clientship and Ethnicity in Rwanda, 1860–1960* (New York: Columbia University Press, 1989).

2. René Lemarchand, *Rwanda and Burundi* (New York: Praeger, 1970).

3. Ibid., pp. 285–286.

4. Michael Lofchie, *Zanzibar: Background to Revolution* (Princeton: Princeton University Press, 1965).

5. The qualifications about dynastic changes and flouted norms were added after a comment by David Newbury, private communication, 24 May 2000.

6. The empirical information in this section derives from Lemarchand, *Rwanda and Burundi*, pp. 96, 97, 99, 102–103, 105, 111–112, 266.

7. Ibid., p. 99.

8. Cited in ibid.

9. Ibid., pp. 104–105.

10. Ibid., p. 112.

11. M. Audrey I. Richards, ed., *Economic Development and Tribal Change: A Study of Immigrant Labour in Buganda* (Nairobi: Oxford University Press, 1973).

12. Mararo Bucyalimwe, "Land Conflicts in Masisi, Eastern Zaire: The Impact and Aftermath of Belgian Colonial Policy (1920–1989)," Ph.D. diss., Indiana University, 1990.

13. Newbury, *The Cohesion of Oppression: Clientship and Ethnicity in Rwanda, 1860–1960.* The next paragraph is based on information from pp. 112, 163–164, 166, 175, 177, 178.

14. Ibid., p. 166.

15. Ibid., pp. 163–164.

16. G. F. Powesland, "History of the Migration in Uganda," in Richards, *Economic Development and Tribal Change*, pp. 30, 36.

17. A. I. Richards, "The Assimilation of the Immigrants," in Richards, *Economic Development and Tribal Change*, pp. 161–193.

18. Ibid., p. 178. Also see, René Lemarchand, "Review of Catharine Newbury, *The Cohesion of Oppression: Clientship and Ethnicity in Rwanda, 1860–1960,*" *Canadian Journal of African Studies* 24 (1990): 474–476; and Johan Pottier, "Review of Catharine Newbury, *The Cohesion of Oppression: Clientship and Ethnicity in Rwanda, 1860–1960,*" *Journal of Peasant Studies* 18, no. 2 (1991): 346–347.

19. Lemarchand, *Rwanda and Burundi*, p. 138.

20. Ibid., p. 139; also see Antoine Lema, *Africa Divided: The Creation of "Ethnic Groups"* (Lund: Lund University Press, 1993), p. 62; and Buluda Itandala, "Ethnicity versus Nationalism in Rwanda," unpublished manuscript, p. 19.

21. Cited in Lemarchand, *Rwanda and Burundi*, p. 133.

22. Ibid., p. 135.

23. Ibid., p. 137.

24. Newbury, *The Cohesion of Oppression*, pp. 145–147; Martin Plaut, "Rwanda—Looking beyond the Slaughter," *World Today* 50, no. 8–9 (1994): 150; Reyntjens (1985, p. 208), cited in Tharcisse Gatwa, "The Churches and Ethnic Ideology in the Rwandan Crises (1900–1994)," Ph.D. diss., University of Edinburgh, 1998, pp. 90–91.

25. Newbury cites examples from Kinyaga: *Soma*, a newspaper launched in 1956, was "oriented towards publicizing the arbitrary use of power by the chiefs and the discrimination in the society against the powerless." The trend grew in 1958 when *Kinyamateka*, the Catholic weekly, carried a series of articles "castigating the system of unrestrained chiefly power and the exploitation by Tuutsi, particularly in the Bukunzi-busoozo-Bugarama chiefdom of Kinyaga." See Newbury, *The Cohesion of Oppression*, pp. 182–183.

26. Gérard Prunier, *The Rwanda Crisis: History of a Genocide* (London: Hurst & Co., 1995), p. 43; also see Lemarchand, *Rwanda and Burundi*, p. 82.

27. Newbury, *The Cohesion of Oppression*, pp. 190–191.

28. Fillip Reyntjens, *Pouvoir et droit au Rwanda*, Musée Royal de l'Afrique Centrale, Annales—Serie—80—Sciences Humaines—No. 117, Tervuren, 1985,

pp. 186–189; Lema, *Africa Divided*, p. 68. An English translation of the "Statement of Views" is reproduced in UN Trusteeship Council, Report of the Visiting Mission T/1402 (1957), Annex II.

29. L. Dorsey, *Historical Dictionary of Rwanda* (London: Scarecrow Press, 1994); cited in Tor Sellstom and Lennart Wohlgemuth, *The International Response to Conflict and Genocide: Lessons from the Rwanda Experience*, Study 1, *Historical Perspective: Some Explanatory Factors* (Uppsala, Sweden: The Nordic Africa Institute, 1997), p. 25.

30. F. Nkundabagenzi, *Rwanda politique, 1958–1960* (Brussels: CRISP, 1961), pp. 21–22; cited in Newbury, *The Cohesion of Oppression*, p. 191; also Nkundabagenzi, *Rwanda politique, 1958–1960*, pp. 20–29, cited Gatwa, "The Churches and Ethnic Ideology in the Rwandan Crises (1900–1994)," pp. 92–93.

31. The information in this paragraph is based on Lemarchand, *Rwanda and Burundi*, pp. 148, 150; Newbury, *The Cohesion of Oppression*, pp. 188–189.

32. Fillip Reyntjens, *L'Afrique des Grands Lacs en crise: Rwanda. Burundi: 1988—1994* (Brussels, 1995), and "Sujets d'inquiétude au Rwanda, en Octobre 1994," *Dialogue* 179: 3–14; both cited in Sellstom and Wohlgemuth, *The International Response to Conflict and Genocide*, p. 25. Nkundabagenzi provides a slightly different translation of this text, but in the full. It is worth considering:

> The ancestors of the Banyiginya (the reigning lineage) is Kigwa. He arrived in Rwanda with his brother Tutsi Mutusi and their sister Nyampundu. . . . To reclaim resources sharing, one must prove a brotherhood. But the relations between us (Tutsi) and them (Hutu) have always been built on servitude. Thus, there is no foundation of brotherhood. . . . The Hutu have also pretended that Kinyarwanda is our common ancestor, the "mediator" of all the Hutu, Tutsi and Batwa families. But Kinyarwanda is the son of Gihanga, of Kazi, of Mirano, of Randa, of Kobo, of Gisa, of Kijuru, of Kimanuka, of Kigwa. This Kigwa found the Hutu in Rwanda. How then Kanyarwanda far posterior to the existence of the three races, Hutu, Tutsi and Batwa, found existing, can be their common ancestor? Our history says that Ruganzu had killed many 'Bahinza (Hutu monarchs) and then conquered the Hutu counties of which those Bahinza were kings. How then the Hutu could pretend being our brothers? All the details are available in Inganji Karinga (Kagame, 1943).

Nkundabagenzi, *Rwanda politique, 1958–60*, pp. 35–36; cited in Gatwa, "The Churches and Ethnic Ideology in the Rwandan Crises (1900–1994)," p. 92.

33. Nkundabagenzi, *Rwanda politique, 1958–60*, p. 37; cited in Gatwa, "The Churches and Ethnic Ideology in the Rwandan Crises (1900–1994)," pp. 92–93.

34. Lemarchand, *Rwanda and Burundi*, p. 155.

35. See Catharine Newbury and David Newbury, "Was the Genocide in Rwanda an Ethnic Struggle?" mimeo, University of North Carolina–Chapel Hill, p. 9; and Lemarchand, *Rwanda and Burundi*, pp. 158, 199.

36. Lemarchand, *Rwanda and Burundi*, pp. 160–161.

37. Ibid., p. 176.

38. Ibid., pp. 154, 159–160.

39. Prunier, *The Rwanda Crisis*, p. 48.

40. "In the end RADER served mainly as a symbol of dissent within the pow-erholding elite." Newbury and Newbury, "Was the Genocide in Rwanda an Ethnic Struggle?" p. 10; also see Newbury, *The Cohesion of Oppression*, p. 200.

41. Lemarchand, *Rwanda and Burundi*, p. 160.

42. "APROSOMA initially welcomed Tuutsi who shared its goals of working for social and political changes and an end to the arbitrary power of the chiefs." Newbury, *The Cohesion of Oppression*, p. 199.

43. Newbury and Newbury, "Was the Genocide in Rwanda an Ethnic Strug-gle?" p. 10.

44. This, it seems to me, is the answer to the question posed by Elizabeth Hop-kins in her review of Catharine Newbury: "Newbury's suspension of a regional perspective at this critical point in her analysis is most unfortunate, for her explora-tion of the 'social preconditions to revolution' offers no insight into why the feroc-ity of Hutu action remained confined to northern and central Rwanda and was not, despite the many facets of Kinyagan discontent, at issue in southern Rwanda." Elizabeth Hopkins, "Review of *The Cohesion of Oppression: Clientship and Ethnicity in Rwanda, 1860–1960*," *Contemporary Sociology* 20, no. 1–3 (1991): 366.

45. The major postgenocide writings convey two different points of view on this question. While Gérard Prunier tends to identify the two parties with "quite distinct regional bases," Catharine and David Newbury point out that while APROSOMA was more of a regional party, PARMEHUTU had more of a coun-trywide support. See Prunier, *The Rwanda Crisis*, p. 48; Newbury and Newbury, "Was the Genocide in Rwanda an Ethnic Struggle?" p. 10. Prunier's analysis, on this point at least, seems to fit the processes of 1959 a little too neatly into the outcomes of 1994.

46. Cited in Lemarchand, *Rwanda and Burundi*, p. 151.

47. According to Lemarchand:
The most important source of disharmony lay in the widely different career opportunities to which each group could aspire by virtue of career and training. Unlike the ex-seminarists, who lacked the necessary qualifications to hold ad-ministrative posts, the Astridiens knew that they would be the first to reap the benefits of constitutional and administrative reforms. Their reformist, gradualist outlook, the logical consequence of their professional training, gave them an overwhelming inclination to join APROSOMA. The ex-seminarists, on the other hand, stood little chance of making their mark in life so long as the Centre Scolaire d'Astride remained the only channel of recruitment to government posts. Faced with a denial of career opportunities, they were naturally predis-posed to reject political reforms. Nothing short of a revolution of the kind advo-cated by the PARMEHUTU would enable them to satisfy their aspirations for leadership.
Lemarchand, *Rwanda and Burundi*, p. 234.

48. Lema, *Africa Divided*, p. 68.

49. Ibid., p. 38.

50. Sellstom and Wohlgemuth, *The International Response to Conflict and Genocide*, p. 26.

51. Gatwa, "The Churches and Ethnic Ideology in the Rwandan Crises (1900–1994)," pp. 192–194.

52. That role has been depicted in starkly opposed terms by contemporary Rwandan writers. Two examples will suffice. Captain Haguma of the RPF writes: "A reactionary HUTU—extremist party—MDR—PARMEHUTU was created by the colonial officials in collaboration with the Catholic church and especially Bishop PERRAUDIN with the intention of effectively blocking the Nationalist Independence programme of King MUTARA RUDAHIGWA." Tharcisse Gatwa writes of the same development: "It seems, from the point of view of this thesis, that it would not be an insult to the quality of organisation and determination of Kayibanda and his colleagues to say that their sudden success and the penetration of the PARMEHUTU propaganda on the hills heavily relied on Colonel Logiest and the Catholic Church resolute support." See Captain Eugene M. Haguma, "The Rwandese Crisis: A Political Economy of Genocide," Symposium on Interface, Dialogue and Co-Operation between Government and NGO's for Popular Participation in National Reconstruction, Conflict and Psycho-Social Trauma Management, Organized Jointly by Africa Humanitarian Action and the UN Economic Commission for Africa, Kigali, 28 February 1995, mimeo, p. 10; Gatwa, "The Churches and Ethnic Ideology in the Rwandan Crises (1900–1994)."

53. The point is made by Wamba-dia-Wamba:

The politics of independence faced other considerations than the mere replacement of colonialists in the State posts. The mere replacement in Rwanda context, would have favoured only a Tutsi domination. Some kind of "social revolution" breaking a Tutsi hierarchy had to take place. *That it was in line with colonialists' interests does not make it unreal.* It gave rise to a political prescription on the state in favour of Hutu domination. Of course, this is a state of possible ethnic wars and not that of civil peace, it is true. In the main, opposition to this "Hutu majority" State has been basically based on an ethnic politics of state entryism—including by military invasion/conquest (emphasis mine).

Ernest Wamba-dia-Wamba, "The State of All Rwandese: Political Prescriptions and Disasters," paper presented to CODESRIA conference, Arusha, 1995, p. 13.

54. Lema, *Africa Divided*, pp. 70–71.

55. Cited in Lemarchand, *Rwanda and Burundi*, p. 169.

56. Gatwa, "The Churches and Ethnic Ideology in the Rwandan Crises (1900–1994)," p. 96.

57. Cited in Lemarchand, *Rwanda and Burundi*, p. 189.

58. Sellstom and Wohlgemuth, *The International Response to Conflict and Genocide*, p. 27.

59. Cited in Lemarchand, *Rwanda and Burundi*, p. 203; James Murray, "Rwanda's Bloody Roots," *New York Times*, 3 September 1994.

60. Lemarchand, *Rwanda and Burundi*, pp.198–206.

61. Wm. Cyrus Reed, "Exile, Reform, and the Rise of the Rwandan Patriotic Front," *Journal of Modern African Studies* 34, no. 3 (1996): 481.

62. Lemarchand, *Rwanda and Burundi*, pp. 217–219.

63. Ibid., pp. 223–224.

64. Colin Legum, ed., *Africa Contemporary Record, 1968–1969* (New York: Africana Publishing), p. 193.

65. Sellstom and Wohlgemuth, *The International Response to Conflict and Genocide*, p. 28.

66. Newbury and Newbury, "Was the Genocide in Rwanda an Ethnic Struggle?" p. 13.

67. Human Rights Watch Arms Project, "Arming Rwanda: The Arms Trade and Human Rights Abuses in the Rwanda War," *Human Rights Watch* 6, no. 1 (January 1994): 8.

68. See Haguma, "The Rwandese Crisis," p. 11. Similarly, Africa Rights claimed that 10,000 Tutsi lost their lives during the 1959 Revolution; see African Rights, *Rwanda: Death, Dispair and Defiance* (London, 1995), p. 11.

CHAPTER FIVE
THE SECOND REPUBLIC

1. "The other," says Paul Theroux, "is the brother." I thought of Hutu and Tutsi. See Theroux, *Sir Vidia's Shadow* (New York: Houghton Mifflin, 1998).

2. Prunier continues: "In fact, under the banner of 'democratic majority rule' on one side and 'immediate independence' on the other, it was a fight between two competing élites, the newly-developed Hutu counter-élite produced by the church and the older neo-traditionalist Tutsi elite which the colonial authorities had promoted since the 1920s. Poor Hutu were used by their new leaders as a battle-axe against a mixed body of Tutsi where, because of the elaborately constructed 'Rwandese ideology' we have sought to outline, the poor stood by the rich on the basis of the myth of 'racial superiority.' " See Gérard Prunier, *The Rwanda Crisis: History of a Genocide* (London: Hurst & Co., 1995), p. 50.

3. Tharcisse Gatwa, "The Churches and Ethnic Ideology in the Rwandan Crises (1900–1994)," Ph.D. diss., University of Edinburgh, 1998, p. 53

4. This is how Gatwa sums up the aspirations of 1959: "that of liberating both the oppressed and the oppressors from the chains of an obscurantist and degrading system so as to rehabilitate them in their dignity as the children of God." Ibid.

5. Catharine Newbury, *The Cohesion of Oppression: Citizenship and Ethnicity in Rwanda, 1860–1960* (New York: Columbia University Press, 1989), p. 222.

6. Colin Legum, ed., *Africa Contemporary Record, 1973–74* (New York: Africana Publishing), p. B237.

7. Prunier, *The Rwanda Crisis*, pp. 57–58.

8. Vidal, an anthropologist who conducted numerous interviews at all levels during 1967–73 confirmed that the hostility directed at Tutsi came almost exclusively from educated Hutu, not from the mass of the population. In the rural areas that she visited, access to land was a far more important issue of concern than the Tutsi question. That the land question was separated from the Tutsi question, one may note, was of course also a consequence of the revolution: by redistributing land in Tutsi hands, it had decisively separated the two questions. See Vidal, "Situations ethniques au Rwanda," in J.-L. Amselle and E. M'bokolo, eds., *Au cœur de l'ethnie* (Paris, 1985), p. 170; cited in Catharine Newbury and David Newbury, "Was the Genocide in Rwanda an Ethnic Struggle?" mimeo, University of North Carolina–Chapel Hill, p. 46, fn. 43.

9. *Urmuli rwa Demokrasi*, 3 July 1966; cited in René Lemarchand, *Rwanda and Burundi* (New York: Praeger, 1970), p. 239.

10. Lemarchand, *Rwanda and Burundi*, p. 260.

11. Ibid., pp. 258–259.

12. The reconstruction of events is from Legum, ed., *Africa Contemporary Record, 1973–74*, p. B237; Jean-Pierre Chrétien, "Hutu et Tutsi au Rwanda et au Burundi," in Amselle and M'bokolo, eds., *Au cœur de l'ethnie*, p. 159, cited in Newbury and Newbury, "Was the Genocide in Rwanda an Ethnic Struggle?" p. 14, fn. 15; Tor Sellstom and Lennart Wohlgemuth, *The International Response to Conflict and Genocide: Lessons from the Rwanda Experience*, Study 1, *Historical Perspective: Some Explanatory Factors* (Uppsala, Sweden: The Nordic Africa Institute, 1997), p. 29.

13. Prunier says the number killed were "officially only six, but probably two dozen or more" (*The Rwanda Crisis*, p. 61). *Africa Contemporary Record, 1973–74* estimated those killed at between 300 and 500!

14. "At the 5 July 1979 celebrations of the Second Republic, Habyarimana decorated Rwandans who had contributed to the 'National' Revolution of 1959 and to the 'Moral' Revolution of 1973." Legum, ed., *Africa Contemporary Record, 1979–80*, p. B283. The designations for the 1959 Revolution and the 1973 coup d'état were several. At a state banquet during his 1978 visit to the People's Republic of China, President Habyarimana returned to the earlier designation of 1959 as the "social" revolution and 1973 as a corrective action "in face of elements bent on a policy of hatred, division and intrigue," a reference to those determined to keep any Tutsi presence out of the political arena. See "Speech by Rwandan President," Xinhua General Overseas News Service, 9 June 1978.

15. Gatwa writes: "Father Muvala was named coadjutor bishop of the Catholic diocese of Butare. An announcement regarding his 'resignation' was made a few days only before the date of the ordination. The official explanation given in the announcement about the incident was 'for personal reasons' but everyone in Rwanda knew that it was an ethnic plot organised by the regime with the full cooperation of (the) Archbishop." The Archbishop also "insisted that some Catholic orders including the Benebikira Sisters' Congregation should practise the politics

of ethnic balance in naming a Hutu Superior." Gatwa, "The Churches and Ethnic Ideology in the Rwandan Crises (1900–1994)," p. 166.

16. *Africa Contemporary Record, 1985–86*, ed. Legum, p. B381.

17. Wm. Cyrus Reed, "The Rwandan Patriotic Front: Politics and Development in Rwanda," *Issue: A Journal of Opinion* 33, no. 2 (1995): 51, African Studies Association of USA.

18. Thus, the southern Tutsi, though they comprise the vast majority of the Tutsi within the country, would have access to only 4 percent of the posts, whereas their counterparts in the north, a much smaller group, would have access to 6 percent of the posts. The 10 percent figure was said to reflect the relative size of the Tutsi/Twa population in the country. Whereas the 1956 census counted the Tutsi at 16 percent, the count in the 1978 census was down to slightly less than 10 percent. J.-P. Chrétien, "La crise politique rwandaise," *Genève Afrique* 30(2): 121–141

19. F. Reyntjens, "Démocratisation et conflits ethniques au Rwanda et au Burundi," *Cahiers Africains—Afrika Studies* 4–5: 209–227; cited in Scott Grosse, "The Roots of Conflict and State Failure in Rwanda," School of Public Health, University of Michigan, Ann Arbor, mimeo, 15 November 1994, p. 8; also L. Uwezeyimana, "L'équilibre ethnique et régional dans l'emploi," *Dialogue* 146 (May–June 1989): 15–31; cited in Grosse, "The Roots of Conflict and State Failure in Rwanda," p. 8.

20. *Africa Contemporary Record, 1977–78*, ed. Legum, p. B350.

21. Vidal, "Situations ethniques au Rwanda," cited in Grosse, "The Roots of Conflict and State Failure in Rwanda," p. 9.

22. "Rwanda," in Legum, ed., *Africa Contemporary Record, 1973–74*, p. B236.

23. Ibid., p. B254.

24. Ibid., p. B239.

25. René Lemarchand, "Recent History," in section on "Rwanda," in *Africa South of the Sahara, 1974* (London: Europa Publications Ltd., 1975), p. 660.

26. Philippe Decraene, *Le Monde* (Paris), 31 March 1974; cited in "Rwanda," in Legum, ed., *Africa Contemporary Record, 1974–75*, p. B255.

27. Ethnic relations were said to be "tense" in 1978. On the one hand, "the Tutsi minority continued to complain that government hiring quotas were handled incorrectly and were prejudicial to their community"; at the same time, "a number of Tutsi left the country and others in government or state agencies complained of harassment." On the other hand, the anti-Tutsi sentiment was identified with potential rivals of Habyarimana: following the discovery of the Kalinga drum in April 1978 and its being placed in the national museum, there were "veiled threats against the Tutsi community—despite official assurances that the government continued to seek national reconciliation and unity as its basic principles." Close journalistic observers of the local scene concluded: "The President's re-election may well put an end to this tension, as he stands for ethnic reconciliation." See "Rwanda," in Legum, ed., *Africa Contemporary Record, 1978–79*, p. B354.

28. See ibid., p. B281. Théonaste Lizinde later joined the RPF and by 1995 was "a key RPF personality." René Lemarchand, "Rwanda: The Rationality of Genocide," *Issue* 23, no. 2 (1995): 9, African Studies Association of USA.

29. René Lemarchand, private communication, August 23, 2000.

30. Lemarchand, "Recent History," in section on "Rwanda," in *Africa South of the Sahara, 1982–83*, p. 821.

31. Catherine Watson, "Exile from Rwanda: Background to an Invasion," prepared for the U.S. Committee for Refugees, Washington, D.C., February 1991, p. 6.

32. Prunier, *The Rwanda Crisis*, p. 75.

33. J.-P. Chrétien, "Pluralisme démocratique, ethnismes et stratégies politiques," in Conac, ed., *L'Afrique en transition vers le pluralisme politique*, pp. 139–147, as cited in Sellstom and Wohlgemuth, *The International Response to Conflict and Genocide*, p. 31.

34. Prunier, however, says this of both the First and the Second Republics. In my view, he underestimates and underplays the difference between them. Prunier, *The Rwanda Crisis*, p. 84.

35. See Timothy Longman, "Anarchy and the State in Africa: Power, Democratization and the Rwandan Catastrophe," mimeo, Drake University, Des Moines, Iowa, no date, p. 8.

36. Lemarchand, "Recent History," in "Rwanda," *Africa South of the Sahara, 1982–83*, p. 691; also see Lemarchand, *Rwanda and Burundi*, pp. 280–282.

37. "Rwanda," in Legum, ed., *Africa Contemporary Record, 1977–78*, p. B349.

38. Ibid., p. B353.

39. Ibid., p. B309. A slightly different version of the reorganization is given by Reyntjens, writing in 1985. According to this version, the country was divided into ten prefectures and 143 communes, with 4–5 *secteurs* per commune. Each *secteur* was in turn divided into ten cells, and each cell comprised ten households of some eighty people. This would make the 1960 reform a far more literal reproduction of the Tanzanian model, also known as the ten-cell system. See F. Reyntjens, *Pouvoir et droit au Rwanda* (A Tervuren: Musée Royal de l'Afrique Centrale); cited in Sellstom and Wohlgemuth, *The International Response to Conflict and Genocide*, p. 25.

40. The figures are compiled in Filip Reyntjens, *L'Afrique des Grands Lacs en crise: Rwanda, Burundi, 1988–1994* (Brussels, 1995), pp. 31–32; and Prunier, *The Rwanda Crisis*, pp. 78–79. Prunier concludes with the benefit of hindsight: "Revisited, like a poisonous snake still unborn inside its egg, the Habyarimana regime till 1988 was in general one of the least bad in Africa if one considers only its actions and not its intellectual underpinnings" (p. 83). I have already pointed out that Prunier tends to underplay the shift in the institutional underpinning of the post-1959 state from the First to the Second Republic, just as he underplays the shift following Habyarimana's death.

41. "Rwanda," in Legum, ed., *Africa Contemporary Record, 1975–76*, p. B292.

42. Harrison (1987), cited in Scott Grosse, "More People, More Trouble: Population Growth and Agricultural Change in Rwanda," School of Public Health, University of Michigan, Ann Arbor, manuscript, prepared for the Africa Bureau, U.S. Agency for International Development, revised draft, 16 November 1994, p. 17.

43. Peter Uvin, "Tragedy in Rwanda: The Political Ecology of Conflict," *Environment*, April 1996, p. 10.

44. Nzisabira, *Accumulation du peuplement rural et ajustements agro-pastoraux au Rwanda*, Cahiers du CIDEP, no. 1 (Louvain-la-Neuve: CIDEP, 1989); L. Cambrezy, *Le Surpeuplement en question: Organisation spatiale et écologie des migrations au Rwanda*. Collection Travaux et Documents, no. 182 (Paris: Ed. ORSTOM, 1984); both cited in Scott Grosse, "More People, More Trouble: Population Growth and Agricultural Change in Rwanda," School of Public Health, University of Michigan, Ann Arbor, manuscript, prepared for the Africa Bureau, U.S. Agency for International Development, revised draft, 16 November 1994, pp. 18–19.

45. An additional factor making for the increase in crop was the colonization of higher-elevation forests.

46. World Bank, *World Development Report 1992* (Oxford: Oxford University Press, 1992), cited in Grosse, "More People, More Trouble," pp. 20–21.

47. Uvin, "Tragedy in Rwanda," p. 10. It is from the national parks that the postgenocide RPF government would carve out land to settle some of the returning Tutsi refugees.

48. "Rwanda," in Legum, ed., *Africa Contemporary Record, 1975–76*, p. B289.

49. Philippe Decraene in *Le Monde* (Paris), 31 March 1974; cited in "Rwanda," in Legum, ed., *Africa Contemporary Record, 1974–75*, p. B254.

50. Shao Tung, "Rwanda Takes on New Look," Xinhua General Overseas News Service, 8 June 1978, item no. 060728, p. 222.

51. See, for example, Longman, "Anarchy and the State in Africa," p. 8.

52. Shao Tung, "Rwanda Takes on New Look," p. 223.

53. Olson (1994), cited in Grosse, "The Roots of Conflict and State Failure in Rwanda," pp. 14–15.

54. Grosse, "The Roots of Conflict and State Failure in Rwanda," p. 15.

55. U.S. Department of State, "Rwanda Human Rights Practices, 1993," in *1993 Human Rights Report*, 31 January 1994, p. 17.

56. Newbury and Newbury, "Was the Genocide in Rwanda an Ethnic Struggle?" pp. 16–17.

57. Uvin, "Tragedy in Rwanda," p. 11.

58. For information on SAP and its consequence, see Sellstom and Wohlgemuth, *The International Response to Conflict and Genocide,* pp. 34–36. The report cites S. Marysse, T. de Herdt, and E. Ndayambaje, *Rwanda: Appauvrissement et ajustement structurel* (Brussels: CEDAF/L'Harmattan, 1994).

59. Economist Intelligence Unit Country Report, no. 1, 1994, cited in Africa Direct, *Submission to the United Nations Tribunal on Rwanda*, Appendix 1: "The

Making of War" (London, 1996), p. 7. The Africa Direct submission summed up more elaborate articles appearing in *Living Marxism*, March 1996, London.

60. Economist Intelligence Unit (1995), cited in Sellstom and Wohlgemuth, *The International Response to Conflict and Genocide*, p. 15.

61. "The myth of an 'egalitarian republic' had evaporated: a quaternary bourgeoisie (military, administrative, business and technocratic) embezzles for its own benefit an important part of the national income." F. Bézy, *Rwanda: Bilan Socio-économique d'un régime, 1962–1989* (Louvain: Institut d'étude des Pays en Développement, University of Louvain-la-Neuve, 1990); cited in Sellstom and Wohlgemuth, *The International Response to Conflict and Genocide*, p. 30.

62. "Trafipro's regional bias, corruption, and the climate of terror it supported led to determined opposition." Pottier (1993, p. 11), cited in Rachel Yeld, "Repatriation of Rwandan Refugees," Refugee Studies Programme, Oxford University, 4 December 1995, p. 7.

63. See, for example, A. Hannsen, *Le désenchantement de la cooperation* (Paris: L'Harmattan, 1989), p. 128; cited in Scott Grosse, e-mail, 22 November 1995.

64. Sellstom and Wohlgemuth, *The International Response to Conflict and Genocide*, p. 30 (citing Reyntjens, 1994). For further details, see Legum, ed., *Africa Contemporary Record, 1976–77*, p. B309; Lemarchand, "Rwanda: Recent History," *Africa South of the Sahara 1980–81*, p. 804.

For example, Colin Legum wrote in 1985:

Senior government staff apointments announced on 18 January created a feeling of discontent amongst southerners, as most positions were filled by individuals from the north. In 12 of the 15 ministries, either the Minister or the Secretary-General is from one of the three northern prefectures. Three ministry heads are from Gisenyi, three from Ruhengeri, and one from Byumba. The reduction in the total number of ministries resulted in a net loss of two southerners from the cabinet. Of nine new Secretary-Generals appointed, eight are northerners—four from Gisenyi, three from Ruhengeri, and one from Byumba. Three of the six services at the Presidency (Economy and Finances, Security and the Secretariat) are led by northerners. Of five new parastatal directors appointed, three are from Gisenyi. This favouratism has occurred at the expense of southerners and, in particular, those from the once influential Butare prefecture. The effort to reduce Butare's importance was also reflected in the decentralization of Rwanda's national university by adding a campus at Ruhengeri to the original one at Butare. See Legum, ed., *Africa Contemporary Record, 1984–85*, p. B320.

65. The 1978 census gave the following figures:

Prefectures	Area	Population	Density
	(sq km)		(per sq km.)
Butare	1,830	602,550	329.3
Byumba	4,987	521,351	104.5
Cyangugu	2,226	333,187	149.7
Gikongoro	2,192	370,596	169.1
Gisenyi	2,395	468,882	195.8

Gitarama	2,241	606,212	270.5
Kibungo	4,134	361,249	87.4
Kibuye	1,320	336,588	255.0
Kigali	3,251	698,442	214.8
Ruhengeri	1,762	531,927	301.9
Total	26,338	4,830,984	183.4

The principal towns, with their population figures in parantheses, were Kigali (117,749), Butare (21,691), Ruhengeri (16,025), and Gisenyi (12,436). See Reyntjens, "Rwanda: Economy," *Africa South of the Sahara, 1991*, p. 824.

66. F. Reyntjens, "Démocratisation et conflits ethniques au Rwanda et au Burundi," *Cahiers Africains—Afrika Studies* 4–5 (1993): 209–227.

67. "The long-standing traditional antagonism which had existed between the two districts came to the fore in the 'Lizinde affair' in April 1980 when Théonaste Lizinde, a former security chief and a Mugoyi, was arrested, with about 30 other people, for allegedly planning a coup. At his trial, eventually held in late 1981, Lizinde was sentenced to death, but later reprieved. He was, however, re-tried in 1985, charged on this occasion with the murder in the mid-1970s of a number of politicians of the first republic. Lizinde, together with five others, was convicted and condemned to death." Reyntjens, "Rwanda: Recent History," *Africa South of the Sahara, 1989*, p. 827.

68. The information in the following two paragraphs is culled from Sellstom and Wohlgemuth, *The International Response to Conflict and Genocide*, p. 37; and Reyntjens, "Rwanda: Recent History," *Africa South of the Sahara, 1992*, pp. 679–680.

69. Peter Uvin, *Aiding Violence* (West Hartford: Kumarian Press, 1998), p. 48.

70. My summary description of the four parties relies on Prunier, *The Rwanda Crisis*, pp. 122–126.

71. Landwald Ndasingwa, one of the PL leaders, was fond of saying: "I am a Tutsi, my wife is a white Canadian, several members of my family are married to Hutu, in fact we are all tired of this ethnic business." Prunier, *The Rwanda Crisis*, p. 125.

CHAPTER SIX
THE POLITICS OF INDIGENEITY IN UGANDA

1. Catherine Watson, "Exile from Rwanda: Background to an Invasion," prepared for the U.S. Committee for Refugees, Washington, D.C., February 1991, p. 5.

2. Writing toward the end of 1990, Catherine Watson estimated the total number of Banyarwanda refugees at "probably about half a million, not one to two million, as is often said." Filip Reyntjens cited Guichaoua's estimate that "a total of 600,000" Tutsi refugees had left Rwanda between 1959 and 1990. Catharine Newbury and David Newbury estimated the number as "between 400,000 and 600,000." Kagabo and Vidal estimated that there were "over 600,000" Tutsi in

exile by 1992, constituting 9 percent of the population of Rwanda at the time. Chrétien estimated that the Tutsi who fled into neighboring countries after 1959 may have multiplied to 600,000 by the early 1990s. In 1994, Human Rights Watch estimated the number of "those who fled Rwanda as well as their descendents" at "between 400,000 and 500,000."

Catherine Watson, "Exile from Rwanda," p. 6. Filip Reyntjens, *L'Afrique des Grands Lacs en crise: Rwanda, Burundi: 1988–1994* (Brussels, 1995), p. 13. Catharine Newbury and David Newbury, "Was the Genocide in Rwanda an Ethnic Struggle?" mimeo, University of North Carolina–Chapel Hill, no date, p. 19. J. Kagabo and C. Vidal, "L'extermination des Rwandais Tutsi," *Cahiers d'études Africaines* 34, np. 4 (1994): 538; cited in Jibrin Ibrahim, "The Narcissism of Minor Difference and the Rise of Genocidal Tendencies in Africa: Lessons from Rwanda and Burundi," paper presented to CODESRIA 8th General Assembly, 26 June–2 July 1995, p. 13. J.-P Chrétien, "La crise politique rwandaise," *Jeune Afrique* 30, no. 2 (1992): 121–141. Human Rights Watch Arms Project, "Arming Rwanda: The Arms Trade and Human Rights Abuses in the Rwandan War," Washington, D.C., January 1994, p. 8.

3. Prunier's estimates were strongly criticized by Scott Grosse on Rwandanet: Prunier repeatedly contradicts his own numbers. Regarding the population of Rwanda, in footnote 15 on page 51 he says it was "about 2.7 million" in late 1963. He says in footnote 19 on page 53 that "In 1961 the total population in Rwanda was about 2,800,000."

Similarly, Prunier gives conflicting estimates of the size of the Tutsi population in Rwanda before the ethnic purges. In footnote 19 on page 53, he states, based on a population estimate of 2,800,000 in 1961, "as 15% of the population, the Tutsi numbered about 420,000. Of these, about 120,000 went into exile." On page 62, he says that the Tutsi population in 1959 was "about 500,000" without any explanation of the inconsistency. The 500,000 figure would imply that the Tutsi fraction was close to 20% of the roughly 2.6 million population of Rwanda as of 1959. . . .

Finally, Prunier gives wildly conflicting estimates of the number of Tutsi refugees from Rwanda. As noted above, on page 53 he indicates that only 120,000 of 420,000 left Rwanda, which implies that the vast majority of Rwandan Tutsis remained in Rwanda. . . . Yet, on pages 62–63, Prunier contends that the Tutsi refugee population as of 1964 totalled 400,000. Given his reasoned estimate of a Tutsi population of 420,000 as of 1961, this implies that virtually the entire Tutsi population of Rwanda had fled the country by 1964. Prunier cannot have his cake and eat it too. That is, he cannot double-count the same people as having left Rwanda and joining the refugee diaspora and as remaining in Rwanda.

Scott Grosse, communication on Rwandanet, 22 January 1996.

4. Captain Eugene M. Haguma, "The Rwandese Crisis: The Political Economy of Genocide," unpublished manuscript, Kigali, February 1995, p. 5.

5. Take, for example, these conflicting reports on how many Rwandese refugees were registered with UNHCR in Uganda. Both accounts come from what are considered to be credible sources of annual reports on African countries. Thus, *Africa Contemporary Record* reported in its 1986–87 publication that UNHCR "recognized" 30,000 Rwandan refugees in Uganda. *Africa South of the Sahara* reported in its 1988 publication: "In 1986 the UN High Commissioner for Refugees (UNHCR) reported that there were about 110,000 registered Rwandan refugees living in Uganda, while an even greater number of refugees were believed to have settled in Uganda without registering with the UNHCR." Catherine Watson reported the number registered with UNHCR in Uganda in early 1991 at "about 81,000." See "Rwanda," in Legum, ed., *Africa Contemporary Record, 1986–87,* p. B385. Réne Lemarchand, "Recent History" in "Rwanda," in *Africa South of the Sahara, 1988* (London: Europa Publications Ltd.), p. 803. Watson, "Exile from Rwanda," p. 6.

6. Here is Watson's account:

The total number of Banyarwanda refugees today is probably about half a million, not one to two as is often said. This lower figure can be derived from the following calculation. Rwanda's population in 1959, before the present exodus, was 2.6 million. An estimated 14% were Tutsi, making the number of Rwandese Tutsi about 364,000. About 20,000 were murdered, leaving 344,000. Since then, populations in East Africa have roughly tripled. This means that the Tutsi today number slightly more than a million, in and outside the country. Figures suggest that between 40 and 70% of Rwanda's Tutsi fled between 1959 and 1964. That would put between 400,000 and 700,000 Tutsi outside the country. In Rwanda, according to the 1978 census, 9.64% of the population was Tutsi. Some sources allege, however, that this figure is smaller than it should be, either due to Tutsi identifying themselves as Hutu out of fear of discrimination, or deliberate tempering by the Hutu-controlled Rwanda government.

See Watson, "Exile from Rwanda," p. 6.

7. A report by Guichaoua, as cited in Filip Reyntjens, *L'Afrique des Grands Lacs en crise,* p. 139.

8. Watson, "Exile from Rwanda," p. 5.

9. Ibid., p. 6.

10. Audrey Richards, "The Travel Routes and the Travellers," in *Economic Development and Tribal Change: A Study of Immigrant Labour in Buganda* (Cambridge: Cambridge University Press, 1956), p. 70.

11. Augustine Ruzindana, interview, Kampala, 31 August 1995.

12. J. M. Fortt, "The Distribution of the Immigrant and the Ganda Population within Buganda," pp. 77–118, and Cynthia Postan, "Changes in the Immigrant Population in Buganda, 1948–59," appendix F, table 8, p. 307; both cited in Richards, *Economic Development and Tribal Change.*

13. Archie Mafeje, "The Agrarian Revolution and the Land Question in Uganda," in Roger Leys, ed., *Dualism and Rural Development in East Africa* (Co-

penhagen: Institute of Development Research, 1973), p. 145. Also see Archie Mafeje and A. I. Richards, "The Commercial Farmer and His Labour Supply," in A. I. Richards, Ford Sturrock, and Jean M. Fortt, eds., *Subsistence to Commercial Farming in Present-day Buganda* (Cambridge: Cambridge University Press, 1973).

14. Dramatic instances as that of the RPF's second-in-command, Lt. Col. Adam Wasswa, who was considered a Muganda even by close colleagues in the NRA, must be considered an exception, however notable.

15. Watson, "Exile from Rwanda," p. 6.

16. Martin R. Doornbos and Michael F. Lofchie, "Ranching and Scheming: A Case Study of the Ankole Ranching Scheme," in Michael F. Lofchie, ed., *The State of the Nations: Constraints on Development in Independent Africa* (Berkeley: University of California Press, 1971), p. 186; Nyangabyaki Bazaara, "Ugandan Politics and the Crisis of Rwandese Refugees and Immigrants," paper presented to the 10th All-African Student Conference, Temple University, Philadelphia, 16–18 May 1997.

17. As the memory of UNAR got dim and the mystique of return to Rwanda faded, a variety of social clubs and cultural associations mushroomed in Canada, Germany, Los Angeles, Washington, D.C., Lomé, Bujumbura, Brazaville, Nairobi, and Kampala. It is in Kampala that the Rwandese Refugee Welfare Foundation (RRWF) was created in 1979 to help victims of political repression after the fall of Idi Amin. The following year, RRWF changed its name to RANU. My information is primarily based on interviews with Patrick Mazimpaka, a leader of RANU and a minister in the present Rwanda government. The interview took place in Kigali in 1995. Also see Gérard Prunier, *The Rwanda Crisis: History of a Genocide* (London: Hurst & Co., 1995), pp. 64–67.

18. Charles David Smith, "The Geopolitics of Rwandan Settlement: Uganda and Tanzania," *Issue* 23, no. 2 (1995): 54, African Studies Association, USA.

19. Watson, "Exile from Rwanda," pp. 9–10.

20. Odonga Ori Amaza, "Rwanda and Uganda: Post-War Prospects for Regional Peace and Security," paper presented at CODESRIA conference on Academic Freedom, Social Research and Conflict Resolution in the Countries of the Great Lakes, 4–7 September 1995, Arusha, Tanzania, pp. 21–22.

21. This paragraph is based on my own experience and also on ibid., p. 22.

22. Leon Dash, "Many Rwandan Refugees Moving North in Uganda to Escape Attacks," *Washington Post*, 2 December 1983, final edition.

23. Legum, ed., *Africa Contemporary Record, 1982–83*, p. B245; also see idem, *Africa Contemporary Record, 1983–84*, p. B230.

24. Watson, "Exile from Rwanda," p. 10.

25. Legum, ed., *Africa Contemporary Record, 1984–85*, p. B325.

26. Lemarchand, "Recent History: Rwanda," in *Africa South of the Sahara, 1983–84*, p. 669; also see Legum, ed., *Africa Contemporary Record, 1986–87*, pp. B383–384.

27. Watson, "Exile from Rwanda," p. 10.

28. Lemarchand, "Recent History: Rwanda," p. 771.

29. Legum, ed., *Africa Contemporary Record, 1985–86*, p. B380; also see idem, *Africa Contemporary Record, 1986–87*, p. B387.

30. I chaired this Commission of Inquiry for its duration of two years (1986–88), which took the commission to each district around the country. See National Commission of Inquiry into Local Government, "Report," Entebbe, Uganda, 1986.

31. Rwigyema went to Mozambique in 1976 as part of a small band under the leadership of Museveni. Kagame joined Museveni's anti-Amin forces in Uganda in 1979. See Catherine Watson, "War and Waiting," *Africa Report*, November–December 1992, p. 54.

32. Catherine Watson, personal communication, September 1995.

33. "There is no evidence to suggest that the Rwandese Banyarwanda who joined the NRA during its early days did so with the aim of preparing to invade their country to facilitate their return home. The majority of them, like most of their Ugandan comrades, were forced to join by getting caught up in the fray or simply fled to the bush to save their lives. However, beginning around 1984, several fairly well-educated Rwandese Banyarwanda began to stream into NRA from recruiting bases in Nairobi. There is reason to believe these later Rwandese Banyarwanda joined NRA with a definite political agenda with regard to their mother country, and it might have been around this time that the conspiracy to desert from the NRA as a prelude to the invasion of Rwanda began to be hatched. The most important of the 1984 group of educated Rwandese Banyarwanda was Dr. Peter Baingana." Amaza, "Rwanda and Uganda: Post-War Prospects for Regional Peace and Security," p. 23. At the time of writing, Amaza was a major in the NRA.

Scott Grosse cites Barbara Harrell-Bond, the director of the Refugee Studies Centre at Oxford University who toured Rwandan refugee camps in Uganda in 1986, as saying that "at that time the RPF was openly conducting military training and making preparations for its eventual invasion of Rwanda." Scott Grosse, "Summary and Comments on 'Exile from Rwanda: Background to an Invasion,' by Catherine Watson, U.S. Committee on Refugees, 1991," Ann Arbor, Michigan, 26 June 1995, p. 6.

34. Cited in William Cyrus Reed, "The Rwandan Patriotic Front: Politics and Development in Rwanda," *Issue* 23, no. 2 (1995): p. 49.

35. Legum, ed., *Africa Contemporary Record, 1983–84*, p. B234.

36. Lemarchand, "Recent History: Rwanda," in *Africa South of the Sahara, 1988*, p. 803.

37. Previously, the most serious attempt at mass naturalization of Banyarwanda refugees had been in Tanzania, though it had floundered at the implementation stage. In Uganda of the late 1980s, however, the political environment was considered far more favorable to mass naturalization. See Charles P. Gasarasi, "The Mass Naturalization and Further Integration of Rwandese Refugees in Tanzania: Pro-

cess, Problems and Prospects," *Journal of Refugee Studies* (Oxford) 3, no. 2 (1990): 90–95.

38. Catherine Watson writes that Banyarwanda numbered "an estimated 2,000–3,000" of 14,000 when the NRA entered Kampala on 26 January 1986. Faced with a civil war in the northern and eastern districts in 1987, when it faced "about 45,000 rebels," NRA "embarked on massive recruitment." In this context, "probably between 1,000 and 2,000 additional Banyarwanda joined." The figure of 4,000 officers and men at the time of the RPF invasion comes from the letter by Uganda's ambassador to the U.S. to Human Rights Watch, 26 August 1993. See Watson, "Exile from Rwanda," pp. 11, 13; Human Rights Watch Arms Project, *Arming Rwanda: The Arms Trade and Human Rights Abuses in the Rwandan War* 6, issue 1 (January 1994), appendix.

39. Prunier is mistaken when he states that Rwigyema was by then army commander-in-chief and minister of defense. See Gérard Prunier, *The Rwanda Crisis*, p. 73.

40. Interview, Kigali, 1995.

41. RANU began preparations for its transformation into a mass-based activist organization at its 1985 congress, which empowered its political bureau to form a task force to develop a strategy to guide its expansion, keeping in mind the existence in Uganda of a cadre with experience in fighting a guerrilla war. William Cyrus Reed, "Exile, Reform and the Rise of the Rwandan Patriotic Front," in *The Journal of Modern African Studies* 34, no. 3 (1996): 485.

42. Some of the grasslands in the county had become infested with the tsetse fly in the 1950s. In 1962, a combined USAID/International Development Agency (World Bank) program financed tsetse eradication on this grazing land, with a pledge from the Uganda government that the land reclaimed would be allocated for commercial ranching to entrepreneurs with a background in cattle keeping. A total of 59 ranches, each measuring up to 5 square kilometers, were allocated in two phases, 17 between 1962 and 1968, and the remaining 42 after 1971 when the Ranch Selection Board had become inoperative and ranch allocation had become the prerogative of leading politicians. For background to the ranching schemes and subsequent developments, see Commission of Inquiry into Government Ranching Schemes, "Report to the Government of Uganda," Entebbe, December 1988.

43. Minister for Animal Industries and Fisheries, National Resistance Council, Wednesday, 22 August 1990, in Parliament of Uganda, *Parliamentary Debates (Hansard)*, Official Report, 4th sess., 2nd meeting, issue no. 14, 28 June–23 August 1990, Kampala, p. 377.

44. Expedit Ddungu, "The Other Side of Land Issues in Buganda: Pastoral Crisis and the Squatter Movement in Sembabule Sub-District," mimeo, Centre for Basic Research, Kampala, no date, pp. 2–3; Frank Emmanuel Muhereza, "The Struggles for Land Rights and 1990 Squatter Uprisings in the Former Govern-

ment Ranching Schemes of Uganda," mimeo, Centre for Basic Research, Kampala, March 1998, pp. 4–5.

45. Mr. A. Okullu quoted from a memo submitted by Mawogola ranchers to the president. It identified three groups as "the source of squatters": "a small fraction" being pastoralists "moving from place to place," the second being Ugandan migrants "who came during the Liberation wars from Ankole, Luwero and Mtukula areas," and finally the Banyarwanda, described as "victims of Rwakasisi's evacuation of non-citizens from Mbarara and Bushenyi." No numbers were given, except for a hint in the contribution by the minister of state for defense. Maj.-Gen. Tinyefuza gave two sets of figures: a figure of "about 120,000 or more" when speaking of "Ugandan human beings who were displaced from their lands some twenty years or so in their sixties" ("Ugandans who have a right to bury their dead"), and 200,000 when referring to the total number of "homeless." The implication was that the refugee squatters numbered in the vicinity of 80,000.

46. For a detailed discussion of the evolution of rental relations, see Ddungu, "The Other Side of Land Issues in Buganda," pp. 4–8.

47. The total of 112 ranches were to be found in five different parts of the country. See Commission of Inquiry into Government Ranching Schemes, "Report to the Government of Uganda," pp. 81–82 and annexes 3 and 8.

48. Muhereza, "The Struggles for Land Rights," p. 11.

49. "Ranches Fight to Retain Land," *New Vision*, 9 February 1990. This paragraph is constructed on the basis of Ddungu, "The Other Side of Land Issues in Buganda," p. 18.

50. When the RC III chairperson of Mijwala tried to intervene, he was temporarily arrested and charged with helping ranchers to deny squatters access to water. "Telephone Ranchers Stand to Lose Most," and "Ranchers Policy Was Child of Injustice," *Weekly Topic*, 24–31 August, 1990; "NRC Holds Special Session on Ranches," *New Vision*, 23 August 1990; both cited in Muhereza, "The Struggles for Land Rights and 1990 Squatter Uprisings in the Former Government Ranching Schemes of Uganda," pp. 8–9. Ddungu, "The Other Side of Land Issues in Buganda," p. 21. President Museveni claimed in Parliament that "the resistance" to squatter demands "was in the technocracy; in the Ministry of Lands, in the Ministry of Veterinary Services." Chairman (president of Uganda), National Resistance Council, Wednesday, 22nd August 1990, in Parliament of Uganda, *Parliamentary Debates (Hansard)*, Official Report, 4th sess., 2nd meeting, issue no. 14, 28 June–23 August 1990, Kampala, p. 416. The information in the rest of the paragraph is from pp. 427–428 and 431 of the parliamentary proceedings.

51. The first attack took place on 5 August 1990. By 13 August Lyatonde police station reported twelve different clashes on ranches, leaving cows, goats, sheep, and buildings destroyed. "Ministers Visit Troubled Ranches," *New Vision*, 17 August 1990; cited in Ddungu, "The Other Side of Land Issues in Buganda," p. 13.

52. "The Other Side of Land Issues in Buganda," p. 13.

53. "Mr. Chairman, I come to another group—the instigators. Here, I can see the instigators apparently are combined together with some squatters against the ranchers and the issue here is to remove the ranchers forcefully." Mr. A. Okulu, National Resistance Council, Wednesday, 22nd August 1990, in Parliament of Uganda, *Parliamentary Debates (Hansard)*, Official Report, 4th sess., 2nd meeting, issue no. 14, 28 June–23 August 1990, Kampala, p. 452.

"Mr. Chairman, if we let people get things of the mighty they have used, the saying will be confirmed. My mighty is my right instead of right is mighty. We shall be saying, mighty is right—my strength, I mean strength. . . . These people are really well armed. Some have spears and they dress in rags but those who dress in rags are really looking gentlemanly and they are not really real squatters. So, these people are really supported by those who disguise to be squatters and if you let this continue, the situation will be explosive." Mr. Kajubi, in ibid., p. 413.

54. Why else, they asked, were nineteen ranches from Buganda (Masaka) targeted for repossession, but only three from Ankole? In his remarks in Parliament, the minister acknowledged both the force and impact of this argument: "Now, people went around saying that the government was repossessing all the ranches in Buganda and they had left alone the ranches in Ankole. People said this and still they say it now. . . . So, we went back to cabinet and said we are being accused of being sectarian and the innuendoes are very clear as to why people are saying that Ankole ranches were being left alone. . . . They said, why do you not go across the board and reduce all the ranches? The cabinet accepted our recommendation." The Minister for Animal Industry and Fisheries (Prof. G. Kagonyera), in ibid., p. 378.

55. Mr. Gasatura said: "What we discuss today, Mr. Chairman, is nothing but a class struggle in which those who have are refusing to allow a little bit to those who have little or none." In support, Mr. Rwakakooko contributed: "I think we are trying right now to answer a problem of social injustice where the government in the past dispossessed people in those areas and gave to people, some of them have developed, some of them have not." Mr. Gasatura's contribution is on p. 383, and that of Mr. Rwakakooko is on p. 401 of ibid.

56. See Mrs. Matembe (Women, Mbarara) in ibid., pp. 396–397, 397–399; Mr. Muruli Mukasa (Nakasongola County, Luwero), pp. 416–417; Prof. Kagonyera, p. 429; Mr. Kasaija (Kampala), p. 426.

The question of military training assumed a greater significance after the RPF invasion of October 1990. The minister of state for defense at first flatly denied the allegations—"there is no such training"—and concluded: "That is rumour-mongering again centred on heaping up the Banyarwanda issue." When pressed further, however, he conceded that Local Defence Unit personnel were indeed being trained in the county. "These are local defence units being trained like anywhere in the country and they are being trained there, and some of those who passed out actually come from the area of the Hon. Member himself—Hon. Kasaija—in Matete. So these are not bandits. They are being trained to keep law and order." Maj. Gen. Tinyefuza, ibid., pp. 425–426.

Based on extensive local research, Ddungu had this to say about military training of squatters:

It is alleged by many local people that some light training went on prior to the
actual uprising. This training is claimed to have taken place in some centres such
as Kasasa area near Rwemiyaga (in Ranch no. 20). This training is said to have
been arranged to coincide with the training of the official local defence personnel. As a characteristic that has remained more or less a permanent legacy of the
uprising, a large section of squatters still carry guns disguised as local defence
personnel. This way there is a local defence personnel in almost every homestead.
Some district officials interviewed over the matter sounded resigned whereas
others did not see any problem in it. Squatters/local defence personnel move
with their guns during the day in their numbers and without any security problem. In other areas of the country there are usually three to four local defense
personnel. The guns are usually kept in a nearby barracks and they are collected
every evening for night duty.

Ddungu, "The Other Side of Land Issues in Buganda," p. 16.

Significantly, government did not deny that military training was taking place
on ranches. It only pointed out that the people being trained were Local Defence
Forces. "Minister Accused of Manipulating President," *The Star*, 24 August 1990;
"Ranches: Tinyefuza Defends Army," *New Vision*, 24 August 1990 cited in Muhereza, "The Struggles for Land Rights," p. 14.

57. Maj. Gen. Tinyefuza on p. 420 and Dr. Ruhakana Rugunda on p. 421,
The National Resistance Council, Wednesday, 22 August 1990, in Parliament of
Uganda, *Parliamentary Debates (Hansard)*.

58. See Mrs. Matembe, ibid., p. 423.

59. Mr. Mwandha said, "Mr. Chairman, the question of citizenship goes hand
in hand with the question of land. Although, Mr. Chairman, you said that this is
not a major problem, I think it is a problem because even this afternoon and this
morning, I have observed that some of the Members of this House who hardly
contribute in this House, when the question came to that of citizenship, they
contributed and very strongly, and they showed that there is a lot of strong feelings
about the question of citizenship. . . . Do we have a system, Mr. Chairman, when
we come to implementing government policy to ensure that only citizens of this
country will be the people to benefit from what has been improvised by government in this resolution. Do we have that system of making sure that we are actually
catering for the citizens of this country? This to me is a very important question."
See ibid., p. 450.

60. The president elaborated: "Now, on this issue of ranches, another campaign
which was going on underground; after talking about Museveni wants to get land
for Banyarwanda, then they talk about Banyankole that this move is in order to
get land for Banyankole from other groups, from other Ugandans. Now, do you
see the opportunists are really wizards." See ibid., p. 407.

61. Maj.-Gen. Tinyefuza, in ibid., p. 425. He was supported by Mr. Pulkol: "These people now, the squatters, are no longer where they used to be," pointed out Mr. Pulkol in Parliament, "you know, some of them have been fighters even in this revolution, they are there now! They are now more enlightened with the RC system; they are now qualified to demand for what they were denied. So, actually, whether you would wait for somebody to instigate you or not, it is just a question of time. If we do not move with speed, we might still experience even a bigger one because as we speak today, these squatters are holding these ranches, they are there physically. Therefore, we must come to terms with this." Mr. Pulkol in ibid., p. 412.

62. The president was forthright when it came to pinning the chairman; see ibid., p. 395.

63. The chairman, in ibid., p. 427.

64. Ibid., p. 406.

65. After discussing the case of non-Africans, those usually referred to as "foreign investors," the president continued (ibid., p. 407): "Then there is the question of the Africans from Africa but who are not Ugandans, from the neighbouring territories especially, Sudan, Rwanda, Kenya and Zaire. What do we do about these? I think that one should be discussed because these are more, they are also peasants unlike the other ones who are industrialists. . . . The question of the property rights of non-Ugandan Africans here in Uganda, it should be discussed." Later on in the debate, Maj. Gen. Tumwine pointed out that the law does not really distinguish between indigenous and non-indigenous Africans (p. 475): "The information that I have according to our present Law, the Chapter 202 of the Land Transfer Act, 1969, Section 13, it says, 'any African can get a lease or buy completely. . . .' " Whereupon Miss Kadaga intervened to point out (p. 475) that the Hon. Member was misleading the House "about the interpretation of the Land Transfer Act when it clearly defines an African there as an indigenous person born here."

66. The distinction was made by the representative from Mufumbira, Dr. Mateke, who carefully distanced himself as one of the Ugandan Banyarwanda from Rwandese refugees: "I was informing the speaker on the Floor that in South Western Uganda, we have got a very big population called Banyarwanda and I am one of them. We have got very many Ugandans about four millions in Uganda who are Banyarwanda and I am one of them. We have got very many Ugandans about four millions in Uganda who are Banyarwanda and are Uganda citizens." Ibid., p. 417.

67. Dr. Kanyeihamba in ibid., p. 489.

68. The chairman in ibid., pp. 489–490.

69. Mr. Kandole in ibid., p. 490; the chairman, pp. 490–491; and Prof. Kanyeihamba, p. 491.

70. Amaza, "Rwanda and Uganda: Post-War Prospects for Regional Peace and Security," p. 24. Uganda's ambassador to the United States stated in his letter to

Human Rights Watch: "Major General Fred Rwigyema was no longer on active duty with the NRA at the time of the invasion in October 1990. Because he opted to remain a Rwandese national, he and many other Rwandese in this category were removed from the NRA by a decision of the National Resistance Council (Parliament)." Human Rights Watch Arms Project, *Arming Rwanda: The Arms Trade and Human Rights Abuses in the Rwandan War* 6, issue 1 (January 1994), appendix.

71. Though none of them grasp the significance of the squatter uprising and its consequences, a number of commentators have understood that the RPF invasion was not a response to developments internal to Rwanda. Yet, without an understanding of the social dynamics shaping refugee options within Uganda, and with an exclusive focus on the individual dilemmas of leading personalities in the RPF, such accounts tend to present the invasion as no more than an initiative (or conspiracy, depending on the point of view of the author) of individuals.

> Thus the RPF attack of 1990 can be seen as having resulted from the convergence of multiple interests. Many refugees (both elites and non-elites, though for different reasons) may have felt that this provided an escape from the burden of discrimination they felt in Uganda. At the same time Museveni may have found it expedient to divest his government of an increasing liability within the Ugandan political arena. The timing of the invasion, however, may have been more affected by initiatives within Rwanda, as the Habyarimana regime moved—very cautiously—towards a more open political system and a new position on refugee issues. Both policies—the move to "political liberalization" and the move to address the "refugee problem"—undercut RPF claims to moral superiority. So the RPF attack on October 1, 1990 carries the appearance of an attempt to preempt two issues on which the Rwanda government had indicated a willingness to act; by attacking when they did, the RPF seemed intent on maintaining the moral "high ground."

Catharine Newbury and David Newbury, "Was the Genocide in Rwanda an Ethnic Struggle?" mimeo, University of North Carolina–Chapel Hill, pp. 20–21. The authors then cite, in a footnote, support from Reyntjens, *L'Afrique des Grands Lacs en crise*, p. 180: "As Reyntjens points out, pressures from within Uganda also probably influenced the timing of the attack. There had been threats of a renewed round of hostility against Rwandans living in Uganda, and two key RPF leaders (Fred Rwigyema and Paul Kagame) had recently been removed from their high positions in the Uganda military."

Filip Reyntjens (p. 181), in turn, quotes Prunier to the effect that the RPF attacked in October 1990 because they were afraid that if they waited, the two main elements of their propaganda, the right of refugees to return and democracy in Rwanda, might be realized peacefully. The Prunier article is "Eléments pour une histoire du Front Patriotique Rwandais," *Politique Africaine* 51 (October 1993): 121–138.

"Some observers question the wisdom of the RPF in taking military action at that particular time (Prunier, 1993). The invasion occurred only two months after the 30-month talks supervised by UNHCR and OAU on the refugee problem had led to a (third) ministerial agreement between Rwanda and Uganda that might have led to concrete results, and during a gradually developing political liberalization process within Rwanda. Although it seems as if the negotiations might have led to a breakthrough, the RPF, however, was not prepared to wait any more; it was apparently tired of the continued stalling by the Rwandese government. It is, however, argued that RPF attacked at that time because a possible breakthrough in the areas of democratization, human rights and refugee repatriation would have diminished the legitimacy of an attack. (Reyntjens, 1994)." Cited in Tor Sellstrom and Lennart Wohlgemuth, *The International Response to Conflict and Genocide: Lessons from the Rwanda Experience*, Study 1, *Historical Perspective: Some Explanatory Factors* (Uppsala, Sweden: The Nordic Africa Institute, 1997), pp. 32–33.

A very similar argument is given by William Cyrus Reed in two related articles. "By legalising political activities domestically and softening its stand on the right of return of refugees, the regime in Kigali was taking a major initiative on the two central demands of the RPF, without their participation." And then: "With their careers blocked, growing pressure to remove them from the military, and plenty of time on their hands, the RPF leaders organised a mass desertion from the NA and focused on preparing an invasion into Rwanda." The first quote is from Reed, "Exile, Reform and the Rise of the Rwandan Patriotic Front," in *Journal of Modern African Studies* 34, no. 3 (1996): 486; the source of the second quote is Reed, "The Rwandan Patriotic Front: Politics and Development in Rwanda," *Issue* 23, no. 2 (1995): 50.

72. The letter was dated 26 August 1993. For details, see *Human Rights Watch Arms Project, Arming Rwanda*.

73. William Cyrus Reed cites Filip Reyntjens as the authority for the following statement: "The success of the withdrawal stemmed from the fact that within the NRA a parallel command structure, headed by Rwigyema, existed in the form of the Rwandan Patriotic Army—code-named '*Inkotanyi*,' a Kinyarwanda word meaning tough fighters." He then adds in a footnote: " '*Inkotanyi*' was also the name of the élite fighters in the ancient Rwandan monarchy, though it is unclear that the RPA was aware of the historical reference." The Reyntjens reference is to *L'Afrique des Grands Lacs en crise*, p. 91, fn. 7; cited in Reed, "Exile, Reform and the Rise of the Rwandan Patriotic Front," p. 488.

74. "RPF Is the Uganda Army, Says Expert," *Economist Intelligence Review*, 19 August 1994.

75. Statement by H. E. Yoweri Kaguta Museveni, president of the Republic of Uganda, in "The Background to the Situation in the Great Lakes," 9 August 1998, Harare/Zimbabwe; excerpted in *East African Alternatives*, March/April 1999, Nairobi, Kenya, p. 39.

CHAPTER SEVEN
THE CIVIL WAR AND THE GENOCIDE

1. Charles Onyango-Obbo, "Inside Rebel-Controlled Rwanda," *Africa News Service*, 26 April 1993.

2. Gérard Prunier, *The Rwanda Crisis: History of a Genocide* (London: Hurst & Co., 1995), pp. 135–136.

3. Tor Sellstom and Lennart Wohlgemuth, *The International Response to Conflict and Genocide: Lessons from the Rwanda Experience*, Study 1, *Historical Perspective: Some Explanatory Factors* (Uppsala, Sweden: The Nordic Africa Institute, 1997), pp. 39, 45.

4. Catherine Watson, "Rwanda: War and Waiting," *Africa Report*, November/December 1992, p. 55.

5. Prunier, *The Rwanda Crisis*, p. 175, fn. 33.

6. Onyango-Obbo, "Inside Rebel-Controlled Rwanda."

7. Catharine Newbury and David Newbury, "Identity, Genocide and Reconstruction in Rwanda," paper presented at the conference "Les racines de la violence dans la région des Grands-Lacs," European Parliament, Brussels, 12–13 January 1995, p. 17.

8. Amy Waldman, "Is It Too Late for Rwanda?" *Houston Chronicle*, 12 June 1994. Waldman quotes another RPF leader: "You cannot have democracy where you have an ignorant population." And then another, "Democracy is rule by the majority for those who are conscious of what they are doing."

9. Human Rights Watch Arms Project, *Arming Rwanda: The Arms Trade and Human Rights Abuses in the Rwandan War*, vol. 4, issue 1, January 1994, p. 13. This section quotes extensively from the report of the January 1993 investigation of human rights abuses in Rwanda carried out by an international commission comprising Africa Watch, the International Federation of Human Rights (Paris), the Inter-African Union of Human Rights (Ouagadougou), and the International Center for Human Rights and Democratic Development (Montreal). See "Report of The International Commission of Investigation on Human Rights Violations in Rwanda since October 1, 1990," March 1993.

10. "They continued to avoid establishing administrative structures in the territory they conquered. Rather, they sought to increase the political costs of the war for the Habyarimana regime by displacing the local population and halting production. . . . Because of the massive displacement of the local population during the war, the RPF did not effectively expand its base through the political activities which normally accompany guerrilla warfare." William Cyrus Reed, "The Rwandan Patriotic Front: Politics and Development in Rwanda," *Issue* 23, no. 2 (1995): 50.

11. "The perceptions that the RPF leaders had of themselves—that of liberators, dedicated to the overthrow of a thoroughly corrupt and oppressive dictator-

ship—turned out to be sadly out of sync with the image that a great many Hutu had of their would-be 'liberators.' " René Lemarchand, "Rwanda: The rationality of Genocide," *Issue* 23, no. 2 (1995): p. 8.

12. William Cyrus Reed, "Exile, Reform and the Rise of the Rwanda Patriotic Front," *Journal of Modern African Studies* 34, no. 3 (1996): 492.

13. Todd Shields, "Invasion Stirs Tribal Tension in Rwanda," *Washington Post*, 13 October 1990.

14. African Rights, *Rwanda: Death, Despair and Defiance*, rev. ed., (London, 1995), pp. 42–43.

15. Robert M. Press, "Escape from Kigali: Odyssey of a Hutu Family," *Christian Science Monitor*, 14 November 1994, p. 9.

16. Bill Berkeley, "Sounds of Violence," *New Republic*, 22 August 1994, p. 18.

17. David Lamb, "Rwanda Tragedy May Reflect Larger Africa Problem," *The Dallas Morning News*, 12 June 1994, p. 21A.

18. Human Rights Watch/Africa, *Genocide in Rwanda, April/May 1994*, vol. 6, no. 4 (May 1994), p. 7.

19. René Lemarchand has summed up these events in a short postgenocide reflection. See Lemarchand, "Rwanda: The Rationality of Genocide," *Issue* 23, no. 2 (1995): 9–10.

20. Catharine Newbury and David Newbury, "Was the Genocide in Rwanda an Ethnic Struggle?" mimeo, University of North Carolina–Chapel Hill, p. 22.

21. U.S. State Department, *1990 Human Rights Report*, 1991.

22. Prunier, *The Rwanda Crisis*, p. 168.

23. Unlike, for example in Uganda under Idi Amin, where it was the central state apparatus that organized the expulsion of residents of Asian origin and appropriated and redistributed their property.

24. Prunier, *The Rwanda Crisis*, pp. 142, 137–138.

25. Timothy Longman, "Democratization and Disorder: Political Transformation and Social Deterioration in Rwanda," Drake University, Des Moines, Iowa, mimeo, no date, p. 8. Longman was one of the few scholars to carry out local interviews soon after the genocide.

26. Human Rights Watch/Africa, *Rwanda: A New Catastrophe?*, vol. 6, no. 12 (December 1994): 7.

27. Human Rights Watch reported in May 1994: "Although much of the violence is still controlled by authorities of the hardline parties, the rump government or the Rwandan army, random killing, especially in the course of banditry and pillage, is growing as well. As food becomes more difficult to obtain, violence linked to the struggle for survival will increase." See Human Rights Watch/Africa, *Genocide in Rwanda, April/May 1994*, p. 6.

28. Press, "Escape from Kigali," p. 9.

29. I have not found the complete text of Mugesera's speech, but sections are widely quoted in different sources, including in communications on Rwandanet.

For an earlier communication, see Dr. Peter L. Hall, Rwandanet, 5 February 1996; also Prunier, *The Rwanda Crisis*, pp. 171–172.

30. Alison des Forges, "The Ideology of Genocide," *Issue* 23, no. 23 (1995): 46.

31. Philip Gourevitch, "After the Genocide," *New Yorker*, 18 December 1995, pp. 84–85; also see Gourevitch, *We wish to inform you that tomorrow we will be killed with our families: Stories from Rwanda* (New York: Picador, 1998), pp. 96–99.

32. D. C. Clay, "Fighting an Uphill Battle: Demographic Pressure, the Structure of Land Holding, and Land Degradation in Rwanda," Department of Agricultural Economics, Michigan State University, East Lansing, mimeo, 1993; cited in Scott Grosse, "More People, More Trouble: Population Growth and Agricultural Change in Rwanda," Department of Population Planning and International Health, School of Public Health, University of Michigan, Ann Arbor, 16 November 1994, paper prepared for the Africa Bureau, U.S. Agency for International Development, work order no. 001 of Requirements Contract no. DHR-5555-Q-00187–00 by the Environmental and Natural Resources Policy and Training (EPAT/MUCIA) Project.

33. Sellstom and Wohlgemuth, *The International Response to Conflict and Genocide*, p. 14.

34. Grosse, "More People, More Trouble," p. 41. Grosse cites two sources. See F. Bart, *Montagnes d'Afrique, Terres Paysannes. Le cas du Rwanda* (Bordeaux: Presses Universitaires de Bordeaux, 1993); L. A. Lewis, "Terracing and Accelerated Soil Loss on Rwandan Steeplands: A Preliminary Investigation of the Implications of Human Activities Affecting Soil Movement," *Land Degradation and Rehabilitation* 3: (1992): 241–246.

35. D. Clay et al., "Promoting Food Security in Rwanda through Sustainable Agricultural Productivity: Meeting the Challenges of Population Pressure, Land Degradation and Poverty," staff paper 95–08 for Department of Agricultural Economics, Michigan State University, March 1995; cited in Peter Uvin, "Tragedy in Rwanda: The Political Economy of Conflict," *Environment*, April 1996, p. 11.

36. *Africa News Report*, 12 September 1994; cited in Prunier, *The Rwanda Crisis*, p. 353. Others labeled the millions of Rwandese refugees in Zaire as "environmental refugees" and explained the conflict as the outcome of "demographic entrapment." See J. Patterson, "Rwandan Refugees," *Nature* 373, no. 6511 (19 January 1995): 185, and M. King, "Rwanda, Malthus and Medicus Mundi," *Medicus Mundi Bulletin*, no. 54 (August 1994); both cited in Uvin, "Tragedy in Rwanda," p. 7.

37. Michael R. Marrus, *The Holocaust in History* (New York: Meridian Penguin, 1987), pp. 10–11, 18, 46.

38. Final report, "International Conference on Genocide, Impunity and Accountability," Kigali, 1–5 November 1995, mimeo, p. 3.

39. Uvin, "Tragedy in Rwanda," *Environment*, April 1996, p. 13. In his more recent book, Peter Uvin combines state-society ("profound racism") with state-centered ("elite manipulation") explanations: "Without the profound racism, we would not find genocide but 'ordinary' communal violence, of which there is so much in Africa; without elite manipulation, structural violence would lead to more diffuse, anomic modes of violence such as petty criminality, sorcery, or domestic abuse—all of which are on the rise in most of Africa." Peter Uvin, *Aiding Violence: The Development Enterprise in Africa* (West Hartford, Conn.: Kumarian Press, 1998), pp. 138–139.

40. Prunier, *The Rwanda Crisis*, pp. 141–142.

41. I should add that Prunier does not always assume an opposition between two kinds of societies: those preliterate and thus prerational, and others literate and rational. If he did, the following comparison between pregenocide Rwanda and pre-Holocaust Prussia would make little sense: "As we saw in chapter 1, there had always been a strong tradition of unquestioning obedience to authority in the pre-colonial kingdom of Rwanda. This tradition was of course reinforced by both the German and the Belgian colonial administrations. And since independence the country had lived under a well-organised tightly-controlled state. When the highest authorities in that state told you to do something you did it, even if it included killing. There is some similarity here to the Prussian tradition of the German state and its ultimate perversion into the disciplined obedience to Nazi orders." Prunier, *The Rwanda Crisis*, p. 245.

42. Gourevitch, "After the Genocide," pp. 83–84; also see Gourevitch, *We wish to inform you*, pp. 22–23.

43. Gourevitch, "After the Genocide," p. 91.

44. Uvin, *Aiding Violence*, p. 215.

45. He then adds: "There is of course one further added cause: overpopulation." See Prunier, *The Rwanda Crisis*, p. 353.

46. Human Rights Watch Arms Project, *Arming Rwanda: The Arms Trade and Human Rights Abuses in the Rwandan War*, p. 4.

47. Des Forges, "The Ideology of Genocide," p. 44.

48. Cited in Patrick McDowell, "342 Women Implicated in Genocide," *Rocky Mountain News*, 26 September 1995, p. 30A.

49. Cited in Amy Waldman, "Is It Too Late for Rwanda?" *Houston Chronicle*, 12 June 1994, sec. A, p. 1.

50. See "Africa Direct, Submission to the UN Tribunal on Rwanda," p. 5. This submission sums up several articles on Rwanda that appeared in the London-based periodical, *Living Marxism*, December 1995 and March 1996.

51. S. Marysse and T. de Herdt, *L'ajustement structurel en Afrique: Les expériences du Mali et du Rwanda* (Antwerp: UFSIA/Centre for Development Studies, 1993); cited in Sellstom and Wohlgemuth, *The International Response to Conflict and Genocide*, p. 34.

52. U.S. State Department, "Rwanda Human Rights Practices, 1993," in *1993 Human Rights Report*, February 1994.

53. Timothy Longman, "Democratization and Disorder," p. 7.

54. United Nations Information Center, "United Nations Observer Mission Uganda-Rwanda," *Africa News Service*, 23 August 1993. The Center also reported that, following the signing of the Kinihira Agreement of 30 May 1993, an estimated 500,000 displaced persons were allowed to return to the demilitarized zone in northern Rwanda. Their respite was, however, temporary since the war continued, and with it the numbers of the displaced. In May 1994, Human Rights Watch estimated the number of the displaced sheltering in RPF-controlled areas at 200,000. See Human Rights Watch/Africa, *Genocide in Rwanda, April/May 1994*, vol. 6, no. 4 (May 1994) p. 8.

55. Prunier, *The Rwanda Crisis*, p. 241.

56. Africa Rights, cited in Sellstom and Wohlgemuth, *The International Response to Conflict and Genocide*, p. 45.

57. U.S. Department of State, *1993 Human Rights Report*, February 1994, section on Rwanda.

58. U.S. Department of State, *1990 Human Rights Report*, February 1991, section on Rwanda. For UN estimates, see, Stephen Nisbet, "60,000 Frightened Refugees Give Burundi Little to Celebrate," Reuters, AM cycle, 2 September 1988.

59. Human Rights Watch/Africa, *Genocide in Rwanda, April/May 1994*, vol. 6, no. 4 (May 1994), p. 8. Once again, as with every other estimate of victims of political violence in Rwanda, and I would add, in Africa generally, a researcher is usually faced with a wide range of estimates. The choice he or she makes usually provides a clue to his/her predilection. On the question of the Barundi refugees in Rwanda during the 1994 genocide, I have seen three estimates, ranging from 200,000 at the outset and 80,000 two months later (Human Rights Watch) to constant estimates of 200,000 (René Lemarchand) to 400,000 (Catharine Newbury). I picked the first because it pays attention to the change in numbers as the situation deteriorated, and because the choice of the lowest available estimate from a credible source makes my point all the more forcefully and convincingly. See Lemarchand, "Rwanda: The Rationality of Genocide," p. 10, and Newbury, "Background to Genocide: Rwanda," p. 16; both in *Issue* 23, no. 2 (1995).

60. Letter of 18 November 1993 to Minister of External Affairs, cited in Africa Rights, *Rwanda: Death, Despair and Defiance*, p. 59, and in Prunier, *The Rwanda Crisis*, pp. 246–247.

61. Newbury and Newbury, "Was the Genocide in Rwanda an Ethnic Struggle?" p. 21.

62. The lower estimate comes from René Lemarchand, the higher from Gérard Prunier. See Lemarchand, "Rwanda: The Rationality of Genocide," p. 10; Prunier, *The Rwanda Crisis*, p. 243.

63. In Rwanda, it is the *Force publique* from neighboring Belgian-ruled Congo that was expected to take on the military function in the case of civil strife.

64. I am indebted to Nurrudin Farah for the insight on Somalia.

65. These events are narrated in Timothy Longman, "Anarchy and the State in Africa: Power, Democratization, and the Rwandan Catastrophe," Drake University, Des Moines, Iowa, pp. 13–14, and Newbury and Newbury, "Was the Genocide in Rwanda an Ethnic Struggle?" p. 23.

66. Christophe Mfizi, *Le réseau zéro*, open letter to the president of the MRND (Kigali: Editions Uruhimbi, July–August 1992); cited in Longman, "Anarchy and the State in Africa," p. 15.

67. Sellstrom and Wohlgemuth, *The International Response to Conflict and Genocide*, p. 40.

68. Bruce D. Jones, "Roots, Resolution and Reaction: Civil War, the Peace Process and Genocide in Rwanda," in Ali Taisier et al., eds., mimeo, Toronto, 1999, p. 20.

69. Longman, "Democratization and Disorder," p. 8.

70. Filip Reyntjens, "Recent History," in *Africa South of the Sahara, 1994* (London: Europa Publications) p. 699.

71. Prunier, *The Rwanda Crisis*, p. 163.

72. For an analysis of the agreement, see Bruce D. Jones, "Roots, Resolution and Reaction," pp. 21–23.

73. That the agreement also stipulated that no refugee who had been ten years or so out of the country could reclaim property could be treated and dismissed as small print by this same media.

74. D. Jones, "Roots, Resolution and Reaction," pp. 25, 45 (fn. 41).

75. Cited in Prunier, *The Rwanda Crisis*, p. 156.

76. Angeline Oyog, "Human Rights-Media: Voices of Hate Test Limits of Press Freedom," Inter-Press Service, 5 April 1995.

77. African Rights, *Rwanda*, p. 30.

78. Lindsey Hilsum, "Hutu Warlord Defends Child Killings," *The Observer* (London), 3 July 1994, p. 15.

79. Human Rights Watch, *Genocide in Rwanda, April/May 1994*, vol. 6, no. 4 (May 1994), p. 9.

80. More than a month into the genocide, on 11 May the Security Council finally authorized a force of 5,500 troops and enlarged its mandate "to protect displaced persons, refugees and civilians at risk." But the force failed to take off since the United States insisted that only a small force of several hundred troops take off in the first instance. The rest would be deployed only after "progress towards a new ceasefire between the RPF and the Government, the availability of resources and further review and action by the Security Council." See Human Rights Watch, *Genocide in Rwanda, April/May 1994*, vol. 6, no. 4 (May 1994), p. 10.

81. See http://www.pbs.org/wgbh/pages/frontline/shows/evil/warning/ cable.html, p. 2.

82. *Baltimore Sun*, 24 July 1994.

83. David Rieff, "Rwanda: The Big Risk," *New York Review*, 31 October 1996.

84. On Burundi, see, René Lemarchand, *Ethnic Conflict and Genocide* (New York: Woodrow Wilson Center Press and Columbia University Press, 1994).

85. "With the assassination of President Melchior Ndadaye of Burundi on 21 October 1993, genocide came to be seen increasingly by MNRD politicians as the only rational option, and compromise, along the lines of Arusha, as synonymous with political suicide. As the first Hutu president in the history of Burundi, Ndadaye's election brought to a close twenty-eight years of Tutsi hegemony. His death at the hands of an all-Tutsi army had an immediate and powerful demonstration effect on the Hutu of Rwanda. As ethnic violence swept across the country, causing some 200,000 panic-stricken Hutu to seek refuge in Rwanda, the message conveyed by Ndadaye's assassination came through clear and loud: 'Never trust the Tutsi!' " Lemarchand, "Rwanda: The Rationality of Genocide," p. 10.

86. Human Rights Watch and Fédération Internationale des Ligues des Droits de l'Homme, *Leave None to Tell the Story: Genocide in Rwanda* (New York: Human Rights Watch, 1999), pp. 55–56.

87. Robert Block, "The Tragedy of Rwanda," *New York Review*, 20 October 1994, pp. 3–8; cited in Longman, "Anarchy and the State in Africa," p. 17.

88. "With Ndadaye's death vanished what few glimmers of hope remained that Arusha might provide a viable formula for a political compromise with the RPF. Though formally committed to implement the accords, Habyarimana was fast losing his grip on the situation." Lemarchand, "Rwanda: The Rationality of Genocide," p. 10.

89. Ibid.

90. Human Rights Watch and Fédération Internationale des Ligues des Droits de l'Homme, *Leave None to Tell the Story*, p. 6.

91. Ibid., p. 7.

92. This account is based on Monique Mujawamariya, "Report of a Visit to Rwanda: September 1–22, 1994," *Issue* 23, no. 2 (1995), pp. 32–33; Prunier, *The Rwanda Crisis*, p. 244; see also African Rights, *Death, Despair and Defiance*, pp. 583–584.

In an account of massacres in two different communities in Kibuye Prefecture, Timothy Longman stresses the importance of outside force. In Buguhu, the violence was "initiated clearly from the outside": "The burgomaster, who lived some distance from Biguhu, came with a mob and with several gendarmes and gathered a few local supporters to assist." The case of Kirinda sheds more light on who these "local supporters" may be. More than a week after the killing began in Kigali, "the local Hutu elite, including the burgomaster and some church leaders, organized a mob to kill Kirinda's Tutsi." While "most local residents refused to participate in the slaughter of their neighbours," the "unemployed youth and some other residents" responded enthusiastically. A lot of the violence, most observers agree, came from the youth. See Longman, "Genocide and Socio-Political Change: Massacres in Two Rwandan Villages," *Issue* 23, no. 2 (1995), pp. 19–20.

93. Villia Jefremovas, "Acts of Human Kindness: Tutsi, Hutu and the Genocide," *Issue* 23, no. 2 (1995), p. 28.

94. Human Rights Watch/Africa, *Rwanda: A New Catastrophe?*, vol. 6, no. 12 (December 1994), pp. 6–7.

95. Rev. Kodjo Ankrah, Church World Action, interview, Kigali, 19 July 1995.

96. François Nsamsuwera, interview, Arusha, 6 September 1995.

97. Faustin, interview, Kigali, 22 July 1995.

98. Professor Marie-Thérèse Kampire, interview, Butare, 21 July 1995.

99. Mectile Kantarama, interview, Kigali, 18 December 1995.

100. McDowell, "342 Women Implicated in Genocide."

101. Calixte Karake, interview, Ntarama, 22 July 1995.

102. A. Inyumba, interview, Kigali, 20 July 1995.

103. Peter Maser, "Crimes of the Children," *The Gazette* (Montreal), 23 September 1995.

104. Prunier, *The Rwanda Crisis*, p. 244; see African Rights, p. 250. That the Church was a bystander is a view comfortably adopted by many of its responsible persons. Even those who have dared to face the role of the Church through individual cases of complicity and direct involvement, like Jean Carbonnarre, honorary president of the Paris-based NGO Survie, tend to take refuge in this notion when it comes to underlining the role of the Church: "The danger does not come just from those who commit evil, but from those who watch and say nothing. The Church in Rwanda mostly stood silent, watching." The quote is cited in "Rwanda: Priests Who Failed Moral Test Face Another Kind of Trial," Inter-Press Service, Paris, 17 May 1995.

105. Raymond Bonner, "Clergy in Rwanda Is Accused of Abetting Atrocities," *New York Times*, 7 July 1995, sec. A, p. 3.

106. Alan Zarembo, "The Church's Shameful Acts," *Houston Chronicle*, 29 January 1995, p. 22.

107. Leslie Scrivener, "Rage and Religion: What Role Did the Churches Play in Rwanda's Genocide?" *Toronto Star*, 5 August 1995.

108. Bonner, "Clergy in Rwanda Is Accused of Abetting Atrocities."

109. Sellstom and Wohlgemuth, *The International Response to Conflict and Genocide*, pp. 49–50.

110. Cited in "Rwanda: Priests Who Failed Moral Test Face Another Kind of Trial."

111. See African Rights, pp. 381–385; Bonner, "Clergy in Rwanda is Accused of Abetting Atrocities."

112. See http://www.uimondo.org/AfricanRights/html/pope_en.html, p. 7.

113. "Human Rights Group Condemns UN in Rwanda," *British Medical Journal* 309 (8 October 1994), p. 895.

114. African Rights, "Dr. Sosthene Munyemana, the Butcher of Tumba, at Liberty in France," *Witness to Genocide*, issue 2, February 1996, pp. 3–4.

115. Patrick de Saint-Exupéry, "Rwanda: Les assassins racontent leurs massacres," in François-Xavier Verschave, *Complicité de génocide? La politique de la France au Rwanda* (Paris: La Découverte, 1994); cited in Prunier, *The Rwanda Crisis*, pp. 254–255.

116. African Rights, "Presumption of Innocence: The Case against Innocent Mazimpaka," *Witness to Genocide*, issue 3, May 1996.

117. Rakiya Omaar, "Introduction," in African Rights, "Burying the Truth in the Name of 'Human Rights': Antoine Sibomana and His Supporters," *Witness to Genocide*, issue 7, May 1997, p. 2.

118. See, for example, African Rights, *Death, Despair and Defiance*, rev. ed. (London, 1995); Fergal Keene, *Season of Blood: A Rwandan Journey* (London: Viking, 1995).

119. Carl Schmitt, *The Concept of the Political* (Chicago: University of Chicago Press, 1996).

CHAPTER EIGHT
TUTSI POWER IN RWANDA AND THE CITIZENSHIP
CRISIS IN EASTERN CONGO

1. The interviews that I quote in this chapter were gathered by a two-person mission to North and South Kivu, Kisangani and Kinshasa, undertaken in September 1997. The mission was put together by the Dakar-based Council for the Development of Social Research in Africa (CODESRIA) and comprised Professor Jacques Depelchin, then of Kinshasa, and myself. We met individuals from academic, civil society, and state organizations with a view to making sense of the rapidly expanding crisis in eastern Congo. Depelchin and I conducted most interviews together; the interpretation advanced here, though, is exclusively mine. I would like to make particular mention of Professor Arsène Kirhero (Bukavu), who gave generously of his time and knowledge in discussing the historical context of ethnic conflict in the region. The list of those interviewed can be found in the appendix.

2. Interview, Bukavu, September 1997.

3. This explanation was given to me by Professor Arsene Kirhero, Interview, Bukavu.

4. Bwisha in Ruchuru was a part of the precolonial Rwandan kingdom. It is said that a Tutsi chief governed it before colonial rule and paid homage to the Mwami in the Central Kingdom. When colonial frontiers were consolidated in 1918 and Bwisha was made a part of Congo, Belgian colonialism replaced the Tutsi chief with a Hutu, Daniel Ndeze. The point of conflict in Bwisha has been whether that authority should be Tutsi (as before 1918) or Hutu (as after 1918).

5. Mararo Bucyalimwe, "Land Conflicts in Masisi, Eastern Zaire: The Impact and Aftermath of Belgian Colonial Policy (1920–1989)," Ph.D. diss., Indiana University, 1990, pp. 61–64, 74–80, 101–102, 298.

6. The missionaries of Bobandana described the situation in 1916 as follows: "We pity sincerely our beloved people, overburdened with daily corvees and requisitions in food and men. Many of them emigrate to Ufamando, three or four days from here, on order to free the corvees. Thus, entire villages suddenly disappear. Yesterday, all seemed quiet; you went there for the weekly instruction; but, during the night, all the village has found it prudent to run away when informed that the chief received a new requisition for them. Thus, six villages are abandoned and already invaded by bush." Cited in Bucyalimwe, "Land Conflicts in Masisi, Eastern Zaire," pp. 127–128.

7. Ibid., pp. 135–136, 137.

8. Catharine Newbury, *The Cohesion of Oppression* (New York: Columbia University Press, 1989), pp. 143–144, 210–211.

9. Bucyalimwe, "Land Conflicts in Masisi, Eastern Zaire," p. 150.

10. Ibid., p. 301.

11. Even though the 1936 immigrants were mainly Hutu, Belgium appointed a Mututsi as chief of Gishari.

12. Bucyalimwe, "Land Conflicts in Masisi, Eastern Zaire," p. 6.

13. Ibid., pp. 218–219.

14. Koen Vlassenroot, "The Promise of Ethnic Conflict: Militarisation and Enclave-Formation in South Kivu," in Didier Goyvaerts, ed., *Conflict and Ethnicity in Central Africa* (Toyko: Institute for the Study of Languages and Cultures of Asia and Africa), pp. 62, 67–68.

15. Ibid., p. 68.

16. Two examples from the city of Kisangani illustrate this tendency. The first relates to a sociocultural center formed in 1987 by a number of the city's college-educated youth in response to the ruling party's attempt to monopolize cultural activities for young people. The focal point of the center's cultural activities was to "denounce injustice through theater." But the center had found it difficult to work openly. This changed with the CNS. When the CNS was suspended in 1992, members of the center joined other youth in public protest. Many were arrested. That provided the impulse for further organization: members of the centre created *Les Amis de Nelson Mandela* as a human rights organization on 6 October 1992 and launched a publication, *Liberté*. "We felt in the National Conference we had found the medium of our emancipation," concluded one of the youthful organizers of *Les Amis*.

Another group that followed in the wake of the CNS was Groupe Lotus, O.N.G. des Droits de l'Homme et du Développement. The president of the group explained the circumstances of its formation in April 1992:

Many of us used to meet from 1991 to discuss what was going on in the country. Then, we would meet at the parish meeting hall. The population of Kisangani and surrounding areas had very little idea of their rights. The other characteristic peculiar of Kisangani was a wait and see attitude, that problems will somehow be solved from the outside. This was reinforced by the fact that while people were following the Sovereign National Conference on television, few had any idea of what it was all about. This is how the Lotus Group was born. There were 12 of us and we decided to call ourselves LOTUS. We wanted to convey the idea of unity of diversity by reference to the flower lotus—since we came from many different environments. There was a biologist amongst us whose thesis supervisor was from India and who suggested that in Indian culture, whenever there is disagreement and difference, they bring out the lotus flower!

Like many other civil society organisations, the Lotus Group concentrated on recruiting from amongst the educated youth. They concentrated on recruiting those young people above the age of 21 with a secondary education at the minimum. Their activities were carried out in Kiswahili and Lingala. Once a member was accepted, they would go through a training workshop, focusing on both the objectives of the group and a social analysis of Congo, with a specific emphasis on human rights issues. The group had political scientists, medical doctors, and economists amongst its members, but not lawyers and jurists, who tended to gravitate to Les Amis. Their activities were concentrated around publications, lobbying, and concrete support to people whose rights had been violated. Anyone approaching the group with a rights violation would be assigned two individuals to accompany them through all legal and related procedures.
See Mahmood Mamdani, "Kivu, 1997: An Essay on Citizenship and the State Crises in Africa," CODESRIA, 1998, mimeo.

17. Historically, the population in the *collectivité* has been Hutu but the chief a Mututsi. This changed in 1994, when Mobutu decided to play with the Hutu; he replaced the Mututsi chief with a Hutu chief.

18. Both explanations are given in Newbury, *The Cohesion of Oppression*, pp. 48–49, 59. Also see Jan Vansina, *L'Evolution du royaume Rwanda des origines à 1900* (Brussels: Arsom, 1962), p. 90; Jacques J. Maquet, "Les pasteurs de l'Itombwe," *Science et Nature* 8 (1955): 3–12.

19. Newbury, *The Cohesion of Oppression*, pp. 161–164.

20. Professor Arsène Kirhero, interview, Bukavu, September 1997.

21. Vlassenroot, "The Promise of Ethnic Conflict," p. 73.

22. Senzeyi Ryamukuru, former president, UMOJA, interview, Goma, September 1997.

23. Arsène Kirhero (Bukavu) and Bakashi (Goma), interviews, September 1997.

24. Father Piere Cobambo, interview, Bukavu, September 1997.

25. Vlassenroot, "The Promise of Ethnic Conflict," p. 79.

26. Arsene Kirhero, interview, Bukavu, September 1997.

27. Interview, Bukavu, September 1997.

28. Lt.-Col. James Kabarebe, interview, Kigali, 3 January 1996.

29. Crawford Young, ed., "Rebellion and the Congo," in Robert Rotberg, *Rebellion in Black Africa* (London: Oxford University Press, 1971), p. 225.

30. Vlassenroot, "The Promise of Ethnic Conflict," p. 96.

31. Laurent Kabila, interview, Goma, 3 January 1996.

32. *Maji* (pronounced *Mayi* in Kivu) means water in Kiswahili, referring to the powers claimed for ritually blessed water to render all those on whom it is sprinkled immune to the life-destroying effect of bullets.

33. Laurent Kabila, interview, Goma, 3 January 1996.

34. Bakashi, interview, Goma, September 1997.

35. Interview, Kinshasa, September 1997.

36. James Kabarebe, interview, Kinshasa, September 1997.

CONCLUSION
POLITICAL REFORM AFTER GENOCIDE

1. The call for separate Hutu and Tutsi homelands was previously identified with extreme tendencies—such as Tutsi Power of President Bagaza in Burundi or Hutu Power of the Interahamwe in Rwanda—but seemed to get broader and more mainstream support after the Kibeho massacre in Rwanda. To take a few examples, President Moi of Kenya said, "One way of solving the problem would be for all the Hutus to settle in Burundi and all the Tutsis in Rwanda, or vice versa." Agence France Press, 29 April 1995. The same agency also reported Assistant Secretary of State George Moose of the United States confirming that the U.S. was indeed considering the possibility of a Hutuland and a Tutsiland.

2. I. Inyumba, interview, Kigali, 20 July 1995.

3. Patrick Mazimpaka, interview, Kigali, 11 July 1997; Philip Gourevitch cites several estimates, from a million (Vice-President Kagame) to three million (Dusaidi, aide to the vice-president). See Philip Gourevitch, *We wish to inform you that tomorrow we will be killed with our families: Stories from Rwanda* (New York: Farrar, Straus, and Giroux, 1998), p. 244.

4. Saskia Van Hoyweghen, "The Rwandan Villagisation Programme: Resettlement or Reconstruction?" in Didier Goyvaerts, *Conflict and Ethnicity in Central Africa* (Tokyo: Institute for the Study of Languages and Cultures of Asia and Africa, 2000), p. 212.

5. Ibid.

6. Filip Reyntjens writes:
The tutsisation of the state machinery was further reaffirmed. Even while the government, the country's international 'business card' has grosso modo equal representation (14 Hutu, 12 Tutsi, 1 unidentified), out of the 18 general secretaries identified, 14 are Tutsi from the RPF; with the exception of 2 ministers, all the non-RPF ministers are flanked by a general secretary from the RPF. While the National Assembly already has a Tutsi majority, it continues to be subject to purges. . . . Out of the twelve prefects, nine are Tutsi, two Hutu and one position is vacant. The number of Tutsi mayors is established to be over 80%. Eleven of the fourteen ambassadors are Tutsi, with nine coming from the ranks of the RPF. Among the fourteen officers comprising the high command of the army and gendarmerie, there is only one Hutu. . . . The tutsisation of the judiciary

has been reinforced in a very pronounced manner after the suspension of six Hutu judges of the *Cour de Cassation* and the Council of State on March 24, 1998; they were later dismissed.
See Filip Reyntjens, *Talking or Fighting? Political Evaluation in Rwanda and Burundi, 1998–99*, Current African Issues, no. 21 (Nordiska Afrikainstitutet, 1999), pp. 5, 15.

7. "At the end of 1998, 125,028 persons remained officially detained, though the actual number is probably much higher. According to the Rwandan government, in 1998 several thousand detainees died as a result of AIDS, malnutrition, dysentery and typhus. During the month of November 1998, 400 prisoners died from typhus in the Rilima prison alone." See ibid., p. 14.

8. This is the sense in which Abraham Lincoln used the term in the aftermath of the Civil War in the United States. Though dipped in religious terminology, he called for survivors to be born again, to reconcile. See Robert Meister, "Forgiving and Forgetting," in Carla Hesse and Robert Post, eds., *Human Rights in Political Transitions: Gettysburg to Bosnia* (New York: Zone Books, 1999), pp. 135–176.

9. See Mahmood Mamdani, "The Truth According to the TRC," in Ifi Amadiume and Abdullahi An-Nai'im, eds., *The Politics of Memory: Truth, Healing and Social Justice* (London: Zed Press, 2000).

10. This, indeed, is Basil Davidson's solution to Africa's political problems. See Davidson, *The Black Man's Burden: Africa and the Curse of the Nation-State* (New York: Times Books, 1992).

11. See Mahmood Mamdani, *Citizen and Subject: Contemporary Africa and the Legacy of Late Colonialism* (Princeton: Princeton University Press, 1996).

Bibliography

Administration Coloniale, Ruanda-Urundi. *Report administratif.* Brussels, 1925.

Africa Direct. *Submission to the United Nations Tribunal on Rwanda.* Appendix One: "The Making of War." London, 1996.

Africa News Report, 12 September 1994.

African Rights. *Rwanda: Death, Despair and Defiance.* Rev. ed. London, 1995.

———. "Dr. Sosthene Munyemana, the Butcher of Tumba, at Liberty in France." *Witness to Genocide,* issue 2, February 1996.

———. "Presumption of Innocence: The Case against Innocent Mazimpaka." *Witness to Genocide,* issue 3, May 1996.

Amaza, Major Ondonga Ari. "Rwanda and Uganda: Post-War Prospects for Regional Peace and Security." Paper presented to CODESRIA Conference on Academic Freedom, Social Research and Conflict Resolution in the Countries of the Great Lakes, 4–7 September 1995, Arusha, Tanzania.

Amin, Samir. *Accumulation on a World Scale: A Critique of the Theory of Underdevelopment.* New York: Monthly Review Press, 1974.

Amselle, Jean-Loup, and Elikia M'bokolo, eds. *Au coeur de l'ethnie: Ethnies, tribalisme et état en Afrique.* Paris: La Découverte, 1985.

Arendt, Hannah. *The Origins of Totalitarianism.* New York: Harcourt Brace, 1975.

Bart, F. *Montagnes d'Afrique, terres paysannes: Le cas du Rwanda.* Bordeaux: Presses Universitaires de Bordeaux, 1993.

Bayoumi, R.A.L., N. Saha, A. S. Salih, A. E. Bekkar, and G. Flatz. "Distribution of the Lactose Phenotype in the Population of the Democratic Republic of the Sudan." *Human Genetics* 57 (1981): 279–281.

Bayoumi, R.A.L., S. D. Flatz, W. Kuhnow, and G. Flatz. "Beja and Nilotes: Nomadic Pastoralist Groups in the Sudan with Opposite Distributions of the Adult Lactose Phenotypes." *Amer. J. of Physical Anthropology* 58 (1982): 173–178.

Bazaara, Nyangabyaki. "Ugandan Politics and the Crisis of Rwandese Refugees and Immigrants." Paper presented to the 10th All-African Student Conference, Temple University, Philadelphia, 16–18 May 1997.

Belgian Congo and Ruanda-Urundi Information and Public Relations Office. *Ruanda Urundi* 60, no. 4, September.

Berkeley, Bill. "Sounds of Violence." *New Republic,* 22 August 1994.

Bernal, Martin. *Black Athena: The Afroasiatic Roots of Classical Civilization.* Vol. 1: *The Fabrication of Ancient Greece, 1785–1985.* New York: Vintage, 1991.

Bessell, M. J. "Nyabingi." *Uganda Journal* 6 (1938–39).

Bézy, F. *Rwanda: Bilan socio-économique d'un régime, 1962–1989.* Louvain: Inst. d'étude des pays en développement, Université de Louvain-la-Neuve, 1990.

Bizimungu, H. E. Pasteur. President of the Republic of Rwanda, Opening Speech, International Conference on Genocide, Impunity, and Accountability, Kigali, 1–5 November 1995.

Block, Robert. "The Tragedy of Rwanda." *New York Review,* 20 October 1994.

Bonner, Raymond. "Clergy in Rwanda Is Accused of Abetting Atrocities." *New York Times,* 7 July 1995, sec. A, p. 3.

Botte, Roger. "Rwanda and Burundi, 1889–1930: Chronology of a Slow Assassination, Part 1." *International Journal of African Historical Studies* 18, no. 1 (1985): 53–91.

———. "Rwanda and Burundi, 1889–1930—Chronology of a Slow Assassination, Part 2. *International Journal of African Historical Studies* 18, no. 2 (1985): 289–314.

Brasseur, D., P. Goyens, and H. L. Vis. "Some Aspects of Protein-Energy Malnutrition in the Highlands of Central Africa." In R. E. Eeckels, O. Ransome-Kuti, and C. C. Kroonenberg, eds., *Child Health in the Tropics,* pp. 167–178. The Hague: Martinus Nijhoff, 1985.

Bright, Martin. "Rwanda: Blurred Roots of Conflict." *The Guardian* (London), 9 May 1994, p. E13.

Bucyalimwe, Mararo. "Land Conflicts in Masisi, Eastern Zaire: The Impact and Aftermath of Belgian Colonial Policy (1920–1989)." Ph.D. diss., Indiana University, 1990.

Cambrezy, L. *Le surpeuplement en question: Organisation spatiale et écologie des migrations au Rwanda.* Collection Travaux et Documents no. 182. Paris: Ed. Orstom, 1984.

Chairman (President of Uganda). National Resistance Council, Wednesday, 22 August 1990, in Parliament of Uganda, *Parliamentary Debates (Hansard),* Official Report, 4th sess., 2nd meeting, issue no. 14, 28 June–23 August 1990, Kampala.

Chatterjee, Partha. *The Partha Chatterjee Omnibus.* Delhi: Oxford University Press, 1999.

Chrétien, Jean-Pierre. "Hutu et Tutsi au Rwanda et au Burundi." In Jean-Loup Amselle and Elikia M'bokolo, eds., *Au cœur de l'ethnie: Ethnies, tribalisme et état en Afrique.* Paris: La Découverte, 1985.

———. "La crise politique Rwandaise." *Genève Afrique* 30, no. 2 (1992): 121–141.

———. *Burundi: Histoire retrouvée: 25 ans de métier d'historien en Afrique.* Paris: Karthala, 1993.

Clay, D. C. "Fighting an Uphill Battle: Demographic Pressure, the Structure of Land Holding, and Land Degradation in Rwanda." East Lansing: Department of Agricultural Economics, Michigan State University, 1993.

Clay, D., et al. "Promoting Food Security in Rwanda through Sustainable Agricultural Productivity: Meeting the Challenges of Population Pressure, Land Degradation and Poverty." Staff paper 95-08, Department of Agricultural Economics, Michigan State University, East Lansing, March 1995.

Commission of Inquiry into Government Ranching Schemes. *Report to the Government of Uganda.* Entebbe, December 1988.

Dash, Leon. "Many Rwandan Refugees Moving North in Uganda to Escape Attacks." *Washington Post,* 2 December 1983, final edition.

Davidson, Basil. *The Black Man's Burden: Africa and the Curse of the Nation-State.* New York: Times Books, 1992.

Ddungu, Expedit. "The Other Side of Land Issues in Buganda: Pastoral Crisis and the Squatter Movement in Sembabule Sub-District." Mimeo, Centre for Basic Research, Kampala, no date.

Dedering, Tilman. " 'A Certain Rigorous Treatment of all Parts of the Nation': The Annihilation of the Herero in German South West Africa, 1904." In Mark Levene and Penny Roberts, eds., *The Massacre in History,* pp. 204–222. New York: Berghahn Books, 1999.

Deng, Francis M. "An African Reflects on Race and Ethnicity." *Brookings Review* 13, no. 3 (1995).

Denon, V. *Travels in Upper and Lower Egypt.* London, 1903.

Des Forges, Alison. "Kings without Crowns: The White Fathers in Rwanda." In D. F. McCall, N. R. Bennett, and J. Butler, eds., *Eastern African History.* New York: Praeger, 1969.

———. " 'The Drum Is Greater than the Shout': The 1912 Rebellion in Northern Rwanda." In Donald Crummey, ed., *Banditry, Rebellion and Social Protest in Africa.* London: James Currey, 1986.

———. "The Ideology of Genocide." *Issue* 23, no. 2 (1995).

———. *"Leave None to Tell the Story": Genocide in Rwanda.* New York: Human Rights Watch, 1999.

d'Hertefelt, M. "The Rwanda of Rwanda." In J. L. Gibbs, ed., *Peoples of Africa.* New York: Holt, Reinhart and Winston, 1965.

———. *Les clans du Rwanda ancien.* Tervuren: MRAC, 1971.

Diller, L. "Human Rights Group Condemns UN in Rwanda." *British Medical Journal* 309 (8 October 1994): 895.

Diop, Cheikh Anta. *The African Origin of Civilization: Myth of Reality.* Westport: Lawrence Hill, 1974.

Doornbos, Martin R., and Michael F. Lofchie. "Ranching and Scheming: A Case Study of the Ankole Ranching Scheme." In Michael F. Lofchie, ed., *The State of the Nations: Constraints on Development in Independent Africa.* Berkeley: University of California Press, 1971.

Dorsey, L. *Historical Dictionary of Rwanda.* London: Scarecrow Press, 1994.

Drechsler, Horst. *"Let Us Die Fighting": The Struggle of the Herero and the Nama against German Imperialism (1884–1915).* London: Zed Press, 1980.

Exoffier, Laurent, Beatrice Pellegrini, Alicia Sanchez-Mazas, Christian Simon, and Andre Langaney. "Genetics and History of Sub-Saharan Africa." *Yearbook of Physical Anthropology* 30 (1987): 151–194.

Fanon, Frantz. *The Wretched of the Earth*. London: Penguin, 1967.

Flatz, Gebhard. "Genetics of Lactose Digestion in Humans." *Advances in Human Genetics* 1 (1987): 1–77.

Fleming, Neil. "Rwanda and Burundi—Africa's Northern Ireland?" United Press International, BC Cycle, Internet, 7 October 1990.

Fortt, J. M. "The Distribution of the Immigrant and the Ganda Population within Buganda." In Audrey Richards, ed., *Economic Development and Tribal Change: A Study of Immigrant Labour in Buganda*, pp. 77–118. Nairobi: Oxford University Press, 1973.

Franche, Dominique. "There's Only One Ethnic Group in Rwanda: Rwandan." *Le Monde Diplomatique/Guardian Weekly*, 24 November 1996.

Gasarasi, Charles P. "The Mass Naturalization and Further Integration of Rwandese Refugees in Tanzania: Process, Problems and Prospects." *Journal of Refugee Studies* (Oxford) 3, no. 2, (1990).

Gatwa, Tharcisse. "The Churches and Ethnic Ideology in the Rwandan Crises (1900–1994)." Ph.D. diss., University of Edinburgh, 1998.

Gewald, Jan-Bart. *Herero Heroes: A Socio-Political History of the Herero of Namibia, 1890–1923*. Oxford: James Currey, 1999.

Gossett, T. F. *Race—the History of an Idea in America*. New York: Oxford University Press, 1997.

Gourevitch, Philip. "After the Genocide." *New Yorker*, 18 December 1995.

———. *We wish to inform you that tomorrow we will be killed with our families: Stories from Rwanda*. New York: Farrar, Straus, and Giroux, 1998.

Goyvaerts, Didier. *Conflict and Ethnicity in Central Africa*, p. 194, fn. 28. Tokyo: Institute for the Study of Languages and Cultures of Asia and Africa, Tokyo University of Foreign Studies, 2000.

Graves, R., and R. Patai. *Hebrew Myths: The Book of Genesis*. New York: Doubleday, 1964.

Greene, J. "The American Debate on the Negro's Place in Nature, 1780–1815." *Journal of History of Ideas* 15 (1954): 384.

Grosse, Scott. "The Roots of Conflict and State Failure in Rwanda: The Political Exacerbation of Social Cleavages in a Context of Growing Resource Scarcity." School of Public Health, University of Michigan, Ann Arbor, Mimeo, 15 November 1994.

———. "More People, More Trouble: Population Growth and Agricultural Change in Rwanda." School of Public Health, University of Michigan, Ann Arbor, *manuscript*, prepared for the Africa Bureau, U.S. Agency for International Development, revised draft, 16 November 1994.

Haguma, Captain Eugene M. "The Rwandese Crisis: A Political Economy of Genocide." Symposium on Interface, Dialogue, and Co-Operation between

Government and NGO's for Popular Participation in National Reconstruction, Conflict and Psycho-Social Trauma Management. Organized jointly by Africa Humanitarian Action and the UN Economic Commission for Africa, Kigali, 28 February 1995.

Hannsen, A. *Le désenchantement de la coopération.* Paris: L'Harmattan, 1989.

Hegel, G.F.W. *The Philosophy of Right.* Amherst, N.Y.: Prometheus Books.

———. "Introduction: Reason in History." in *Lectures on the Philosophy of World History,* trans. from the German edition of Johannes Hoffmeister by H. B. Nisbet. London: Cambridge University Press, 1975 (Hegel's second draft is dated 1830).

———. *The Philosophy of History.* Trans. J. Sibree. New York: Dover, 1956.

Heusch, Luc de. *Rwanda: Tableau d'une monarchie féodale.* Brussels, 1954 (film produced in cooperation with Jacques Maquet).

———. "Rwanda: Responsibilities for Genocide." *Anthropology Today* 11, no. 4 (August 1995).

Hiernaux, Jean. "Heredity and Environment: Their Influence on Human Morphology. A Comparison of Two Independent Lines of Study." *American Journal of Physical Anthropology* 21 (1963): 579–590.

———. *La croissance des écoliers rwandais.* Brussels: Académie Royale des Sciences d'Outre-Mer, 1965.

———. *The People of Africa.* New York: Charles Scribner's Sons, 1974.

Hilsum, Lindsey. "Hutu Warlord Defends Child Killings." *The Observer* (London), 3 July 1994.

Hopkins, Elizabeth. "The Nyabingi Cult of Southwestern Uganda." In Robert I. Rotberg, ed., *Rebellion in Black Africa.* London: Oxford University Press, 1971.

———. "Review of Catharine Newbury, *The Cohesion of Oppression: Clientship and Ethnicity in Rwanda 1860–1960.*" *Contemporary Sociology* 20, nos. 1–3 (1991): 365–366.

Human Rights Watch Arms Project. *Arming Rwanda: The Arms Trade and Human Rights Abuses in the Rwandan War.* Vol. 6, issue 1, January 1994, Appendix.

Human Rights Watch/Africa. *Genocide in Rwanda, April/May 1994.* Vol. 6, no. 4, May 1994.

———. *Rwanda: A New Catastrophe?* Vol. 6, no. 12, December 1994, p. 7.

Human Rights Watch and Fédération Internationale des Ligues des Droits de l'Homme. *Leave None to Tell the Story: Genocide in Rwanda.* London and New York: Human Rights Watch; and Paris: Fédération Internationale des Ligues des Droits de l'Homme, 1999.

Huntington, Samuel. *The Clash of Civilizations and the Remaking of World Order.* New York: Simon and Schuster, 1996.

Ibrahim, Jibrin. "The Narcissism of Minor Difference and the Rise of Genocidal Tendencies in Africa: Lessons from Rwanda and Burundi." Paper presented to CODESRIA, 8th General Assembly, 26 June–2 July 1995.

International Conference on Genocide, Impunity and Accountability. Final report, Kigali, 1–5 November 1995.

Itandala, Buluda. "Ethnicity versus Nationalism in Rwanda." Paper presented at the Conference on Academic Freedom, Social Research, and Conflict Resolution in the Countries of the Great Lakes, organized by CODESRIA in collaboration with the University of Dar-es-Salaam and the Centre for Basic Research (Kampala), Arusha, Tanzania, 4–7 September 1995.

Jefremovas, Villia. "Acts of Human Kindness: Tutsi, Hutu and the Genocide." *Issue* 23, no. 2 (1995).

Jere-Malanda, Regina. "The Tribe Germany Wants to Forget." *New African* (London), no. 383 (March 2000): 16–21.

Jones, Bruce D. "Roots, Resolution and Reaction: Civil War, the Peace Process and Genocide in Rwanda." Mimeo, Toronto, 1999.

Kagabo, J., and C. Vidal. "L'extermination des Rwandais Tutsi." *Cahiers d'études Africaines* 34, no. 4 (1994) 538.

Kagame, Alexis. *Un abrégé de l'ethno-histoire du Rwanda.* 2 vols. Collection "Muntu," 3–4 Butare: Editions Universitaires du Rwanda, 1972–75.

Keene, Fergal. *Season of Blood: A Rwandan Journey.* London: Viking, 1995.

King, M. "Rwanda, Malthus and Medicus Mundi." *Medicus Mundi Bulletin*, no. 54 (August 1994).

Lacger, Louis de. *Ruanda.* Kigali: Kabgayi, 1961.

Lamb, David. "Rwanda Tragedy May Reflect Larger Africa Problem." *Dallas Morning News*, 12 June 1994, p. 21A.

Lema, Antoine. *Africa Divided: The Creation of "Ethnic Groups."* Lund Dissertations in Sociology 6. Lund, Sweden: Lund University Press, 1993.

Lemarchand, René. *Rwanda and Burundi.* New York: Praeger, 1970.

———. "Recent History." In section on "Rwanda," in *Africa South of the Sahara, 1974.* London: Europa Publications, 1975.

———. "Review of Catharine Newbury, *The Cohesion of Oppression: Clientship and Ethnicity in Rwanda, 1860–1960.*" *Canadian Journal of African Studies* 24 (1990): 473–475.

———. "Rwanda: The Rationality of Genocide." *Issue* 23, no. 2 (1995), African Studies Association of USA.

Levene, M. and P. Roberts, eds. *The Massacre in History.* NY: Berghahn, 1993.

Lewis, L. A. "Terracing and Accelerated Soil Loss on Rwandan Step Lands: A Preliminary Investigation of the Implications of Human Activities Affecting Soil Movement." *Land Degradation and Rehabilitation* 3 (1992): 241–246.

Leys, Colin. *Under-development in Kenya.* London: Heinemann.

Linden, Ian. *Church and Revolution in Rwanda.* Manchester: Manchester University Press, 1977.

Lofchie, Michael. *Zanzibar: Background to Revolution.* Princeton: Princeton University Press, 1965.

Longman, Timothy. "Anarchy and the State in Africa: Power, Democratization and the Rwandan Catastrophe." Mimeo, Drake University, Des Moines, Iowa, no date.

———. "Democratisation and Disorder: Political Transformation and Social Deterioration in Rwanda." *Mimeo*, Drake University, no date.

Loupais, P. "Tradition et légende des Tutsi sur la création du monde et leur etablissement au Rwanda." In *Anthropos* 3, no. 9 (1908) 1–33.

Lwanga-Lunyigo, S.L., and J. Vansina. "The Bantu-Speaking Peoples and Their Expansion." In M. El Fasi, ed., *UNESCO General History of Africa*, vol. 3. London: Heinemann, 1988.

Mafeje, Archie. "The Agrarian Revolution and the Land Question in Uganda." In Roger Leys, ed., *Dualism and Rural Development in East Africa*, p. 145. Copenhagen: Institute of Development Research, 1973.

———. "The Ideology of Tribalism." *Journal of Modern African Studies* 9, no. 2 (1971).

———. *The Theory and Ethnography of African Social Formations: The Case of the Intralacustrine Kingdoms*. Dakar: CODESRIA, 1991.

Mafeje, Archie, and A. I. Richards. "The Commercial Farmer and his Labour Supply." In A. I. Richards, Ford Sturrock, and Jean M. Fortt, eds., *Subsistence to Commercial Farming in Present-day Buganda*. Cambridge: Cambridge University Press, 1973.

Mamdani, Mahmood. *Politics and Class Formation in Uganda*. New York: Monthly Review Press, 1976.

———. *Citizen and Subject: Contemporary Africa and the Legacy of Late Colonialism*. Princeton: Princeton University Press, 1996.

———. "Babu: A Personal Tribute." *Review of African Political Economy* (London), no. 19 (1996).

———. "From Conquest to Consent Is the Basis of State Formation: Reflections on Rwanda." *New Left Review*, no. 216 (March/April 1996).

———. *Kivu, 1997: An Essay on Citizenship and the State Crises in Africa*. Mimeo, Dakar, CODESRIA, 1998.

———. "When Does a Settler Become a Native? Reflections on the Colonial Roots of Citizenship in Equatorial and South Africa." Inaugural Lecture, University of Cape Town, new series no. 208, 13 May 1998.

———. "The Truth According to the TRC." In Ifi Amadiume and Abdullahi An-Nai'im, eds., *The Politics of Memory: Truth, Healing and Social Justice*. London: Zed Press, 2000.

Mao Tse-tung. "Analysis of the Classes in Chinese Society." In *Selected Works of Mao Tse-tung*, vol. 1. Beijing: Foreign Language Press, 1967.

Maquet, Jacques J. "Les pasteurs de l'Itombwe." *Science et Nature* 8 (1955): 3–12.

————. *The Premise of Inequality in Ruanda: A Study of Political Relations in a Central African Kingdom.* London: Oxford University Press, 1961.

Marrus, Michael R. *The Holocaust in History.* New York: Meridian Penguin, 1987.

Martin, S. "Boserup Revisited: Population and Technology in Tropical African Agriculture, 1900–1940." *Journal of Imperial and Commonwealth History* 16 (October 1987): 109–123.

Marysse, S., and T. de Herdt. *L'ajustement structurel en Afrique: Les expériences du Mali et du Rwanda.* Antwerp: UFSIA/Centre for Development Studies, 1993.

Marysse, S., T. de Herdt, and E. Ndayambaje. *Rwanda: Appauvrissement et ajustement structurel.* Brussels: CEDAF/L'Harmattan, 1994.

Maser, Peter. "Crimes of the Children." *The Gazette* (Montreal), 23 September 1995.

Mazimpaka, Patrick. *Interview.* Kigali, 11 July 1997.

McDowell, Patrick. "342 Women Implicated in Genocide," *Rocky Mountain News*, Denver, Colorado, 26 September 1995, p. 30A.

Meister, Robert. *Political Identity: Thinking through Marx.* New York: Blackwell, 1991.

————. "Forgiving and Forgetting." In Carla Hesse and Robert Post, eds., *Human Rights in Political Transitions: Gettysburg to Bosnia*, pp. 135–176. New York: Zone Books, 1999.

Mfizi, Christophe. *Le réseau zéro.* Open letter to the president of the MRND. Kigali: Editions Uruhimbi, July–August 1992.

Minister for Animal Industry and Fisheries (Prof. G. Kagonyera). National Resistance Council, Wednesday, 22 August 1990, in Parliament of Uganda, *Parliamentary Debates (Hansard)*, Official Report, 4th sess., 2nd meeting, issue no. 14, 28 June–23 August 1990, Kampala.

Muhereza, Frank Emmanuel. "The Struggles for Land Rights and 1990 Squatter Uprisings in the Former Government Ranching Schemes of Uganda." Mimeo, Centre for Basic Research, Kampala, March 1998.

Mujawamariya, Monique. "Report of a Visit to Rwanda: September 1–22, 1994." *Issue* 23, no. 2 (1995).

Murray, James. "Rwanda's Bloody Roots." *New York Times*, 3 September 1994.

Museveni, H. E. Yoweri Kaguta. President of the Republic of Uganda, Speech on "The Background to the Situation in the Great Lakes." Harare, Zimbabwe, 9 August 1998.

Muvala, F. *Introduction à l'histoire de l'evangélisation.* Kigali: Pallotti Presse, 1990.

National Commission of Inquiry into Local Government. Report, Entebbe, Uganda, 1986.

Newbury, Catharine. *The Cohesion of Oppression: Clientship and Ethnicity in Rwanda, 1860–1960.* New York: Columbia University Press, 1989.

————. "Ubureetwa and Thangata: Catalysts to Peasant Political Consciousness in Rwanda and Malawi." *Canadian Journal of African Studies* 14, no. 1 (1980).

————. "Ethnicity in Rwanda: The Case of Kinyage." *Africa* 48, no. 1 (1978).

Newbury, Catharine, and David S. Newbury. "Was the Genocide in Rwanda an Ethnic Struggle?" Mimeo, University of North Carolina–Chapel Hill.

————. "Identity, Genocide and Reconstruction in Rwanda." Paper presented at the conference "Les racines de la violence dans la région des Grands-Lacs," European Parliament, Brussels, 12–13 January 1995.

Newbury, David S. "The Invention of Rwanda: The Alchemy of Ethnicity." Mimeo, University of North Carolina–Chapel Hill.

————. "The Clans of Rwanda: An Historical Hypothesis." *Africa* 50, no. 4 (1980).

————. "Trick Cyclists? Recontextualizing Rwandan Domestic Chronology." *History in Africa* 21 (1994): 191–217.

————. " 'Bunyabungo': The Western Rwandan Frontier, c. 1750–1850." In Igor Kopytoff, ed., *The African Frontier: The Reproduction of Traditional African Societies*. Bloomington: Indiana University Press, 1987.

Nisbet, Stephen. "60,000 Frightened Refugees Give Burundi Little to Celebrate." Reuters, AM cycle, 2 September 1988.

Nkundabagenzi, F. *Rwanda Politique, 1958–1960*. Brussels: CRISP, 1961.

Nkurikiyimfura, Jean-Népomucene. *Le gros bétail et la société rwandaise: Evolution historique: Des XIIe–XIVe siècles à 1958*. Paris: L'Harmattan, 1994.

Nzisabira, J. *Accumulation du peuplement rural et ajustements agro-pastoraux au Rwanda*. Cahiers du CIDEP no. 1. Louvain-la-Neuve: CIDEP, 1989.

Ogot, B.A. "The Great Lakes Region." In D. T. Niane, ed., *UNESCO General History of Africa*, vol. 4. London: Heinemann, 1988.

Omaar, Rakiya. "Introduction." In African Rights, "Burying the Truth in the Name of 'Human Rights': Antoine Sibomana and His Supporters." *Witness to Genocide*, issue 7, May 1997.

Onyango-Obbo, Charles. "Inside Rebel-Controlled Rwanda." Africa News Service, 26 April 1993.

Oyog, Angeline. "Human Rights-Media: Voices of Hate Test Limits of Press Freedom." Inter-Press Service, 5 April 1995.

Pagès, A. *Au Rwanda, sur le bord du Lac Kivu (Congo Belge): Un royaume Hamite au centre de l'Afrique*. Brussels: IRCB, 1933.

Patterson, J. "Rwandan Refugees." *Nature* 373, no. 6511 (19 January 1995).

Philips, J.E.T. "The Nyabingi: An Anti-European Secret Society in Africa." *Congo* 1 (1928).

Plaut, Martin. "Rwanda—Looking beyond the Slaughter." *The World Today* 50, no. 8–9 (1994).

Postan, Cynthia. "Changes in the Immigrant Population in Buganda, 1948–59." In M. Audrey I. Richards, *Economic Development and Tribal Change: A Study of Immigrant Labour in Buganda*, appendix F. table 8, p. 307. Nairobi: Oxford University Press, 1973.

Pottier, Johan. "Review of Catharine Newbury, *The Cohesion of Oppression: Clientship and Ethnicity in Rwanda, 1860–1960.*" *Journal of Peasant Studies* 18, issue 2, (1991): 346–347.

Powesland, G. F. "History of the Migration in Uganda." In M. Audrey I. Richards, ed., *Economic Development and Tribal Change: A Study of Immigrant Labour in Buganda.* Nairobi: Oxford University Press, 1973.

Press, Robert M. "Escape from Kigali: Odyssey of a Hutu Family." *Christian Science Monitor*, 14 November 1994.

Prunier, Gérard. "Elements pour une histoire du Front Patriotique Rwandais." *Politique Africaine* 51 (October 1993): 121–138.

———. *The Rwanda Crisis: History of a Genocide, 1959–1994.* London: Hurst & Co., 1995.

Reed, William Cyrus. "Exile, Reform and the Rise of the Rwandan Patriotic Front." In *Journal of Modern African Studies* 34, no. 3 (1996).

———. "The Rwandan Patriotic Front: Politics and Development in Rwanda." *Issue* 23, no. 2 (1995).

Rennie, J. K. "The Precolonial Kingdom of Rwanda: A Reinterpretation." *Transafrican Journal of History* 2, no. 2 (1972).

Report of the International Commission of Investigation on Human Rights Violations in Rwanda since October 1, 1990. March 1993, Geneva.

Reyntjens, Filip. *Pouvoir et droit au Rwanda.* Musée Royal de l'Afrique Centrale, Annales—Serie—80—Sciences Humaines—no. 117, Tervuren, 1985.

———. "Démocratisation et conflits ethniques au Rwanda et au Burundi." *Cahiers Africains—Afrika Studies* 4–5 (1993): 209–227.

———. "Sujets d'inquiétude au Rwanda, en Octobre 1994." *Dialogue*, no. 179: 3–14.

———. *L'Afrique des Grands Lacs en crise: Rwanda, Burundi, 1988–1994.* Paris: Karthala, 1994.

———. *Talking or Fighting? Political Evaluation in Rwanda and Burundi, 1998–99.* Nordiska Afrikainstitutet, 1999, Current African Issues, no. 21.

Richards, M. Audrey, ed. *Economic Development and Tribal Change, A Study of Immigrant Labour in Buganda.* Nairobi: Oxford University Press, 1973.

———. "The Assimilation of the Immigrants." In M. Audrey I. Richards, ed., *Economic Development and Tribal Change: A Study of Immigrant Labour in Buganda.* Nairobi: Oxford University Press, 1973.

Rieff, David. "Rwanda: The Big Risk." *New York Review*, 31 October 1996.

Rodney, Walter. *How Europe Underdeveloped Africa.* Dar-es-Salaam: Tanzania Publishing House, 1971.

Report Administration Coloniale. *Ruanda-Urundi*, 1927.

Rotberg, Robert, ed. *Rebellion in Black Africa.* London: Oxford Uiversity Press, 1971.

Rutanga, Murindwa. "The Agrarian Crisis and Peasant Struggles in Kigezi, 1910–1995." Ph.D. diss., Jadavpur University, Calcutta, 1999.

"Rwanda: Priests Who Failed Moral Test Face Another Kind of Trial." Final report, Kigali, 1–5 November 1995.

Saint-Exupéry, Patrick de. "Rwanda: Les assassins racontent leurs massacres." In François-Xavier Verschave, *Complicité de génocide? La politique de la France au Rwanda*. Paris: La Découverte, 1994.

Sanders, Edith R. "The Hamitic Hypothesis: Its Origin and Functions in Time Perspective." *Journal of African History* 10, no. 4 (1969).

Schmitt, Carl. *The Concept of the Political*. Trans. and with an introduction by George Schwab. Chicago: University of Chicago Press, 1996.

Schoenbrun, David Lee. *A Green Place, A Good Place Agrarian Change, Gender, and Social Identity in the Great Lakes Region to the 15th Century*. Kampala: Fountain, 1998.

———. "Cattle Herds and Banana Gardens: The Historical Geography of the Western Great Lakes Region." *African Archeology Review* 11, (1993): 41–75.

Scott, David. *Refashioning Futures*. Princeton: Princeton University Press, 1998.

Scrivener, Leslie. "Rage and Religion: What Role Did the Churches Play in Rwanda's Genocide?" *Toronto Star*, 5 August 1995.

Seligman, Charles Gabriel. *Races of Africa*, 4th ed. London: Oxford University Press, 1966.

Sellstom, Tor, and Lennart Wohlgemuth. *The International Response to Conflict and Genocide: Lessons from the Rwanda Experience*, Study 1, *Historical Perspective: Some Explanatory Factors*. Uppsala, Sweden: Nordic Africa Institute, 1997.

Shields, Todd. "Invasion Stirs Tribal Tension in Rwanda." *Washington Post*, 13 October 1990.

Shivji, Issa. *Silent Class Struggle*. Dar-es-Salaam: Tanzania Publishing House, 1973.

———. *Class Struggles in Tanzania*. Dar-es-Salaam: Tanzania Publishing House, 1976.

Smith, Charles David. "The Geopolitics of Rwandan Settlement: Uganda and Tanzania." *Issue* 23, no. 2 (1995): 54–57.

Speke, J. H. *Journal of the Discovery of the Source of the Nile*. New York: Harper and Brothers, 1864.

Stalin, Joseph. *Marxism and the National Question: Selected Writings and Speeches*. New York: International Publishers, 1942.

———. *The Essential Stalin*. Ed. Bruce Franklin. London: Croom Helm, 1973.

Takeuchi, Shinichi. "Hutu and Tutsi: A Note on Group Formation in Pre-colonial Rwanda." In Didier Goyvaerts, ed., *Conflict and Ethnicity in Central Africa*. Tokyo: Institute for the Study of Languages and Cultures of Asia and Africa, pp. 190–191, appendix 1, Tokyo University of Foreign Studies, 2000.

Theroux, Paul. *Sir Vidia's Shadow: A Friendship Across Five Continents*. New York: Houghton Mifflin, 1998.

Tung, Shao. "Rwanda Takes on New Look." Xinhua General Overseas News Service, 8 June 1978, item no. 060728.

United Nations Commission of Experts Established Pursuant to Security Council Resolution 935 (1994) on Rwanda. *Final Report.* Geneva, 25 November 1994.

United Nations Information Center. "United Nations Observer Mission Uganda-Rwanda." Africa News Service, 23 August 1993.

U.S. Department of State. *1990 Human Rights Report,* 1 February 1991, section on Rwanda.

———. *1993 Human Rights Report,* February 1994, section on Rwanda.

Uvin, Peter. "Tragedy in Rwanda: The Political Ecology of Conflict." *Environment,* April 1996.

———. *Aiding Violence: The Development Enterprise in Africa.* West Hartford, Conn.: Kumarian Press, 1998.

Uwezeyimana, L. "L'équilibre ethnique et régional dans l'emploi." *Dialogue* 146 (May–June 1989): 15–31.

Van Hoyweghen, Saskia. "The Rwandan Villagisation Programme: Resettlement or Reconstruction?" In Didier Goyvaerts, ed., *Conflict and Ethnicity in Central Africa,* p. 212. Tokyo: Institute for the Study of Languages and Cultures of Asia and Africa, Tokyo University of Foreign Studies, 2000.

Vansina, Jan. *L'évolution du royaume Rwanda des origines à 1900.* Brussels: Arsom, 1962.

Vidal, Claudine. "Situations ethniques au Rwanda." In Jean-Loup Amselle and E. M'bokolo, eds., *Au cœur de l'ethnie: Ethnies, tribalisme et état en Afrique.* Paris: La Découverte, 1985.

Vlassenroot, Koen. "The Promise of Ethnic Conflict: Militarisation and Enclave-Formation in South Kivu." In Didier Goyvaerts, ed., *Conflict and Ethnicity in Central Africa.* Tokyo: Institute for the Study of Languages and Cultures of Asia and Africa, Tokyo University of Foreign Studies, 2000.

Volney, Constantin-François. *Travels through Syria and Egypt, 1783–1784–1785.* Published 1787.

Waldman, Amy. "Is It Too Late for Rwanda?" *Houston Chronicle,* 12 June 1994, sec. A, p. 1.

Waller, D. *Rwanda: Which Way Now?* Oxford: Oxfam, 1993.

Wallerstein, Immanuel. "The Uses of Racism." *London Review of Books* 22, no. 10 (18 May 2000): 11–14.

Wamba-dia-Wamba, Ernest. "The State of all Rwandese: Political Prescriptions and Disasters." Paper presented to CODESRIA conference, Arusha, Tanzania.

Watson, Catherine. *Exile from Rwanda: Background to an Invasion.* Issue paper. Washington, D.C.: U.S. Committee for Refugees, February 1991.

———. "War and Waiting." *Africa Report,* November/December 1992, p. 54.

World Bank. *World Development Report, 1992.* Oxford: Oxford University Press, 1992.

Wrigley, C. "Some Thoughts on the Bachwezi." *Uganda Journal* 22, no. 1 (1958): 11–21.

Yeld, Rachel. "Repatriation of Rwandan Refugees." Refugee Studies Programme, Oxford University, 4 December 1995.

Young, Crawford. "Rebellion and the Congo." In Robert Rotberg, ed., *Rebellion in Black Africa*. London: Oxford University Press, 1971.

Zarembo, Alan. "The Church's Shameful Acts." *Houston Chronicle*, 29 January 1995, p. 22.

Index